Book of
Humorous Quotations

For customers interested in other titles from Wordsworth Editions

Visit our web-site at
www.wordsworth-editions.com

Or for our latest list and a full mail order service contact:

Bibliophile Books
5 Thomas Road
London
E14 7BN

Tel: (0044) 020 7515 9222
Fax: (0044) 020 7538 4115
e-mail: orders@bibliophilebooks.com

This edition published 1993 by Wordsworth Editions Limited
8b East Street, Ware, Hertfordshire SG12 9HJ

ISBN 1-85326-759-7

Printed and bound in Great Britain by Mackays of Chatham PLC.

The Wordsworth
Book of
Humorous Quotations

—

Edited by Connie Robertson

Wordsworth Reference

Editor's Introduction

How often I read or hear a witty remark or statement and wish I had said it myself. The gift of being able to provide a particularly apt rejoinder and brighten a conversation is not given to many. In this collection I hope I have provided some of the best examples of the ways in which both the famous and the less well known have demonstrated this ability over the years, and in contexts as varied as literature, politics, and sport. For this gift is not limited to the comic genius, but is also found in those with professions of the most sober kind.

Although this book is intended mainly as a source of amusement for the reader, it may also provide examples of the type of humorous quotation which, should the opportunity arise, may enable the reader to make that really amusing remark that everyone else will wish they had made.

Arrangement of Entries

Entries have been arranged alphabetically by author/speaker and also indexed by keywords (usually at least two) so that if the originator is not known it should not prove difficult to find a quotation by using the index.

Authors are listed under their most commonly used names, for example where a pseudonym or titled form is the best known version. Where joint authors are responsible for a quotation, they are listed under the first name by which the pairing is commonly known, but this is not intended to diminish the importance of the contribution of the other author.

The source of the quotation is shown where it is known to come from a published work by that author. Where the source is a part-work such as a story or poem within a larger work, it is given within single quotation marks. Notes that clarify the context of the quotation are shown in brackets.

The index is arranged by keyword. In most cases singular and plural forms of a noun are grouped separately, but in seeking to locate a quotation it is advisable to check under both forms. Where an unusual spelling of a keyword occurs in the quotation, it is indexed under the more usual form unless there is no equivalent.

If you wish to write to suggest an amendment or to request the inclusion of a favourite humorous quotation that you would like to see included in a revised edition, your letters will be most welcome.

Please write to me:
c/o Wordsworth Editions Ltd, 6 London Street, London W2 1HL

Connie Robertson
June 1998

Contents

Book of Humorous Quotations

ABBOTT Diane 1953-

1

Being an MP is the sort of job all working class parents want for their children - clean, indoors and no heavy lifting.

ACE Goodman

2

The best cure for hypochondria is to forget about your own body and get interested in someone else's.

ACE Jane

3

Doctor, feel my purse.

4

Time wounds all heels.

ACHESON Dean 1893-1971

5

The first requirement of a statesman is that he be dull.

ADAMOV Arthur 1908-1970

6

The only thing to know is how to use your neuroses.

ADAMS Cindy

7

Success has made failures of many men.

ADAMS Douglas 1952-

8 *The Hitch Hiker's Guide to the Galaxy*

The Answer to the great Question of...Life, the Universe and Everything...is Forty-two.

ADAMS Franklin P. 1881-1960

9

Christmas is over, and Business is Business.

10

Health is the thing that makes you feel that now is the best time of the year.

11 *Nods and Becks*

Years ago we discovered the exact point, the dead centre of middle age. It occurs when you are too young to take up golf and too old to rush up to the net.

12 *Nods and Becks*

Elections are won by men and women chiefly because most people vote against somebody rather than for somebody.

13

There are plenty of good five-cent cigars in the country. The trouble is they cost a quarter. What the country really needs is a good five-cent nickle.

ADAMS Henry Brooks 1838-1918

14 *The Education of Henry Adams*

They know enough who know how to learn.

15 *The Education of Henry Adams*

Accident counts for much in companionship as in marriage.

16 *The Education of Henry Adams*

A friend in power is a friend lost.

ADAMS Joey

17

Bankruptcy is a legal proceeding in which you put your money in your pants pocket and give your coat to your creditors.

ADAMS John Quincy 1767-1848

18

In esse I am nothing; in posse I am everything.

ADDISON Joseph 1672-1719

19 *(of Cowley)*

He more had pleased us, had he pleased us less.

20 *The Spectator*

Sir Roger told them, with the air of a man who would not give his judgement rashly, that much might be said on both sides.

21 *The Spectator*

A woman seldom asks advice until she has bought her wedding clothes.

22

Sunday clears away the rust of the whole week.

23
I have often thought, says Sir Roger, it happens very well that Christmas should fall out in the Middle of Winter.

ADE George 1866-1944
24 *Fables in Slang*
After being turned down by numerous publishers, he had decided to write for posterity.

25
He had been kicked in the head by a mule when young, and believed everything he read in the Sunday papers.

26
One man's poison ivy is another man's spinach.

27
A people so primitive that they did not know how to get money except by working for it.

28
If it were not for the presents, an elopement would be preferable.

29 *'The Steel Box'*
`Whom are you?' he asked, for he had attended business college.

30 *The Sultan of Sulu.*
R-E-M-O-R-S-E.
Those dry Martinis did the work for me;
Last night at twelve I felt immense,
Today I feel like thirty cents.

31
In uplifting, get underneath.

ADENAUER Konrad 1876-1967
32
The good Lord set definite limits on man's wisdom, but set no limits on his stupidity - and that's just not fair.

33
I havn't asked you to make me young again. All I want is to go on getting older.

34
History is the sum total of the things that could have been avoided.

35
A thick skin is a gift from God.

ADLER Mortimer J.
36
In the case of good books, the point is not to see how many of them you can get through, but rather how many can get through to you.

37
The telephone book is full of facts but it doesn't contain a single idea.

ADLER Polly 1900-1962
38 *(referring to a brothel)*
A House is not a Home.

AESCHYLUS c.525-456 BC
39 *(of Helen)*
Hell to ships, hell to men, hell to cities.

AESOP c.550 BC
40 *Fables 'The Milkmaid and her Pail'*
Don't count your chickens before they are hatched.

AGA KHAN III 1877-1957
41 *(defending his taste for alcohol)*
I'm so holy that when I touch wine, it turns into water.

AGAR Herbert 1897-1980
42
Snobs talk as if they had begotten their ancestors.

AGATE James 1877-1947
43 *Ego 6*
My mind is not a bed to be made and re-made.

44
The English instinctively admire any man who has no talent and is modest about it.

45
Long experience has taught me that in England nobody goes to the theatre unless he or she has bronchitis.

AHMANSON Howard
46
I'm so happy to be rich, I'm willing to take all the consequences.

ALBEE Edward 1928-
47 *Who's afraid of Virginia Woolf?*
I have a fine sense of the ridiculous, but no sense of humour.

ALDINGTON Richard 1892-1962
48 *The Colonel's Daughter*
Patriotism is a lively sense of collective responsibility. Nationalism is a silly cock crowing on its own dunghill.

ALDRICH Thomas Bailey 1836-1907
49
The man who suspects his own tediousness has yet to be born.

50
The possession of gold has ruined fewer men than the lack of it.

ALEXANDER The Great 356-323 BC
51
I am dying with the help of too many physicians.

ALGREN Nelson 1909-1981
52 *A Walk on the Wild Side*
Never eat at a place called Mom's. Never play cards with a man called Doc. Never go to bed with a woman whose troubles are greater than your own.

ALI Muhammad (Cassius Clay) 1942-53
You don't want no pie in the sky when you die. You want something here on the ground while you're still around.

54 *(motto)*
Float like a butterfly, sting like a bee.

55
When you're as great as I am, it's hard to be humble.

ALLEN Fred 1894-1956
56 *(attributed)*
Committee - a group of men who individually can do nothing but as a group decide that nothing can be done.

57
I don't want to own anything that won't fit into my coffin.

58
(A gentleman) is any man who wouldn't hit a woman with his hat on.

ALLEN George 1902-1989
59
Winning can be defined as the science of being totally prepared.

ALLEN Marty
60
A study of economics usually reveals that the best time to buy anything is last year.

ALLEN William 1889-1949
61
America - the best poor man's country in the world.

ALLEN Woody 1935-
62 *All You Ever Wanted to Know About Sex*
Is sex dirty? Only if it's done right.

63 *Annie Hall*
[Sex] was the most fun I ever had without laughing.

64 *Annie Hall (of masturbation)*
Don't knock it. It's sex with someone you love.

65
I believe that sex is a beautiful thing between two people. Between five, it's fantastic.

66 *Clown Prince of American Humour*
I want to tell you this terrific story about contraception. I asked this girl to sleep with me, and she said no.

67
I don't want to achieve immortality through my work. I want to achieve immortality through not dying.

68 *Without Feathers*
I'm not afraid to die. I just don't want to be there when it happens.

69 *Without Feathers*
Money is better than poverty, if only for financial reasons.

70
Love is the answer, but while you're waiting for the answer, sex raises some pretty good questions.

71 *'My Philosophy', Getting Even*
Not only is there no God, but try getting a plumber on weekends.

72 *'Notebooks'*
If only God would give me some clear sign! Like making a large deposit in my name at a Swiss bank.

73
Showing up is eighty percent of life.

74 *Sleeper*
My Brain? It's my second favourite organ.

ALLINGHAM Margery 1904-1966
75 *Flowers for the Judge*
Once sex rears its ugly 'ead it's time to steer clear.

ALLINGHAM William 1828-1899
76 *The Fairies*
Up the airy mountain,
Down the rushy glen,
We daren't go a-hunting,
For fear of little men.

ALTMAN Robert 1925-
77
What's a cult? It just means not enough people to make a minority.

AMES Adelbert
78
The things we see are the mind's best bet as to what is out front.

AMHERST Earl 1773-1857
79
In the bad old days, there were three easy ways of losing money - racing being the quickest, women the pleasantest and farming the most certain.

AMIEL Henri Frédéric 1821-1881
80
Doing easily what others find is difficult is talent; doing what is impossible for talent is genius.

81
A thousand things advance; nine hundred and ninety-nine retreat, that is progress.

AMIS Sir Kingsley 1922-1995
82 *'A Bookshop idyll'*
We men have got love well weighed up; our stuff
Can get by without it.
Women don't seem to think that's good enough;
They write about it.

83 *'A Bookshop idyll'*
Women are really much nicer than men:
No wonder we like them.

84 *'Delivery Guaranteed'*
Death has got something to be said for it:
There's no need to get out of bed for it;
Wherever you may be,
They bring it to you, free.

85 *One Fat Englishman*
Outside every fat man there was an even fatter man trying to close in.

86 *One Fat Englishman*
He was of the faith chiefly in the sense that the church he currently did not attend was Catholic.

87 *Lucky Jim*
The light did him harm, but not as much as looking at things did; he resolved, having done it once, never to move his eyeballs again.

ANDERSON Patrick
88
Power is like a woman you want to stay in bed with forever.

ANDERSON Robert 1917-
89 *Tea and Sympathy*
All you're supposed to do is every once in a while give the boys a little tea and sympathy.

ANNE Princess, The Princess Royal 1950-
90 *(attributed)*
When I appear in public, people expect me to neigh, grind my teeth and swish my tail.

91 *(on her first encounter with a horse)*
One was presented with a small hairy individual and out of general curiosity, one climbed on.

92 *(on pregnancy)*
It's a very boring time. I am not particularly   maternal - it's an occupational hazard of being a wife.

ANONYMOUS
93
Been there, done that, got the T-shirt.

94 *(placard at Countryside March, 1998)*
Eat British Lamb: 50,000 foxes can't be wrong.

95 *(1940s saying)*
If it moves, salute it; if it doesn't move, pick it up; and if you can't pick it up, paint it white.

96
Alimony: the cash surrender value of a husband.

97
All marriages are happy. It's living together afterwards that is difficult.

98
If all the world were paper,
And all the sea were ink,
And all the trees were bread and cheese
What should we do for drink?

99 *(by an American Lawyer)*
Obscenity is whatever gives a judge an erection.

100 *(annotation to a ministerial brief)*
This is a rotten argument, but it should be good enough for their lordships on a hot summer afternoon.

101
Anything which parents have not learned from experience they can now learn from their children.

102
Every April, God rewrites the Book of Genesis.

103
The average girl would rather have beauty than brains because she knows the average man can see much better than he can think.

104
The beginning is easy; what happens next is much harder.

105
The bible tells us to forgive our enemies; not our friends.

106
Bigamy is having one husband too many. Monogamy is the same.

107
The bigger they are, the further they fall.

108
Book lovers never go to bed alone.

109
One boy's a boy, two boys are half a boy; three boys are no boy at all.

110
A bred-in-the-bone Boston lady, when asked why she never travelled, said 'Why should I? I'm already there.'

111 *(on the British monarchy)*
At certain times of grave national stress, when that rag-bag called the British Constitution is in grave danger of coming unstuck, thank heaven for the big safety-pin at the top that keeps it together.

112
A camel is a horse designed by a committee.

113 *(car bumper sticker)*
Life is uncertain - eat dessert first

114
In his chamber, weak and dying,
While the Norman Baron lay,
Loud, without, his men were crying,
'Shorter hours and better pay'.

115 *(Charles E. Wilson's defence policy)*
A bigger bang for a buck.

116
Child: Mamma, are Tories born wicked,
or do they go wicked afterwards?
Mother: They are born wicked, and grow
worse.

117
The Church of England is the Tory party
at prayer.

118
The cleverest woman finds a need for
foolish admirers.

119
If a cluttered desk is an indication of a
cluttered mind, what is indicated by an
empty desk?

120
Coffee in England is just toasted milk.

121
Confirmation at Eton: like a huge garden
party, faintly over-shadowed by a sense
of religion.

122
Conscience is a cur that will let you get
past it but that you cannot keep from
barking.

123 *(of David Lloyd George)*
He uses figures as if they were adjectives.

124
A dead man
Who never caused others to die
Seldom rates a statue.

125
Death is terrible to Cicero, desirable to
Cato, and indifferent to Socrates.

126 *(Decca Recording Company rejecting
The Beatles)*
We don't like their sound, and guitar
music is on the way out.

127
Deep down he is shallow.

128 *(definition of a lie)*
An abomination unto the Lord, but a
very present help in time of trouble.

129
There is a difference between a
pyschopath and a neurotic. A
pyschopath thinks two and two are five.
A neurotic knows that two and two are
four, but he worries about it.

130
A distinguished diplomat could hold his
tongue in ten languages.

131
To dream of the person you would like to
be is to waste the person you are.

132
The early North American Indians made
a great mistake by not having an
immigration bureau.

133
To eat is human, to digest, divine.

134
The Eiffel Tower is the Empire State
Building after taxes.

135 *Epperson's Law*
When a man says it's a silly, childish
game, it's probably something his wife
can beat him at.

136
Her face looks as if it had worn out two
bodies.

137
A fair price for oil is whatever you can
get plus ten to twenty per cent.

138
There was a faith-healer from Deal
Who said, 'Although pain isn't real,
If I sit on a pin
And it punctures my skin,
I dislike what I fancy I feel'.

139
I feel no pain dear mother now
But oh, I am so dry!
O take me to a brewery
And leave me there to die.

140
He that fights and runs away,
May live to fight another day.

141
The final test of fame is to have a crazy person imagine he is you.

142
If it flies, floats or fucks....don't buy it, rent it.

143
Any fool can make a rule, and every fool will mind it.

144 *(forecasting advance of science in 1949)*
Computers in the future will weigh no more than 1.5 tons.

145
The four-letter word for psychotherapy is 'talk'.

146
The French have a passion for revolution but an abhorrence of change.

147 *(of G.B. Shaw)*
John the Baptist pretending to be Karl Marx.

148
A genealogist is one who traces your family back as far as your money will go.

149
Gentleman: one who never hurts anyone's feelings unintentionally.

150
From ghoulies to ghosties and long-leggety beasties
And things that go bump in the night,
Good Lord, deliver us!

151
He wouldn't give a duck a drink if he owned Lake Michigan.

152
The glances over cocktails
That seemed to be so sweet
Don't seem quite so amorous
Over Shredded Wheat.

153
If God lived on earth, people would break his windows.

154
Good judgement comes from experience, and experience - well, that comes from poor judgement.

155
There is so much good in the worst of us and so much bad in the best of us, that it's rather hard to tell which of us ought to reform the rest of us.

156 *(graffito found on a London Underground)*
Life is a sexually transmitted disease.

157 *(graffito seen on toilet wall at Athens airport)*
Aestheticism is the last resort of the bourgeois.

158
It's not as great a day for the bride as she thinks. She's not marrying the best man.

159
The hard rubs of the world are what makes a man bright.

160
Harpists spend half their life tuning and the other half playing out of tune.

161
He'd give the devil ulcers.

162
Hell is truth seen too late.

163
A hobby is hard work you wouldn't do for a living.

164
A husband always prefers his wife's mother-in-law to his own.

165 *(IBM engineer on the microchip in 1968)*
But what...is it good for?

166 *(Illinois Institute of Technology)*
After an eight-hour day, workers require three overtime hours to produce two regular hours of results.

167 *(on impartiality)*
Like Caesar's wife, all things to all men.

168
Inflation is defined as the quality that makes balloons larger and candy bars smaller.

169 *(inscription on a sundial)*
Time wastes our bodies and our wits;
But we waste time, so we are quits.

170
An Intelligent Russian once remarked to us, `Every country has its own constitution; ours is absolutism moderated by assassination'.

171 *(on investing in the radio in 1920s)*
The wireless music box has no imaginable commercial value. Who would pay for a message sent to nobody in particular?

172 *(Jaws 2: film advertising copy)*
Just when you thought it was safe to go back in the water.

173
If there were any justice in the world, people would be able to fly over pigeons for a change.

174
No more Latin, no more French,
No more sitting on a hard board bench.
No more beetles in my tea,
Making googly eyes at me;
No more spiders in my bath
Trying hard to make me laugh.

175
The law locks up both man and woman
Who steals the goose from off the common,
But lets the great felon loose
Who steals the common from the goose.

176
Let's all give God a great big hand. I've seen the last page of the Bible and it's all going to turn out all right.

177
Liberty is always unfinished business.

178
Here lies Fred,
Who was alive and is dead:

Had it been his father,
I had much rather;
Had it been his brother,
Still better than another;
Had it been his sister,
No one would have missed her;
Had it been the whole generation,
Still better for the nation:

179
There is no such thing as a little garlic.

180
A little nonsense now and then is relished by the wisest men.

181
There is little serenity comparable to the serenity of the inexperienced giving advice to the experienced.

182
Little wit in the head makes much work for the feet.

183
Lizzie Borden took an axe
And gave her mother forty whacks;
When she saw what she had done
She gave her father forty-one!

184
If every man would mend a man, then all the world would be mended.

185
If a man can remember what he worried about last week, he has a very good memory.

186
If it weren't for marriage, men would spend their lives thinking they had no faults at all.

187
I married my husband for life, not for lunch.

188 *The Masque of Balliol*
My name is George Nathianel Curzon, I am a most superior person.

189
'Mean to' don't pick no cotton.

190 *(on microbes)*
Adam
Had'em.

191
Middle age is when you have a choice of two temptations and choose the one that will get you home earlier.

192
Even moderation ought not to be practised to excess.

193
Modern kitchen - where the pot calls the kettle chartreuse.

194
A mother is a person who if she is not there when you get home from school you wouldn't know how to get your dinner, and you wouldn't feel like eating it anyway.

195
Muscular Christianity.

196
The nearest thing to death in life
Is David Patrick Maxwell Fyfe,
Though underneath that gloomy shell
He does himself extremely well.

197
Ne'er of the living can the living judge -
Too blind the affection, or too fresh the grudge.

198 *(negro spiritual)*
God gave Noah the rainbow sign,
No more water, the fire next time.

199
Never pick a quarrel with a man who buys his ink by the gallon.

200 *(news headline on evolution findings)*
Man is more mushroom than tulip.

201
Nil carborundum illegitimi
(Cod Latin for) 'Don't let the bastards grind you down'.

202
Nostalgia ain't what it used to be.

203
There is nothing wrong with making mistakes. Just don't respond with encores.

204 *(notice in an English doctor's waiting-room)*
To avoid delay, please have all your symptoms ready.

205
Oboe - an ill woodwind that nobody blows good.

206 *(oil drillers in 1859)*
Drill for oil? You mean drill into the ground to try and find oil? You're crazy.

207
There was an old lady from Riga
Who rode with a smile on a tiger
They returned from the ride
With the lady inside
And a smile on the face of the tiger.

208
Old men and far travellers may lie with authority.

209 *(overheard at a performance of Cleopatra)*
How different, how very different from the home life of our own very dear Queen!

210
Some people handle the truth carelessly; others never touch it at all.

211
Pretty much all the honest truthtelling there is in the world is done by children.

212
Psychiatry is the care of the id by the odd.

213
Reality is an illusion caused by lack of alcohol.

214
If you really do put a small value upon yourself, rest assured that the world will not raise your price.

215 *(report to Admiralty)*
We shelled the Turks from 9 to 11: and then, it being Sunday, had Divine Service.

216 *(results of a 1997 tourist survey)*
The overall impression from the British and Germans is that they love France itself but would rather that the French didn't live there.

217 *(Rugby Football rules in Toronto)*
If a player continues transgressing the rules, his side shall lose him.

218 *(Scottish toast)*
Here's tae us; wha's like us? Gey few, and they're a'deid.

219
The secret of teaching is to appear to have known all your life what you learned this afternoon.

220
See the happy moron,
He doesn't give a damn,
I wish I were a moron,
My God! perhaps I am.

221
Keep a thing seven years and you will find a use for it.

222
His shortcoming is his long staying.

223 *(sign on lawn, University of Iowa)*
If allowed to survive, this grass will produce enough oxygen for two students to breathe for one semester.

224
A smile is a curve that can set things straight.

225 *(song)*
O Death, where is thy sting-a-ling-a-ling
O grave, thy victory?
The bells of hell go ting-a-ling-a-ling
For you but not for me.

226 *(song)*
It is good to be merry and wise,
It is good to be honest and true,
It is best to be off with the old love,
Before you are on with the new.

227
There's no such thing as a free lunch.

228
There's a wonderful family called Stein,
There's Gert, and there's Epp and there's Ein:
Gert's poems are bunk,
Epp's statues are junk,
And no one can understand Ein.

229
Every time a man puts a new idea across he finds ten men who thought of it before he did - but they only thought of it.

230
It takes time to be a success, but time is all it takes.

231
'Tis better than riches
To scratch when it itches.

232 *(title of BBC Television series)*
Not So Much a Programme, More a Way of Life.

233
There are two reasons for doing things - a very good reason and the real reason.

234 *(two-line comic song)*
Lloyd George knew my father,
My father knew Lloyd George.

235
War does not determine who is right - only who is left.

236 *(Weller's Law)*
Nothing is impossible for the person who doesn't have to do it.

237 *(Western Union memo, 1876)*
This 'telephone' has too many shortcomings to be seriously considered as a means of communication. The device is inherently of no value to us.

238
What costs nothing is worth nothing.

239
What men usually ask of God when they pray is that two and two not make four.

240
When you want really big money, you usually find yourself talking to people who didn't go to Eton.

241
Where is the man who has the power and skill
To stem the torrent of a woman's will?
For if she will, she will, you may depend on't;
And if she won't, she won't; so there's an end on't.

242
Whilst Adam slept, Eve from his side arose;
Strange his first sleep should be his last repose.

243
Who buys has need of two eyes
But one's enough to sell the stuff.

244
He who drinketh by the inch and speaketh by the yard shall be kicketh by the foot.

245
He who laughs, lasts.

246 *(of the Winchester Cathedral organ)*
Audible at five miles, painful at three, and lethal at one.

247
Wit is far more often a shield than a lance.

248
Some women blush when they are kissed; some call for the police; some swear; some bite. But the worst are those who laugh.

249
Women have their faults
Men have only two
Everything they say,
Everything they do.

250
A word to the wise is infuriating.

251
No one in this world needs a mink coat but a mink.

252
Things could be worse. Suppose your errors were counted and published every day, like those of a baseball player.

253
Write something, even if it's just a suicide note.

254
Every year it takes less time to fly across the Atlantic, and more time to drive to the office.

255
There was a young lady from Kent,
Who said she knew what men meant
When they asked her to dine;
Private room, champagne, wine -
She knew what they meant and she went.

256
Young men think old men fools and old men know young men to be so.

257
This is a youth-oriented society, and the joke is on them because youth is a disease from which we all recover.

258
After you've heard two eyewitness accounts of an auto accident it makes you wonder about history.

ANOUILH Jean 1910-1987
259
A good actor must never be in love with anyone but himself.

260
Every man thinks God is on his side. The rich and powerful know he is.

261
We poison our lives with fear of burglary and shipwreck, and, ask anyone, the house is never burgled, and the ship never goes down.

262
What you get free costs too much.

263
When you are forty, half of you belongs to the past ... And when you are seventy, nearly all of you.

ANTHONY Susan B. 1820-1906
264
The only question left to be settled now is, are women persons?

ANTRIM Minna 1861-
265 *Naked Truth and Veiled Allusions*
Experience is a good teacher, but she sends in terrific bills.

266 *Naked Truth and Veiled Allusions*
A fool bolts pleasure, then complains of moral indigestion.

APPLETON Sir Edward 1892-1965
267
I do not mind what language an opera is sung in so long as it is a language I don't understand.

APPLETON Thomas Gold 1812-1884
268
A Boston man is the east wind made flesh.

269
Good Americans, when they die, go to Paris.

APPLEY Lawrence
270
Management is now where the medical profession was when it decided that working in a drug store was not sufficient training to become a doctor.

ARETINO Pietro 1492-1556
271
Age has a good mind and sorry shanks.

ARISTOTLE 384-322 BC
272
Humour is the only test of gravity, and gravity of humour, for a subject which will not bear raillery is suspicious, and a jest which will not bear serious examination is false wit.

ARMOUR J. Ogden
273
The young man who wants to marry happily should pick out a good mother and marry one of her daughters - any one will do.

ARMSTRONG Louis 1901-1971
274
All music is folk music, I ain't never heard no horse sing a song.

275
There are some people that if they don't know, you can't tell 'em.

276
What we play is life.

ARMSTRONG Sir Robert 1927-
277 *(during 'Spycatcher' trial)*
It contains a misleading impression, not a lie. It was being economical with the truth.

ARNOLD George 1834-1865
278 *'The Jolly Old Pedagone'*
The living need charity more than the dead.

ARNOLD Matthew 1822-1888
279
Journalism is literature in a hurry.

280 *Letters of Matthew Arnold*
I am past thirty, and three parts iced over.

281
Nature, with equal mind,
Sees all her sons at play,
Sees man control the wind,
The wind sweep man away.

ASAF George 1880-1951
282 *'Pack up your Troubles in Your Old Kit Bag'*
What's the use of worrying?
It never was worth while,
So pack up your troubles in your old kit bag,
And smile, smile, smile.

ASCH Sholem
283
It has been said that writing comes more easily if you have something to say.

ASHFORD Daisy 1881-1972
284
I am very fond of fresh air and royalties.

ASNAS Max
285
Money is something you got to make in case you don't die.

ASQUITH Herbert H. 1852-1928
286
Greatness is a zigzag streak of lightning in the brain.

ASQUITH Margot 1865-1945
287 *(of David Lloyd George)*
He can't see a belt without hitting below it.

288 *(of F.E. Smith)*
He's very clever, but sometimes his brains go to his head.

289 *(of her husband)*
His modesty amounts to deformity.

290 *(to Jean Harlow, correcting the mispronunciation of her name)*
The 'T' is silent - as in `Harlow'.

291 *(of Lady Desborough)*
She tells enough white lies to ice a wedding cake.

292 *(of Lord Kitchener)*
If Kitchener is not a great man, he is, at least, a great poster.

293 *(of a politician)*
He always has his arm round your waist and his eye on the clock.

294 *(of Sir Stafford Cripps)*
He has a brilliant mind until he makes it up.

ASTOR Lady 1879-1964
295
I married beneath me. All women do.

296
My vigour, vitality and cheek repel me. I am the kind of woman I would run from.

ATKINS Eileen 1934-
297
Fame means absolutely nothing except a good table at a restaurant.

ATKINSON Brooks 1894-1984
298
Life is seldom as unendurable as, to judge by the facts, it logically ought to be.

299
Every man with an idea has at least two or three followers.

ATTLEE Clement 1883-1967
300 *(on himself)*
Few thought he was even a starter.
There were many who thought
themselves smarter.
But he ended PM, CH and OM.
An Earl and a Knight of the Garter.

301
Democracy means government by discussion, but it is only effective if you can stop people talking.

302
I think the British have the distinction above all other nations of being able to put new wine into old bottles without bursting them.

303
Winston Churchill - fifty per cent genius, fifty per cent bloody fool.

ATWOOD Margaret 1939-
304
If the national mental illness of the United States is megalomania, that of Canada is paranoid schizophrenia.

AUDEN W. H. 1907-1973
305 *(of himself)*
My face looks like a wedding-cake left out in the rain.

306
We are all here on earth to help others; what on earth the others are here for I don't know.

307
Almost all of our relationships begin,
and most of them continue, as forms of
mutual exploitation, a mental or
physical barter, to be terminated when
one or both parties run out of goods.

308 *Dog Beneath the Skin*
Happy the hare at morning, for she
cannot read
The Hunter's waking thoughts.

309 *The Dyer's Hand*
Among those whom I like, I can find no
common denominator, but among those
whom I love, I can: all of them make me
laugh.

310
The ear tends to be lazy, craves the
familiar and is shocked by the
unexpected; the eye, on the other hand,
tends to be impatient, craves the novel
and is bored by repetition.

311
Geniuses are the luckiest of mortals
because what they must do is the same
as what they most want to do.

312
Let us humour if we can
The vertical man
Though we value none
But the horizontal one.

313 *'The Love Feast'*
In an upper room at midnight
See us gathered on behalf
Of love according to the gospel
Of the radio-phonograph.

314
Any marriage, happy or unhappy, is
infinitely more interesting and
significant than any romance, however
passionate.

315 *'In memory of Sigmund Freud'*
To us he is no more a person
now but a whole climate of opinion.

316 *'New Year letter'*
To the man-in-the-street, who, I'm sorry
to say,
Is a keen observer of life,

The word 'Intellectual' suggests straight
away
A man who's untrue to his wife.

317
It is nonsense to speak of 'higher' and
'lower' pleasures. To a hungry man it is,
rightly, more important that he eat than
that he philosophize.

318 *'Orators'*
Private faces in public places
Are wiser and nicer
Than public faces in private places.

319
A professor is one who talks in someone
else's sleep.

AUGUSTINE St. 354-430
320 *Confessions*
Give me chastity and continence, but
not yet.

321 *Joannis*
Love and do what you like.

AURELIUS Marcus 121-180
322
The art of living is more like that of
wrestling than of dancing. The main
thing is to stand firm and be ready for an
unforeseen attack.

323
There is no man so blessed that some
who stand by his deathbed won't hail the
occasion with delight.

AUSTEN Jane 1775-1817
324 *Emma*
With men he can be rational and
unaffected, but when he has ladies to
please, every feature works.

325 *Emma*
The sooner every party breaks up the
better.

326 *Emma*
Business, you know, may bring money,
but friendship hardly ever does.

327 *Letter to Fanny Knight*
Single women have a dreadful
propensity for being poor - which is one

very strong argument in favour of matrimony.

328 *Letters*
What dreadful hot weather we have! It keeps me in a continual state of inelegance.

329 *Letters*
I do not want people to be very agreeable, as it saves me the trouble of liking them a great deal.

330 *Letters*
In nine cases out of ten, a woman had better show more affection than she feels.

331 *Letters*
Men are all so good for nothing, and hardly any women at all.

332 *Mansfield Park*
A large income is the best recipe for happiness I ever heard of. It certainly may secure all the myrtle and turkey part of it.

333 *Northanger Abbey*
Oh! who can ever be tired of Bath!

334 *Northanger Abbey*
From politics, it was an easy step to silence.

335
There is nothing like staying at home for real comfort.

336 *Persuasion*
She had been forced into prudence in her youth, she learned romance as she grew older - the natural sequel of an unnatural beginning.

337 *Persuasion*
Next to being married, a girl likes to be crossed in love a little now and then.

338
I have been a selfish being all my life, in practice, though not in principle.

339 *Sense and Sensibility*
An annuity is a very serious business.

AUSTIN Alfred 1835-1913
340 *(attributed: on illness of the Prince of Wales)*
Across the wires the electric message came: `He is not better, he is much the same'.

AUSTIN Warren R. 1877-1962
341 *(in a debate on the Middle East)*
[Jews and Arabs should settle their differences] like good Christians.

AVOT Pirke
342
If I am not myself, who will be?

AYCKBOURN Alan 1939-
343 *Bedroom Farce*
My mother used to say, Delia, if S-E-X ever rears its ugly head, close your eyes before you see the rest of it.

344 *How the Other Half Loves*
Do you realize, Mrs Foster, the hours I've put into that woman? When I met her, you know, she was nothing. Nothing at all. With my own hands I have built her up. Encouraging her to join the public library and make use of her non-fiction tickets.

345 *Table Manners*
I always feel with Norman that I have him on loan from somewhere. Like one of his library books.

AYRES Pam 1947-
346 *'Oh no, I got a cold'*
Medicinal discovery,
It moves in mighty leaps,
It leaps straight past the common cold,
And gives it us for keeps.

BACALL Lauren 1924-
347
Stardom isn't a profession; it's an accident.

BACKUS Jim
348
Many a man owes his success to his first wife and his second wife to his success.

BACON Francis 1561-1626

349
Anger makes dull men witty, but it keeps them poor.

350 *'The Antitheta of Things'*
Riches are a good handmaid, but the worst mistress.

351 *'The Antitheta of Things'*
Silence is the virtue of fools.

352 *Essays*
Some books are to be tasted, others to be swallowed, and some few to be chewed and digested.

353 *Essays 'Of Marriage and the Single Life'*
Wives are young men's mistresses, companions for middle age, and old men's nurses.

354 *Essays 'Of Marriage and the Single Life'*
He was reputed one of the wise men that made answer to the question when a man should marry? 'A young man not yet, an elder man not at all.'

355 *Essays 'Of Seditions and Troubles'*
Money is like muck, not good except it be spread.

356 *Essays 'Of Seeming Wise'*
The French are wiser than they seem, and the Spaniards seem wiser than they are.

357 *Essays 'Of Truth'*
A mixture of a lie doth ever add pleasure.

358
Hope is a good breakfast, but it is a bad supper.

359
Universities incline wits to sophistry and affectation.

360 *The World*
What is it then to have or have no wife,
But single thraldom, or a double strife?

BAEZ Joan 1941-
361 *(of 60s contemporaries)*
Everyone is either bald or dead or looks like a plum pudding.

BAGEHOT Walter 1826-1877
362 *Estimates of some Englishmen and Scotchmen*
No real English gentleman, in his secret soul, was ever sorry for the death of a political economist.

363 *Estimates of some Englishmen and Scotchmen*
Writers, like teeth, are divided into incisors and grinders.

364
The great pleasure in life is doing what people say you cannot do.

365
Poverty is an anomaly to rich people: it is very difficult to make out why people who want dinner do not ring the bell.

BAILEY David 1938-
366
Women love scallywags, but some marry them and then try to make them wear a blazer.

BAILEY John
367
Politics is not a good location or a vocation for anyone lazy, thin-skinned or lacking a sense of humour.

BAIRNSFATHER Bruce 1888-1959
368 *Fragments from France*
Well, if you knows of a better 'ole, go to it.

BAKER Bobby
369
Shopping is the perfect model for the Quest.

BAKER Russell
370
Happiness is a small and unworthy goal for something as big and fancy as a whole lifetime, and should be taken in small doses.

371
I've had an unhappy life, thank God.

BALDWIN James 1924-1987
372
Children have never been very good at listening to their elders, but they have never failed to imitate them.

373
I met a lot of people in Europe. I even encountered myself.

374
Money, it turned out, was exactly like sex, you thought of nothing else if you didn't have it and thought of other things if you did.

BALDWIN Stanley 1867-1947
375
The intelligent are to the intelligentsia what a gentleman is to a gent.

376
There are three classes which need sanctuary more than others - birds, wild flowers, and Prime Ministers.

BALFOUR Arthur James 1848-1930
377 *Letter to Mrs. Drew*
It is unfortunate, considering that enthusiasm moves the world, that so few enthusiasts can be trusted to speak the truth.

378
Winston has written four volumes about himself and called it 'World Crisis'.

BALL George W.
379
Nostalgia is a seductive liar.

BALMAIN Pierre 1914-1982
380
The trick of wearing mink is to look as though you were wearing a cloth coat. The trick of wearing a cloth coat is to look as though you are wearing mink.

BALZAC Honoré De 1799-1850
381
The majority of husbands remind me of an orang-utan trying to play the violin.

382
No man should marry until he has studied anatomy and dissected at least one woman.

BANKHEAD Tallulah 1903-1968
383
I'd rather be strongly wrong than weakly right.

BANKS Tony
384 *(whilst Minister for Sport)*
My mind is very, very open, and so is my mouth.

BANZINI Luigi
385
A gentleman does things no gentleman should do in a way only a gentleman can.

BARAKA Imamu Amiri 1934-
386 *Midstream*
God has been replaced, as he has all over the West, with respectability and air-conditioning.

BARBER James David
387
Trying to make the presidency work these days is like trying to sew buttons on a custard pie.

BARHAM R.H. ('Thomas Ingoldsby')
1788-1845
388 *The Ingoldsby Legends*
So put that in your pipe, my Lord Otto, and smoke it.

BARING Maurice 1874-1945
389
If you would know what the Lord God thinks of money, you have only to look at those to whom he gives it.

BARKER J.M.
390
Only an incompetent mind is content to express itself incompetently.

BARNES Julian 1946-
391 *Flaubert's Parrot*
Do not imagine that Art is something which is designed to give gentle uplift and self-confidence. Art is not a brassiere. At least, not in the English

sense. But do not forget that brassiere is the French for life-jacket.

392 *Talking It Over*
Love is just a system for getting someone to call you darling after sex.

BARNES Peter 1931-
393 *The Ruling Class*
CLAIRE: How do you know you're ... God?
EARL OF GURNEY: Simple. When I pray to Him I find I'm talking to myself.

BARNUM Phineas T. 1810-1891
394 *(attributed)*
There's a sucker born every minute.

395
Every crowd has a silver lining.

BARRAULT Jean-Louis 1910-1994
396
Acting consists of the ability to keep an audience from coughing.

BARRIE J.M. 1860-1937
397
God gave us memories that we might have roses in December.

398
Heaven for climate, hell for company.

399 *What Every Woman Knows*
There are few more impressive sights in the world than a Scotsman on the make.

400 *What Every Woman Knows*
It's a sort of bloom on a woman. If you have it, you don't need to have anything else; and if you don't have it, it doesn't much matter what else you have.

BARRYMORE John 1882-1942
401
The trouble with life is that there are so many beautiful women and so little time.

402
I want him ('Hamlet') to be so male that when I come out on the stage, they can hear my balls clank.

BARTH Karl 1886-1968
403
Laughter is the closest thing to the grace of God.

BARTHES Roland 1915-1980
404 *Mythologies 'La nouvelle Citroën'*
I think that cars today are almost the exact equivalent of the great Gothic cathedrals: I mean the supreme creation of an era, conceived with passion by unknown artists, and consumed in image if not in usage by a whole population which appropriates them as a purely magical object.

BARUCH Bernard 1870-1965
405
To me, old age is always fifteen years older than I am.

406
Vote for the man who promises least; he'll be the least disappointing.

BARZUN Jacques 1907-
407
Whoever wants to know the hearts and minds of America had better learn baseball.

BASINGER Kim
408
The more flesh you show, the further up the ladder you go.

BAUDELAIRE Charles 1821-1867
409
Genius is childhood recaptured.

410
We love women in proportion to their degree of strangeness to us.

411
As a remedy against all ills - poverty, sickness, and melancholy - only one thing is absolutely necessary: a liking for work.

412
A sweetheart is a bottle of wine, a wife is a wine bottle.

BAUGHMAN M. Dale
413
You can never hope to become a skilled conversationalist until you learn how to put your foot tactfully through the television set.

BAX Sir Arnold 1883-1953
414
You should make a point of trying every experience once, excepting incest and folk-dancing.

BEADLE E.R.
415
Half the work that is done in the world is to make things appear what they are not.

BEAUMARCHAIS Pierre-Augustin Caron de 1732-1799
416 *The Barber of Seville*
Drinking when we are not thirsty and making love all year round, madam; that is all there is to distinguish us from the other animals.

417
Vilify! Vilify! Some of it will always stick.

BEAUMONT Francis 1584-1616
418 *The Scornful Lady*
Kiss till the cow comes home.

BEAVERBROOK Lord 1879-1964
419 *(attributed)*
Buy old masters. They fetch a better price than old mistresses.

420 *The Decline and Fall of Lloyd George*
[He] did not seem to care which way he travelled providing he was in the driver's seat.

BECKER May Lamberton
421
We grow neither better nor worse as we get old, but more like ourselves.

BECKETT Samuel 1906-1989
422 *Malone Dies*
If I had the use of my body I would throw it out of the window.

423 *Waiting for Godot*
One of the thieves was saved. (Pause) It's a reasonable percentage.

424 *Waiting for Godot*
We all are born mad. Some remain so.

BEDFORD Harry and SULLIVAN Terry
425 *(song written for Marie Lloyd)*
I'm a bit of a ruin that Cromwell knocked about a bit.

BEECHAM Sir Thomas 1879-1961
426 *Beecham Stories*
There are two golden rules for an orchestra: start together and finish together. The public doesn't give a damn what goes on in between.

427 *Beecham Stories (describing the harpsichord)*
Like two skeletons copulating on a corrugated tin roof.

428 *(to a cellist - attributed)*
Madam, you have between your legs an instrument capable of giving pleasure to thousands - and all you can do is scratch it.

429
The English may not like music, but they absolutely love the noise it makes.

430 *Wit of Music*
Why do we have to have all these third-rate foreign conductors around - when we have so many second-rate ones of our own?

BEECHER Henry Ward 1813-1887
431
Clothes and manners do not make the man; but, when he is made, they greatly improve his appearance.

432
The difference between perseverance and obstinacy is that one often comes from a strong will, and the other from a strong won't.

433
The dog is the god of frolic.

434
It is not well for a man to pray cream and live skim milk.

435
The meanest, most contemptible kind of praise is that which first speaks well of a man, and then qualifies it with a 'but'.

436
Mirthfulness is in the mind and you cannot get it out. It is just as good in its place as conscience or veneration.

437
Where is human nature so weak as in the bookstore?

438
The worst thing in this world, next to anarchy, is government.

BEECHER John
439
Strength is a matter of the made-up mind.

BEERBOHM Sir Max 1872-1956
440 *(attributed)*
I belong to the generation that says goodbye at the front door.

441 *A Defence of Cosmetics*
Most women are not so young as they are painted.

442 *And Even Now 'Hosts and Guests'*
Mankind is divisible into two great classes: hosts and guests.

443
You cannot make a man by standing a sheep on its hind legs. But by standing a flock of sheep in that position you can make a crowd of men.

444
To mankind in general Macbeth and Lady Macbeth stand out as the supreme type of all that a host and hostess should not be.

445
The past is a work of art, free of irrelevancies and loose ends.

446 *More 'Going Back to School'*
I was not unpopular [at school] ... It is Oxford that has made me insufferable.

447 *More 'Going Back to School'*
Undergraduates owe their happiness chiefly to the consciousness that they are no longer at school. The nonsense which was knocked out of them at school is all put gently back at Oxford or Cambridge.

448 *Zuleika Dobson*
The dullard's envy of brilliant men is always assuaged by the suspicion that they will come to a bad end.

449 *Zuleika Dobson*
Women who love the same man have a kind of bitter freemasonry.

BEHAN Brendan 1923-1964
450 *My Brother Brendan (by Dominic Behan)*
There's no such thing as bad publicity except your own obituary.

451
Critics are like eunuchs in a harem: they know how it's done, they've seen it done every day, but they're unable to do it themselves.

452
We had gone out there to pass the beautiful day of high summer like true Irishmen - locked in the dark Snug of a public house.

453 *The Hostage*
PAT: He was an Anglo-Irishman.
MEG: In the blessed name of God what's that?
PAT: A Protestant with a horse.

454 *The Hostage*
When I came back to Dublin, I was court-martialled in my absence and sentenced to death in my absence, so I said they could shoot me in my absence.

455 *The Hostage*
We're here because we're queer
Because we're queer because we're here.

456
It's not that the Irish are cynical. It's rather that they have a wonderful lack of respect for everything and everybody.

457
A Torontonian is a man who leaves culture to his wife.

BEHN Aphra 1640-1689
458 *The Rover*
Come away; poverty's catching.

BELLOC Hilaire 1870-1953
459 *A Bad Child's Book of Beasts 'The Tiger'*
The Tiger, on the other hand, is kittenish and mild,
He makes a pretty play fellow for any little child;
And mothers of large families (who claim to common sense)
Will find a Tiger well repay the trouble and expense.

460 *'To the Balliol Men Still in Africa'*
Balliol made me, Balliol fed me,
Whatever I had she gave me again:
And the best of Balliol loved and led me.
God be with you, Balliol men.

461 *More Beasts for Worse Children 'The Microbe'*
The Microbe is so very small
You cannot make him out at all.
But many sanguine people hope
To see him through a microscope.

462 *More Beasts for Worse Children 'The Microbe'*
Oh! let us never, never doubt
What nobody is sure about!

463 *'On His Books'*
When I am dead, I hope it may be said:
'His sins were scarlet, but his books were read.'

464 *Cautionary Tales 'Henry King'*
Physicians of the Utmost Fame
Were called at once; but when they came
They answered, as they took their Fees,
'There is no Cure for this Disease'.

465 *Cautionary Tales 'Jim'*
And always keep a-hold of Nurse
For fear of finding something worse.

466 *Cautionary Tales 'Lord Lundy'*
In my opinion, Butlers ought
To know their place, and not to play
The Old Retainer night and day.

467 *Cautionary Tales 'Lord Lundy'*
Sir! you have disappointed us!
We had intended you to be
The next Prime Minister but three:
The stocks were sold; the Press was squared;
The Middle Class was quite prepared.
But as it is! ... My language fails!
Go out and govern New South Wales!

468 *Cautionary Tales 'Matilda'*
For every time She shouted 'Fire!'
They only answered 'Little Liar!'
And therefore when her Aunt returned,
Matilda, and the House, were Burned.

469 *Cautionary Tales 'Rebecca'*
A Trick that everyone abhors
In Little Girls is slamming Doors.

470 *Fatigue*
I'm tired of Love: I'm still more tired of Rhyme.
But money gives me pleasure all the Time.

471 *'On a Great Election'*
The accursed power which stands on Privilege
(And goes with Women, and Champagne, and Bridge)
Broke - and Democracy resumed her reign:
(Which goes with Bridge, and Women and Champagne).

472 *'Heroic Poem upon Wine'*
Strong brother in God and last companion, Wine.

473
Just as there is nothing between the admirable omelette and the intolerable, so with autobiography.

474
The Llama is a woolly sort of fleecy hairy goat
With an indolent expression and an

undulating throat
Like an unsuccessful literary man.

475 *The Modern Traveller*
Whatever happens we have got
The Maxim Gun, and they have not.

476 *New Cautionary Tales 'About John'*
Like many of the Upper Class
He liked the Sound of Broken Glass

477 *New Cautionary Tales 'Peter Goole'*
And even now, at twenty-five,
He has to WORK to keep alive!
Yes! All day long from 10 till 4!
For half the year or even more;
With but an hour or two to spend
At luncheon with a city friend.

478 *'Newdigate Poem'*
A smell of burning fills the startled Air -
The Electrician is no longer there!

479 *On Nothing 'On Tea'*
Is there no Latin word for Tea? Upon my
soul, if I had known that I would have let
the vulgar stuff alone.

480 *More Peers 'Lord Finchley'*
Lord Finchley tried to mend the Electric
Light
Himself. It struck him dead: And serve
him right!
It is the business of the wealthy man
To give employment to the artisan.

481 *'On a Sundial'*
I am a sundial, and I make a botch
Of what is done much better by a watch.

BELLOW Saul 1915-
482
A man is only as good as what he loves.

483
I have never turned over a fig leaf yet
that didn't have a price tag on the other
side.

BELTAIRE Mark
484
The nicest thing about the promise of
spring is that sooner or later she'll have
to keep it.

BENCHLEY Robert 1889-1945
485
Anyone can do any amount of work
provided it isn't the work he is supposed
to be doing at that moment.

486 *Chips off the old Benchley 'Safety
Second'*
My only solution for the problem of
habitual accidents ... is to stay in bed all
day. Even then, there is always the
chance that you will fall out.

487
It took me fifteen years to discover that I
had no talent for writing, but I couldn't
give it up because by that time I was too
famous.

488 *Pluck and Luck*
In America there are two classes of travel
- first class, and with children.

489 *Wits End (on Venice)*
Streets Flooded. Please advise.

BENEDICT Francis G.
490
The extra calories needed for one hour
of intense mental effort would be
completely met by eating one oyster
cracker or one half of a salted peanut.

BENÉT Stephen Vincent 1898-1943
491
(Abraham Lincoln's) weathered face was
homely as a plowed field.

492
He could fiddle all the bugs off a sweet-
potato vine.

493
Honesty is as rare as a man without self-
pity.

494
As for what you're calling hard luck -
well, we made New England out of it.
That and codfish.

BENN Tony 1925-
495
If you file your waste-paper basket for 50
years you build a public library.

BENNETT Alan 1934-
496 *'Place Names of China'*
Here I sit, alone and sixty,
Bald, and fat, and full of sin,
Cold the seat and loud the cistern,
As I read the Harpic tin.

497 *Dinner at Noon*
What keeps us in our place is
embarrassment.

498 *Enjoy*
I don't want to give you the idea I'm
trying to hide anything, or that anything
unorthodox goes on between my wife
and me. It doesn't. Nothing goes on at
all ... No foreplay. No afterplay. And
fuck all in between.

499 *Forty Years On*
HEADMASTER: Of course they're out of
date. Standards are always out of date.
That is what makes them standards.

500 *Getting On*
We started off trying to set up a small
anarchist community, but people
wouldn't obey the rules.

501 *The Old Country*
We were put to Dickens as children but it
never quite took. That unremitting
humanity soon had me cheesed off.

502 *'Take a Pew' from Beyond the Fringe*
Life is rather like a tin of sardines - we
are all of us looking for the key. I wonder
how many of you have wasted years of
your life looking behind the kitchen
dressers of this life for the key. Others
think they have found the key. They roll
back the sardine tin of life, they reveal
the sardines, the riches of life therein,
they get them out and enjoy them. You
know there is always a little bit in the
corner you can't quite get out.

BENNETT Arnold 1867-1931
503 *The Card*
His opinion of himself, having once
risen, remained at 'set fair'.

504 *Things that have Interested Me*
The price of justice is eternal publicity.

505
A man of sixty has spent twenty years in
bed and over three years in eating.

506 *(attributed to his tailor)*
Trousers should shiver on the shoe, but
not break.

507 *The Title*
Being a husband is a whole-time job.
That is why so many husbands fail. They
cannot give their entire attention to it.

BENNETT James Gordon 1795-1872
508
Remember, son, many a good story has
been ruined by over-verification.

BENNETT Jill 1931-1990
509
Never marry a man who hates his
mother, because he'll end up hating you.

BENNETT W.A.C.
510
Yes, I'm 68, but when I was a boy I was
too poor to smoke, so knock off ten
years. That makes me 58. And since I
never developed the drinking habit, you
can knock off ten more years. So I'm 48 -
in the prime of my life. Retire? Retire to
what?

BENOIT Madame
511
I feel a recipe is only a theme, which an
intelligent cook can play each time with
a variation.

BENTHAM Jeremy 1748-1832
512 *Anarchical Fallacies*
Natural rights is simple nonsense:
natural and imprescriptible rights,
rhetorical nonsense - nonsense upon
stilts.

BENTLEY E. C. 1875-1956
513 *Biography for Beginners 'Sir
Christopher Wren'*
Sir Christopher Wren
Said, 'I am going to dine with some men.
If anybody calls
Say I am designing St. Paul's.'

514 *Biography for Beginners 'Clive'*
What I like about Clive
Is that he is no longer alive.
There is a great deal to be said
For being dead.

515 *Biography for Beginners -*
Introduction
The Art of Biography
Is different from Geography.
Geography is about Maps,
But Biography is about Chaps.

516 *More Biography 'George the Third'*
George the Third
Ought never to have occurred.
One can only wonder
At so grotesque a blunder.

BENTLEY Eric 1916-
517
Ours is the age of substitutes: instead of
language, we have jargon; instead of
principles, slogans; and, instead of
genuine ideas, Bright Ideas.

BENTLEY John
518
Making money is fun, but it's pointless if
you don't use the power it brings.

BENTLEY Richard 1662-1742
519 *Bentley, his judgement on claret*
It would be port if it could.

520 *The Works of Samuel Johnson*
It is a pretty poem, Mr. Pope, but you
must not call it Homer.

BENTLEY Thomas 1730-1780
521
No man is demolished but by himself.

BERENSON Bernhard 1865-1919
522
Consistency requires you to be as
ignorant today as you were a year ago.

523
We define genius as the capacity for
productive reaction against one's
training.

524
Governments last as long as the
undertaxed can defend themselves
against the overtaxed.

BERESFORD Lord Charles 1846-1919
525 *The World of Fashion 1837-1922*
Very sorry can't come. Lie follows by
post.

BERLIN Irving 1888-1989
526
The toughest thing about success is that
you've got to keep on being a success.

BERLIOZ Hector 1803-1869
527
The luck of having talent is not enough;
one must also have a talent for luck.

528
Time is a great teacher, but
unfortunately it kills all its pupils.

BERNANOS Georges 1888-1948
529
Hell, madame, is to love no longer.

BERNARD Dorothy
530
Courage - fear that has said its prayers.

BERRA Yogi
531
You can't think and hit at the same time.

532
The game isn't over until it's over.

533
You can observe a lot just by watching.

534
Ninety per cent of this game is half-
mental.

BETJEMAN Sir John 1906-1984
535 *'Death in Leamington'*
Oh! Chintzy, Chintzy cheeriness,
Half dead and half alive!

536 *'Henley-on-Thames'*
Oh shall I see the Thames again?
The prow-promoted gems again,
As beefy ATS
Without their hats
Come shooting through the bridge?

And 'cheerioh' or 'cheeri-bye'
Across the waste of waters die
And low the mists of evening lie
And lightly skims the midge.

537 *'How to get on in Society'*
Phone for the fish-knives, Norman
As Cook is a little unnerved;
You kiddies have crumpled the serviettes
And I must have things daintily served.

538 *'Middlesex'*
Gaily into Ruislip Gardens
Runs the red electric train,
With a thousand Ta's and Pardon's
Daintily alights Elaine;
Hurries down the concrete station
With a frown of concentration,
Out into the outskirt's edges
Where a few surviving hedges
Keep alive our lost Elysium - rural
Middlesex again.

539 *'Slough'*
Come friendly bombs, and fall on
Slough!
It isn't fit for humans now,
There isn't grass to graze a cow.
Swarm over, Death!

540 *'A Subaltern's Love-Song'*
Miss J. Hunter Dunn, Miss J. Hunter
Dunn,
Furnish'd and burnish'd by Aldershot
sun,
What strenuous singles we played after
tea,
We in the tournament - you against me.

541 *'A Subaltern's Love-song'*
Around us are Rovers and Austins afar,
Above us, the intimate roof of the car,
And here on my right is the girl of my
choice,
With the tilt of her nose and the chime of
her voice.

542 *Summoned by Bells*
The dread of beatings! Dread of being
late!
And, greatest dread of all, the dread of
games!

BETTI Ugo 1882-1954
543
This free-will business is a bit terrifying
anyway. It's almost pleasanter to obey,
and make the most of it.

544
A vague uneasiness; the police. It's like
when you suddenly understand you
have to undress in front of the doctor.

BEUDOIN Patricia C.
545
The toughest thing about being a
housewife is you have no place to stay
home from.

BEVAN Aneurin 1897-1960
546 *Aneurin Bevan*
Damn it all, you can't have the crown of
thorns and the thirty pieces of silver.

547 *(debate on Suez crisis)*
I am not going to spend any time
whatsoever in attacking the Foreign
Secretary ... If we complain about the
tune, there is no reason to attack the
monkey when the organ grinder is
present.

548 *(of Robert Boothby)*
Why read the crystal when he can read
the book?

549 *(speech at Blackpool)*
This island is made mainly of coal and
surrounded by fish. Only an organizing
genius could produce a shortage of coal
and fish at the same time.

550 *(on unilateral disarmament)*
If you carry this resolution you will send
Britain's Foreign Secretary naked into the
conference chamber.

551
We know what happens to people who
stay in the middle of the road. They get
run down.

BEVERIDGE Karl
552
My favourite example (of ex-patriotism)
is James Joyce, who left Ireland at
nineteen and never came back. But he
spent the rest of his life writing about

Ireland from the perspective of living in Paris.

DEVIN Ernest 1801-1951
553 *Ernest Bevin and the Foreign Office*
If you open that Pandora's Box, you never know what Trojan 'orses will jump out.

554
My [foreign] policy is to be able to take a ticket at Victoria Station and go anywhere I damn well please.

BIDAULT Georges 1899-1983
555
The weak have one weapon: the errors of those who think they are strong.

BIERCE Ambrose 1842-c.1914
556 *The Devil's Dictionary*
Acquaintance, n: a person whom we know well enough to borrow from, but not well enough to lend to.

557 *The Devil's Dictionary*
Apologize, v: to lay the foundation for a future offence.

558 *The Devil's Dictionary*
Christian, n: one who believes that the New Testament is a divinely inspired book admirably suited to the spiritual needs of his neighbour.

559 *The Devil's Dictionary*
Commendation, n: the tribute that we pay to achievements that resemble, but do not equal, our own.

560 *The Devil's Dictionary*
Cynic, n: a blackguard whose faulty vision sees things as they are, not as they ought to be.

561 *The Devil's Dictionary*
Destiny, n: a tyrant's authority for crime and a fool's excuse for failure.

562 *The Devil's Dictionary*
Debauche, n: one who has so earnestly pursued pleasure that he has had the misfortune to overtake it.

563 *The Devil's Dictionary*
Education, n: that which discloses to the wise and disguises from the foolish their lack of understanding.

564 *The Devil's Dictionary*
Epitaph, n: an inscription on a tomb showing that virtues acquired by death have a retroactive effect.

565 *The Devil's Dictionary*
History, n: an account mostly false, of events, mostly unimportant, which are brought about by rulers, mostly knaves, and soldiers, mostly fools.

566 *The Devil's Dictionary*
Idiot, n: a member of a large and powerful tribe whose influence in human affairs has always been dominant and controlling.

567 *The Devil's Dictionary*
Ignoramus, n: a person unacquainted with certain kinds of knowledge familiar to yourself, and having certain other kinds that you know nothing about.

568 *The Devil's Dictionary*
Infidel, n: in New York, one who does not believe in the Christian religion; in Constantinople, one who does.

569 *The Devil's Dictionary*
Litigant, n: a person about to give up his skin for the hope of retaining his bone.

570 *The Devil's Dictionary*
Love, n: a temporary insanity often curable by marriage.

571 *The Devil's Dictionary*
Mausoleum, n: the final and funniest folly of the rich.

572 *The Devil's Dictionary*
Marriage, n: the state or condition of a community consisting of a master, a mistress, and two slaves, making, in all, two.

573 *The Devil's Dictionary*
Painting, n: the art of protecting flat surfaces from the weather and exposing them to the critic.

574 *The Devil's Dictionary*
Peace, n: in international affairs, a period of cheating between two periods of fighting.

575 *The Devil's Dictionary*
Philanthropist, n: a rich (and usually bald) old gentleman who has trained himself to grin while his conscience is picking his pocket.

576 *The Devil's Dictionary*
Piracy, n: commerce without its folly-swaddles - just as God made it.

577 *The Devil's Dictionary*
To be positive: to be mistaken at the top of one's voice.

578 *The Devil's Dictionary*
Pray, v: to ask that the laws of the universe be annulled in behalf of a single petitioner confessedly unworthy.

BIFFEN John 1930-
579 *(of Margaret Thatcher)*
She was a tigress surrounded by hamsters.

BILLINGS Josh 1818-1885
580
Adversity has the same effect on a man that severe training has on the pugilist - it reduces him to his fighting weight.

581
My advice to those who are about to begin, in earnest, the journey of life, is to take their heart in one hand and a club in the other.

582
To bring up a child in the way he should go, travel that way yourself once in a while.

583
It is a very delicate job to forgive a man, without lowering him in his estimation, and yours too.

584
As a general thing, when a woman wears the pants in a family, she has a good right to them.

585
The happiest time in any man's life is when he is in red-hot pursuit of a dollar with a reasonable prospect of overtaking it.

586 *Josh Billings' Wit and Humour*
'Vote early and vote often' is the Politishun's golden rule.

587
Laughter is the sensation of feeling good all over, and showing it principally in one spot.

588
Every man has his follies - and often they are the most interesting things he has got.

589
Most men would rather be charged with malice than with making a blunder.

590
Nature never makes any blunders; when she makes a fool she means it.

591
It is not only the most difficult thing to know oneself, but the most inconvenient one, too.

592
There are some people so addicted to exaggeration that they can't tell the truth without lying.

593
There are many people who mistake their imagination for their memory.

594
Pity costs nothin' and ain't worth nothin'.

595
As scarce as truth is, the supply has always been in excess of the demand.

596
The trouble ain't that people are ignorant: it's that they know so much that ain't so.

597
The truly innocent are those who not only are guiltless themselves, but who think others are.

598
When a man comes to me for advice, I find out the kind of advice he wants, and I give it to him.

599
When a man gets talking about himself, he seldom fails to be eloquent and often reaches the sublime.

BINGER William
600
A man is a person who will pay two dollars for a one-dollar item he wants. A woman will pay one dollar for a two-dollar item she doesn't want.

BISMARCK Prince Otto von 1815-1898
601
You can trust all Englishmen except those who speak French.

602
When you say that you agree to a thing in principle, you mean that you have not the slightest intention of carrying it out.

BISSONETTE David
603
I recently read that love is entirely a matter of chemistry. That must be why my wife treats me like toxic waste.

BLACK Conrad 1944-
604
Humility is a good quality, but it can be overdone.

BLACKBURN Tony
605
Why should the Pope be any closer to God than I am?

BLADE Toledo
606
A great many open minds should be closed for repairs.

BLAKE Eubie 1883-1983
607 *(on reaching 100)*
If I'd known I was gonna live this long, I'd have taken better care of myself.

BLAKE William 1757-1827
608
Improvement makes straight roads; but the crooked roads without improvement are roads of genius.

609 *The Marriage of Heaven and Hell*
Damn braces: Bless relaxes.

BLIXEN Karen 1885-1962
610 *Out of Africa*
A herd of elephant ... pacing along as if they had an appointment at the end of the world.

611 *Seven Gothic Tales 'The Dreamers'*
What is man, when you come to think upon him, but a minutely set, ingenious machine for turning, with infinite artfulness, the red wine of Shiraz into urine?

BLOCH Arthur
612
A conclusion is the place where you got tired of thinking.

BLOOMFIELD Harold H.
613
The irony of love is that it guarantees some degree of anger, fear and criticism.

BLUM Norbert
614
Politics is like football - it doesn't matter whether you win 3-1 or 1-0, you still get 2 points.

BLYTHE Ronald 1922-
615 *The Age of Illusion*
As for the British churchman, he goes to church as he goes to the bathroom, with the minimum of fuss and with no explanation if he can help it.

BODENHEIM Maxwell 1893-1954
616
Poetry is the impish attempt to paint the colour of the wind.

BOESE Paul
617
Nature thrives on patience; man on impatience.

BOGART Humphrey 1899-1957
618
The whole world is about three drinks behind.

BOILEAU Nicolas 1636-1711
619 *L'Art poétique*
A fool can always find a greater fool to admire him.

620 *Satire (2) A M.Molière*
Of every four words I write, I strike out three.

BOK Derek 1930-
621
If you think education is expensive - try ignorance.

BOLINGBROKE 1st Viscount 1678-1751
622 *Observations, Anecdotes, and Characters*
The great mistake is that of looking upon men as virtuous, or thinking that they can be made so by laws.

623 *Observations, Anecdotes, and Characters*
The greatest art of a politician is to render vice serviceable to the cause of virtue.

BOLT Robert 1924-1995
624 *A Man for All Seasons*
It profits a man nothing to give his soul for the whole world ... But for Wales - !

BOMBECK Erma 1927-
625
Guilt: the gift that goes on giving.

BOND Edward 1934-
626
Law and order is one of the steps taken to maintain injustice.

BOORSTIN Daniel J. 1914-
627
Some are born great, some achieve greatness, and some hire public relations officers.

628 *The Image*
A best-seller was a book which somehow sold well simply because it was selling well.

629
A sign of a celebrity is often that his name is worth more than his services.

BOREN James H. 1925-
630
Guidelines for bureaucrats:
(1) When in charge, ponder.
(2) When in trouble, delegate.
(3) When in doubt, mumble.

BORGE Victor 1909-
631
Laughter is the shortest distance between two people.

632
Ah Mozart! He was happily married - but his wife wasn't.

633 *(playing to a half-filled house)*
Flint must be an extremely wealthy town; I see that each of you bought two or three seats.

BORGES Jorge Luis 1899-1986
634
The Falklands thing was a fight between two bald men over a comb.

BÖRNE Ludwig 1786-1837
635
Women are most adorable when they are afraid; that's why they frighten so easily.

BORROW George 1803-1881
636 *Lavengro*
A losing trade, I assure you, sir: literature is a drug.

BORSODI Ralph
637
There is less leisure now than in the Middle Ages, when one third of the year consisted of holidays and festivals.

BOSSIDY John Collins 1860-1928
638 *(at Holy Cross College)*
And this is good old Boston,
The home of the bean and the cod,

Where the Lowells talk to the Cabots
And the Cabots talk only to God.

BOSWELL James 1740-1795
639 *The Life of Samuel Johnson*
JOHNSON: Well, we had a good talk.
BOSWELL: Yes Sir; you tossed and gored
several persons.

640 *The Life of Samuel Johnson*
A man, indeed, is not genteel when he
gets drunk; but most vices may be
committed very genteelly: a man may
debauch his friend's wife genteelly: he
may cheat at cards genteelly.

BOTTOMLEY Virginia 1948-
641
Smoking is a dying habit.

BOUCICAULT Dion c.1820-1890
642
I wish Adam had died with all his ribs in
his body.

BOULDING Kenneth
643
Canada has no cultural unity, no
linguistic unity, no religious unity, no
economic unity, no geographic unity. All
it has is unity.

644
Nothing fails like success because we
don't learn from it. We learn only from
failure.

BOULTON Sir Harold Edwin 1859-1935
645 *'Glorious Devon'*
When Adam and Eve were dispossessed
Of the garden hard by Heaven,
They planted another one down in the
west,
'Twas Devon, glorious Devon!

BOURJAILY Vance
646
Every man, even the most blessed, needs
a little more than average luck to survive
this world.

BOWEN Elizabeth 1899-1973
647 *(of Edith Sitwell)*
A high altar on the move.

BOWEN Ezra
648
If thee marries for money, thee surely
will earn it.

BOWEN Lord 1835-1894
649
The rain, it raineth on the just
And also on the unjust fella:
But chiefly on the just, because
The unjust steals the just's umbrella.

650
When I hear of an 'equity' in a case like
this, I am reminded of a blind man in a
dark room - looking for a black hat -
which isn't there.

BOWER Walter
651
The wolf was sick, he vowed a monk to
be;
But when he got well, a wolf once more
was he.

BOWMAN Louis Nelson
652
Another thing about capitalism -
everybody knows who's in Grant's tomb.

BOWMAN Peter
653
Only man, among living things, says
prayers. Or needs to.

BOWRA Sir Maurice 1898-1971
654 *John Betjeman Summoned by Bells*
I'm a man more dined against than
dining.

BOYD-ORR Lord 1880-1971
655
If people have to choose between
freedom and sandwiches they will take
sandwiches.

BOYER Charles 1899-1978
656
A French woman, when double-crossed,
will kill her rival. The Italian woman
would rather kill her deceitful lover. The
Englishwoman simply breaks off
relations - but they will all console
themselves with another man.

BOYSE J.F.
657
It would be a great advantage to some schoolmasters if they would steal two hours a day from their pupils, and give their own minds the benefit of the robbery.

BRADBURY Malcolm 1932-
658 *Eating People is Wrong*
The English have the most rigid code of immorality in the world.

BRADLEE Benjamin 1921-
659
News is the first rough draft of history.

BRADLEY F.H. 1846-1924
660 *Appearance and Reality [preface]*
Where everthing is bad it must be good to know the worst.

661
Few people would not be the worse for complete sincerity.

BRADLEY Omar 1893-1981
662
We have grasped the mystery of the atom, and rejected the Sermon on the Mount.

BRANDEN Nathaniel
663
For the rational, psychologically healthy man, the desire for pleasure is the desire to celebrate his control over reality. For the neurotic, the desire for pleasure is the desire to escape from reality.

BRANDO Marlon 1924-
664
An actor's a guy who, if you ain't talking about him, ain't listening.

665 *in On The Waterfront*
"I coulda been a contender. I coulda had class and been somebody."

BRAUN Wernher von 1912-1977
666
Basic research is when I'm doing what I don't know what I'm doing.

BRECHT Bertholt 1898-1956
667
People are too durable, that's their main trouble. They can do too much to themselves, they last too long.

668 *The Threepenny Opera*
Food comes first, then morals.

669 *The Threepenny Opera*
What is robbing a bank compared with founding a bank?

670
What happens to the hole when the cheese is gone?

BRENAN Gerald 1894-1987
671 *Thoughts in a Dry Season*
In a happy marriage, it is the wife who provides the climate, the husband the landscape.

BRIDGMAN Percy Williams 1882-1961
672
There is no adequate defence, except stupidity, against the impact of a new idea.

BRINKLEY David
673
This is the first convention of the space age - where a candidate can promise the moon and mean it.

BRITTEN Benjamin 1913-1976
674
I am an arrogant and impatient listener, but in the case of a few composers, a very few, when I hear a work I do not like, I am convinced that it is my own fault. Verdi is one of those composers.

BRONTÉ Charlotte 1816-1855
675 *Shirley*
Of late years an abundant shower of curates has fallen upon the North of England.

676 *Shirley*
Be a governess! Better be a slave at once!

BROOKE Rupert 1887-1915
677 *'The Old Vicarage, Grantchester'*
For Cambridge people rarely smile,

Being urban, squat, and packed with guile.

BROOKS Mel 1926-
678
Humour is just another defence against the universe.

679
Look at Jewish history. Unrelieved lamenting would be intolerable. So, for every ten Jews beating their breasts, God designated one to be crazy and amuse the breast-beaters. By the time I was five I knew I was that one.

BROOKS Thomas 1608-1680
680
No good deed ever goes unpunished.

BROOKS Van Wyck 1886-1963
681
Nothing is so soothing to our self-esteem as to find our bad traits in our forebears. It seems to absolve us.

BROUN Heywood 1888-1939
682
Men build bridges and throw railroads across deserts, and yet they contend successfully that the job of sewing on a button is beyond them. Accordingly, they don't have to sew buttons.

BROWN Bob
683
Behind every successful man there's a lot of unsuccessful years.

BROWN Jerry 1938-
684
The government is becoming the family of last resort.

BROWN John Mason 1900-
685
To many people dramatic criticism must seem like an attempt to tattoo soap bubbles.

BROWN Thomas 1663-1704
686
I do not love thee, Doctor Fell,
The reason why I cannot tell;
But this alone I know full well,
I do not love thee, Doctor Fell.

BROWNE Sir William 1692-1774
687 *Literary Anecdotes Reply to Trapp's epigram*
The King to Oxford sent a troop of horse,
For Tories own no argument but force:
With equal skill to Cambridge books he sent,
For Whigs admit no force but argument.

BROWNING Robert 1812-1889
688 *'Bishop Blougram's Apology'*
He said true things, but called them by wrong names.

689 *'Easter-Day'*
'Tis well averred,
A scientific faith's absurd.

690 *'My Last Duchess'*
She had
A heart - how shall I say? - too soon made glad,
Too easily impressed: she liked whate'er
She looked on, and her looks went everywhere.

691 *Sordello*
Any nose
May ravage with impunity a rose.

BRUCE Lenny 1925-1966
692
The whole motivation for any performer is 'Look at me, Ma.'

BRUYERE Jean de la 1645-1696
693
It is a great misfortune neither to have enough wit to talk well nor enough judgement to be silent.

694
As long as men are liable to die and are desirous to live, a physician will be made fun of, but he will be well paid.

695
A man often runs the risk of throwing away a witticism if he admits that it is his own.

BUCHAN John 1875-1940
696
An atheist is a man who has no invisible means of support.

697 *Mr. Standfast*
Its a great life if you don't weaken.

BUCHANAN Robert 1841-1901
698 *'White Rose and Red'*
She just wore
Enough for modesty - no more.

BUCHMAN Frank 1878-1961
699 *Remaking the World*
Suppose everybody cared enough,
everybody shared enough, wouldn't
everybody have enough? There is
enough in the world for everyone's need,
but not enough for everyone's greed.

BUCHWALD Art
700
Television has a real problem. They have
no page two.

701
When it came to writing about wine, I
did what everyone else did - faked it.

BUCK Pearl 1892-1973
702 *The Good Earth*
It is better to be first with an ugly woman
than the hundredth with a beauty.

BULLER Arthur 1874-1944
703 *'Relativity'*
There was a young lady named Bright,
Whose speed was far faster than light;
She set out one day
In a relative way
And returned on the previous night.

BULWER-LYTTON Edward 1803-1873
704
A good cigar is as great a comfort to a
man as a good cry is to a woman.

705
Life would be tolerably agreeable if it
were not for its amusements.

706 *The Parisians*
Revolutions are not made with
rosewater.

707 *What will he do with it?*
There is no man so friendless but what
he can find a friend sincere enough to
tell him disagreeable truths.

BUÑUEL Luis 1900-1983
708
Thanks to God, I am still an atheist.

BURBANK Luther 1849-1926
709
Heredity is nothing but stored
environment.

BURKE Billie
710
I am constantly amazed when I talk to
young people to learn how much they
know about sex and how little about
soap.

711
A woman past forty should make up her
mind to be young - not her face.

BURKE Edmund 1729-1797
712
By gnawing through a dyke, even a rat
may drown a nation.

BURNET Dana
713
I'd rather have an inch of dog than miles
of pedigree.

BURNETT Carol 1934-
714
Comedy is tragedy - plus time.

BURNEY Fanny (Mme D'Arblay) 1752-
1840
715 *Camilla*
A little alarm now and then keeps life
from stagnation.

716 *Camilla*
It's a delightful thing to think of
perfection; but it's vastly more amusing
to talk of errors and absurdities.

717 *Camilla*
No man is in love when he marries. He
may have loved before; I have even
heard he has sometimes loved after: but
at the time never. There is something in
the formalities of the matrimonial
preparations that drive away all the little
cupidons.

718 *Cecilia*
Travelling is the ruin of all happiness!
There's no looking at a building here
after seeing Italy.

BURNS George 1896-1996
719
Too bad that all the people who know
how to run the country are busy driving
taxicabs and cutting hair.

720
With the collapse of vaudeville new
talent has no place to stink.

721
I must be getting absent-minded.
Whenever I complain that things aren't
what they used to be, I always forget to
include myself.

722
Happiness? A good cigar, a good meal,
and a good woman - or a bad woman; it
depends on how much happiness you
can handle.

BURNS Robert 1759-1796
723 *'The Author's Earnest Cry and Prayer'*
Freedom and Whisky gan thegither!

724 *'Death and Dr Hornbook'*
I wasna fou, but just had plenty.

725 *'The Deil's awa wi' th'Exciseman'*
There's threesome reels, there's foursome
reels,
There's hornpipes and strathspeys, man,
But the ae best dance e'er cam to the
land
Was, the deil's awa wi' th'Exciseman.

726 *'Green Grow the Rashes'*
Green grow the rashes, O,
Green grow the rashes, O;
The sweetest hours that e're I spend,
Are spent among the lasses, O.

727 *'The Jolly Beggars'*
Life is all a VARIORUM,
We regard not how it goes;
Let them cant about DECORUM,
Who have characters to lose.

728 *'To a Louse'*
O wad some Pow'r the giftie gie us
To see oursels as others see us!
It wad frae mony a blunder free us,
And foolish notion.

729 *(said shortly before his death)*
Don't let the awkward squad fire over
me.

BURROUGHS William 1914-1997
730
Americans have a special horror of
letting things happen their own way,
without interference. They would like to
jump down their stomachs, digest the
food, and shovel the shit out.

BURROWS Sir Fred 1887-1973
731 *(speech as last Governor of undivided
Bengal)*
Unlike my predecessors I have devoted
more of my life to shunting and hooting
than to hunting and shooting.

BURTON Sir Richard 1821-1890
732 *(note to his wife)*
Pay, pack, and follow at convenience.

BURTON Robert 1577-1640
733
Set a beggar on horseback, and he will
ride a gallop.

BUSCH Wilhelm 1832-1908
734
To become a father is not hard,
To be a father is, however.

BUSH Barbara 1925-
735
Somewhere out in this audience may
even be someone who will one day
follow in my footsteps, and preside over
the White House as the President's
spouse. I wish him well.

BUSSY-RABUTIN Comte de 1618-1693
736
God is usually on the side of big
squadrons and against little ones.

BUSTON Charles
737
To make pleasure pleasant, shorten.

BUTLER Nicholas Murray 1862-1947
738 *(attributed)*
An expert is one who knows more and
more about less and less.

BUTLER Samuel 1835-1902
739 *(attributed)*
Brigands demand your money or your
life; women require both.

740
All philosophies, if you ride them home,
are nonsense; but some are greater
nonsense than others.

741
An apology for the Devil - it must be
remembered that we have only heard
one side of the case. God has written all
the books.

742
I do not mind lying, but I hate
inaccuracy.

743 *Further Extracts from Notebooks*
The three most important things a man
has are, briefly, his private parts, his
money, and his religious opinions.

744 *Further Extracts from Notebooks*
Jesus! with all thy faults I love thee still.

745 *Further Extracts from Notebooks*
Conscience is thoroughly well-bred and
soon leaves off talking to those who do
not wish to hear it.

746
It is the function of vice to keep virtue
within reasonable grounds.

747
I can generally bear the separation, but I
don't like the leave-taking.

748
It has been said that though God cannot
alter the past, historians can; it is
perhaps because they can be useful to
Him in this respect that He tolerates
their existence.

749
The great pleasure of a dog is that you
may make a fool of yourself with him

and not only will he not scold you, but
he will make a fool of himself too.

750
It is hard to come down the social ladder
without tumbling off.

751
A hen is only an egg's way of making
another egg.

752
A lawyer's dream of heaven - every man
reclaimed his property at the
resurrection, and each tried to recover it
from all his forefathers.

753 *Letters between Samuel Butler and
Miss E.M.Savage*
It was very good of God to let Carlyle and
Mrs Carlyle marry one another and so
make only two people miserable instead
of four.

754
Life is like playing a violin solo in public
and learning the instrument as one goes
on.

755
If life must not be taken too seriously -
then so neither must death.

756 *Notebooks*
Life is one long process of getting tired.

757 *Notebooks*
All progress is based upon a universal
innate desire on the part of every
organism to live beyond its income.

758 *Notebooks*
The history of art is the history of
revivals.

759 *Notebooks*
Our ideas. They are for the most part
like bad sixpences and we spend our
lives in trying to pass them on one
another.

760 *Notebooks*
To live is like to love - all reason is
against it, and all healthy instinct for it.

761
To put one's trust in God is only a longer way of saying that one will chance it.

762
I reckon being ill is one of the greatest pleasures of life, provided one is not too ill and is not obliged to work till one is better.

763
Silence is not always tact, and it is tact that is golden, not silence.

764 *The Way of All Flesh*
The advantage of doing one's praising for oneself is that one can lay it on so thick and exactly in the right places.

765 *The Way of All Flesh*
Young as he was, his instinct told him that the best liar is he who makes the smallest amount of lying go the longest way.

766
When you have told anyone you have left him a legacy, the only decent thing to do is to die at once.

BUTLER Samuel 'Hudibras' 1612-1680
767 *Hudibras*
He'd run in debt by disputation,
And pay with ratiocination.

768 *Hudibras*
For all a rhetorician's rules
Teach nothing but to name his tools.

769 *Hudibras*
He knew what's what, and that's as high
As metaphysic wit can fly.

770 *Hudibras*
Compound for sins, they are inclined to,
By damning those they have no mind to.

771 *Hudibras*
Great actions are not always true sons
Of great and mighty resolutions.

772 *Hudibras*
What makes all doctrines plain and clear?
About two hundred pounds a year.
And that which was proved true before,
Prove false again? Two hundred more.

BUXTON Charles
773
Pounds are the sons, not of pounds, but of pence.

BYRON Lord 1788-1824
774 *'The Age of Bronze'*
For what were all these country patriots born?
To hunt, and vote, and raise the price of corn?

775 *Don Juan*
And thus they form a group that's quite antique,
Half naked, loving, natural, and Greek.

776 *Don Juan*
Dreading that climax of all human ills,
The inflammation of his weekly bills.

777 *Don Juan*
There is a tide in the affairs of women,
Which, taken at the flood, leads - God knows where.

778 *Don Juan*
A lady of a 'certain age', which means
Certainly aged.

779 *Don Juan*
Of all the horrid, hideous notes of woe,
Sadder than owl-songs or the midnight blast,
Is that portentous phrase, 'I told you so.'

780 *Don Juan*
Let us have Wine and Women, Mirth and Laughter
Sermons and soda-water the day after.

781 *Don Juan*
Society is now one polished horde,
Formed of two mighty tribes,
The Bores and the Bored.

782 *Don Juan*
What men call gallantry, and gods adultery,
Is much more common where the climate's sultry.

783 *Don Juan*
A little still she strove, and much repented,

And whispering 'I will ne'er consent' -
consented.

784 *Don Juan*
Merely innocent flirtation.
Not quite adultery, but adulteration.

785 *Don Juan*
Now hatred is by far the longest
pleasure;
Men love in haste, but they detest at
leisure.

786 *Don Juan*
The English winter - ending in July,
To recommence in August.

787 *Letter to Thomas Moore*
Like other parties of the kind, it was first
silent, then talky, then argumentative,
then disputatious, then unintelligible,
then altogethery, then inarticulate, and
then drunk.

788 *The Vision of Judgement*
Yet still between his Darkness and his
Brightness
There passed a mutual glance of great
politeness.

CABELL James Branch 1879-1958
789 *The Silver Stallion*
The optimist proclaims that we live in
the best of all possible worlds; and the
pessimist fears this is true.

CAHN Peggy
790
I believe that the sign of maturity is
accepting deferred gratification.

CAINE Marti 1945-1995
791 *(when told she had malignant
limphoma)*
Does that mean I'm a lymphomaniac?

CAINE Michael 1933-
792 *in Alfie*
"My understanding of Women goes only
as far as the pleasure."

793
The British Film Industry is alive and
well and living in Los Angeles.

CAJAL Santiago Ramon y
794
That which enters the mind through
reason can be corrected. That which is
admitted through faith, hardly ever.

CALVERLEY C.S. 1831-1884
795 *'Contentment'*
Life is with such all beer and skittles;
They are not difficult to please
About their victuals.

CAMERON Simon
796
An honest politician is one who when he
is bought will stay bought.

CAMPBELL Bushrod H.
797
If I've learned anything in my seventy
years it's that nothing's as good or as bad
as it appears.

CAMPBELL Patrick
798
It seems to me that you can go
sauntering along for a certain period,
telling the English some interesting
things about themselves, and then all at
once it feels as if you had stepped on the
prongs of a rake.

CAMPBELL Mrs Patrick 1865-1940
799
Do you know why God withheld the
sense of humour from women? So that
we might love men instead of laugh at
them.

800
It doesn't matter what you do in the
bedroom as long as you don't do it in the
street and frighten the horses.

801 *(on her recent marriage)*
The deep, deep peace of the double-bed
after the hurly-burly of the chaise-
longue.

CAMPBELL Thomas 1777-1844
802 *'The Jilted Nymph'*
Better be courted and jilted
Than never be courted at all.

CAMUS Albert 1913-1960

803

We call first truths those we discover after all the others.

804

Charm is a way of getting the answer yes without having asked any clear question.

805 *The Fall*

We seldom confide in those who are better than ourselves.

806 *The Fall*

I'll tell you a great secret, my friend. Don't wait for the last judgement. It happens every day.

807 *The Fall*

A single sentence will suffice for modern man: he fornicated and read the papers.

808

The innocent is the person who explains nothing.

809

I know myself too well to believe in pure virtue.

810 *Notebooks*

An intellectual is someone whose mind watches itself.

811 *The Rebel*

What is a rebel? A man who says no.

CANNING George 1770-1827

812

Give me the avowed, the erect, and manly foe,
Bold I can meet, perhaps may turn the blow;
But of all plagues, good Heaven, thy wrath can send,
Save, save, oh save me from the candid friend!

813

In matters of commerce the fault of the Dutch
Is offering too little and asking too much.
The French are with equal advantage content,
So we clap on Dutch bottoms just 20%.

814 *'The Oracle'*

Pitt is to Addington
As London is to Paddington.

CAPOTE Truman 1924-1984

815

In California everyone goes to a therapist, is a therapist, or is a therapist going to a therapist.

816 *(of Jack Kerouac)*

That's not writing, that's typing.

817

Venice is like eating an entire box of chocolate liqueurs in one go.

CAPRA Frank 1897-1991

818

Automatic simply means that you can't repair it yourself.

CARLYLE Jane 1801-1866

819 *Letter to Thomas Carlyle*

I am not at all the sort of person you and I took me for.

CARLYLE Thomas 1795-1881

820 *Critical and Miscellaneous Essays*

A well-written Life is almost as rare as a well-spent one.

821 *Critical and Miscellaneous Essays*

The three great elements of modern civilization, Gunpowder, Printing, and the Protestant Religion.

822

God Almighty never created a man half as wise as he looks.

823

He that can work is a born king of something.

CARMAN Bliss 1861-1929

824

The greatest joy in nature is the absence of man.

825

Indifference may not wreck a man's life at any one turn, but it will destroy him with a kind of dryrot in the long run.

CARROLL Lewis (Charles L. Dodgson)
1832-1898
826 *Alice's Adventures in Wonderland*
'What is the use of a book' thought Alice,
'without pictures or conversations?'

827 *Alice's Adventures in Wonderland*
How cheerfully he seems to grin,
How neatly spreads his claws,
And welcomes little fishes in
With gently smiling jaws!

828 *Alice's Adventures in Wonderland*
'You are old, Father William,' the young
man said,
'And your hair has become very white;
And yet you incessantly stand on your
head-
Do you think, at your age, it is right?'

829 *Alice's Adventures in Wonderland*
Speak roughly to your little boy,
And beat him when he sneezes;
He only does it to annoy,
Because he knows it teases.

830 *Alice's Adventures in Wonderland*
Everything's got a moral, if you can only
find it.

831 *Through the Looking-Glass*
'Twas brillig, and the slithy toves
Did gyre and gimble in the wabe;
All mimsy were the borogoves,
And the mome raths outgrabe.'

'Beware the Jabberwock, my son!
The jaws that bite, the claws that catch!'

832 *Through the Looking-Glass*
'The time has come,' the Walrus said,
'To talk of many things:
Of shoes - and ships - and sealing wax -
Of cabbages - and kings -
And why the sea is boiling hot -
And whether pigs have wings.'

833 *Through the Looking-Glass*
The rule is, jam tomorrow and jam
yesterday - but never jam today.

834 *Through the Looking-Glass*
It's as large as life and twice as natural!

835 *Through the Looking-Glass*
'The horror of that moment,' the King
went on, 'I shall never, never forget!'
'You will, though,' the Queen said, 'if you
don't make a memorandum of it.'

836 *Through the Looking-Glass*
Now here, you see, it takes all the
running you can do to keep in the same
place. If you want to get somewhere
else, you must run at least twice as fast
as that!

837 *Through the Looking-Glass*
What I tell you three times is true.

838 *Through the Looking-Glass*
It's one of the most serious things that
can possibly happen to one in a battle -
to get one's head cut off.

839 *Through the Looking-Glass*
Take care of the sense and the sounds
will take of themselves.

CARRUTHERS Charles Edwin
840
In judging others, folks will work
overtime for no pay.

CARSON Jack
841
A fan club is a group of people who tell
an actor he is not alone in the way he
feels about himself.

CARSON Lord 1854-1935
842
My only great qualification for being put
at the head of the Navy is that I am very
much at sea.

CARSON Marco
843
And by my grave you'd pray to have me
back
So I could see how well you look in
black.

CARTER Dyson
844
I feel age like an icicle down my back.

CARTER Hodding
845
There are only two lasting bequests we

CARTER Jimmy 1924-
846
I've looked on a lot of women with lust. I've committed adultery in my heart many times. This is something God recognizes I will do - and I have done it - and God forgives me for it.

CARTLAND Barbara 1901-
847
A historical romance is the only kind of book where chastity really counts.

CARY Joyce 1888-1957
848 *The Horse's Mouth*
Sara could commit adultery at one end and weep for her sins at the other, and enjoy both operations at once.

849
A man of eighty has outlived probably three new schools of painting, two of architecture and poetry, and a hundred in dress.

CASSON Herbert
850
Net - the biggest word in the language of business.

CASTRO Fidel 1926-
851 *(on battledress)*
Practical, simple, cheap and does not go out of fashion.

CATLIN Wynn
852
Diplomacy; the art of saying 'nice doggie' till you can find a rock.

CATULLUS c.84-c.54 BC
853 *Carmina*
For there is nothing sillier than a silly laugh.

CÉLINE Louis-Ferdinand 1894-1961
854
If you aren't rich, you should always look useful.

855
History doesn't pass the dishes again.

CENTLIVRE Susannah c.1667-1723
856
'Tis my opinion every man cheats in his way, and he is only honest who is not discovered.

CERVANTES Miguel de 1547-1616
857
God bears with the wicked, but not forever.

858
Every one is as God made him and oftentimes a good deal worse.

859
The guts carry the feet, not the feet the guts.

860 *Don Quixote*
Let them eat the lie and swallow it with their bread. Whether the two were lovers or no, they'll have accounted to God for it by now. I have my own fish to fry.

861
You must not think, sir, to catch old birds with chaff.

CHAGALL Marc 1889-1985
862
The fingers must be educated, the thumb is born knowing.

CHAMFORT Sebastien c.1741-1794
863
Society is composed of two great classes: those who have more dinners than appetite, and those who have more appetite than dinners.

CHANDLER Raymond 1888-1959
864 *Farewell My Lovely*
She gave me a smile I could feel in my hip pocket.

865
A good title is the title of a successful book.

866 *The Long Good-Bye*
Alcohol is like love: the first kiss is magic, the second is intimate, the third is routine. After that you just take the girl's clothes off.

CHANEL Coco 1883-1971
867
There is time for work. And time for love. That leaves no other time.

868 *(on being asked where one should wear perfume)*
Wherever one wants to be kissed.

CHAR René 1907-
869
In action, be primitive; in foresight, a strategist.

870
That which comes into the world to disturb nothing deserves neither respect nor patience.

871
For an inheritance to be really great, the hand of the defunct must not be seen.

CHARCOT Jean-Martin
872
Symptoms, then, are in reality nothing but the cry from suffering organs.

CHASE Alexander
873
The banalities of a great man pass for wit.

874
Memory is the thing you forget with.

CHAUCER Geoffrey c.1343-1400
875 *The Canterbury Tales*
Wel loved he garleek, oynons, and eek lekes,
And for to drynken strong wyn, reed as blood.

876 *The Canterbury Tales*
Kepe wel they tonge, and thenk upon the crowe.

877 *The Canterbury Tales*
Derk was the nyght as pich, or as the cole,
And at the wyndow out she putte hir hole,
And Absolon, hym fil no bet be wers,
But with his mouth he kiste hir naked ers.

878 *The Canterbury Tales*
'By God,' quod he, 'for pleynly, at a word,
Thy drasty rymyng is nat worth a toord!'

879 *The Canterbury Tales*
'My lige lady, generally,' quod he,
'Wommen desiren to have sovereynetee
As wel over hir housbond as hir love.'

880 *Tale of Melibee*
What is bettre than wisedoom?
Womman. And what is bettre than a good womman? Nothyng.

881 *Troilus and Criseyde*
It is nought good a slepyng hound to wake.

CHAZAI
882
A woman knows how to keep quiet when she is in the right, whereas a man, when he is in the right, will keep on talking.

CHEKHOV Anton 1860-1904
883
Any idiot can face a crisis - it's this day-to-day living that wears you out.

884
A man and a woman marry because both of them don't know what to do with themselves.

CHEPIK Nikolai 1966-1985
885 *(from his diary)*
Believing that a girl will wait is just like jumping with a parachute packed by someone else.

CHER 1946-
886
The trouble with some women is they get all excited about nothing - and then they marry him!

CHESTERFIELD Lord 1694-1773
887 *Letters to his Son*
An injury is much sooner forgotten than an insult.

888
Patience is a most necessary quality for business; many a man would rather you heard his story than grant his request.

41

889
Many people enjoy the inferiority of their best friends.

890
When a man is once in fashion, all he does is right.

CHESTER Henry
891
Enthusiasm is the greatest asset in the world. It beats money and power and influence.

CHESTERTON G.K. 1874-1936
892
I am not absent-minded. It is the presence of mind that makes me unaware of everything else.

893
Angels fly because they take themselves lightly.

894
The classes that wash most are those that work least.

895 *The Defendant*
There is a road from the eye to the heart that does not go through the intellect.

896
Democracy means government by the uneducated, while aristocracy means government by the badly educated.

897
We make our friends; we make our enemies; but God makes our next-door neighbour.

898 *The Man who was Thursday*
Thieves respect property. They merely wish the property to become their property that they may more perfectly respect it.

899
One may understand the cosmos, but never the ego; the self is more distant than any star.

900
Merely having an open mind is nothing. The object of opening the mind, as of opening the mouth, is to shut it again on something solid.

901
There is nothing the matter with Americans except their ideals. The real American is all right; it is the ideal American who is all wrong.

902
Psychoanalysis is confession without absolution.

903 *'The Rolling English Road'*
Before the Roman came to Rye or out to Severn strode,
The rolling English drunkard made the rolling English road.
A reeling road, a rolling road, that rambles round the shire,
And after him the parson ran, the sexton and the squire;
A merry road, a mazy road, and such as we did tread
The night we went to Birmingham by way of Beachy Head.

904
Silence is the unbearable repartee.

905 *What's Wrong with the World*
The Christian ideal has not been tried and found wanting. It has been found difficult; and left untried.

906 *What's Wrong with the World*
The prime truth of woman, the universal mother ... that if a thing is worth doing, it is worth doing badly.

907
The word 'good' has many meanings. For example, if a man were to shoot his grandmother at a range of five hundred yards, I should call him a good shot, but not *necessarily* a good man.

CHEVALIER Maurice 1888-1972
908 *(attributed)*
Many a man has fallen in love with a girl in a light so dim he would not have chosen a suit by it.

909
Old age is not so bad when you consider the alternatives.

CHILDS Richard S.
910
A reformer is one who sets forth cheerfully towards sure defeat.

CHING Cyrus
911
I learned long ago never to wrestle with a pig. You get dirty, and besides, the pig likes it.

CHRISTIE Dame Agatha 1890-1976
912 *(of her own marriage)*
An archaeologist is the best husband any woman can have. The older she gets, the more interested he is in her.

CHRISTINA Queen of Sweden
913
I love men, not because they are men, but because they are not women.

CHURCHILL Charles 1731-1764
914 *Night*
Keep up appearances; there lies the test;
The world wil give thee credit for the rest.

915 *The Rosciad*
The two extremes appear like man and wife,
Coupled together for the sake of strife.

CHURCHILL Lord Randolph 1849-1894
916
Whenever by an unfortunate occurrence of circumstances an opposition is compelled to support the government, the support should be given with a kick and not a caress and should be withdrawn at the first available moment.

CHURCHILL Sir Winston 1874-1965
917
He has all of the virtues I dislike and none of the vices I admire.

918
We are all worms, but I do believe that I am a glow-worm.

919 *(attributed)*
An appeaser is one who feeds a crocodile - hoping it will eat him last.

920 *(of Clement Attlee)*
A sheep in sheep's clothing.

921
It has been said that Democracy is the worst form of government except all those other forms that have been tried from time to time.

922 *My Early Life*
Headmasters have powers at their disposal with which Prime Ministers have never yet been invested.

923 *My Early Life*
It is a good thing for an uneducated man to read books of quotations.

924 *While England Slept*
Dictators ride to and fro on tigers from which they dare not dismount. And the tigers are getting hungry.

925
The English never draw a line without blurring it.

926
A fanatic is one who can't change his mind and won't change the subject.

927 *The Gathering Storm*
When you have to kill a man it costs nothing to be polite.

928
If you have an important point to make, don't try to be subtle or clever. Use a pile-driver. Hit the point once. Then come back and hit it again. Then hit it a third time - a tremendous whack!

929
To jaw-jaw is always better than to war-war.

930
Say what you have to say and the first time you come to a sentence with a grammatical ending - sit down.

931
This is the sort of English up with which I will not put.

932
When I am abroad, I always make it a rule never to criticize or attack the government of my own country. I make up for lost time when I come home.

933
Where does the family start? It starts with a young man falling in love with a girl - no superior alternative has yet been found.

CIARDI John 1916-
934
Gentility is what is left over from rich ancestors after the money is gone.

935
Modern art is what happens when painters stop looking at girls and persuade themselves they have a better idea.

936
A savage is simply a human organism that has not received enough news from the human race.

937
A university is what a college becomes when the faculty loses interest in students.

CIBBER Colley 1671-1757
938 *The Double Gallant*
Oh! how many torments lie in the small circle of a wedding-ring!

939 *Richard III*
Perish the thought!

CICERO Marcus Tullius 106-43 BC
940
I am not ashamed to confess that I am ignorant of what I do not know.

941 *De Divinatione*
There is nothing so absurd but some philosopher has said it.

942
Old age, especially an honoured old age, has so great authority, that this is of more value than all the pleasures of youth.

943
Old age is by nature rather talkative.

944
When you have no basis for an argument, abuse the plaintiff.

CIORAN E.M.
945
No one can keep his griefs in their prime; they use themselves up.

CLAPHAM Lady Elisabeth 1911-1994
946
I never drink gin. It makes me, by turns, bellicose, lachrymose and comatose.

CLARE John 1793-1864
947 *'Child Harold'*
They took me from my wife, and to save trouble
I wed again, and made the error double.

CLARK Jane
948
All girlfriends are like bluebottles. Some are just a bit harder to swat.

CLARK Kenneth 1903-1983
949 *Civilisation*
Medieval marriages were entirely a matter of property, and, as everyone knows, marriage without love means love without marriage.

CLARKE John d. 1658
950 *Paraemiologia Anglo-Latina 'Diligentia'*
He that would thrive
Must rise at five;
He that hath thriven
May lie till seven.

CLARK Joe 1939-
951
One of the luxuries of a politician's life is that you see yourself as others see you.

CLAY Henry 1777-1852
952 *(to Senator Preston of South Carolina)*
I had rather be right than be President.

CLEAVER Eldridge 1935-
953
Too much agreement kills a chat.

CLEMENCEAU Georges 1841-1929
954 *(attributed)*
War is too serious a matter to entrust to
military men.

955
All the great pleasures in life are silent.

956
All that I know I learned after I was
thirty.

CLOUGH Arthur Hugh 1819-1861
957 *The Bothie of Tober-na-Vuolich*
Grace is given of God, but knowledge is
bought in the market.

958 *Dipsychus*
And almost everyone when age,
Disease, or sorrows strike him,
Inclines to think there is a God,
Or something very like Him.

959 *'The Latest Decalogue'*
Thou shalt not kill; but need'st not strive
Officiously to keep alive.

960 *'The Latest Decalogue'*
Do not adultery commit;
Advantage rarely comes of it.

961 *'The Latest Decalogue'*
Thou shalt not steal; an empty feat,
When it's so lucrative to cheat.

962 *'The Latest Decalogue'*
Thou shalt not covet; but tradition
Approves all forms of competition.

COBB Irvin S.
963
If a woman likes another woman, she's
cordial. If she doesn't like her, she's very
cordial.

COCKER Joe
964
England to me was always the 3 o'clock
break - that endless gap between lunch
and the pub opening again.

COCTEAU Jean 1889-1963
965
The greatest masterpiece in literature is
only a dictionary out of order.

966 *Journal d'un inconnu*
Poetry is a religion with no hope.

967 *Opium*
Life is a horizontal fall.

968 *Opium*
Victor Hugo was a madman who thought
he was Victor Hugo.

COFFIN Harold
969
A consumer is a shopper who is sore
about something.

COFFIN Rev. William Sloane 1924-
970
I'm not ok - you're not ok, and that's ok.

971
The world is too dangerous for anything
but truth, and too small for anything but
love.

COLBERT Jean Baptiste 1619-1683
972
The art of taxation consists in so
plucking the goose as to get the most
feathers with the least hissing.

COLBY Frank Moore
973
Many people lose their tempers merely
from seeing you keep yours.

COLEMAN John S.
974
The point to remember is that what the
government gives, it must first take away.

COLERIDGE Samuel Taylor 1772-1834
975
The most happy marriage I can imagine
to myself would be the union of a deaf
man to a blind woman.

976
Only the wise possess ideas; the greater
part of mankind are possessed by them.

977 *Table Talk*
The man's desire is for the woman; but
the woman's desire is rarely other than
for the desire of the man.

COLETTE (Sidonie-Gabrielle) 1873-1954

978

The woman who thinks she is intelligent demands equal rights with men. A woman who is intelligent does not.

COLLIE G. Norman

979

To make certain that crime does not pay, the government should take it over and try to run it.

COLLINS John Churton 1848-1908

980

To ask advice is in nine cases out of ten to tout for flattery.

981

The world, like an accomplished hostess, pays most attention to those whom it will soonest forget.

COLLINS Mortimer 1827-1876

982 *The Unknown Quantity*

A man is as old as he's feeling.
A woman as old as she looks.

COLTON Charles Caleb c.1780-1832

983

Applause is the spur of noble minds, the end and aim of weak ones.

984

Body and mind, like man and wife, do not always agree to die together.

985

To dare to live alone is the rarest courage; since there are many who had rather meet their bitterest enemy in the field, than their own hearts in their closet.

986

We hate some persons because we do not know them; and will not know them because we hate them.

987

If you cannot inspire a woman with love of you, fill her above the brim with love of herself; all that runs over will be yours.

988 *Lacon*

When you have nothing to say, say nothing.

989 *Lacon*

If you would be known, and not know, vegetate in a village; if you would know, and not be known, live in a city.

990

Men will wrangle for religion, write for it, fight for it, die for it, anything but live for it.

991

Never join with your friend when he abuses his horse or his wife unless the one is to be sold, and the other to be buried.

992

There is a paradox in pride: it makes some men ridiculous, but prevents others from becoming so.

COMFORT Alex 1920-

993

Sex ought to be a wholly satisfying link between two affectionate people from which they emerge unanxious, rewarded, and ready for more.

994

The telephone is the most important single technological resource of later life.

995

Two weeks is about the ideal length of time to retire.

COMMONER Barry

996

The first law of ecology is that everything is related to everything else.

COMPTON-BURNETT Dame Ivy 1884-1969

997

There is more difference within the sexes than between them.

998 *A Family and a Fortune*

Well, of course, people are only human ... But it really does not seem much for them to be.

999 *A Family and a Fortune*
People don't resent having nothing nearly as much as too little.

1000 *The Mighty and their Fall*
There are different kinds of wrong. The people sinned against are not always the best.

1001 *Orion*
My point is that it [wickedness] is not punished, and that is why it is natural to be guilty of it. When it is likely to be punished, most of us avoid it.

1002
There is probably nothing like living together for blinding people to each other.

1003
Real life seems to have no plots.

CONANT James Bryant 1898-1978
1004
Behold the turtle. He makes progress only when he sticks his neck out.

CONE Fairfax
1005
Advertising is what you do when you can't go to see somebody. That's all it is.

CONGREVE William 1670-1729
1006 *The Double Dealer*
There is nothing more unbecoming a man of quality than to laugh; Jesu, 'tis such a vulgar expression of the passion!

1007 *The Double Dealer*
She lays it on with a trowel.

CONNOLLY Cyril 1903-1974
1008
All charming people have something to conceal, usually their total dependence on the appreciation of others.

1009 *Enemies of Promise*
There is no more sombre enemy of good art than the pram in the hall.

1010 *The Unquiet Grave*
Imprisoned in every fat man a thin one is wildly signalling to be let out.

1011 *The Unquiet Grave*
There is no fury like an ex-wife searching for a new lover.

1012
The one way to get thin is to re-establish a purpose in life.

CONNOR Ralph 1860-1937
1013
I would often be a coward, but for the shame of it.

CONRAD Joseph 1857-1924
1014
Caricature: putting the face of a joke upon the body of a truth.

CONRAN Shirley 1932-
1015 *Superwoman*
Life's too short to stuff a mushroom.

COOK Dan
1016
The opera ain't over 'til the fat lady sings.

COOK Joe
1017
Of all my wife's relations I like myself the best.

COOLIDGE Calvin 1872-1933
1018
If you don't say anything, you won't be called on to repeat it.

1019
I have noticed that nothing I never said ever did me any harm.

1020
I think the American public wants a solemn ass as a president, and I think I'll go along with them.

1021
When more and more people are thrown out of work, unemployment results.

COPLAND Aaron 1900-1990
1022
If a literary man puts together two words about music, one of them will be wrong.

CORELLI Marie 1855-1924
1023
I never married because I have three

pets at home that answer the same purpose as a husband. I have a dog that growls every morning, a parrot that swears all afternoon, and a cat that comes home late at night.

COREY Professor Irwin
1024
Marriage is like a bank account. You put it in, you take it out, you lose interest.

CORT David
1025
Sex is the great amateur art.

COSBY Bill 1937-
1026
Human beings are the only creatures on earth that allow their children to come back home.

COSSMAN Joseph E.
1027
The best way to remember your wife's birthday is to forget it once.

1028
Middle age is when your broad mind and narrow waist begin to change places.

1029
Obstacles are things a person sees when he takes his eyes off his goal.

COTGRAVE Randle
1030
Eat bread at pleasure, drink wine by measure.

COTY René 1882-1962
1031
It's taken me all my life to understand that it is not necessary to understand everything.

COURTELINE Georges
1032
A woman never sees what we do for her, she only sees what we don't do.

COUTELI
1033
We are dying of accuracy.

COWARD Noël 1899-1973
1034
My body has certainly wandered a good deal, but I have an uneasy suspicion that my mind has not wandered enough.

1035
As one gets older, one discovers everything is going to be exactly the same with different hats on.

1036
Good heavens, television is something you appear on, you don't watch.

1037 *(of Randolph Churchill)*
Dear Randolph, utterly unspoiled by failure!

1038 *(attributed - of the retreat from Dunkirk)*
The noise, my dear! And the people!

COWLEY Abraham 1618-1667
1039 *'To Dr Scarborough'*
Life is an incurable disease.

COWLEY Hannah 1743-1809
1040 *Who's the Dupe?*
But what is woman? - only one of Nature's agreeable blunders.

COWLEY Malcolm 1898-1989
1041
They tell you that you'll lose your mind when you grow older. What they don't tell you is that you won't miss it very much.

COWPER William 1731-1800
1042 *'Conversation' (on tobacco)*
Pernicious weed! whose scent the fair annoys.

1043
A fool must now and then be right by chance.

1044
How much a dunce that has been sent to roam
Excels a dunce that has been kept at home!

1045 *'The Progress of Error'*
Remorse, the fatal egg by pleasure laid.

1046 *The Task*
Knowledge is proud that he has learned
so much;
Wisdom is humble that he knows no
more.

1047 *The Task 'The Sofa'*
Thus first necessity invented stools,
Convenience next suggested elbow-
chairs,
And luxury the accomplished sofa last.

1048 *'Tirocinium'*
The parson knows enough who knows a
duke.

CRABBE George 1754-1832
1049 *Tales of the Hall*
Secrets with girls, like loaded guns with
boys,
Are never valued till they make a noise.

1050 *The Village*
I grant indeed that fields and flocks have
charms,
For him that gazes or for him that farms.

CRIPPS Agnes
1051
Educate a man and you educate an
individual - educate a woman and you
educate a family.

CRITCHLEY Julian 1930-
1052
The only safe pleasure for a
parliamentarian is a bag of boiled
sweets.

CRYSTAL Billy
1053
Women need a reason to have sex - men
just need a place.

CUDLIPP Hugh 1913-
1054 *(of William Randolph Hearst)*
Truth for him was a moving target; he
never aimed for the bull and rarely
pierced the outer ring.

CUMMINGS E. E. 1894-1962
1055
a politician is an arse upon which
everyone has sat except a man.

CUNNINGHAM James Vincent 1911-
1985
1056 *Epigrams*
I married in my youth a wife.
She was my own, my very first.
She gave the best years of her life.
I hope nobody gets the worst.

CUPPY Will
1057
Etiquette means behaving yourself a
little better than is absolutely essential.

1058
Henry VIII had so many wives because
his dynastic sense was very strong
whenever he saw a maid of honour.

CURTIS Tony
1059
I wouldn't be caught dead marrying a
woman old enough to be my wife.

CUSHMAN Charlotte 1816-1876
1060
Goethe said there would be little left of
him if you were to discard what he owed
to others.

DAACON George
1061
If absolute power corrupts absolutely,
where does that leave God?

DALEY Cass
1062
Marriage is a matter of give and take, but
so far I haven't been able to find anybody
who'll take what I have to give.

DANGERFIELD Rodney 1921-
1063
I am at the age where food has taken the
place of sex in my life. In fact, I've just
had a mirror put over my kitchen table.

DARROW Clarence 1857-1938
1064
I do not pretend to know what many
ignorant men are sure of.

1065
The first half of our lives is ruined by our
parents and the second half by our
children.

D'AUREVILLY Barbey
1066
Next to the wound, what women makes best is the bandage.

DAVIES Robertson 1913-1995
1067
The eye sees only what the mind is prepared to comprehend.

1068
Female beauty is an important minor sacrament ... I am not at all sure that neglect of it does not constitute a sin of some kind.

1069
As a general thing, people marry most happily with their own kind. The trouble lies in the fact that people usually marry at an age when they do not really know what their own kind is.

1070 (on a biography of himself)
It's an exellent life of somebody else. But I've really lived inside myself, and she can't get in there.

DAVIS Bette 1908-1989
1071 in All About Eve
"Fasten your seatbelts. It's going to be a bumpy night."

1072 in The Cabin in the Cotton
"I'd luv to kiss ya, but I just washed my hair."

DAVIS Jr. Sammy 1925-1990
1073 Yes I Can
Being a star has made it possible for me to get insulted in places where the average negro could never hope to go and get insulted.

DAVIS William T.
1074
Only a few human beings should grow to the square mile; they are commonly planted too close.

DAY Clarence 1874-1935
1075
Father expected a good deal of God. He didn't actually accuse God of inefficiency, but when he prayed his tone was loud and angry, like that of a dissatisfied guest in a carelessly managed hotel.

DAY-LEWIS Tamasin
1076
I haven't yet been able to find a happy adulterer.

DE BEAUVOIR Simone 1908-1986
1077
The role of a retired person is no longer to possess one.

DE BONO Edward 1933-
1078
Many highly intelligent people are poor thinkers. Many people of average intelligence are skilled thinkers. The power of a car is separate from the way the car is driven.

1079
Removing the faults in a stagecoach may produce a perfect stagecoach, but it is unlikely to produce the first motor car.

1080
The solid wealth of insurance companies and the success of those who organize gambling are some indication of the profits to be derived from the efficient use of chance.

DEDDOES Dick
1081
Horses and jockeys mature earlier than people - which is why horses are admitted to race tracks at the age of two, and jockeys before they are old enough to shave.

DEFOE Daniel 1660-1731
1082 The Farther Adventures of Robinson Crusoe
In trouble to be troubled
Is to have your trouble doubled.

1083
It is better to have a lion at the head of an army of sheep, than a sheep at the head of an army of lions.

1084
Middle age is youth without its levity,
And age without decay.

1085 *Moll Flanders*
Vice came in always at the door of
necessity, not at the door of inclination.

1086 *The True-Born Englishman*
Wherever God erects a house of prayer,
The Devil always builds a chapel there;
And 'twill be found, upon examination,
The latter has the largest congregation.

1087 *The True-Born Englishman*
From this amphibious ill-born mob
began
That vain, ill-natured thing, an
Englishman.

DE GAULLE Charles 1890-1970
1088
Diplomats are useful only in fair
weather. As soon as it rains, they drown
in every drop.

1089
It will not be any European statesman
who will unite Europe: Europe will be
united by the Chinese.

1090
How can you govern a country which has
246 varieties of cheese?

1091
Since a politician never believes what he
says, he is quite surprised to be taken at
his word.

1092 *(replying to Clement Attlee)*
Politics are too serious a matter to be left
to the politicians.

1093
A true leader always keeps an element of
surprise up his sleeve, which others
cannot grasp but which keeps his public
excited and breathless.

DELANO Anthony
1094
She was not a woman likely to settle for
equality when sex gave her an
advantage.

DELORIA Jr. Vine
1095
When asked by an anthropologist what
the Indians called America before the

white man came, and Indian said simply
'Ours'.

DEMPSEY Jack 1895-1983
1096 *(on losing World Heavyweight title)*
Honey, I just forgot to duck.

DE NIRO Robert 1943-
1097 *in The King of Comedy*
"Better to be king for a night than a
schmuck for a lifetime."

DEPEW Chauncey 1834-1928
1098
It's pleasant to hear these nice words
while I'm still alive. I'd rather have the
taffy than the epitaphy.

DERBY Lord 1799-1869
1099
The duty of an Opposition [is] very
simple ... to oppose everything, and
propose nothing.

DESCARTES René 1596-1650
1100 *Discourse on Method*
Common sense is the best distributed
commodity in the world, for every man
is convinced that he is well supplied with
it.

DESTOUCHES Philippe Néricault 1680-
1754
1101 *L'Obstacle imprévu*
The absent are always in the wrong.

DE VOTO Bernard 1897-1955
1102
The proper union of gin and vermouth is
a great and sudden glory; it is one of the
happiest marriages on earth, and one of
the shortest lived.

DE VRIES Peter 1910-1993
1103
Celibacy is the worst form of self-abuse.

1104 *The Mackerel Plaza*
It is the final proof of God's omnipotence
that he need not exist in order to save us.

1105
If there's anything I hate it's the word
humorist - I feel like countering with the
word seriousist.

1106
The universe is like a safe to which there is a combination, but the combination is locked up in the safe.

1107
Who of us is mature enough for offspring before the offspring themselves arrive? The value of marriage is not that adults produce children but that children produce adults.

DEWAR Lord 1864-1930
1108
Love is an ocean of emotions entirely surrounded by expenses.

1109
[There are] only two classes of pedestrians in these days of reckless motor traffic - the quick, and the dead.

DEWAR Sir James 1842-1923
1110 *(attributed)*
Minds are like parachutes. They only function when they are open.

DEWEL Duane
1111
Any married man should forget his mistakes - no use two people remembering the same thing.

DEWEY John 1859-1952
1112
We only think when we are confronted with a problem.

DEWEY Thomas E. 1902-1971
1113
No man should be in public office who can't make more money in private life.

DEWING Thomas W.
1114
Why, if you're not in New York you are camping out.

DIANE Comtesse (Marie de Beausacq)
1115
Wealth makes everything easy - honesty most of all.

DIAZ Porfirio 1830-1915
1116 *(attributed)*
Poor Mexico, so far from God and so close to the United States.

DIBDIN Thomas 1771-1841
1117 *'The Snug Little Island'*
Oh! what a snug little Island,
A right little, tight little Island!

DICKENS Charles 1812-1870
1118
If there were no bad people, there would be no good lawyers.

1119 *The Chimes 'The Second Quarter'*
O let us love our occupations,
Bless the squire and his relations,
Live upon our daily rations,
And always know our proper stations.

1120 *A Christmas Carol*
'Bah,' said Scrooge. 'Humbug!'

1121 *Pickwick Papers*
Never sign a walentine with your own name.

DICKINSON Angie
1122
I dress for women - and I undress for men.

DICKINSON Emily 1830-1886
1123
The pedigree of honey
Does not concern the bee;
A clover, anytime, to him
Is aristocracy.

DICKMAN Franklin J.
1124
The glittering generalities of the speaker have left an impression more delightful than permanent.

DICKSON Paul 1939-
1125
Rowe's Rule: the odds are five to six that the light at the end of the tunnel is the headlight of an oncoming train.

DIDION Joan 1934-
1126
There is one last thing to remember: writers are always selling somebody out.

DIETRICH Marlene 1901-1991
1127 *(attributed)*
Most women set out to try to change a man - and when they have changed him, they do not like him.

1128
The average man is more interested in a woman who is interested in him than he is in a woman - any woman - with beautiful legs.

1129
How do you know when love is gone? If you said that you would be there at seven and get there by nine, and he or she has not called the police - it's gone.

DILLARD Annie
1130
I read about an Eskimo hunter who asked the local missionary priest, 'If I did not know about God and sin, would I go to hell?' 'No,' said the priest, 'not if you did not know.' 'Then why,' asked the Eskimo earnestly, 'did you tell me?'

1131
In literary history, generation follows generation in a rage.

DILLER Phyllis 1917-
1132 *Phyllis Diller's Housekeeping Hints*
Never go to bed mad. Stay up and fight.

DIOGENES c.400-c.325 BC
1133
Calumny is only the noise of madmen.

1134 *Plutarch Parallel Lives 'Alexander'*
Alexander ... asked him if he lacked anything. 'Yes,' said he, 'that I do: that you stand out of my sun a little.'

DIRKSEN Everett 1896-1969
1135
The U.S. Senate - an old scow which doesn't move very fast, but never sinks.

1136
Three Laws of Politics:
1. Get elected.
2. Get re-elected
3. Don't get mad, get even.

DISRAELI Benjamin 1804-1881
1137 *(attributed)*
Damn your principles! Stick to your party.

1138 *(advice to a young man)*
Talk as much as possible to women. They ask so many questions.

1139
Anybody amuses me for once. A new acquaintance is like a new book. I prefer it, even if bad, to a classic.

1140 *(on becoming Prime Minister)*
I have climbed to the top of the greasy pole.

1141 *Contarini Fleming*
Read no history: nothing but biography, for that is life without theory.

1142 *(on death bed, declining a visit from the Queen)*
'No, it is better not, she would only ask me to take a message to Albert.'

1143
Departure should be sudden.

1144 *(on his elevation to the House of Lords)*
I am dead; dead, but in the Elysian fields.

1145 *Endymion*
Said Waldershare, 'Sensible men are all of the same religion.' ' And pray what is that?' ... 'Sensible men never tell.'

1146 *(of Gladstone)*
A sophistical rhetorician, inebriated with the exuberance of his own verbosity.

1147
My idea of an agreeable person is a person who agrees with me.

1148
An insular country, subject to fogs and with a powerful middle class, requires grave statesmen.

1149
Yes, I am a Jew, and when the ancestors of the right honourable gentlemen were brutal savages in an unknown land,

mine were priests in the Temple of Solomon.

1150 *Lothair*
Every day when he looked into the glass, and gave the last touch to his consummate toilette, he offered his grateful thanks to Providence that his family was not unworthy of him.

1151 *Lothair*
A Protestant, if he wants aid or advice on any matter can only go to his solicitor.

1152 *Lothair*
When a man fell into his anecdotage it was a sign for him to retire from the world.

1153 *Lothair*
Every woman should marry - and no man.

1154
No man is regular in his attendance at the House of Commons until he is married.

1155
I will not go down to posterity talking bad grammar.

1156
Pray remember, Mr. Dean, no dogma, no Dean.

1157
The right hon. Gentleman caught the Whigs bathing, and walked away with their clothes.

1158 *(of the Treasury Bench)*
You behold a range of exhausted volcanoes.

DOBIE J. Frank
1159
Luck is being ready for the chance.

DOBSON Henry Austin 1840-1921
1160 *'Fame is a Food'*
Fame is a food that dead men eat, -
I have no stomach for such meat.

1161 *'The Paradox of Time'*
Time goes, you say? Ah no!
Alas, Time stays, we go.

DODD Ken 1931-
1162
Freud's theory was that when a joke opens a window ... you get a marvellous feeling of relief and elation. The trouble with Freud is that he never had to play the old Glasgow Empire on a Saturday night after Rangers and Celtic had both lost.

DONATUS Aelius c.300-399
1163
Confound those who have said our remarks before us.

DONLEAVY J.P. 1926-
1164 *The Ginger Man*
When you don't have any money, the problem is food. When you have money, it's sex. When you have both it's health.

DONNE John 1572-1631
1165 *(to his wife on being dismissed from service)*
John Donne, Anne Donne, Un-done.

DOREN Carl Van 1885-1950
1166
The race of man, while sheep in credulity, are wolves for conformity.

DOSTOEVSKY Fedor 1821-1881
1167
It seems, in fact, as though the second half of a man's life is made up of nothing but the habits he has accumulated during the first half.

DOUGLAS Keith 1920-1944
1168 *'Simplify me when I'm Dead'*
Remember me when I am dead
And simplify me when I'm dead.

DOUGLAS Norman 1868-1952
1169 *Almanac*
To find a friend one must close one eye.
To keep him - two.

1170
Justice is too good for some people, and not good enough for the rest.

1171
A man can believe in a considerable deal of rubbish, and yet go about his daily work in a rational and cheerful manner.

1172 *South Wind*
Many a man who thinks to found a
home discovers that he has merely
opened a tavern for his friends.

1173
It takes a wise man to handle a lie. A fool
had better remain honest.

DOWNES Donald
1174
Fear can be headier than whisky, once
man has acquired a taste for it.

DOYLE Sir Arthur Conan 1859-1930
1175 *The Adventures of Sherlock Holmes*
A man should keep his little brain attic
stocked with all the furniture that he is
likely to use, and the rest he can put
away in the lumber room of his library,
where he can get it if he wants it.

1176 *The Adventures of Sherlock Holmes*
It is quite a three-pipe problem, ...

1177 *A Study in Scarlet*
London, that great cesspool into which
all the loungers and idlers of the Empire
are irresistibly drained.

DOYLE Sir Francis 1810-1888
1178 *'The Unobstrusive Christian'*
His creed no parson ever knew,
For this was still his 'simple plan',
To have with clergymen to do
As little as a Christian can.

DRABBLE Margaret 1939-
1179 *A Natural Curiosity*
England's not a bad country ... It's just a
mean, cold, ugly, divided, tired, clapped-
out, post-imperial, post-industrial slag-
heap covered in polystyrene hamburger
cartons.

1180 *A Summer Bird-Cage*
Perhaps the rare and simple pleasure of
being seen for what one is compensates
for the misery of being it.

DRUCKER Peter 1909-
1181
There is nothing so useless as doing
efficiently that which should not be done
at all.

1182
Profitability is the sovereign criterion of
the enterprise.

1183
The really important things are said over
cocktails and are never done.

1184
Along this tree
From root to crown
Ideas flow up
And vetoes down.

DRYDEN John 1631-1700
1185 *Absalom and Achitophel*
In pious times, ere priestcraft did begin,
Before polygamy was made a sin.

1186 *Absalom and Achitophel*
Plots, true or false, are necessary things,
To raise up commonwealths and ruin
kings.

1187 *Absalom and Achitophel*
But far more numerous was the herd of
such
Who think too little and who talk too
much.

1188 *Absalom and Achitophel*
A man so various that he seemed to be
Not one, but all mankind's epitome.
Stiff in opinions, always in the wrong;
Was everything by starts, and nothing
long:
But, in the course of one revolving
moon,
Was chemist, fiddler, statesman, and
buffoon.

1189 *Absalom and Achitophel*
In squandering wealth was his peculiar
art:
Nothing went unrewarded, but desert.
Beggared by fools, whom still he found
too late:
He had his jest, and they had his estate.

1190 *Absalom and Achitophel*
Never was patriot yet, but was a fool.

1191 *Alexander's Feast*
War, he sung, is toil and trouble;
Honour but an empty bubble.

1192 'The Character of a Good Parson'
Refined himself to soul, to curb the
sense
And made almost a sin of abstinence.

1193 Cymon and Iphigenia
He trudged along unknowing what he
sought,
And whistled as he went, for want of
thought.

**1194 Epistle 'To my honoured kinsman
John Driden'**
The wise, for cure, on exercise depend;
God never made his work, for man to
mend.

1195 The Hind and the Panther
By education most have been misled;
So they believe, because they so were
bred.
The priest continues what the nurse
began,
And thus the child imposes on the man.

1196
Every inch that is not fool is rogue.

1197 The Maiden Queen
I am resolved to grow fat and look young
till forty, and then slip out of the world
with the first wrinkle and the reputation
of five-and-twenty.

1198 The Medal
We loathe our manna, and we long for
quails.

1199 Mithridates
For, Heaven be thanked, we live in such
an age,
When no man dies for love, but on the
stage.

1200 Palamon and Arcite
Repentance is but want of power to sin.

1201 'The Prologue at Oxford, 1680'
But 'tis the talent of our English nation,
Still to be plotting some new
reformation.

**1202 (translation of Ovid: The Art of
Love)**
To see and be seen, in heaps they run;
Some to undo, and some to be undone.

DUDEK Louis
1203
A critic at best is a waiter at the great
table of literature.

1204
There are two kinds of people: those who
are always well and those who are always
sick. Most of the evils of the world come
from the first sort and most of the
achievements from the second.

1205
What is forgiven is usually well-
remembered.

DUMAS Alexandre ('Pere') 1802-1870
1206
All human wisdom is summed up in two
words - wait and hope.

DUMAS Alexandre ('Fils') 1824-1895
1207 (attributed)
It is only rarely that one can see in a little
boy the promise of a man, but one can
almost always see in a little girl the
threat of a woman.

1208
Business? It's quite simple. It's other
people's money.

DUNCAN Sara Jeannette
1209
If you have anything to tell me of
importance, for God's sake begin at the
end.

1210
A human being isn't an orchid, he must
draw something from the soil he grows
in.

1211
One loses so many laughs by not
laughing at oneself.

1212
Why is it that when people have no
capacity for private usefulness they
should be so anxious to serve the public?

DUNNE Dominick
1213
Let me tell you something about silence:
The bullshit stops.

DUNNE Finley Peter 1867-1936
1214
An appeal is when ye ask wan court to show its contempt for another court.

1215
Comfort the afflicted and afflict the comfortable.

1216
You can lead a man up to the university, but you can't make him think.

1217
Many a man that couldn't direct ye to th' drug store on th' corner when he was thirty will get a respectful hearin' when age has further impaired his mind.

1218
A man's idee in a card game is war - crool, devastatin' and pitiless. A lady's idee iv it is a combynation iv larceny, embezzlement an' burglary.

1219
No matter whether the Constitution follows the flag or not, the Supreme Court follows the election return.

1220
I see gr-reat changes takin' place ivry day, but no change at all ivry fifty years.

1221
Th' prisidincy is th' highest office in th' gift iv th people. Th' vice-prisidincy is th' next highest an' the lowest. It isn't a crime exactly. Ye can't be sint to jail f'r it, but it's a kind iv a disgrace.

1222
Vice goes a long way tow'rd makin' life bearable. A little vice now an' thin is relished by th' best iv men.

1223
Whin a man gets to be my age, he ducks political meetin's, an' reads th' papers an' weighs th' ividence an' th' argymints - pro-argymints an' con-argymints, an' makes up his mind ca'mly, an' votes th' Dimmycratic Ticket.

DURANT Will 1885-1981
1224 *(on his 90th Birthday)*
The love we have in our youth is superficial compared to the love that an old man has for his old wife.

1225
Our knowledge is a receding mirage in an expanding desert of ignorance.

1226
One of the lessons of history is that nothing is often a good thing to do and always a clever thing to say.

1227
Most of us spend too much time on the last twenty-four hours and too little on the last six thousand years.

1228
Tired mothers find that spanking takes less time than reasoning and penetrates sooner to the seat of the memory.

DURRELL Lawrence 1912-1990
1229 *Justine*
There are only three things to be done with a woman. You can love her, you can suffer for her, or you can turn her into literature.

DYLAN Bob 1941-
1230
I'm just glad to be feeling better. I really thought I'd be seeing Elvis soon.

EBAN Abba 1915-
1231
History teaches us that men and nations behave wisely once they have exhausted all other alternatives.

EDGEWORTH Maria 1768-1849
1232 *Leonora*
What a misfortune it is to be born a woman! ... Why seek for knowledge, which can prove only that our wretchedness is irremediable?

EDISON Thomas Alva 1847-1931
1233
Everything comes to him who hustles while he waits.

1234
I am long on ideas, but short on time. I expect to live only about a hundred years.

1235
Results! Why, man, I have gotten a lot of results. I know several thousand things that won't work.

EDWARD VIII (Duke of Windsor) 1894-1972
1236
The thing that impresses me most about America is the way parents obey their children.

EDWARDS Murray D.
1237
Men of genius are the worst possible models for men of talent.

EDWARDS Oliver 1711-1791
1238
For my part not, I consider supper as a turnpike through which one must pass, in order to get to bed.

1239
I have tried too in my time to be a philosopher; but, I don't know how, cheerfulness was always breaking in.

EDWARDS Robert C.
1240
Never exaggerate your faults; your friends will attend to that.

1241
Whisky drowns some troubles and floats a lot more.

EHRLICH Paul R. 1932-
1242
The first rule of intelligent tinkering is to save all the parts.

EINSTEIN Albert 1879-1955
1243
I can't believe that God plays dice with the universe.

1244
If you are out to describe the truth, leave elegance to the tailor.

1245
The environment is everything that isn't me.

1246
No amount of experimentation can ever prove me right; a single experiment can prove me wrong.

1247
How do I work? I grope.

1248
I never think of the future. It comes soon enough.

1249
Reading after a certain (time) diverts the mind too much from its creative pursuits. Any man who reads too much and uses his own brain too little falls into lazy habits of thinking.

1250 *(of Relativity)*
I simply ignored axiom.

1251
If A is a success in life, then A equals x plus y plus z. Work is x; y is play; and z is keeping your mouth shut.

1252
We should take care not to make the intellect our god; it has, of course, powerful muscles, but no personality.

1253
If my theory of relativity is proven correct, Germany will claim me as a German and France will declare that I am a citizen of the world. Should my theory prove untrue, France will say that I am a German and Germany will declare that I am a Jew.

1254
I think and think for months and years. Ninety-nine times, the conclusion is false. The hundredth time I am right.

1255
When you sit with a nice girl for two hours, you think it's only a minute. But when you sit on a hot stove for a minute, you think it's two hours. That's relativity.

EISENHOWER Dwight D. 1890-1969
1256
An intellectual is a man who takes more words than necessary to tell more than he knows.

1257
What counts is not necessarily the size of the dog in the fight - it's the size of the fight in the dog.

ELBRIDGE Gerry
1258
A standing army is like a standing member: an excellent assurance of domestic tranquillity but a dangerous temptation to foreign adventure.

ELIOT George 1819-1880
1259
It's them that takes advantage that gets advantage i' this world.

1260
Blessed is the man who, having nothing to say, abstains from giving us wordy evidence of the fact.

1261 *Daniel Deronda*
A difference of taste in jokes is a great strain on the affections.

1262 *Felix Holt*
An election is coming. Universal peace is declared, and the foxes have a sincere interest in prolonging the lives of the poultry.

1263 *Felix Holt*
'Abroad', that large home of ruined reputations.

1264
Men's men: be they gentle or simple, they're much of a muchness.

1265 *Middlemarch*
A woman dictates before marriage in order that she may have an appetite for submission afterwards.

1266 *Middlemarch*
Among all forms of mistake, prophecy is the most gratuitous.

1267 *Middlemarch*
Plain women he regarded as he did the other severe facts of life, to be faced with philosophy and investigated by science.

1268 *The Mill on the Floss*
I should like to know what is the proper function of women, if it is not to make reasons for husbands to stay at home, and still stronger reasons for bachelors to go out.

1269
There is nothing will kill a man so soon as having nobody to find fault with but himself.

1270 *Scenes of Clerical Life*
Errors look so very ugly in persons of small means - one feels they are taking quite a liberty in going astray; whereas people of fortune may naturally indulge in a few delinquencies.

1271
Speech may be barren; but it is ridiculous to suppose that silence is always brooding on a nestful of eggs.

ELIOT T.S. 1888-1965
1272
An editor should tell the author his writing is better than it is. Not a lot better, a little better.

1273 *'The Love Song of J. Alfred Prufrock'*
I have measured out my life with coffee spoons.

1274 *Old Possum's Book of Practical Cats*
Macavity, Macavity, there's no one like Macavity,
There never was a Cat of such deceitfulness and suavity.
He always has an alibi, and one or two to spare:
At whatever time the deed took place - MACAVITY WASN'T THERE!

1275
A play should give you something to think about. When I see a play and understand it the first time, then I know it can't be much good.

1276
Poetry is a mug's game.

1277 *The Rock*
And the wind shall say: 'Here were
decent godless people:
Their only monument the asphalt road
And a thousand lost golf balls.'

1278 *The Sacred Wood*
Immature poets imitate; mature poets
steal.

1279
I suppose some editors are failed writers
- but so are most writers.

1280 *Sweeney Agonistes*
Birth, and copulation, and death.
That's all the facts when you come to
brass tacks:

1281 *The Waste Land*
When lovely woman stoops to folly and
Paces about her room again, alone,
She smoothes her hair with automatic
hand,
And puts a record on the gramophone.

1282 *'Whispers of Immortality'*
Grishkin is nice: her Russian eye
Is underlined for emphasis;
Uncorseted, her friendly bust
Gives promise of pneumatic bliss.

ELIZABETH I Queen 1533-1603
1283 *(to Edward de Vere)*
My Lord, I had forgot the fart.

1284 *(to leaders of her Council)*
I will make you shorter by the head.

1285 *(to William Cecil, who suffered from
gout)*
My lord, we make use of you, not for
your bad legs, but for your good head.

ELIZABETH II Queen 1926-
1286
In the words of one of my more
sympathetic correspondents, it has
turned out to be an 'annus horribilis'.

1287 *(on her 25th Wedding Anniversary)*
I think everybody really will concede that
on this, of all days, I should begin my

speech with the words 'My husband and
I'.

ELLERTON Alf
1288
Belgium put the kibosh on the Kaiser.

ELLIOT Henry Rutherford
1289
It it's sanity you're after
There's no recipe like
Laughter.
Laugh it off.

ELLIOTT Ebenezer 1781-1849
1290 *'Epigram'*
What is a communist? One who hath
yearnings
For equal division of unequal earnings.

ELLIOTT Jr. John
1291
Big ideas are so hard to recognize, so
fragile, so easy to kill. Don't forget that,
all of you who don't have them.

ELLIS George 1753-1815
1292 *'The Twelve Months'*
Snowy, Flowy, Blowy,
Showery, Flowery, Bowery,
Hoppy, Croppy, Droppy,
Breezy, Sneezy, Freezy.

ELLIS Havelock 1859-1939
1293 *Impressions and Comments*
What we call 'progress' is the exchange of
one nuisance for another nuisance.

EMERSON Ralph Waldo 1803-1882
1294
All the great speakers were bad speakers
at first.

1295
Can anything be so elegant as to have
few wants, and to serve them one's self?

1296 *(of architecture)*
The flowering of geometry.

1297
There is always a best way of doing
everything, if it be only to boil an egg.
Manners are the happy ways of doing
things.

1298
Character is that which can do without success.

1299 *The Conduct of Life*
The louder he talked of his honour, the faster we counted our spoons.

1300
There is a crack in everything God has made.

1301 *Essays*
Men are conservatives when they are least vigorous, or when they are most luxurious. They are conservatives after dinner.

1302 *Essays*
Every man is wanted, and no man is wanted much.

1303
Extremes meet, and there is no better example than the naughtiness of humility.

1304 *Fortune of the Republic*
What is a weed? A plant whose virtues have not been discovered.

1305
A good indignation brings out all one's powers.

1306
I hate quotations.

1307
Every hero becomes a bore at last.

1308
A hero is no braver than an ordinary man, but he is brave five minutes longer.

1309 *Journal*
Old age brings along with its uglinesses the comfort that you will soon be out of it.

1310
Every man is an impossibility until he is born.

1311
No man should travel until he has learned the language of the country he visits, otherwise he voluntarily makes himself a great baby - so helpless and ridiculous.

1312
Men are what their mothers made them.

1313
The merit claimed for the Anglican Church is that, if you let it alone, it will let you alone.

1314
Nature is reckless of the individual. When she has points to carry, she carries them.

1315
Some natures are too good to be spoiled by praise.

1316
A person seldom falls sick but the bystanders are animated with a faint hope that he will die.

1317 *Representative Men*
Is not marriage an open question, when it is alleged, from the beginning of the world, that such as are in the institution wish to get out; and such as are out wish to get in.

1318
Sanity is very rare; every man almost, and every woman, has a dash of madness.

1319
No sensible person ever made an apology.

1320
If you shoot at a king you must kill him.

1321
The sky is the daily bread of the eyes.

1322
Speak what you think today in words as hard as cannon balls, and tomorrow speak what tomorrow thinks in hard words again, though it contradict everything you said today.

1323
Take egotism out, and you would castrate the benefactor.

EPICTETUS AD c.50-130
1324
First learn the meaning of what you say, and then speak.

1325
Nature has given to men one tongue, but two ears, that we may hear from others twice as much as we speak.

EPSTEIN Joseph
1326
There is no word equivalent to 'cuckold' for women.

ERSKINE John 1879-1951
1327
Temperance is the control of all the functions of our bodies. The man who refuses liquor, goes in for apple pie and develops a paunch, is no ethical leader for me.

ERTZ Susan 1894-1985
1328
He talked with more claret than clarity.

ESAR Evan
1329
Housework is what woman does that nobody notices unless she hasn't done it.

1330
The quizzical expression of the monkey at the zoo comes from his wondering whether he is his brother's keeper, or his keeper's brother.

ESCHENBACH Marie Ebner von 1830-1916
1331 *Aphorism*
We don't believe in rheumatism and true love until after the first attack.

ESTIENNE Henri 1531-1598
1332 *Les Prémices*
If youth knew; if age was able.

EURIPIDES c.485-406 BC
1333
Money is the wise man's religion.

1334
There's nothing like the sight of an old enemy down on his luck.

EUWER Anthony
1335
As a beauty I am not a star,
There are others more handsome by far,
But my face - I don't mind it
For I am behind it.
It's the people in front get the jar.

EVANS Edith 1888-1976
1336
I seem to have an awful lot of people inside me.

EWER William Norman 1885-1976
1337 *Week-End Book*
How odd
Of God
To choose
The Jews.

FADIMAN Clifton
1338
Cheese - milk's leap toward immortality.

1339
One newspaper a day ought to be enough for anyone who still prefers to retain a little mental balance.

1340
One's first book, kiss, home run is always the best.

1341
There are two kinds of writers - the great ones who can give you truths, and the lesser ones, who can only give you themselves.

1342
When you travel, remember that a foreign country is not designed to make you comfortable. It is designed to make its own people comfortable.

FAROUK (ex-King) 1920-1965
1343
The whole world is in revolt. Soon there will be only five Kings left - the King of England, the King of Spades, the King of Clubs, the King of Hearts and the King of Diamonds.

FARQUHAR George 1678-1707
1344 *The Beaux' Stratagem*
No woman can be a beauty without a fortune.

1345 *The Inconstant*
Crimes, like virtues, are their own rewards.

1346 *The Recruiting Officer*
Hanging and marriage, you know, go by Destiny.

FARRELL Warren
1347
When women hold off from marrying men, we call it independence. When men hold off from marrying women, we call it fear of commitment.

FAULKNER William 1897-1962
1348
An artist is a creature driven by demons. He doesn't know why they choose him and he's usually too busy to wonder why.

1349
A man shouldn't fool with booze until he's fifty; then he's a damn fool if he doesn't.

1350
The Swiss are not a people so much as a neat, clean, quite solvent business.

FEATHER William
1351
A man of fifty looks as old as Santa Claus to a girl of twenty.

1352
The petty economies of the rich are just as amazing as the silly extravagances of the poor.

1353
If you're naturally kind, you attract a lot of people you don't like.

FEMINA Jerry Della
1354
Advertising is the most fun you can have with your clothes on.

FERBER Edna 1887-1968
1355
Being an old maid is like death by drowning, a really delightful sensation after you cease to struggle.

FIELDING Henry 1707-1754
1356
His designs were strictly honourable, as the phrase is: that is, to rob a lady of her fortune by way of marriage.

1357
There is no greater folly than to seek to correct the natural infirmities of those we love.

1358 *Joseph Andrews*
Public schools are the nurseries of all vice and immorality.

1359 *Love in Several Masques*
Love and scandal are the best sweeteners of tea.

1360
It requires a penetrating eye to discern a fool through the disguise of gaiety and good breeding.

1361
Thwackum was for doing justice, and leaving mercy to heaven.

1362 *Tom Jones*
That monstrous animal, a husband and wife.

1363 *Tom Jones*
What is commonly called love, namely the desire of satisfying a voracious appetite with a certain quantity of delicate white human flesh.

FIELDS W.C. 1880-1946
1364 *You Can't Cheat an Honest Man*
Some weasel took the cork out of my lunch.

1365
We frequently hear of people dying from too much drinking. That this happens is a matter of record. But the blame almost always is placed on whisky. Why this should be I never could understand. You can die from drinking too much of anything - coffee, water, milk, soft drinks and all such stuff as that. And so long as the presence of death lurks with anyone

who goes through the simple act of swallowing, I will make mine whisky.

1366
Hell, I never vote for anybody. I always vote against.

1367
Last week I went to Philadelphia, but it was closed.

1368
Never give a sucker an even break.

1369
I always keep a supply of stimulant handy in case I see a snake - which I also keep handy.

1370 *(when caught reading the Bible)*
I'm looking for loopholes.

1371
It was a woman who drove me to drink - and, you know, I never even thanked her.

1372
Women are like elephants. They are interesting to look at, but I wouldn't like to own one.

1373 *in You're Telling Me*
"It's a funny old world - a man's lucky if he gets out of it alive."

FINLEY John
1374
Maturity is the capacity to endure uncertainty.

FIRBANK Ronald 1886-1926
1375 *The Flower Beneath the Foot*
I remember the average curate at home as something between a eunuch and a snigger.

1376 *Vainglory*
All millionaires love a baked apple.

FISHER H.A.L. 1856-1940
1377 *A History of Europe*
Purity of race does not exist. Europe is a continent of energetic mongrels.

FISHER Irving 1857-1947
1378 *(in 1929)*
Stocks have reached what looks like a permanently high plateau.

FISHER John Arbuthnot 1841-1920
1379 *Memories*
The best scale for an experiment is 12 inches to a foot.

FISHER Martin H.
1380
Knowledge is a process of piling up facts; wisdom lies in their simplification.

1381
The practice of medicine is a thinker's art, the practice of surgery a plumber's.

1382
The specialist is a man who fears the other subjects.

FITZGERALD Edward 1809-1883
1383 *The Rubáiyát of Omar Khayyám*
Ah, make the most of what we yet may spend,
Before we too into the dust descend;
Dust into dust, and under dust, to lie,
Sans wine, sans song, sans singer, and - sans End!

1384
Taste is the feminine of genius.

FITZGERALD F. Scott 1896-1940
1385 *All the Sad Young Men*
Let me tell you about the very rich. They are different from you and me.

1386 *The Crack-Up*
Show me a hero and I will write you a tragedy.

1387
No grand idea was ever born in a conference, but a lot of foolish ideas have died there.

1388 *The Great Gatsby*
Her voice is full of money.

1389
Grown up, and that is a terribly hard thing to do. It is much easier to skip it and go from one childhood to another.

1390 *The Last Tycoon*
There are no second acts in American lives.

1391 *The Last Tycoon*
One girl can be pretty - but a dozen are only a chorus.

FITZWATER Marlin
1392 *(on inexperience at the White House)*
A few more fat, old bald men wouldn't hurt the place.

FLANDERS Michael and SWANN Donald 1922-1975 and 1923-1994
1393
Have some madeira, M'dear.

FLAUBERT Gustave 1821-1880
1394 *(letter to Louis Bouilhet)*
Things seem to be going at a dizzy rate. We are dancing not on a volcano, but on the rotten seat of a latrine.

FLEMING Alexander D. 1881-1955
1395
A good gulp of hot whisky at bedtime - it's not very scientific, but it helps.

FLORIO John c.1553-1625
1396 *Second Frutes*
England is the paradise of women, the purgatory of men, and the hell of horses.

FOCH Ferdinand 1851-1929
1397
Airplanes are interesting toys but of no military value.

FONDA Henry 1905-1982
1398
The best actors do not let the wheels show.

FOOTE Shelby
1399
Longevity conquers scandal every time.

FORBES Malcolm S. 1919-1990
1400
Ability will never catch up with the demand for it.

FORD Gerald 1909-
1401
I've had a lot of experience with people smarter than I am.

1402
When a man is asked to make a speech, the first thing he has to decide is what to say.

FORD Henry 1863-1947
1403 *(on choice of colour for the Model T Ford)*
Any colour - so long as it's black.

1404
History is more or less bunk.

FORGY Howell 1908-1983
1405 *(at Pearl Harbor)*
Praise the Lord and pass the ammunition.

FORSTER E.M. 1879-1970
1406 *A Passage to India*
The so-called white races are really pinko-grey.

1407 *Two cheers for Democracy 'What I Believe'*
If I had to choose between betraying my country and betraying my friend, I hope I should have the guts to betray my country.

1408 *Two cheers for Democracy 'What I Believe'*
So Two cheers for Democracy: one because it admits variety and two because it permits criticism.

FORSTER W.E. 1878-1969
1409
What is the use of lying when truth, well distributed, serves the same purpose?

FOSDICK Harry Emerson 1878-1969
1410
God is not a cosmic bellboy for whom we can press a button to get things done.

1411
Liberty is always dangerous - but it is the safest thing we have.

1412
Nothing in human life, least of all in religion, is ever right until it is beautiful.

FOWLER Gene
1413
Writing is easy: all you do is sit staring at the blank sheet of paper until the drops of blood form on your forehead.

FOWLES John Robert 1926-
1414 *The Aristos*
Passion destroys passion; we want what puts an end to wanting what we want.

1415
Men love war because it allows them to look serious; because it is the only thing that stops women laughing at them.

FRANCE Anatole 1844-1924
1416
Chance is the pseudonym of God when he did not want to sign.

1417
I do not know any reading more easy, more fascinating, more delightful than a catalogue.

1418
If fifty million people say a foolish thing, it is still a foolish thing.

1419
It is human nature to think wisely and to act in an absurd fashion.

1420
Never lend books - nobody ever returns them; the only books I have in my library are those which people have lent me.

1421
I prefer the errors of enthusiasm to the indifference of wisdom.

FRANCIS Brendan
1422
The big difference between sex for money and sex for free is that sex for money usually costs a lot less.

FRANCIS of Sales, Saint 1567-1622
1423
While I am busy with little things, I am not required to do greater things.

1424
Nothing is more like a wise man than a fool who holds his tongue.

FRANCIS Xavier, Saint 1506-1552
1425
Give me the children until they are seven and anyone may have them afterwards.

FRANK Lawrence K.
1426
Don't quote me; that's what you heard, not what I said.

FRANKENBERG Lloyd
1427
The apparent serenity of the past is an oil spread by time.

FRANKFURTER Felix 1882-1965
1428
It is a fair summary of history to say that the safeguards of liberty have frequently been forged in cases involving not very nice people.

FRANKLIN Benjamin 1706-1790
1429
A child thinks twenty shillings and twenty years can scarce ever be spent.

1430
There is a difference between imitating a good man and counterfeiting him.

1431
God heals, and the doctor takes the fees.

1432
The greatest monarch on the proudest throne is obliged to sit upon his own arse.

1433 *(letter to Georgiana Shipley)*
Here Skugg
Lies snug
As a bug
In as rug.

1434 *(letter to Jean Baptiste Le Roy)*
In this world nothing can be said to be certain, except death and taxes.

1435
If a man empties his purse into his head, no one can take it from him.

1436
Were the offer made true, I would engage to run again, from beginning to end, the same career of life. All I would ask should be the privilege of an author, to correct, in a second edition, certain errors of the first.

1437 *Poor Richard's Almanac*
He that lives upon hope will die fasting.

1438
Praise to the undeserving is severe satire.

1439 *(at the Signing of Declaration of Independence)*
We must indeed all hang together, or, most assuredly, we shall all hang separately.

1440
There are three faithful friends: an old wife, and old dog, and ready money.

1441
If you want a thing done, go - if not, send.

1442
Who is wise? He that learns from everyone.
Who is powerful? He that governs his passions.
Who is rich? He that is content.
Who is that? Nobody.

1443
Nothing is more fatal to health than an overcare of it.

FRANKS Baron 1905-
1444
A secret in the Oxford sense: you may tell it to only one person at a time.

FRAYN Michael 1933-
1445
I feel bad that I don't feel worse.

FRAZER Sir James 1854-1941
1446 *The Golden Bough*
The awe and dread with which the untutored savage contemplates his mother-in-law are amongst the most familiar facts of anthropology.

FREUD Clement 1924-
1447
If you resolve to give up smoking, drinking and loving, you don't actually live longer; it just seems longer.

FREUD Martin 1895-1982
1448
I didn't know the full facts of life until I was 17. My father [Sigmund Freud] never talked about his work.

FREUD Sigmund 1856-1939
1449
From error to error one discovers the entire truth.

1450
A hero is a man who stands up manfully against his father and in the end victoriously overcomes him.

1451 *(letter to Marie Bonaparte)*
The great question that has never been answered and which I have not yet been able to answer, despite my thirty years of research into the feminine soul, is 'What does a woman want?'

1452
The only unnatural sexual behaviour is none at all.

FRIEDENBERG Edgar Z.
1453
Part of the American dream is to live long and die young.

1454
The 'teenager' seems to have replaced the Communist as the appropriate target for public controversy and foreboding.

FRIEDMAN Milton 1912-
1455
Inflation is one form of taxation that can be imposed without legislation.

FRISCH Max 1911-1991
1456
Technology - the knack of so arranging the world that we don't have to experience it.

FROMM Erich 1900-1980

1457
Giving is the highest expression of potency.

1458
I think if you ask people what their concept of heaven is, they would say, if they are honest, that it is a big department store, with new things every week - all the money to buy them, and maybe a little more than the neighbours.

FROST David 1939-

1459
Television is an invention that permits you to be entertained in your living room by people you wouldn't have in your home.

FROST Robert 1874-1963

1460
Americans are like a rich father who wishes he knew how to give his son the hardships that made him rich.

1461
The best things and best people rise out of their separateness; I'm against a homogenized society because I want the cream to rise.

1462 *'Cluster of Faith'*
Forgive, O Lord, my little jokes on Thee
And I'll forgive Thy great big one on me.

1463 *'The Death of the Hired Man'*
Home is the place where, when you have to go there,
They have to take you in.

1464
Don't be agnostic - be something.

1465
You don't have to deserve your mother's love. You have to deserve your father's. He's more particular.

1466
Don't ever take a fence down until you know why it was put up.

1467
Education is the ability to listen to almost anything without losing your temper or your self-confidence.

1468 *'Fire and Ice'*
Some say the world will end in fire,
Some say in ice.
From what I've tasted of desire
I hold with those who favour fire.
But if it had to perish twice,
I think I know enough of hate
To say that for destruction ice
Is also great
And would suffice.

1469
Happiness makes up in height for what it lacks in length.

1470 *'The Hardship of Accounting'*
Never ask of money spent
Where the spender thinks it went.
Nobody was ever meant
To remember or invent
What he did with every cent.

1471
Humour is the most engaging cowardice. With it myself I have been able to hold some of my enemy in play far out of gunshot.

1472
A jury consists of twelve persons chosen to decide who has the better lawyer.

1473
A Liberal is a man too broadminded to take his own side in a quarrel.

1474 *'Mending Wall'*
Good fences make good neighbours.

1475
The only way round is through.

1476
Poetry is a way of taking life by the throat.

1477 *'Precaution'*
I never dared be radical when young
For fear it would make me conservative when old.

1478
To be social is to be forgiving.

1479
A successful lawsuit is the one worn by a policeman.

1480
There's nothing I'm afraid of like scared people.

1481
In three words I can sum up everything I've learned about life. It goes on.

1482
Writing free verse is like playing tennis with the net down.

1483
You've got to love what's lovable, and hate what's hateable. It takes brains to see the difference.

FRYE Northrop 1912-1991
1484
Historically, a Canadian is an American who rejects the Revolution.

1485
The simplest questions are the hardest to answer.

1486
We are being swallowed up by the popular culture of the United States, but then the Americans are being swallowed up by it too. It's just as much a threat to American culture as it is to ours.

1487
War appeals to young men because it is fundamentally auto-eroticism.

FULLER Buckminster 1895-1983
1488
Don't fight forces; use them.

1489 *Operating Manual for Spaceship Earth*
Now there is one outstandingly important fact regarding Spaceship Earth, and that is that no instruction book came with it.

1490
Pollution is nothing but resources we're not harvesting.

FULLER Thomas 1608-1661
1491
If an ass goes travelling, he'll not come back a horse.

1492
Cheat me in the price but not in the goods.

1493
We could be cowards, if we had courage enough.

1494
The Devil himself is good when he is pleased.

1495
Don't let your will roar when your power only whispers.

1496
Even doubtful accusations leave a stain behind them.

1497
He that flings dirt at another dirtieth himself most.

1498
A fox should not be on the jury at a goose's trial.

1499
Good is not good, where better is expected.

1500
Great and good are seldom the same man.

1501
He that has a great nose thinks everybody is speaking of it.

1502
He is idle that might be better employed.

1503
Old foxes want no tutors.

1504
Pride, perceiving humility honourable, often borrows her cloak.

1505
Pride had rather go out of the way than go behind.

1506
He that resolves to deal with none but honest men, must leave off dealing.

1507
The scalded cat fears even cold water.

1508
Seeing's believing, but feeling's the truth.

GABIROL Solomon Ibn c.1020-1070
1509
What is the test of good manners? Being able to bear patiently with bad ones.

GABOR Zsa Zsa 1919-
1510 *(attributed)*
Never despise what it says in the women's magazines. It may not be subtle, but neither are men.

1511 *(asked which of the Gabor women was the oldest)*
She'll never admit it, but I believe it is Mama.

1512
Husbands are like fires. They go out when unattended.

1513
I'm an excellent housekeeper. Everytime I get a divorce, I keep the house.

1514
Macho does not prove mucho.

1515
A man is incomplete until he has married. Then he's finished.

1516
I never hated a man enough to give him his diamonds back.

1517
I know nothing about sex, because I was always married.

GALBRAITH J.K. 1908-
1518 *The Affluent Society*
It is a far, far better thing to have a firm anchor in nonsense than to put out on the troubled seas of thought.

1519 *The Affluent Society*
The greater the wealth, the thicker will be the dirt.

1520
More die in the United States of too much food than of too little.

1521
In economics, the majority is always wrong.

1522
One of the greatest pieces of economic wisdom is to know what you do not know.

1523
Humour is richly rewarding to the person who employs it. It has some value in gaining and holding attention. But it has no persuasive value at all.

1524
Meetings are indispensable when you don't want to do anything.

1525
People of privilege will always risk their complete destruction rather than surrender any material part of their advantage.

1526
The more underdeveloped the country, the more overdeveloped the women.

1527
Washington is a place where men praise courage and act on elaborate personal cost-benefit calculations.

GALLANT Mavis 1922-
1528
There are a great many opinions in this world, and a good half of them are professed by people who have never been in trouble.

GALLICO Paul 1897-1976
1529
No one can be as calculatedly rude as the British, which amazes Americans,

who do not understand studied insult and can only offer abuse as a substitute.

GALSWORTHY John 1867-1933
1530
One's eyes are what one is, one's mouth what one becomes.

GANDHI Mahatma 1869-1948
1531
To a man with an empty stomach food is god.

GARBETT Archbishop C. 1875-1955
1532
Any fool can criticize, and many of them do.

GARCIA Jerry d.1995
1533
Truth is something you stumble into when you think you're going some place else.

GARDNER Ed 1901-1963
1534 *Duffy's Tavern*
Opera is when a guy gets stabbed in the back and, instead of bleeding, he sings.

GARDNER Dr Howard
1535
It isn't necessary to be a bastard to be a genius, but a disregard for others does seem necessary.

GARDNER John W. 1912-
1536
If one defines the term 'dropout' to mean a person who has given up serious effort to meet his responsibilities, then every business office, government agency, golf club and university faculty would yield its quota.

1537
History never looks like history when you are living through it. It always looks confusing and messy, and it always feels uncomfortable.

GARIBALDI Giuseppe 1807-1882
1538
Bacchus has drowned more men than Neptune.

GARNER John Nance 1868-1967
1539
The vice-presidency isn't worth a pitcher of warm piss.

GARY Romain 1914-1990
1540
Humour is an affirmation of dignity, a declaration of man's superiority to all that befalls him.

GASKELL Elizabeth 1810-1865
1541 *Cranford*
A man ... is *so* in the way in the house!

1542 *Cranford*
I'll not listen to reason ... Reason always means what someone else has got to say.

GASSET José Ortega y 1883-1955
1543
I am I plus my circumstances.

GATES Bill 1955-
1544 *(of computer memory - in 1981)*
640K ought to be enough for anybody.

GATEWOOD W. Boyd
1545
Very few people go to the doctor when they have a cold, they go to the theatre instead.

GAY John 1685-1732
1546 *The Beggar's Opera*
Do you think your mother and I should have lived comfortably so long together, if ever we had been married?

1547 *The Beggar's Opera*
The comfortable estate of widowhood, is the only hope that keeps up a wife's spirits.

1548 *The Beggar's Opera*
If with me you'd fondly stray.
Over the hills and far away.

1549 *The Beggar's Opera*
Fill ev'ry glass, for wine inspires us,
And fires us
With courage, love and joy.
Women and wine should life employ.
Is there ought else on earth desirous?

1550 *The Beggar's Opera*
In one respect indeed, our employment
may be reckoned dishonest, because,
like great Statesmen, we encourage those
who betray their friends.

1551 *The Beggar's Opera*
How happy could I be with either,
Were t'other dear charmer away!

1552 *Dione*
Behold the victim of Parthenia's pride!
He saw, he sighed, he loved, was scorned
and died.

1553 *'My Own Epitaph'*
Life is a jest; and all things show it.
I thought so once; but now I know it.

1554 *Fables 'The Dog and the Fox'*
I know you lawyers can, with ease,
Twist words and meanings as you please;
That language, by your skill made pliant,
Will bend to favour ev'ry client.

1555 *Fables 'The Man, the Cat, the Dog
and Fly'*
Studious of elegance and ease,
Myself alone I seek to please.

1556 *Fables 'The Squire and his Cur'*
That politician tops his part,
Who readily can lie with art.

1557 *'Polly'*
Whether we can afford it or no, we must
have superfluities.

1558
Who friendship with a knave hath made,
Is judged a partner in the trade.

GEDDES Sir Eric 1875-1937
1559
The Germans, if this Government is
returned, are going to pay every penny;
they are going to be squeezed as a lemon
is squeezed - until the pips squeak.

GENEEN Harold 1910-
1560
I don't believe in just ordering people to
do things. You have to sort of grab an
oar and row with them.

GEORGE Daniel
1561 *The Perpetual Pessimist*
O Freedom, what liberties are taken in
thy name!

GEORGE I King 1660-1727
1562
I hate all Boets and Bainters.

GEORGE II King 1683-1760
1563 *(of General Wolfe)*
Mad, is he? Then I hope he will *bite*
some of my other generals.

1564
We are come for your good, for all your
goods.

GEORGE IV King 1762-1830
1565 *(on first meeting his wife to be)*
Harris, I am not well; pray get me a glass
of brandy.

GEORGE V King 1865-1936
1566
Bugger Bognor.

GEORGE VI King 1895-1952
1567
Abroad is bloody.

GEORGE W.L. 1882-1926
1568
The true America is the Middle West, and
Columbus discovered nothing at all
except another Europe.

GETTY Paul 1892-1976
1569
Going to work for a large company is like
getting on a train. Are you going sixty
miles an hour or is the train going sixty
miles an hour and you're just sitting still?

GIBBON Edward 1737-1794
1570 *Memoirs of My Life*
Dr - well remembered that he had a
salary to receive, and only forgot that he
had a duty to perform.

GIBBON John Murray
1571
I always suspect an artist who is
successful before he is dead.

GIBBONS Stella 1902-1989
1572 *Cold Comfort Farm*
Something nasty in the woodshed.

GIBLIN II Frank J
1573
Be yourself. Who else is better qualified?

GIESE W.
1574
Contemporary literature can be classified under three headings: the neurotic, the erotic and the tommy-rotic.

GIFFORD Frank
1575
Pro football is like nuclear warfare. There are no winners, only survivors.

GILBERT W.S. 1836-1911
1576
Darwinian Man, though well-behaved, At best is only a monkey shaved!

1577 *The Gondoliers*
Of that there is no manner of doubt -
No probable, possible shadow of doubt -
No possible doubt whatever.

1578 *The Gondoliers*
All shall equal be,
The Earl, the Marquis, and the Dook,
The Groom, the Butler, and the Cook,
The Aristocrat who banks with Coutts,
The Aristocrat who cleans the boots.

1579 *The Gondoliers*
But the privilege and pleasure
That we treasure beyond measure
Is to run on little errands for the
Ministers of State.

1580 *The Gondoliers*
Take a pair of sparkling eyes,
Hidden, ever and anon,
In a merciful eclipse.

1581 *The Gondoliers*
Ambassadors cropped up like hay,
Prime Ministers and such as they
Grew like asparagus in May,
And dukes were three a penny.

1582 *The Gondoliers*
When every one is somebodee,
Then no one's anybody.

1583 *HMS Pinafore*
What, never?
No, never!
What, *never*?
Hardly ever!

1584 *HMS Pinafore*
Though 'Bother it' I may
Occasionally say,
I never use a big, big D -

1585 *HMS Pinafore*
And so do his sisters, and his cousins
and his aunts!
His sisters and his cousins,
Whom he reckons up by dozens,
And his aunts!

1586 *HMS Pinafore*
When I was a lad I served a term
As office boy to an Attorney's firm.
I cleaned the windows and I swept the
floor,
And I polished up the handle of the big
front door.
I polished up that handle so carefullee
That now I am the Ruler of the Queen's
Navee!

1587 *HMS Pinafore*
I always voted at my party's call,
And I never thought of thinking for
myself at all.

1588 *HMS Pinafore*
Stick close to your desks and never go to
sea,
And you all may be Rulers of the Queen's
Navee!

1589 *HMS Pinafore*
Things are seldom what they seem,
Skim milk masquerades as cream.

1590 *HMS Pinafore*
He is an Englishman!
For he himself has said it,
And it's greatly to his credit,
That he is an Englishman!

1591 *HMS Pinafore*
For he might have been a Roosian,
A French, or Turk, or Proosian,
Or perhaps Ital-ian!
But in spite of all temptations

To belong to other nations,
He remains an Englishman!

1592 *HMS Pinafore*
The other, upper crust,
A regular patrician.

1593
As innocent as a new-laid egg.

1594 *Iolanthe*
Bow, bow, ye lower middle classes!
Bow, bow, ye tradesmen, bow, ye masses.

1595 *Iolanthe*
The Law is the true embodiment
Of everything that's excellent.
It has no kind of fault or flaw,
And I, my Lords, embody the Law.

1596 *Iolanthe*
Spurn not the nobly born
With love affected,
Nor treat with virtuous scorn
The well-connected.

1597 *Iolanthe*
Hearts just as pure and fair
May beat in Belgrave Square
As in the lowly air
Of Seven Dials.

1598 *Iolanthe*
I often think it's comical
How Nature always does contrive
That every boy and every gal,
That's born into the world alive,
Is either a little Liberal,
Or else a little Conservative!

1599 *Iolanthe*
When in that House MPs divide,
If they've a brain and cerebellum too,
They have to leave that brain outside,
And vote just as their leaders tell 'em to.

1600 *Iolanthe*
The prospect of a lot
Of dull MPs in close proximity,
All thinking for themselves is what
No man can face with equanimity.

1601 *Iolanthe*
The House of Peers, throughout the war,
Did nothing in particular,
And did it very well.

1602 *Iolanthe*
When you're lying awake with a dismal
headache, and repose is taboo'd by
anxiety,
I conceive you may use any language
you choose to indulge in, without
impropriety.

1603 *Iolanthe*
For you dream you are crossing the
Channel, and tossing about in a steamer
from Harwich -
Which is something between a large
bathing machine and a very small
second class carriage.

1604 *Iolanthe*
And bound on that journey you find
your attorney (who started that morning
from Devon);
He's a bit undersized, and you don't feel
surprised when he tells you he's only
eleven.

1605 *Iolanthe*
In your shirt and your socks (the black
silk with gold clocks), crossing Salisbury
Plain on a bicycle.

1606 *Iolanthe*
The shares are a penny, and ever so
many are taken by Rothschild and
Baring,
And just as a few are allotted to you, you
awake with a shudder despairing.

1607 *The Mikado*
A wandering minstrel I -
A thing of shreds and patches.
Of ballads, songs and snatches,
And dreamy lullaby!

1608 *The Mikado*
I can trace my ancestry back to a
protoplasmal primordial atomic globule.
Consequently, my family pride is
something in-conceivable. I can't help it.
I was born sneering.

1609 *The Mikado*
As some day it may happen that a victim
must be found,
I've got a little list - I've got a little list
Of society offenders who might well be
under ground

And who never would be missed - who
never would be missed!

1610 *The Mikado*
The idiot who praises, with enthusiastic
tone,
All centuries but this, and every country
but his own.

1611 *The Mikado*
Three little maids from school are we,
Pert as a schoolgirl well can be,
Filled to the brim with girlish glee.

1612 *The Mikado*
Life is a joke that's just begun.

1613 *The Mikado*
Three little maids who, all unwary,
Come from a ladies' seminary.

1614 *The Mikado*
Awaiting the sensation of a short, sharp
shock,
From a cheap and chippy chopper on a
big black block.

1615 *The Mikado*
Here's a how-de-doo!

1616 *The Mikado*
Here's a state of things!

1617 *The Mikado*
Matrimonial devotion
Doesn't seem to suit her notion.

1618 *The Mikado*
My object all sublime
I shall achieve in time -
To let the punishment fit the crime -
The punishment fit the crime.

1619 *The Mikado*
The music-hall singer attends a series
Of masses and fugues and 'ops'
By Bach, interwoven
With Spohr and Beethoven,
At classical Monday Pops.

1620 *The Mikado*
The billiard sharp whom any one
catches,
His doom's extremely hard -
He's made to dwell -
In a dungeon cell
On a spot that's always barred.

And there he plays extravagant matches
In fitless finger-stalls
On a cloth untrue
With a twisted cue
And elliptical billiard balls.

1621 *The Mikado*
I have a left shoulder-blade that is a
miracle of loveliness. People come miles
to see it. My right elbow has a
fascination that few can resist.

1622 *The Mikado*
Something lingering, with boiling oil in
it, I fancy.

1623 *The Mikado*
Merely corroborative detail, intended to
give artistic verisimiltude to an
otherwise bald and unconvincing
narrative.

1624 *The Mikado*
The flowers that bloom in the spring,
Tra la,
Have nothing to do with the case.

1625 *The Mikado*
I've got to take under my wing,
Tra la,
A most unattractive old thing,
Tra la,
With a caricature of a face.

1626 *The Mikado*
'Is it weakness of intellect, birdie?' I
cried,
'Or a rather tough worm in your little
inside?'
With a shake of his poor little head he
replied,
'Oh, Willow, titwillow, titwillow!'

1627 *The Mikado*
He sobbed and he sighed, and a gurgle
he gave,
Then he plunged himself into the billowy
wave,
And an echo arose from the suicide's
grave
'Oh willow, titwillow, titwillow!'

1628 *The Mikado*
There's a fascination frantic
In a ruin that's romantic;

Do you think you are sufficiently
decayed?

1629 *Patience*
If you're anxious for to shine in the high
aesthetic line as a man of culture rare.

1630 *Patience*
You must lie upon the daisies and
discourse in novel phrases of your
complicated state of mind,
The meaning doesn't matter if it's only
idle chatter of a transcendental kind.

1631 *Patience*
Then a sentimental passion of a
vegetable fashion must excite your
languid spleen,
An attachment à la Plato for a bashful
young potato, or a not too French French
bean!
Though the Philistines may jostle, you
will rank as an apostle in the high
aesthetic band,
If you walk down Piccadilly with a poppy
or a lily in your medieval hand.

1632 *Patience*
While this magnetic,
Peripatetic
Lover, he lived to learn,
By no endeavour
Can magnet ever
Attract a Silver Churn!

1633 *Patience*
'High diddle diddle'
Will rank as an idyll,
If I pronounce it chaste!

1634 *Patience*
Francesca di Rimini, miminy, piminy,
Je-ne-sais-quoi young man!

1635 *Patience*
A greenery-yallery, Grosvenor Gallery,
Foot-in-the-grave young man!

1636 *The Pirates of Penzance*
It is, it is a glorious thing
To be a Pirate King.

1637 *The Pirates of Penzance*
The question is, had he not been
A thing of beauty,

Would she be swayed by quite as keen
A sense of duty?

1638 *The Pirates of Penzance*
I'm very good at integral and differential
calculus,
I know the scientific names of beings
animalculous;
In short, in matters vegetable, animal,
and mineral,
I am the very model of a modern Major-
General.

1639 *The Pirates of Penzance*
About binomial theorem I'm teeming
with a lot of news,
With many cheerful facts about the
square on the hypotenuse.

1640 *The Pirates of Penzance*
When constabulary duty's to be done,
A policeman's lot is not a happy one.

1641 *The Pirates of Penzance*
They are no members of the common
throng;
They are all noblemen who have gone
wrong!

1642 *The Pirates of Penzance*
No Englishman unmoved that statement
hears,
Because, with all our faults, we love our
House of Peers.

1643 *Princess Ida*
To everybody's prejudice I know a thing
or two;
I can tell a woman's age in half a minute
- and I do!

1644 *Princess Ida*
Man is Nature's sole mistake!

1645 *Ruddigore*
You must stir it and stump it,
And blow your own trumpet,
Or trust me, you haven't a chance.

1646 *Ruddigore*
He combines the manners of a Marquis
with the morals of a Methodist.

1647 *Ruddigore*
If a man can't forge his own will, whose
will can he forge?

1648 *Ruddigore*
Some word that teems with hidden meaning - like Basingstoke.

1649 *Ruddigore*
This particularly rapid, unintelligible patter
Isn't generally heard, and if it is it doesn't matter.

1650
See how the Fates their gifts allot.
For A is happy - B is not.
Yet B is worthy, I dare say,
Of more prosperity than A.

1651 *The Sorcerer*
I was a pale young curate then.

1652 *Trial by Jury*
So I fell in love with a rich attorney's
Elderly ugly daughter.

1653 *Trial by Jury*
She may very well pass for forty-three
In the dusk with a light behind her!

1654 *The Yeoman of the Guard*
It's a song of a merryman, moping mum,
Whose soul was sad, and whose glance was glum,
Who sipped no sup, and who craved no crumb,
As he sighed for the love of a ladye.

1655 *The Yeoman of the Guard*
'Tis ever thus with simple folk - an accepted wit has but to say 'Pass the mustard', and they roar their ribs out!

1656
And whether you're an honest man, or whether you're a thief,
Depends on whose solicitor has given me my brief.

1657
You've no idea what a poor opinion I have of myself - and how little I deserve it.

GILMAN Charlotte Perkins 1860-1935
1658
The people people work with best are often very queer.

GINSBERG Louis
1659
Life is ever
Since man was born,
Licking honey
From a thorn.

GIORDANO Bruno
1660
With luck on your side you can do without brains.

GLASS Montague
1661
She was an aging singer who had to take every note above 'A' with her eyebrows.

GLEASON Jackie
1662
Thin people are beautiful but fat people are adorable.

GODARD Jean-Luc 1930-
1663
'Movies should have a beginning, a middle and an end,' harrumphed French film maker Georges Franju ... 'Certainly,' replied Jean-Luc Godard. 'But not necessarily in that order.'

GODLEY A.D. 1856-1925
1664 *'The Megalopsychiad'*
Great and good is the typical Don, and of evil and wrong the foe,
Good, and great, I'm a Don myself, and therefore I ought to know.

1665
What is this that roareth thus?
Can it be a Motor Bus?
Yes, the smell and hideous hum
Indicat Motorem Bum!...
How shall wretches live like us
Cincti Bis Motoribus?
Domine, defende nos
Contra hos Motores Bos!

GOERING Hermann 1893-1946
1666
We have no butter ... but I ask you - would you rather have butter or guns? ... preparedness makes us powerful. Butter merely makes us fat.

GOETHE Johann von 1749-1832
1667
If children grew up according to early indications, we should have nothing but geniuses.

1668
From desire I plunge to its fulfilment, where I long once more for desire.

1669
So, lively brisk old fellow, don't let age get you down. White hairs or not, you can still be a lover.

1670
It is said that no man is a hero to his valet. That is because a hero can be recognized only by a hero.

1671
If a man thinks about his physical or moral state, he usually discovers that he is ill.

1672
And here, poor fool, with all my lore, I stand no wiser than before.

GOFFIN Harold
1673
Behind every successful man you'll find a woman who has nothing to wear.

GOGOL Nikolai 1809-1852
1674
Don't blame the mirror if your face is faulty.

GOLAS Thaddeus
1675
When you first learn to love hell, you will be in heaven.

GOLDBERG Justice Arthur 1908-1990
1676
If Columbus had had an advisory committee he would probably still be at the dock.

1677
I am surprised nothing has been made of the fact that astronaut Neil Armstrong carried no sidearms when he landed on the moon.

GOLDBERG Isaac 1887-1938
1678 *The Reflex*
Diplomacy is to do and say
The nastiest thing in the nicest way

GOLDEN Harry 1896-1976
1679
A tablecloth restaurant is still one of the great rewards of civilization.

GOLDMAN Albert
1680
The Jews have always been students, and their greatest study is themselves.

GOLDSMITH Oliver 1730-1774
1681 *The Bee no. 3*
The true use of speech is not so much to express our wants as to conceal them.

1682 *The Deserted Village*
The village all declared how much he knew;
'Twas certain he could write and cypher too.

1683 *The Deserted Village*
In arguing too, the parson owned his skill,
For e'en though vanquished, he could argue still;
While words of learned length, and thund'ring sound
Amazed the gazing rustics ranged around,
And still they gazed, and still the wonder grew,
That one small head could carry all he knew.

1684 *'Elegy on the Death of a Mad Dog'*
The dog, to gain some private ends,
Went mad and bit the man.

1685 *'Elegy on the Death of a Mad Dog'*
The man recovered of the bite,
The dog it was that died.

1686 *'Elegy on Mrs. Mary Blaize'*
The doctor found, when she was dead,
Her last disorder mortal.

1687 *The Good-Natured Man*
This same philosophy is a good horse in the stable, but an arrant jade on a journey.

1688 *'Logicians Refuted'*
Brutes never meet in bloody fray,
Nor cut each other's throats, for pay.

1689 *Retaliation*
Our Garrick's a salad; for in him we see
Oil, vinegar, sugar, and saltness agree.

1690 *Retaliation*
Here lies David Garrick, describe me, who can,
An abridgement of all that was pleasant in man.

1691 *Retaliation (of Edmund Burke)*
Who, too deep for his hearers, still went on refining,
And thought of convincing, while they thought of dining;
Though equal to all things, for all things unfit,
Too nice for a statesman, too proud for a wit.

1692 *Retaliation (of Garrick)*
On the stage he was natural, simple, affecting;
'Twas only that when he was off he was acting.

1693 *Retaliation (of Reynolds)*
When they talked of their Raphaels, Correggios, and stuff,
He shifted his trumpet, and only took snuff.

1694 *She Stoops to Conquer*
Is it one of my well-looking days, child?
Am I in face to-day?

1695 *She Stoops to Conquer*
The very pink of perfection.

1696 *She Stoops to Conquer*
I'll be with you in the squeezing of a lemon.

1697 *She Stoops to Conquer*
It's a damned long, dark, boggy, dirty, dangerous way.

1698 *She Stoops to Conquer*
Was there ever such a cross-grained brute?

1699 *She Stoops to Conquer 'Song'*
Let schoolmasters puzzle their brain,
With grammar, and nonsense, and learning,
Good liquor, I stoutly maintain,
Gives genius a better discerning.

1700
As I take my shoes from the shoemaker, and my coat from the tailor, so I take my religion from the priest.

1701 *The Traveller*
Where'er I roam, whatever realms to see,
My heart untravelled fondly turns to thee;
Still to my brother turns with ceaseless pain,
And drags at each remove a lengthening chain.

1702 *The Traveller*
Pride in their port, defiance in their eye,
I see the lords of human kind pass by.

1703 *The Vicar of Wakefield*
I was ever of opinion, that the honest man who married and brought up a large family, did more service than he who continued single and only talked of population.

1704 *The Vicar of Wakefield*
I ... chose my wife, as she did her wedding gown, not for a fine glossy surface, but such qualities as would wear well.

1705 *The Vicar of Wakefield*
All our adventures were by the fire-side, and all our migrations from the blue bed to the brown.

1706 *The Vicar of Wakefield*
It seemed to me pretty plain, that they had more of love than matrimony in them.

1707 *The Vicar of Wakefield*
When lovely woman stoops to folly
And finds too late that men betray,
What charm can soothe her melancholy,
What art can wash her guilt away?

GOLDWYN Sam 1882-1974
1708
I read part of it all the way through.

1709
Chaplin is no businessman - all he knows is that he can't take anything less.

1710
I'm exhausted from not talking.

1711
Any man who goes to a psychiatrist should have his head examined.

1712
Pictures are for entertainment, messages should be delivered by Western Union.

1713 *(on resigning from Motion Picture Producers)*
Gentlemen, include me out.

1714
If Roosevelt were alive he'd turn in his grave.

1715
From success you get a lot of things, but not that great inside thing that love brings you.

1716
That's the way with these directors, they're always biting the hand that lays the golden egg.

1717
A verbal contract isn't worth the paper it is written on.

1718
Why should people pay good money to go out and see bad films when they can stay at home and see bad television for nothing?

GOODMAN Al
1719
The perfect computer has been developed. You just feed in your problems, and they never come out again.

GOODMAN Paul
1720
Enjoyment is not a goal, it is a feeling that accompanies important ongoing activity.

1721
The family is the American fascism.

1722
Few great men could pass Personnel.

1723
I have learned to have very modest goals for society and myself; things like clean air, green grass, children with bright eyes, not being pushed around, useful work that suits one's abilities, plain tasty food, and occasional satisfying nookie.

GOODMAN Roy M.
1724
Remember that happiness is a way of travel - not a destination.

GORDON Mack 1904-1959
1725 *'Chattanooga Choo-choo'*
Pardon me boy is that the Chattanooga Choo-choo,
Track twenty nine,
Boy you can gimme a shine.
I can afford to board a Chattanooga Choo-choo,
I've got my fare and just a trifle to spare.
You leave the Pennsylvania station 'bout a quarter to four,
Read a magazine and then you're in Baltimore,
Dinner in the diner nothing could be finer
Than to have your ham'n eggs in Carolina.

GORDON Ruth
1726
To be somebody you must last.

GORMAN Teresa 1931-
1727
The Prime Minister has got the Parliamentary Party by the goolies.

GOULBURN Edward Meyrick 1818-1897
1728 *(sermon at Rugby School)*
Let the scintillations of your wit be like the coruscations of summer lightning, lambent but innocuous.

GOULD Bruce
1729
In England I would rather be a man, a horse, a dog or a woman, in that order. In America I think the order would be reversed.

GOURMONT Rémy de 1858-1915
1730
Women still remember the first kiss after men have forgotten the last.

1731
Of all sexual aberrations, perhaps the most peculiar is chastity.

GOWANS Alan
1732
By the laws of probability, North America ought to speak French, not English, today.

GOWERS Sir Ernest 1880-1966
1733
We are all esquires now, and we are none of us gentlemen any more.

GRACIAN Baltasar 1601-1658
1734
A beautiful woman should break her mirror early.

1735
'No' and 'Yes' are words quickly said, but they need a great amount of thought before you utter them.

1736
Time and I against any two.

1737
At twenty a man is a peacock, at thirty a lion, at forty a camel, at fifty a serpent, at sixty a dog, at seventy an ape, at eighty, nothing at all.

GRAHAM Billy 1918-
1738
Everybody has a little bit of Watergate in him.

GRAHAM Clementina Stirling 1782-1877
1739 *Mystifications*
The best way to get the better of temptation is just to yield to it.

GRAHAM Harry 1874-1936
1740 *More Ruthless Rhymes for Heartless Homes*
Weep not for little Léonie
Abducted by a French Marquis!
Though loss of honour was a wrench
Just think how it's improved her French.

1741 *Ruthless Rhymes for Heartless Homes*
O'er the rugged mountain's brow
Clara threw the twins she nursed,
And remarked, 'I wonder now
Which will reach the bottom first?'

1742 *Ruthless Rhymes for Heartless Homes*
Aunt Jane observed, the second time
She tumbled off a bus,
'The step is short from the Sublime
To the Ridiculous.'

1743 *Ruthless Rhymes for Heartless Homes*
'There's been an accident,' they said,
'Your servant's cut in half; he's dead!'
'Indeed!' said Mr Jones, 'and please,
Send me the half that's got my keys.'

1744 *Ruthless Rhymes for Heartless Homes*
Billy, in one of his nice new sashes,
Fell in the fire and was burnt to ashes;
Now, although the room grows chilly,
I haven't the heart to poke poor Billy.

GRAHAME Kenneth 1859-1932
1745
The clever men at Oxford
Know all there is to be knowed -
But they none of them know as half as much
As intelligent Mr. Toad.

1746 *The Golden Age*
Monkeys ... very sensibly refrain from speech, lest they should be set to earn their livings.

1747 *The Wind in the Willows*
There is *nothing* - absolutely nothing - half so much worth doing as simply messing about in boats.

GRAVES Robert 1895-1985
1748
If I were a girl, I'd despair. The supply of good women far exceeds that of the men who deserve them.

1749 *Occupation: Writer*
In love as in sport, the amateur status must be strictly maintained.

1750 *'The Persian Version'*
Truth-loving Persians do not dwell upon
The trivial skirmish fought near
Marathon.

1751
There's no money in poetry, but then there's no poetry in money either.

GRAVINA Gian Vinvenzo
1752
A bore is a man who deprives you of solitude without providing you with company.

GRAY John Chipman 1839-1915
1753 *Restraints on the Alienation of Property*
Dirt is only matter out of place.

GRAY Lord d.1612
1754 *(attributed)*
A dead woman bites not.

GRAY Thomas 1716-1771
1755 *Ode on a Distant Prospect of Eton College*
Alas, regardless of their doom,
The little victims play!
No sense have they of ills to come,
Nor care beyond to-day.

1756 *'Sketch of his own Character'*
Too poor for a bribe, and too proud to importune,
He had not the method of making a fortune.

1757
Where ignorance is bliss
'Tis folly to be wise.

GREELEY Horace 1811-1872
1758
The darkest hour of any man's life is when he sits down to plan how to get money without earning it.

1759 *Hints toward Reforms*
Go West, young man, and grow up with the country.

GREEN Benny 1927-
1760
A jazz musician is a juggler who uses harmonies instead of oranges.

GREEN Matthew 1696-1737
1761 *The Grotto*
They politics like ours profess,
The greater prey upon the less.

GREEN Russell
1762
Heaven is the place where the donkey finally catches up with his carrot: hell is the eternity while he waits for it.

1763
A wife encourages her husband's egoism in order to exercise her own.

GREENBERG Clement
1764
All profoundly original art looks ugly at first.

GREER Germaine 1939-
1765
I didn't fight to get women out from behind the vacuum cleaner to get them onto the board of Hoover.

1766
Women must learn to lighten up if we are to survive.

GREGG Alan
1767
A good education should leave much to be desired.

GREY John
1768
And what's a butterfly? At best,
He's but a caterpillar, drest.

GRICE Glenn le
1769
Florida: God's waiting room.

GROPIUS Walter 1883-1969
1770
Society needs a good image of itself.
That is the job of the architect.

GROSSMITH George and Weedon 1847-
1912 and 1854-1919
1771 *The Diary of a Nobody*
What's the good of a home if you are
never in it?

1772 *The Diary of a Nobody*
I left the room with silent dignity, but
caught my foot in the mat.

1773 *The Diary of a Nobody*
I am a poor man, but I would gladly give
ten shillings to find out who sent me the
insulting Christmas card I received this
morning.

GUEDALLA Philip 1889-1944
1774
I had always assumed that cliché was a
suburb of Paris, until I discovered it to be
a street in Oxford.

1775
The Lord Chief Justice of England
recently said that the greater part of his
judicial time was spent investigating
collisions between propelled vehicles,
each on its own side of the road, each
sounding its horn and each stationary.

1776 *Masters and Men*
Any stigma, as the old saying is, will
serve to beat a dogma.

1777 *(of The Duke of Wellington and Sir
Robert Peel in 1836)*
Their relations sometimes resembled an
exchange of signals between passing
icebergs.

1778 *Supers and Supermen*
The cheerful clatter of Sir James Barrie's
cans as he went round with the milk of
human kindness.

1779 *Supers and Supermen*
History repeats itself. Historians repeat
each other.

GUÉRARD Albert
1780
Chivalry is the most delicate form of
contempt.

GUINNESS Sir Alec 1914-
1781
Acting is happy agony.

GUITERMAN Arthur
1782
Amoebas at the start were not complex;
They tore themselves apart and started
sex.

1783
The porcupine, whom one must handle
gloved,
May be respected, but is never loved.

GUITRY Sacha 1885-1957
1784
Honest women are inconsolable for the
mistakes they haven't made.

1785
An ideal wife is one who remains faithful
to you but tries to be just as if she
weren't.

1786
The little I know, I owe to my ignorance.

1787
You can pretend to be serious, but you
can't pretend to be witty.

1788 *(attributed remark to his fifth wife)*
The others were only my wives. But you,
my dear, will be my widow.

1789
Even the most respectable woman has a
complete set of clothes in her wardrobe
ready for a possible abduction.

1790
When a man marries his mistress, he
creates a job vacancy.

1791
When a man steals your wife, there is no
better revenge than to let him keep her.

GULBENKIAN Nubar 1896-1972
1792
The best number for a dinner party is

two - myself and a dam' good head waiter.

GUNN Thom 1929-
1793 *Carnal Knowledge*
You know I know you know I know you know.

GUNTHER John 1901-1970
1794
All happiness depends on a leisurely breakfast.

1795
The first essence of journalism is to know what you want to know; the second, is to find out who will tell you.

GUTHRIE Woody 1912-1967
1796
Now as through this world I ramble,
I see lots of funny men,
Some rob you with a six gun
Some with a fountain pen.

HABERMAN Jr. Philip W.
1797
A gourmet is just a glutton with brains.

HAIG Earl 1861-1928
1798 *(of the 17th Earl of Derby)*
A very weak-minded fellow I am afraid, and, like the feather pillow, bears the marks of the last person who has sat on him!

HALDANE J.B.S. 1892-1964
1799
I have never yet met a healthy person who worries very much about his health, or a really good person who worries much about his own soul.

HALDEMAN H.R. 1929-
1800 *(of the Watergate affair)*
Once the toothpaste is out of the tube, it is awfully hard to get it back in.

HALIFAX Lord George 1633-1695
1801
Anger raiseth invention, but it overheateth the oven.

1802
A busy fool is fitter to be shut up than a downright madman.

HALLA Sven
1803
The good should be grateful to the bad - for providing the world with a basis for comparison.

HALSER Professor A.H.
1804
The project as understood by feminists is making women more like men, but it ought to be making men more like women.

HALSEY Margaret 1910-
1805 *With Malice Toward Some*
The English never smash in a face. They merely refrain from asking it to dinner.

1806
Some persons talk simply because they think sound is more manageable than silence.

1807
Whatever the rest of the world thinks of the English gentleman, the English lady regards him apprehensively as something between God and a goat and equally formidable on both scores.

HAMILTON Alex 1936-
1808
Those who stand for nothing fall for anything.

HAMILTON Robert B.
1809
Man is a reasoning, rather than a reasonable animal.

HAMPTON Christopher 1946-
1810 *Savages*
A definition of capitalism ... the process whereby American girls turn into American women.

HAND Learned 1872-1961
1811
The aim of law is the maximum gratification of the nervous system of man.

1812
The spirit of liberty is the spirit which is not too sure that it is right.

HANDS Terry 1941-
1813
It is said that Hamlet is the first modern man - so obviously he must be insane.

HARBURG E.Y. 1898-1981
1814
The World would be a safer place,
If someone had a plan,
Before exploring Outer Space,
To find the Inner man.

HARDING Warren G. 1865-1923
1815
My God, this is a hell of a job. I have no trouble with my enemies. I can take care of my enemies all right. But my damn friends, my goddamn friends. They're the ones that keep me walking the floor nights.

HARDWICKE Sir Cedric 1893-1964
1816
I regard England as my wife and America as my mistress.

HARDY Oliver 1892-1957
1817 *in The Laurel and Hardy Murder Case*
"Here's another fine mess you've gotten me into."

HARDY Thomas 1840-1928
1818 *'The Man he Killed'*
Yes; quaint and curious war is!
You shoot a fellow down
You'd treat if met where any bar is,
Or help to half-a-crown.

HARE Julius and HARE Augustus 1795-1855 and 1792-1834
1819
The greatest truths are the simplest, and so are the greatest men.

1820 *Guesses at Truth*
Half the failures in life arise from pulling in one's horse as he is leaping.

HARINGTON Sir John 1561-1612
1821 *Epigrams*
Treason doth never prosper, what's the reason?
For if it prosper, none dare call it treason.

HARKNESS Richard
1822
What is a committee? A group of the unwilling, picked from the unfit, to do the unnecessary.

HARLECH Lord (David Ormsby Gore)
1918-1985
1823
It would indeed be a tragedy if the history of the human race proved to be nothing more than the story of an ape playing with a box of matches on a petrol dump.

HARLOW Jean 1911-1937
1824 *in Hell's Angels*
"Excuse me while I slip into something more comfortable."

HARRIS Joel Chandler 1848-1908
1825
You k'n hide de fier, but what you guine do wid de smoke?

HARRIS Sydney J.
1826
The true test of independent judgement is being able to dislike someone who admires us.

HARTE Bret 1836-1902
1827
One big vice in a man is apt to keep out a great many smaller ones.

HASKINS Henry S.
1828
Disappointments should be cremated, not embalmed.

1829
If a man hears much that a woman says, she is not beautiful.

HAY Ian 1876-1952
1830 *The Housemaster*
What do you mean, funny? Funny-peculiar or funny ha-ha?

HAY John 1838-1905
1831
The best-loved man or maid in the town would perish with anguish could they hear all that their friends say in the course of a day.

HAYAKAWA S.I.
1832
We should keep the Panama Canal. After all we stole it fair and square.

HAYDON A. Eustace
1833
Fortunately for serious minds, a bias recognized is a bias sterilized.

HAYEK Friedrich 1899-1992
1834
Competition means decentralized planning by many separate persons.

HAYES J. Milton 1884-1940
1835 *The Green Eye of the Yellow God*
There's a one-eyed yellow idol to the
north of Khatmandu,
There's a little marble cross below the
town,
There's a broken-hearted woman tends
the grave of Mad Carew,
And the Yellow God forever gazes down.

HAYS Brooks
1836
Back of every achievement is a proud wife and a surprised mother-in-law.

HAZLITT William 1778-1830
1837
Actors are the only honest hypocrites.

1838
Without the aid of prejudice and custom, I should not be able to find my way across the room.

1839
It is essential to the triumph of reform that it shall never succeed.

1840
We are not hypocrites in our sleep.

1841
Landscape painting is the obvious resource of misanthropy.

1842
Man is a make-believe animal - he is never so truly himself as when he is acting a part.

1843
Man is the only animal that laughs and weeps; for he is the only animal that is struck by the difference between what things are and what they might have been.

1844
There is nothing good to be had in the country, or, if there be, they will not let you have it.

1845
Persons who undertake to pry into, or cleanse out all the filth of a common sewer, either cannot have very nice noses, or will soon lose them.

1846 *Sketches and Essays*
But of all footmen the lowest class is *literary footmen*.

1847 *Sketches and Essays*
A nickname is the heaviest stone that the devil can throw at a man.

1848
Those who are fond of setting things to rights have no great objection to setting them wrong.

1849
If we wish to know the force of human genius, we should read Shakespeare. If we wish to see the insignificance of human learning, we may study his commentators.

1850
Wit is the salt of conversation, not the food.

HEARST William Randolph 1863-1951
1851
Don't be afraid to make a mistake, your readers might like it.

HEIN Piet
1852
If no thought
your mind does visit
make your speech
not too explicit.

HEINE Heinrich 1797-1856
1853 *(as he died)*
God will pardon me. It's his business.

1854
The Romans would never have had time to conquer the world if they had been obliged to learn Latin first of all.

HELLER Joseph 1923-
1855 *Catch-22*
Some men are born mediocre, some men achieve mediocrity, and some men have mediocrity thrust upon them. With Major Major it had been all three.

1856
Frankly I'd like to see the government get out of war altogether and leave the whole field to private industry.

1857 *Something Happened*
The company has a policy about getting laid. It's okay ... Talking about getting laid is even more okay than doing it, but doing it is okay too, although talking about getting laid with your own wife is never okay.

1858
When I read something saying I've not done anything as good as *Catch-22*, I'm tempted to reply, 'Who has?'

HEMINGWAY Ernest 1899-1961
1859
The most essential gift for a good writer is a built-in, shockproof shit detector. This is the writer's radar and all great writers have had it.

HENDERSON Nelson
1860
The true meaning of life is to plant trees, under whose shade you do not expect to sit.

HENDREN L.L.
1861
Fathers send their sons to college either because they went to college, or because they didn't.

HENLEY W.E. 1849-1903
1862
Bland as a Jesuit, sober as a hymn.

HENRICH Tommy
1863
Catching a fly ball is a pleasure, but knowing what to do with it is a business.

HENRY O. 1862-1910
1864 *(last words)*
Turn up the lights; I don't want to go home in the dark.

1865 *Memoirs of a Yellow Dog*
If men knew how women pass the time when they are alone, they'd never marry.

HENRY Will
1866
What is research, but a blind date with knowledge?

HENRY William (Duke of Gloucester) 1743-1805
1867
Another damned, thick, square book! Always scribble, scribble, scribble! Eh! Mr. Gibbon?

HEPBURN Katharine 1909-
1868
If you give audiences a chance they'll do half your acting for you.

1869
Only the really plain people know about love - the very fascinating ones try so hard to create an impression that they soon exhaust their talents.

1870
If you're given a choice between money and sex appeal, take the money. As you get older, the money will become your sex appeal.

HERBERT A.P. 1890-1971
1871
A dull speaker, like a plain woman, is credited with all the virtues, for we charitably suppose that a surface so unattractive must be compensated by interior blessings.

1872 *'The Farmer'*
The Farmer will never be happy again;
He carries his heart in his boots;
For either the rain is destroying his grain
Or the drought is destroying his roots.

1873
A highbrow is the kind of person who looks at a sausage and thinks of Picasso.

1874 *'The President of the Board of Trade'*
This high official, all allow,
Is grossly overpaid;
There wasn't any Board, and now
There isn't any Trade.

1875 *Uncommon Law*
The critical period in matrimony is breakfast-time.

1876 *Uncommon Law*
The Common Law of England has been laboriously built about a mythical figure - the figure of 'The Reasonable Man'.

HERBERT George 1593-1633
1877
The chicken is the country's, but the city eats it.

1878
Drink not the third glass - which thou can'st not tame when once it is within thee.

HERBERT Jack
1879
A comedian is a fellow who finds other comedians too humorous to mention.

HERFORD Oliver
1880
Actresses will happen in the best regulated families.

1881
Bigamy is one way of avoiding the painful publicity of divorce and the expense of alimony.

1882
Only the young die good.

HERODOTUS c.485-425 BC
1883
Very few things happen at the right time, and the rest do not happen at all; the conscientious historian will correct these defects.

HEROLD Don
1884
Babies are such a nice way to start people.

1885
A humorist is a man who feels bad but who feels good about it.

1886
There's one thing about baldness - it's neat.

HERRICK Robert 1591-1674
1887
Fain would I kiss my Julia's dainty leg,
Which is as white and hairless as an egg.

1888 *'Upon Julia's Clothes'*
Whenas in silks my Julia goes,
Then, then (methinks) how sweetly flows
That liquefaction of her clothes.
Next, when I cast mine eyes and see
That brave vibration each way free;
O how that glittering taketh me!

HERSCHENSOHN Bruce
1889
Boredom turns a man to sex, a woman to shopping, and it drives newscasters berserk.

HERSHEY Lenore
1890
Do give books - religious or otherwise - for Christmas. They're never fattening, seldom sinful, and permanently personal.

HERZOG Roman 1934-
1891
One cannot cancel out Hitler through Beethoven.

HESS Stephen
1892 *(of John Major)*
The other European leaders actually ARE old: he just acts old.

HEYWOOD John c.1497-1580
1893
Wedding is destiny, and hanging likewise.

HICKS Sir John 1904-1989
1894 *Econometrica* 'The Theory of
Monopoly'
The best of all monopoly profits is a
quiet life.

HILL Rowland 1744-1833
1895
He did not see any reason why the devil
should have all the good tunes.

HILLARY Sir Edmund 1919-
1896 *(on conquering Mount Everest)*
Well, we knocked the bastard off!

HILLINGDON Lady 1857-1940
1897 *The Rise and Fall of the British
Nanny*
I am happy now that Charles calls on my
bedchamber less frequently than of old.
As it is, I now endure but two calls a
week and when I hear his steps outside
my door I lie down on my bed, close my
eyes, open my legs, and think of
England.

HILTON James 1900-1954
1898 *Goodbye, Mr Chips*
Nothing really wrong with him - only
anno domini, but that's the most fatal
complaint of all, in the end.

HIMMEL Sam
1899
A dictatorship is a country where they
have taken the politics out of politics.

HINCKS Clarence H.
1900
Nothing succeeds like one's own
successor.

HINES James
1901
A gentle Quaker, hearing a strange noise
in his house one night, got up and
discovered a burglar busily at work. He
went and got his gun, came back and
stood quietly in the doorway. 'Friend' he
said, 'I would do thee no harm for the
world, but thou standest where I am
about to shoot.'

HIPPOCRATES c.460-377 BC
1902
Wherever a doctor cannot do good, he
must be kept from doing harm.

HISLOP Ian 1960-
1903
What satirist ever toppled the
government? Swift managed to get one
small tax changed in his whole career.

HITCHCOCK Alfred 1899-1980
1904
Drama is life with the dull bits cut out.

1905
Television has brought back murder into
the home - where it belongs.

HITCHCOCK R.D.
1906
In a truly heroic life there is no
peradventure. It is always doing or
dying.

HOCKNEY David 1937-
1907
The thing with high-tech is that you
always end up using scissors.

HODGSON Ralph 1871-1962
1908
Did anyone ever have a boring dream?

1909 *'Bells of Heaven'*
'Twould ring the bells of Heaven
The wildest peal for years,
If Parson lost his senses
And people came to theirs,
And he and they together
Knelt down with angry prayers
For tamed and shabby tigers
And dancing dogs and bears,
And wretched, blind, pit ponies,
And little hunted hares.

HOFFA Jimmy c.1913-1975
1910
I may have faults but being wrong ain't
one of them.

HOFFENSTEIN Samuel
1911
Breathes there a man with hide so tough
Who says two sexes aren't enough?

HOFFER Eric 1902-1983
1912
There is a radicalism in all getting, and a conservatism in all keeping.
Lovemaking is radical, while marriage is conservative.

1913
Rudeness is the weak man's imitation of strength.

HOFFMANN Heinrich 1809-1894
1914 *Struwwelpeter*
Look at little Johnny there,
Little Johnny Head-In-Air!

HOLLAND Agnieszka
1915
In Hollywood they don't feel guilt.

HOLLAND James
1916
The Middle East is a region where oil is thicker than blood.

HOLLAND J.G. 1819-1881
1917
God gives every bird its food, but he does not throw it into the nest.

HOLMAN Libby
1918
I suppose you've heard all those wicked stories about me. Well, I've lived my life as it came and I've done bloody marvels with a bad hand.

HOLMES John Andrew
1919
It is well to remember that the entire population of the universe, with one trifling exception, is composed of others.

HOLMES Oliver Wendell 1809-1894
1920
Apology - a desperate habit, and one that is rarely cured.

1921
Apology is only egotism wrong side out.

1922 *The Autocrat of the Breakfast Table*
Man has his will - but woman has her way.

1923
A general flavour of mild decay,
But nothing local, as one may say.

1924
Heredity is an omnibus in which all our ancestors ride, and every now and then one of them puts his head out and embarrasses us.

1925
Husband and wife come to look alike at last.

1926
A man must get a thing before he can forget it.

1927
A man is a kind of inverted thermometer, the bulb uppermost, and the column of self-valuation is all the time going up and down.

1928
Man's mind stretched to a new idea never goes back to its original dimensions.

1929
Men are idolaters, and want something to look at and kiss and hug, or throw themselves down before; they always did, they always will, and if you don't make it of wood, you must make it of words.

1930
Nature, when she invented, manufactured and patented her authors, contrived to make critics out of the chips that were left.

1931
Rough work, iconoclasm, but the only way to get at the truth.

1932 *(of Samuel Francis Smith)*
Fate tried to conceal him by naming him Smith.

1933
After sixty years the stern sentence of the burial service seems to have a meaning that one did not notice in former years.

There begins to be something personal about it.

1934
When you write in prose you say what you mean. When you write in rhyme you say what you must.

HOLMES Oliver Wendell Jr. 1841-1935
1935
The advice of the elders to young men is very apt to be as unreal as a list of the hundred best books.

1936
This is a court of law, young man, not a court of justice.

1937
Fame usually comes to those who are thinking about something else.

1938
Every calling is great when greatly pursued.

1939
Life is painting a picture, not doing a sum.

1940
Longevity is having a chronic disease and taking care of it.

1941
A man over ninety is a great comfort to all his elderly neighbours: he is a picket-guard at the extreme outpost: and the young folks of sixty and seventy feel that the enemy must get by him before he can come near their camp.

1942
The mind of a bigot is like the pupil of the eye; the more light you pour upon it, the more it will contract.

1943
A person is always startled when he hears himself seriously called an old man for the first time.

1944
The reward of a general is not a bigger tent - but command.

1945
A sense of wrongdoing is an enhancement of pleasure.

1946
To be seventy years young is sometimes far more cheerful and hopeful than to be forty years old.

1947
If you think that I am going to bother myself again before I die about social improvement, or read any of those stinking upward and onwarders - you err - I mean to have some good out of being old.

1948
The trombone age (moving the page back and forth).

HOLYDAY Barten
1949
A man may as well open an oyster without a knife, as a lawyer's mouth without a fee.

HOMOLKA Oscar
1950
To really enjoy the better things in life, one must first have experienced the things they are better than.

HONEGGER Arthur 1892-1955
1951
The first requirement for a composer is to be dead.

HOOD Hugh
1952
Nothing ever tasted any better than a cold beer on a beautiful afternoon with nothing to look forward to but more of the same.

HOOD Thomas 1799-1845
1953 *Faithless Nelly Gray*
The love that loves a scarlet coat
Should be more uniform.

1954 *'Faithless Sally Brown'*
His death, which happened in his berth,
At forty-odd befell:
They went and told the sexton, and
The sexton tolled the bell.

1955 'A Reflection'
When Eve upon the first of Men
The apple pressed with specious cant,
Oh! what a thousand pities then
That Adam was not Adamant!

1956 *Up the Rhine*
Holland ... lies so low they're only saved
by being dammed.

1957 'The Song of the Shirt'
O! men with sisters dear,
O! men with mothers and wives!
It is not linen you're wearing out,
But human creatures' lives!

1958 'The Song of the Shirt'
Oh! God! that bread should be so dear,
And flesh and blood so cheap!

HOPE Anthony 1863-1933
1959 *The Dolly Dialogues*
Economy is going without something
you do want in case you should, some
day, want something you probably won't
want.

HOPE Bob 1903-
1960 *(attributed)*
A bank is a place that will lend you
money if you can prove that you don't
need it.

1961
If you haven't any charity in your heart,
you have the worst kind of heart trouble.

1962
The good news is that Jesus is coming
back. The bad news is that he's really
pissed off.

1963 *(on receiving honorary knighthood)*
I am literally speechless. Where are my
writers when I need them?

1964
People who throw kisses are hopelessly
lazy.

1965
If you watch a game, it's fun. If you play
it, it's recreation. If you work at it, it's
golf.

HOPKINS Anthony 1937-
1966 *in The Silence of the Lambs*
"I have to go now, Clarice, I'm having an
old friend for dinner."

HOPKINS Harry 1890-1946
1967
Hunger is not debatable.

HORACE 65-8 BC
1968 *Ars Poetica*
Not gods, nor men, nor even booksellers
have put up with poets being second-
rate.

1969
Dismiss the old horse in good time, lest
he fail in the lists and the spectators
laugh.

1970 *Epistles*
No verse can give pleasure for long, nor
last, that is written by drinkers of water.

HORNEY Karen 1885-1952
1971
Fortunately, analysis is not the only way
to resolve inner conflicts. Life itself
remains a very effective therapist.

HOUSMAN A.E. 1859-1936
1972
Malt does more than Milton can
To justify God's ways to man.

1973 *A Shropshire Lad*
When I was one-and-twenty
I heard a wise man say,
'Give crowns and pounds and guineas
But not your heart away;
Give pearls away and rubies,
But keep your fancy free.'
But I was one-and-twenty,
No use to talk to me.

HOWARD Elizabeth Jane 1923-
1974
Sex is like petrol. It's a galvaniser, a
wonderful fuel for starting a relationship.

HOWE Edgar Watson
1975 ·
Abuse a man unjustly, and you will make
friends for him.

1976
About all some men accomplish in life is to send a son to Harvard.

1977
If you go to church, and like the singing better than the preaching, that's not orthodox.

1978
Even if a farmer intends to loaf, he gets up in time to get an early start.

1979
Farmers worry only during the growing season, but town people worry all the time.

1980
If a friend is in trouble, don't annoy him by asking if there is anything you can do. Think up something appropriate and do it.

1981
A good scare is worth more to a man than good advice.

1982
A man should be taller, older, heavier, uglier and hoarser than his wife.

1983
A modest man is usually admired - if people ever hear of him.

1984
What people say behind your back is your standing in the community.

HOWELL James
1985
He that hath the name to be an early riser may sleep till noon.

HOWELLS William Dean 1837-1920
1986
Some people can stay longer in an hour than others can in a week.

HOYLE Sir Fred 1915-
1987
Space isn't remote at all. It's only an hour's drive away if your car could go straight upwards.

HSIEH Tehyi
1988
If ignorance is indeed bliss, it is a very low grade of the article.

HUBBARD Elbert 1859-1915
1989
To escape criticism - do nothing, say nothing, be nothing.

1990
God will not look you over for medals, degrees or diplomas, but for scars.

1991
Every man is a damn fool for at least five minutes every day; wisdom consists in not exceeding the limit.

1992
Mystic: a person who is puzzled before the obvious, but who understands the non-existent.

1993
Pessimism is only the name that men of weak nerves give to wisdom.

1994
A pessimist is one who has been compelled to live with an optimist.

1995 *Philistine*
Life is just one damned thing after another.

1996
Polygamy: an endeavour to get more out of life than there is in it.

1997 *The Roycroft Dictionary*
An editor - a person employed on a newspaper, whose business it is to separate the wheat from the chaff, and to see that the chaff is printed.

HUBBARD Kin 1868-1930
1998
I don't know of anything better than a woman if you want to spend money where it will show.

1999
The fellow that owns his own home is always just coming out of a hardware store.

2000
Some fellows pay a compliment like they expected a receipt.

2001
Folks that blurt out just what they think wouldn't be so bad if they thought.

2002
Some folks can look so busy doing nothin' that they seem indispensable.

2003
A friend that ain't in need is a friend indeed.

2004
Gossip is vice enjoyed vicariously - the sweet, subtle satisfaction without the risk.

2005
I haven't heard of anybody who wants to stop living on account of the cost.

2006
Kindness goes a long way lots o' times when it ought t' stay at home.

2007
The only way to entertain some folks is to listen to them.

2008
An optimist is a fellow who believes what's going to be will be postponed.

2009
It's pretty hard to be efficient without being obnoxious.

2010
The world gets better every day - then worse again in the evening.

HUBBARD L. Ron 1911-1986
2011
If you really want to make a million ... the quickest way is to start your own religion.

HUDSON William Henry 1841-1922
2012
You cannot fly like an eagle with the wings of a wren.

HUGHES Charles Evans 1862-1948
2013
We are under a Constitution, but the Constitution is what the judges say it is.

HUGHES J.B.
2014
If Moses had been a committee, the Israelites would still be in Egypt.

HUGHES Rupert
2015
Her face was her chaperone.

HUGO Victor 1802-1885
2016
No army can withstand the strength of an idea whose time has come.

2017
If you would civilize a man, begin with his grandmother.

2018
Everything bows to success, even grammar.

2019
There are fathers who do not love their children; there is no grandfather who does not adore his grandson.

2020
Forty is the old age of youth; fifty is the youth of old age.

HULBERT Harold S.
2021
Children need love, especially when they do not deserve it.

HULBERT James
2022
A company is judged by the president it keeps.

HULL Josephine
2023
Playing Shakespeare is very tiring. You never get to sit down, unless you're a king.

HUME Cardinal Basil 1923-2024 *(asked how he plans to celebrate the Millennium)*
I'll be splashing around in the fountains of Trafalgar Square with everyone else.

HUMPHREY Hubert 1911-1978
2025
I've never thought my speeches were too long; I've rather enjoyed them.

2026
The right to be heard does not automatically include the right to be taken seriously.

HUNT Leigh 1784-1859
2027 *The Examiner 1808*
Never lay yourself open to what is called conviction: you might as well open your waist-coat to receive a knock-down blow.

2028
If you are ever at a loss to support a flagging conversation, introduce the subject of eating.

2029 *'The Story of Rimini' (1816)*
The two divinest things this world has got,
A lovely woman in a rural spot!

HUNTINGTON Collis P. 1821-1900
2030
Whatever is not nailed down is mine. Whatever I can pry loose is not nailed down.

HUROK Sol 1888-1974
2031
When people don't want to come, nothing will stop them.

HUTCHINSON Sir Robert
2032
Vegetarianism is harmless enough, though it is apt to fill a man with wind and self-righteousness.

HUXLEY Aldous 1894-1963
2033
To his dog, every man is Napoleon; hence the constant popularity of dogs.

2034
The natural rhythm of human life is routine punctuated by orgies.

2035 *'Fifth Philosopher's Song'*
A million million Spermatozoa,
All of them alive:
Out of their cataclysm but one poor Noah
Dare hope to survive.
And among that billion minus one
Might have chanced to be
Shakespeare, another Newton, a new Donne -
But the One was me.

2036 *'Ninth Philosopher's Song'*
Beauty for some provides escape,
Who gain a happiness in eyeing
The gorgeous buttocks of the ape
Or Autumn sunsets exquisitely dying.

2037
After silence, that which comes nearest to expressing the inexpressible is music.

2038
What we think and feel and are is to a great extent determined by the state of our ductless glands and our viscera.

2039
Why should human females become sterile in their forties, while female crocodiles continue to lay eggs into their third century?

HUXLEY Sir Julian 1887-1975
2040 *Religion without Revelation*
Operationally, God is beginning to resemble not a ruler but the last fading smile of a cosmic Cheshire cat.

HUXLEY Thomas 1825-1895
2041 *Collected Essays*
If a little knowledge is dangerous, where is the man who has so much as to be out of danger?

2042
If some great power would agree to make me always think what is true and do what is right, on condition of being some sort of clock and wound up every morning before I got out of bed, I should close instantly with the offer.

2043
The great tragedy of Science: the slaying of a beautiful hypothesis by an ugly fact.

2044
I am too much of a sceptic to deny the possibility of anything.

2045 *Science and Culture and Other Essays*
Irrationally held truths may be more harmful than reasoned errors.

2046
Tolerably early in life I discovered that one of the unpardonable sins, in the eyes of most people, is for a man to go about unlabelled. The world regards such a person as the police do an unmuzzled dog.

HUXTABLE Ada Louise
2047
Washington is an endless series of mock palaces clearly built for clerks.

IBARRURI Dolores ('La Pasionaria')
1895-1989
2048
It is better to die on your feet than to live on your knees.

IBSEN Henrik 1828-1906
2049
One should never put on one's best trousers to go out to battle for freedom and truth.

ILES Francis 1893-1970
2050 *Malice Aforethought*
Murder is a serious business.

INGE Charles 1868-1957
2051 *'On Monsieur Coué'*
This very remarkable man
Commends a most practical plan:
You can do what you want
If you don't think you can't,
So don't think you can't think you can.

INGE William R. 1860-1954
2052
A man usually does his best work just before he is found out.

2053
Middle-aged people are often happier than the young: but it by no means follows that they ought to be...

2054
Let none of us delude himself by supposing that honesty is always the best policy. It is not.

2055 *Outspoken Essays*
It takes in reality only one to make a quarrel. It is useless for the sheep to pass resolutions in favour of vegetarianism, while the wolf remains of a different opinion.

2056
Religion is a way of walking, not a way of talking.

2057
Because most of the saints were poor, it does not follow that most of the poor are saints.

2058
There are two kinds of fools: one says, 'This is old, therefore it is good'; the other says, 'This is new, therefore it is better.'

2059
What is originality? Undetected plagiarism.

2060
The whole of nature is a conjugation of the verb to eat, in the active and passive.

INGELOW Jean 1820-1897
2061
I have lived to thank God that all my prayers have not been answered.

INGERSOLL Robert G. 1833-1899
2062
An honest God is the noblest work of man.

2063
In the republic of mediocrity, genius is dangerous.

2064
With soap baptism is a good thing.

2065
I suppose it can be truthfully said that hope is the only universal liar who never loses his reputation for veracity.

IONESCO Eugene 1912-1994
2066
You can only predict things after they've happened.

IRVING Washington 1783-1859
2067
I am always at a loss to know how much to believe of my own stories.

ISHERWOOD Christopher 1904-1986
2068 *'The Common Cormorant'*
The common cormorant (or shag)
Lays eggs inside a paper bag,
You follow the idea, no doubt?
It's to keep the lightning out.

But what these unobservant birds
Have never thought of, is that herds
Of wandering bears might come with buns
And steal the bags to hold the crumbs.

JACKSON Andrew 1767-1845
2069
There goes a man made by the Lord Almighty and not by his tailor.

JACKSON George
2070
Patience has its limits. Take it too far, and it's cowardice.

JACKSON Holbrook 1874-1948
2071 *Platitudes in the Making*
As soon as an idea is accepted it is time to reject it.

JACKSON Jesse 1941-
2072
Your children need your presence more than your presents.

JACKSON Thomas (Stonewall) 1824-1863
2073
I like liquor - its taste and its effects - and that is just the reason why I never drink it.

JACOB Fred
2074
A good husband should always bore his wife.

JAFFREY Saeed
2075 *in My Beautiful Launderette*
"Take my advice, there's money in muck."

JAMES Henry 1843-1916
2076 *'The Given Case'*
Women never dine alone. When they dine alone they don't dine.

2077 *Hawthorne*
He was imperfect, unfinished, inartistic; he was worse than provincial - he was parochial.

JAMES I King (JAMES VI of Scotland) 1566-1625
2078 *A Counterblast to Tobacco*
A branch of the sin of drunkenness, which is the root of all sins.

2079 *A Counterblast to Tobacco*
A custom loathsome to the eye, hateful to the nose, harmful to the brain, dangerous to the lungs, and in the black, stinking fume thereof, nearest resembling the horrible Stygian smoke of the pit that is bottomless.

2080 *(recorded by Archdeacon Plume)*
Dr Donne's verses are like the peace of God; they pass all understanding.

JAMES William 1842-1910
2081
As Charles Lamb says, there is nothing so nice as doing good by stealth and being found out by accident, so I now say it is even nicer to make heroic decisions and to be prevented by 'circumstances beyond your control' from ever trying to execute them.

2082
Footnotes, the little dogs yapping at the heels of the text.

2083
Genius, in truth, means little more than the faculty of perceiving in an unhabitual way.

2084
The great use of life is to spend it for something that will outlast it.

2085
An unlearned carpenter of my acquaintance once said in my hearing: 'There is very little difference between

one man and another, but what there is
is *very important.'*

JARRELL Randall 1914-1965
2086
Ezra Pound - idiosyncrasy on a
monument.

2087
A good poet is someone who manages,
in a lifetime of standing out in
thunderstorms, to be struck by lightning
five or six times.

2088
The novel is a prose narrative of some
length that has something wrong with it.

2089 *Pictures from an Institution*
To Americans, English manners are far
more frightening than none at all.

JEANS Ronald d.1973
2090
Actor-manager - one to whom the part is
greater than the whole.

JEFFERIES Richard
2091
When I look in the glass I see that every
line in my face means pessimism, but in
spite of my face - that is my experience -
I remain an optimist.

JENKINS Dr David (Bishop of Durham)
1925-
2092
There is no doubting my belief in God,
but the Church has driven me close to it.

JEROME Jerome K. 1859-1927
2093
Idleness, like kisses, to be sweet must be
stolen.

2094 *Idle Thoughts of an Idle Fellow*
It is impossible to enjoy idling
thoroughly unless one has plenty of
work to do.

2095 *Idle Thoughts of an Idle Fellow*
Love is like the measles; we all have to go
through it.

JERROLD Douglas 1803-1857
2096
Australia is so kind that, just tickle her

with a hoe, and she laughs with a
harvest.

2097
A Conservative is a man who will not
look at the new moon, out of respect for
that ancient institution, the old one.

2098 *The Life and Remains of Douglas
Jerrold*
If an earthquake were to engulf England
to-morrow, the English would manage to
meet and dine somewhere among the
rubbish, just to celebrate the event.

2099
Love the sea? I dote upon it - from the
beach.

2100
The ugliest of trades have their moments
of pleasure. Now, if I was a grave digger,
or even a hangman, there are some
people I could work for with a great deal
of enjoyment.

2101 *The Wit and Opinions of Douglas
Jerrold*
The best thing I know between France
and England is - the sea.

2102 *The Wit and Opinions of Douglas
Jerrold*
Love's like the measles - all the worse
when it comes late in life.

JIPCHO Ben
2103
Running for money doesn't make you
run fast. It makes you run first.

JOAD C.E.M. 1891-1953
2104
My life is spent in a perpetual alternation
between two rhythms, the rhythm of
attracting people for fear I may be lonely,
and the rhythm of trying to get rid of
them because I know that I am bored.

JOBS Steve 1955-
2105 *(of attempts to get interest in the
Apple PC)*
We went to Atari and said "We've got this
amazing thing..." They said "No". Then
we went to Hewlett-Packard; they said,

"We don't need you. You haven't got through college yet."

JOHN XXIII Pope 1881-1963
2106
Italians come to ruin most generally in three ways - women, gambling and farming. My family chose the slowest one.

2107
See everything: overlook a great deal: correct a little.

JOHNSON Gerald
2108
Heroes are created by popular demand, sometimes out of the scantiest materials ... such as the apple that William Tell never shot, the ride that Paul Revere never finished, the flag that Barbara Frietchie never waved.

JOHNSON Lyndon B. 1908-1973
2109
I may not know much, but I know chicken shit from chicken salad.

2110
What's the difference between a cactus and a caucus>? A cactus has the pricks on the outside.

2111 *(of Gerald Ford)*
So dumb he can't fart and chew gum at the same time.

2112
Only two things are necessary to keep one's wife happy. One is to let her think she is having her own way, and the other, to let her have it.

2113
While you're saving your face you're losing your ass. Never trust a man whose eyes are too close to his nose. I never trust a man unless I've got his pecker in my pocket. Better inside the tent pissing out than outside the tent pissing in.

JOHNSON Paul 1928-
2114
Tories, in short, are atrophied Englishmen, lacking certain moral and intellectual reflexes. They are recognizable, homely - even, on occasions, endearing - but liable to turn very nasty at short notice.

JOHNSON Samuel 1709-1784
2115
Abstinence is as easy for me as temperance would be difficult.

2116
I would advise no man to marry, who is not likely to propagate understanding.

2117 *Boswell - Life*
Norway, too, has noble wild prospects; and Lapland is remarkable for prodigious noble wild prospects. But, Sir, let me tell you, the noblest prospect which a Scotchman ever sees, is the high road that leads him to England.

2118 *Boswell - Life*
Every man has a lurking wish to appear considerable in his native place.

2119 *Boswell - Life*
Patriotism is the last refuge of a scoundrel.

2120 *Boswell - Life*
There is nothing which has yet been contrived by man, by which so much happiness is produced as by a good tavern or inn.

2121 *Boswell - Life*
Marriages would in general be as happy, and often more so, if they were all made by the Lord Chancellor, upon a due consideration of characters and circumstances, without the parties having any choice in the matter.

2122 *Boswell - Life*
We would all be idle if we could.

2123 *Boswell - Life*
No man but a blockhead ever wrote, except for money.

2124 *Boswell - Life*
A man who has not been in Italy, is always conscious of an inferiority, from his not having seen what it is expected a man should see.

2125 *Boswell - Life*
A mere antiquarian is a rugged being.

2126 *Boswell - Life*
Were it not for imagination, Sir, a man would be as happy in the arms of a chambermaid as of a Duchess.

2127 *Boswell - Life*
Claret is the liquor for boys; port, for men; but he who aspires to be a hero (smiling) must drink brandy.

2128 *Boswell - Life*
A man who exposes himself when he is intoxicated, has not the art of getting drunk.

2129 *Boswell - Life*
Every man has a right to utter what he thinks truth, and every other man has a right to knock him down for it. Martyrdom is the test.

2130 *Boswell - Life*
A Frenchman must be always talking, whether he knows anything of the matter or not; an Englishman is content to say nothing, when he has nothing to say.

2131 *Boswell - Life*
Now, Sir, there are people whom one should like very well to drop, but would not wish to be dropped by.

2132 *Boswell - Life*
Sir, I have two very cogent reasons for not printing any list of subscribers; one, that I have lost all the names; the other, that I have spent all the money.

2133 *Boswell - Life*
How few of his friends' houses would a man choose to be at when he is sick.

2134 *Boswell - Life*
If a young or middle-aged man, when leaving a company, does not recollect where he laid his hat, it is nothing; but if the same inattention is discovered in an old man, people will shrug up their shoulders, and say, 'His memory is going'.

2135 *Boswell - Life*
Sir, I have found you an argument; but I am not obliged to find you an understanding.

2136 *Boswell - Life (on biography writing)*
The dogs don't know how to write trifles with dignity.

2137 *Boswell - Life (of Mr Dudley Long)*
Mr Long's character is very *short*. It is nothing. He fills a chair.

2138 *Boswell - Life (on the Giant's Causeway)*
Worth seeing, yes; but not worth going to see.

2139 *Boswell - Life (of Jeremiah Markland)*
I hate a fellow whom pride, or cowardice, or laziness drives into a corner, and who does nothing when he is there but sit and *growl*; let him come out as I do, and *bark*.

2140 *Boswell - Life (letter to Boswell)*
If you are idle, be not solitary; if you are solitary, be not idle.

2141 *Boswell - Life (of a man who remarried)*
A triumph of hope over experience.

2142 *Boswell - Life (on the merits of two minor poets)*
Sir, there is no settling the point of precedency between a louse and a flea.

2143 *Boswell - Life (of Milton's sonnets)*
Milton, Madam, was a genius that could cut a Colossus from a rock; but could not carve heads upon cherry-stones.

2144 *Boswell - Life (parodying Henry Brooke)*
It might as well be said 'Who drives fat oxen should himself be fat.'

2145 *Boswell - Life (on roast mutton served at an inn)*
It is as bad as bad can be; it is ill-fed, ill-killed, ill-kept, and ill-drest.

2146 *Boswell - Life (of Thomas Gray's Odes)*
They are forced plants, raised in a hot-bed; and they are poor plants; they are but cucumbers after all.

2147
Corneille is to Shakespeare ... as a clipped hedge is to a forest.

2148 *A Dictionary of the English Language*
Dull. To make dictionaries is dull work.

2149 *A Dictionary of the English Language*
Lexicographer. A writer of dictionaries, a harmless drudge.

2150 *A Dictionary of the English Language*
Network. Anything reticulated or decussated at equal distances, with interstices between the intersections.

2151
One of the disadvantages of wine is that it makes a man mistake words for thoughts.

2152
Don't think of retiring from the world until the world will be sorry that you retire.

2153
As the faculty of writing has chiefly been a masculine endowment, the reproach of making the world miserable has always been thrown upon the women.

2154
A fly, Sir, may sting a stately horse and make him wince; but one is but an insect, and the other a horse still.

2155 *The Idler*
When two Englishmen meet, their first talk is of the weather.

2156 *The Idler*
Nothing is more hopeless than a scheme of merriment.

2157 *(attributed, in Instructions to Young Sportsmen)*
Fly fishing may be a very pleasant amusement; but angling or float fishing I can only compare to a stick and a string, with a worm at one end and a fool at the other.

2158
Had I learned to fiddle, I should have done nothing else.

2159
Life is a progress from want to want, not from enjoyment to enjoyment.

2160
It is better to live rich than to die rich.

2161
A man should be careful never to tell tales of himself to his own disadvantage. People may be amused at the time, but they will be remembered, and brought out against him upon some subsequent occasion.

2162
A man is in general better pleased when he has a good dinner upon his table, than when his wife talks Greek.

2163
No man is a hypocrite in his pleasures.

2164
Every man has, some time in his life, an ambition to be a wag.

2165
If the man who turnips cries,
Cry not when his father dies,
'Tis a proof that he had rather
Have a turnip than his father.

2166
Your manuscript is both good and original; but the parts that are good are not original, and the parts that are original are not good.

2167
Much may be made of a Scotchman if he be caught young.

2168
Music ... the only sensual pleasure without vice.

2169
None but a fool worries about things he cannot influence.

2170
Nothing flatters a man as much as the happiness of his wife; he is always proud of himself as the source of it.

2171
Oats: A grain which in England is generally given to horses, but in Scotland supports the people.

2172
Is not a patron one who looks with unconcern on a man struggling for life in the water, and, when he has reached ground, encumbers him with help?

2173
Questioning is not the mode of conversation among gentlemen.

2174 *The Rambler*
No place affords a more striking conviction of the vanity of human hopes, than a public library.

2175
Being in a ship is being in a jail, with the chance of being drowned.

2176
When a man knows he is to be hanged in a fortnight, it concentrates his mind wonderfully.

JOHNSON Vera
2177
There's such a thing as moderation, even in telling the truth.

JOHNSTON Eric
2178
The dinosaur's eloquent lesson is that if some bigness is good, an overabundance of bigness is not necessarily better.

JONES Clinton 1848-1936
2179
I never been in no situation where havin' money made it any worse.

JONES Franklin P.
2180
Bargain: something you can't use at a price you can't resist.

2181
Experience enables you to recognize a mistake when you make it again.

2182
An extravagance is anything you buy that is of no earthly use to your wife.

2183
Most people like hard work, particularly when they're paying for it.

JONES Spike
2184
When the audience knows you know better, it's satire, but when they think you can't do any better, it's corn.

JONG Erica 1942-
2185 *Fear of Flying*
Jealousy is all the fun you think they had.

JONSON Ben c.1573-1637
2186
All men are Philosophers, to their inches.

2187 *Bartholomew Fair*
The lungs of the tobacconist are rotted, the liver spotted, the brain smoked like the backside of the pig-woman's booth here, and the whole body within, black as her pan you saw e'en now without.

2188 *Bartholomew Fair*
Neither do thou lust after that tawney weed tobacco.

2189 *Bartholomew Fair (of Ursula, the pig woman)*
The very womb and bed of enormity.

2190 *The Entertainment at Althrope*
This is Mab, the Mistress-Fairy
That doth nightly rob the dairy.

2191 *Every Man in His Humour*
I do honour the very flea of his dog.

2192 *The Poetaster*
Ramp up my genius, be not retrograde;
But boldly nominate a spade a spade.

2193 *The Poetaster*
Detraction is but baseness' varlet;
And apes are apes, though clothed in
scarlet.

2194 *Timber, or Discoveries made upon
Men and Matter*
The players have often mentioned it as
an honour to Shakespeare that in his
writing, whatsoever he penned, he never
blotted out a line. My answer hath been
'Would he had blotted a thousand'.

2195 *Volpone*
Our drink shall be prepared gold and
amber;
Which we will take, until my roof whirl
around
With the *vertigo*: and my dwarf shall
dance.

2196 *Volpone*
Honour! tut, a breath,
There's no such thing in nature; a mere
term
Invented to awe fools.

JORDAN Thomas c.1612-1685
2197 *'How the War began'*
They plucked communion tables down
And broke our painted glasses;
They threw our altars to the ground
And tumbled down the crosses.
They set up Cromwell and his heir -
The Lord and Lady Claypole -
Because they hated Common Prayer,
The organ and the maypole.

JOSEPH Jenny
2198
I was raised to feel that doing nothing
was a sin. I had to learn to do nothing.

JOUBERT Joseph 1754-1824
2199
Words, like eyeglasses, blur everything
that they do not make clear.

2200
Never cut what you can untie.

2201
To teach is to learn twice.

JOWETT Benjamin 1817-1893
2202
There is a great deal of hard lying in the
world: especially among people whose
characters are above suspicion.

2203
No married clergyman should refuse a
bishopric.

2204
Men get lazy, and substitute quantity of
work for quality.

2205
Nowhere probably is there more true
feeling, and nowhere worse taste, than in
a churchyard.

2206
`Research' is a mere excuse for idleness.

2207
We have sought truth, and sometimes
perhaps found it. But have we had any
fun?

2208
No one who has a great deal of energy
will long be popular in Oxford.

JOYCE James 1882-1941
2209
[on being asked by an admirer whether
he might kiss the hand that wrote
Ulysses] No, it did lots of other things
too.

2210 *Finnegans Wake*
The flushpots of Euston and the hanging
garments of Marylebone.

2211 *Finnegans Wake*
All moanday, tearsday, wailsday,
thumpsday, frightday, shatterday till the
fear of the Law.

2212 *Finnegans Wake*
The Gracehoper was always jigging ajog,
hoppy on akkant of his joyicity.

2213 *Finnegans Wake*
If I seen him bearing down on me now
under whitespread wings like he'd come
from Arkangels, I sink I'd die down over
his feet, humbly dumbly, only to
washup.

2214 *A Portrait of the Artist as a Young Man*
Ireland is the old sow that eats her farrow.

2215 *Ulysses*
The snotgreen sea. The scrotumtightening sea.

2216 *Ulysses*
When I makes tea I makes tea. And when I makes water I makes water ... *Begob, ma'am,* says Mrs Cahill, *God send you don't make them in the one pot.*

2217 *Ulysses*
Lawn Tennyson, gentleman poet.

2218 *Ulysses*
He ... saw the dark tangled curls of his bush floating, floating hair of the stream around the limp father of thousands, a languid floating flower.

2219 *Ulysses*
Come forth, Lazarus! And he came fifth and lost the job.

2220 *Ulysses*
Greater love than this, he said, no man hath that a man lay down his wife for his friend. Go thou and do likewise. Thus, or words to that effect, saith Zarathustra, sometime regius professor of French letters to the university of Oxtail.

JOYCE Peggy
2221
It takes all the fun out of a bracelet if you have to buy it yourself.

JUNIUS
2222
If individuals have no virtues, their vices may be of use to us.

JUVENAL AD c.60-c.130
2223 *Satires*
No one ever suddenly became depraved.

KAEL Pauline 1919-
2224
One of the surest signs of the Philistine is his reverence for the superior tastes of those who put him down.

KAHN Gus and EGAN Raymond 1886-1941 and 1890-1952
2225 *'Ain't We Got Fun'*
There's nothing surer,
The rich get rich and the poor get children.
In the meantime, in between time,
Ain't we got fun.

KAISER Henry J. 1882-1967
2226
Trouble is only opportunity in work clothes.

2227
When your work speaks for itself, don't interrupt.

KAN Alphonse
2228
Every man has three characters - that which he exhibits, that which he has, and that which he thinks he has.

KANE Marie Elizabeth
2229 *(when thirteen years old)*
I feel when people say 'bigger and better' they should say 'bigger and badder'.

KANIN Garson
2230
Amateurs hope. Professionals work.

2231
Whenever I'm asked what college I attended, I'm tempted to reply, 'Thornton Wilder'.

KAPP K. William
2232
Had there been a computer a hundred years ago, it would probably have predicted that by now there would be so many horse-drawn vehicles it would be impossible to clear up all the manure.

KAPPEL Frederick
2233
The Bell system is like a damn big dragon. You kick it in the tail, and two years later, it feels it in its head.

KASLUCK Lady
2234
The worst thing about work in the house or home is that whatever you do is

destroyed, laid waste or eaten within twenty-four hours.

KAUFMAN George S. 1889-1961
2235
Satire is what closes Saturday night.

2236
I like terra firma - the more firma, the less terra.

KAUFMAN Gerald 1930-
2237 *(on the Labour Party's New Hope for Britain)*
The longest suicide note in history.

KEATE Stuart
2238
Canada reminds me of vichyssoise - it's cold, half-French and difficult to stir.

KEATS John 1795-1821
2239
In disease Medical Men guess: if they cannot ascertain a disease, they call it nervous.

2240 *Letter to J.H. Reynolds*
It is impossible to live in a country which is continually under hatches ... Rain! Rain! Rain!

2241 *'Lines on the Mermaid Tavern'*
Souls of poets dead and gone,
What Elysium have ye known
Happy field or mossy cavern
Choicer than the Mermaid Tavern?

2242
A proverb is no proverb to you till life has illustrated it.

KEILLOR Garrison 1942-
2243 *The Book of Guys*
Years ago, manhood was an opportunity for achievement, and now it is a problem to be overcome.

KELLY Hugh 1739-1777
2244 *Memoirs of a Magdalen*
Of all the stages in a woman's life, none is so dangerous as the period between her acknowledgement of a passion for a man, and the day set apart for her nuptials.

KELLY William M. 1811-1888
2245
Man is a slow, sloppy and brilliant thinker; the machine is fast, accurate and stupid.

KELVIN Lord 1824-1907
2246 *(whilst President of the Royal Society, 1895)*
Heavier-than-air flying machines are impossible.

KEMPTON Sally
2247
It is hard to fight an enemy who has outposts in your head.

KENNEDY Florynce
2248
If men could get pregnant, abortion would be a sacrament.

KENNEDY John F. 1917-1963
2249 *(asked how he became a war hero)*
It was involuntary. They sank my boat.

KENNEDY Joseph P. 1888-1969
2250
When the going gets tough, the tough get going.

KERR Clark 1911-
2251 *(whilst President, University of California)*
I find the three major administrative problems on a campus are sex for the students, athletics for the alumni and parking for the faculty.

KERR Jean 1923-
2252
The thing about having a baby is that thereafter you have it.

2253
Marrying a man is like buying something you've been admiring for a long time in a shop window. You may love it when you get it home, but it doesn't always go with everything in the house.

2254 *Mary, Mary*
Being divorced is like being hit by a truck - if you survive, you start looking very carefully to the left and right.

KETTERING Charles F. 1876-1958
2255
It is easy to build a philosophy. It doesn't have to run.

2256
My interest is in the future because I am going to spend the rest of my life there.

KEYNES John Maynard 1883-1946
2257 *(of his poor results in the Civil Service exams)*
I evidently knew more about economics than my examiners.

KEYSERLING Hermann 1880-1946
2258
The greatest American superstition is belief in facts.

KHRUSHCHEV Nikita 1894-1971
2259
If anyone believes that our smiles involve abandonment of the teaching of Marx, Engels and Lenin he deceives himself. Those who wait for that must wait until a shrimp learns to whistle.

2260
I don't like the life here in New York. There is no greenery. It would make a stone sick.

2261
Politicians are the same all over. They promise to build a bridge even when there is no river.

2262
If we should promise people nothing better than only revolution, they would scratch their heads and say, 'Isn't it better to have good goulash?'

2263
If you start throwing hedgehogs under me, I shall throw a couple of porcupines under you.

KIERKEGAARD Sören 1813-1855
2264
Anxiety is the dizziness of freedom.

2265
Life can only be understood backwards; but it must be lived forwards.

2266
Most people believe that the Christian commandments are intentionally a little too severe - like setting a clock half an hour ahead to make sure of not being late in the morning.

KILVERT Francis 1840-1879
2267 *Diary*
Of all noxious animals, too, the most noxious is a tourist. And of all tourists the most vulgar, ill-bred, offensive and loathsome is the British tourist.

2268 *Diary*
The Vicar of St Ives says the smell of fish there is sometimes so terrific as to stop the church clock.

KING Benjamin Franklin 1857-1894
2269 *'The Pessimist'*
Nothing to do but work,
Nothing to eat but food,
Nothing to wear but clothes
To keep one from going nude.

Nothing to breathe but air,
Quick as a flash 't is gone;
Nowhere to fall but off,
Nowhere to stand but on.

2270 *'The Pessimist'*
Nowhere to go but out,
Nowhere to come but back.

KINGSLEY Charles 1819-1875
2271 *The Water Babies*
As thorough an Englishman as ever coveted his neighbour's goods.

2272 *Westward Ho!*
Eustace is a man no longer; he is become a thing, a tool, a Jesuit.

KINGSMILL Hugh 1889-1949
2273 *(on friends)*
God's apology for relations.

2274
Society is based on the assumption that everyone is alike and no one is alive.

KIPLING Rudyard 1865-1936
2275 *'The Ballad of the King's Jest'*
And the talk slid north, and the talk slid south,

With the sliding puffs from the hookah-
mouth.
Four things greater than all things are,
Women and Horses and Power and War.

2276 *The Betrothed*
And a woman is only a woman but a
good cigar is a Smoke.

2277 *'Boots'*
Foot - foot - foot - foot - sloggin' over
Africa -
(Boots - boots - boots - boots - movin' up
and down again!)

2278 *'The Conundrum of the Workshops'*
We know that the tail must wag the dog,
for the horse is drawn by the cart;
But the Devil whoops, as he whooped of
old: 'It's clever, but is it Art?'

2279 *'The 'Eathen'*
The 'eathen in 'is blindness bows down
to wood an' stone;
'E don't obey no orders unless they is 'is
own;

2280 *'The 'Eathen'*
The 'eathen in 'is blindness must end
where 'e began.
But the backbone of the Army is the
non-commissioned man!

2281 *'Fuzzy-Wuzzy'*
So 'ere's *to* you, Fuzzy-Wuzzy, at your
'ome in the Soudan;
You're a pore benighted 'eathen but a
first-class fightin' man;
An' 'ere's *to* you, Fuzzy-Wuzzy, with your
'ayrick 'ead of 'air -
You big black boundin' beggar - for you
broke a British square!

2282 *'Gentlemen-Rankers'*
We're poor little lambs who've lost our
way,
Baa! Baa! Baa!
We're little black sheep who've gone
astray,
Baa-aa-aa!
Gentlemen-rankers out on the spree,
Damned from here to Eternity,
God ha' mercy on such as we,
Baa! Yah! Bah!

2283 *'The Glory of the Garden'*
Our England is a garden, and such
gardens are not made
By singing:- 'Oh, how beautiful!' and
sitting in the shade,
While better men than we go out and
start their working lives
At grubbing weeds from gravel paths
with broken dinner-knives.

2284 *'The Gods of the Copybook
Headings'*
As it will be in the future, it was at the
birth of Man -
There are only four things certain since
Social Progress began:-
That the Dog returns to his Vomit and
the Sow returns to her Mire,
And the burnt Fool's bandaged finger
goes wabbling back to the Fire.

2285 *'Gunga Din'*
The uniform 'e wore
Was nothin' much before,
An' rather less than 'arf o' that be'ind.

2286 *'Gunga Din'*
Though I've belted you and flayed you,
By the livin' Gawd that made you,
You're a better man than I am, Gunga
Din!

2287 *'The Islanders'*
Then ye returned to your trinkets; then
ye contented your souls
With the flannelled fools at the wicket or
the muddied oafs at the goals.

2288 *Just So Stories 'The Elephant's Child'*
Then the Elephant's Child put his head
down close to the Crocodile's musky,
tusky mouth, and the Crocodile caught
him by his little nose ... 'Led go! You are
hurtig be!'

2289 *Just So Stories 'The Elephant's Child'*
I keep six honest serving-men
(They taught me all I knew);
Their names are What and Why and
When
And How and Where and Who.

2290 *Just So Stories 'How the Camel got
his Hump'*
The cure for this ill is not to sit still,

Or frowst with a book by the fire;
But to take a large hoe and a shovel also,
And dig till you gently perspire.

2291 *Just So Stories 'How the Whale ...'*
And the small 'Stute Fish said in a small
'stute voice, 'Noble and generous
Cetacean, have you ever tasted Man?'
'No,' said the Whale. 'What is it like?'
'Nice,' said the small 'Stute Fish. 'Nice
but nubbly.'

2292 *Just So Stories 'How the Whale ...'*
He had his Mummy's leave to paddle, or
else he would never have done it,
because he was a man of infinite-
resource-and-sagacity.

2293 *'The Ladies'*
When you get to a man in the case,
They're like as a row of pins -
For the Colonel's Lady an' Judy O'Grady
Are sisters under their skins!

2294 *'The Liner She's a Lady'*
The Liner she's a lady, an' she never looks
nor 'eeds -
The Man-o'-War's 'er 'usband, an' 'e gives
'er all she needs;
But, oh, the little cargo boats that sail the
wet seas roun',
They're just the same as you an' me a-
plyin' up and down!

2295 *'Mandalay'*
An' I seed her first a-smokin' of a
whackin' white cheroot,
An' a-wastin' Christian kisses on an
'eathen idol's foot.

2296 *'Mandalay'*
Ship me somewheres east of Suez, where
the best is like the worst,
Where there aren't no Ten
Commandments an' a man can raise a
thirst.

2297 *The Naulahka*
And the end of the fight is a tombstone
white, with the name of the late
deceased,
And the epitaph drear: 'A fool lies here
who tried to hustle the East'.

2298 *'In the Neolithic Age'*
There are nine and sixty ways of
constructing tribal lays,
And - every - single - one - of - them - is -
right!

2299 *'In Partibus'*
But I consort with long-haired things
In velvet collar-rolls,
Who talk about the Aims of Art,
And 'theories' and 'goals',
And moo and coo with women-folk
About their blessed souls.

2300 *Plain Tales from the Hills*
Every one is more or less mad on one
point.

2301 *'The Power of the Dog'*
There is sorrow enough in the natural
way
From men and women to fill our day;
But when we are certain of sorrow in
store,
Why do we always arrange for more?
*Brothers and Sisters, I bid you beware
Of giving your heart to a dog to tear.*

2302
There was a small boy of Quebec
Who was buried in snow to the neck:
When they said 'Are you friz?'
He replied 'Yes, I is -
But we don't call this cold in Quebec!'

2303 *The Story of the Gadsbys 'Poor Dear
Mamma'*
Being kissed by a man who *didn't* wax his
moustache was - like eating an egg
without salt.

2304 *'Tomlinson'*
For the sin ye do by two and two ye must
pay for one by one!

2305 *Traffics and Discoveries 'Mrs
Bathurst'*
'Tisn't beauty, so to speak, nor good talk
necessarily. It's just It. Some women'll
stay in a man's memory if they once
walked down a street.

2306 *'The Vampire'*
A fool there was and he made his prayer
(Even as you and I!)

To a rag and a bone and a hank of hair
(We called her the woman who did not care)
But the fool he called her his lady fair -
(Even as you and I!)

2307 *'What Dane-geld means'*
It is always a temptation to a rich and lazy nation,
To puff and look important and to say:-
'Though we know we should defeat you, we have not the time to meet you,
We will therefore pay you cash to go away.

2308 *'When Earth's Last Picture is Painted'*
And only the Master shall praise us, and only the Master shall blame;
And no one shall work for money, and no one shall work for fame,
But each for the joy of the working, and each, in his separate star,
Shall draw the Thing as he sees It for the God of Things as They are!

2309 *'The Young British Soldier'*
When you're wounded and left on Afghanistan's plains
And the women come out to cut up what remains
Just roll on your rifle and blow out your brains
An' go to your Gawd like a soldier.

KISSINGER Henry 1923-
2310
The illegal we do immediately. The unconstitutional takes a little longer.

2311
Power is the ultimate aphrodisiac.

2312
Now when I bore people at a party, they think it's their fault.

KLOPSTOCK Friedrich 1724-1803
2313 *(of a passage in one of his poems)*
God and I both knew what it meant once; now God alone knows.

KNOX Ronald 1888-1957
2314 *'Absolute and Abitofhell'*
When suave politeness, tempering bigot zeal,
Corrected *I believe to One does feel.*

2315 *(advertisement placed in a newspaper)*
Evangelical vicar, in want of a portable, second-hand font, would dispose, for the same, of a portrait, in frame, of the Bishop, elect, of Vermont.

2316 *(definition of a baby, attributed)*
A loud noise at one end and no sense of responsibility at the other.

2317
O God, for as much as without Thee
We are not enabled to doubt Thee,
Help us all by Thy grace
To convince the whole race
It knows nothing whatever about Thee.

2318 *'Magister Reformator'*
Hail him like Etonians, without a single word,
Absolutely silent and indefinitely bored.

2319
There once was a man who said, 'God
Must think it exceedingly odd
If he finds that this tree
Continues to be
When there's no one about in the Quad.'

2320 *'After the party'*
The tumult and the shouting dies,
The captains and the kings depart,
And we are left with large supplies
Of cold blancmange and rhubarb tart.

2321 *(on being asked to perform a baptism in English)*
The baby doesn't understand English and the Devil knows Latin.

2322
The room smelt of not having been smoked in.

2323
It's not the taste of water I object to. It's the after-effects.

KOCH William
2324
Frontal attack never works, sneak attack is always the best.

KOESTLER Arthur 1905-1983
2325 *Darkness at Noon*
The definition of the individual was: a multitude of one million divided by one million.

2326 *The Ghost in the Machine*
Behaviourism is indeed a kind of flat-earth view of the mind ... it has substituted for the erstwhile anthropomorphic view of the rat, a ratomorphic view of man.

2327 *The Ghost in the Machine*
God seems to have left the receiver off the hook, and time is running out.

KORZYBSKI Alfred 1879-1950
2328
There are two ways to slide easily through life; to believe everything or doubt everything. Both ways save us from thinking.

KOSINSKI Jerzy 1933-1991
2329
You don't die in the United States, you underachieve.

KRAUS Karl
2330
Stupidity is an elemental force for which no earthquake is a match.

2331
He who gladly does without the praise of the crowd will not miss the opportunity of becoming his own fan.

2332
A writer is someone who can make a riddle out of an answer.

KRUSE Scott M.
2333
As a matter of biology, if something bites you it is probably female.

KRUTCH Joseph Wood 1893-1970
2334
Cats seem to go on the principle that it never does any harm to ask for what you want.

2335
Though many have tried, no one has ever yet explained away the decisive fact that science, which can do so much, cannot decide what it ought to do.

2336 *The Twelve Seasons 'February'*
The most serious charge which can be brought against New England is not Puritanism but February.

2337
When a man wantonly destroys a work of man we call him a vandal; when a man destroys one of the works of God, we call him a sportsman.

KUPCINET Irv
2338
Air pollution is turning Mother Nature prematurely grey.

KUSMENKO Mika
2339
Female empowerment is such vague terminology that I doubt it exists in any language but English.

LA BRUYERE Jean de 1645-1696
2340 *Les Caractères, 'De la société et la conversation'*
There are some who speak one moment before they think.

2341 *Les Caractères, 'De l'homme'*
The majority of men devote the greater part of their lives to making their remaining years unhappy.

2342 *Les Caractères, 'Des femmes'*
Women run to extremes; they are either better or worse than men.

LA FONTAINE Jean de 1621-1695
2343 *Fables 'Le Meunier, son Fils et l'Ane'*
The greatest ass of the three is not the one you would think.

2344 *Fables 'Le Milan et le Rossignol'*
A hungry stomach has no ears.

2345 *Fables 'L'Enfant et le Maître d'École'*
My friend, get me out of danger. You can make your speech afterwards.

2346 *Fables 'Le Renard et le Bouc'*
This fellow did not see further than his own nose.

2347 *Fables 'L'Ours et les deux Compagnons'*
Never sell the bear's skin before one has killed the beast.

2348 *Fables 'Parole de Socrate'*
Everyone calls himself a friend, but only a fool relies on it; nothing is commoner than the name, nothing rarer than the thing.

LA MANCE Thomas
2349
Life is what happens to us while we are making other plans.

LA ROCHEFOUCAULD François Duc de
1613-1680
2350
There are few chaste women who are not tired of their trade.

2351
We often forgive those who bore us, but can't forgive those whom we bore.

2352
Hope, deceitful as it is, serves at least to lead us to the end of life along an agreeable road.

2353
We are lazier in our minds than in our bodies.

2354 *Maxims*
Hypocrisy is a tribute which vice pays to virtue.

2355 *Maxims*
The height of cleverness is to be able to conceal it.

2356 *Maxims*
We need greater virtues to bear good fortune than bad.

2357 *Maxims*
If we had no faults we should not take so much pleasure in noticing them in others.

2358 *Maxims*
If one judges love by the majority of its effects, it is more like hatred than like friendship.

2359 *Maxims*
Everyone complains of his memory, but no one complains of his judgement.

2360 *Maxims*
The intellect is always fooled by the heart.

2361 *Maxims*
One gives nothing so freely as advice.

2362 *Maxims*
One had rather malign oneself than not speak of oneself at all.

2363 *Maxims*
To refuse praise reveals a desire to be praised twice over.

2364 *Maxims*
Flattery is false coin that is only current thanks to our vanity.

2365 *Maxims*
We only confess our little faults to persuade people that we have no large ones.

2366 *Maxims*
We seldom attribute common sense except to those who agree with us.

2367
Quarrels would not last long if the fault was only on one side.

2368
What is perfectly true is perfectly witty.

2369
When our vices leave us, we flatter ourselves with the credit of having left them.

2370
He who lives without folly is not as wise as he thinks.

LACKINGTON James 1746-1815
2371 *Memoirs*
At last, by singing and repeating enthusiastic amorous hymns, and

ignorantly applying particular texts of scripture, I got my imagination to the proper pitch, and thus was I born again in an instant.

LAMB Charles 1775-1834
2372
Here cometh April again, and as far as I can see the world hath more fools in it than ever.

2373
If dirt were trumps, what hands you would hold!

2374 *Essays of Elia 'Mrs Battle's Opinions'*
She unbent her mind afterwards - over a book.

2375 *Essays of Elia 'Mrs Battle's Opinions on Whist'*
They do not play at cards, but only play at playing at them.

2376 *Essays of Elia 'A Chapter on Ears'*
Sentimentally I am disposed to harmony. But organically I am incapable of a tune.

2377 *Essays of Elia 'A Dissertation upon Roast Pig'*
Presents, I often say, endear Absents.

2378 *Essays of Elia 'Imperfect Sympathies'*
I have been trying all my life to like Scotchmen, and am obliged to desist from the experiment of despair.

2379 *Essays of Elia 'The Old and the New Schoolmaster'*
Boys are capital fellows in their own way, among their mates; but they are un-wholesome companions for grown people.

2380 *Essays of Elia 'Oxford in the Vacation'*
A votary of the desk - a notched and cropt scrivener - one that sucks his substance, as certain sick people are said to do, through a quill.

2381 *Essays of Elia 'Quakers' Meeting'*
The uncommunicating muteness of fishes.

2382 *Essays of Elia 'The Two Races of Men'*
The human species, according to the best theory I can form of it, is composed of two distinct races, *the men who borrow,* and *the men who lend.*

2383 *Essays of Elia 'The Two Races of Men'*
Your *borrowers of books* - those mutilators of collections, spoilers of the symmetry of shelves, and creators of odd volumes.

2384 *'A Farewell to Tobacco'*
For thy sake, Tobacco, I
Would do any thing but die.

2385 *Last Essays of Elia 'Popular Fallacies'*
[A pun] is a pistol let off at the ear; not a feather to tickle the intellect.

2386 *Letter to B.W. Proctor*
When my sonnet was rejected, I exclaimed, 'Damn the age; I will write for Antiquity!'

2387 *Letter to Dorothy Wordsworth*
How I like to be liked, and what I do to be liked!

2388 *Letter to Southey*
Anything awful makes me laugh. I mis-behaved once at a funeral.

2389 *Letter to Thomas Manning*
This very night I am going to leave off tobacco! Surely there must be some other world in which this unconquerable purpose shall be realized.

2390 *Letter to Wordsworth (of Coleridge)*
An Archangel a little damaged.

2391
To be sick is to enjoy monarchial prerogatives.

LAMBERT Constant 1905-1951
2392 *(written in a copy of Coeleb's In Search of a Wife)*
If ever I marry a wife,
I'll marry a landlord's daughter,
For then I may sit in the bar,
And drink cold brandy and water.

2393
The average English critic is a don *manqué*, hopelessly parochial when not exaggeratedly teutonophile, over whose desk must surely hang the motto (presumably in Gothic lettering) 'Above all no enthusiasm'.

2394 *Music Ho!*
The whole trouble with a folk song is that once you have played it through there is nothing much you can do except play it over again and play it rather louder.

LAMBTON John George 1792-1840
2395
£40,000 a year a moderate income - such a one as a man *might jog on with.*

LAMPTON William James 1859-1917
2396 *June Weddings*
Same old slippers,
Same old rice,
Same old glimpse of
Paradise.

LANCE Bert 1931-
2397 *Nation's Business*
If it ain't broke, don't fix it.

LANDERS Ann 1918-
2398
Television has proved that people will look at anything rather than each other.

2399
If you want your children to listen, try talking softly - to someone else.

2400
We wouldn't worry so much about what people thought of us if we knew how seldom they did.

LANDOR Walter Savage 1775-1864
2401 *Epigram in The Atlas*
George the First was always reckoned
Vile, but viler George the Second;
And what mortal ever heard
Any good of George the Third?
When from earth the Fourth descended
God be praised the Georges ended!

2402
Great men too often have greater faults than little men can find room for.

2403 *'To Ianthe'*
'Tis verse that gives
Immortal youth to mortal maids.

2404 *Imaginary Conversations*
Fleas know not whether they are upon the body of a giant or upon one of ordinary size.

LANG Andrew 1844-1912
2405
He uses statistics as a drunken man uses lamp-posts - for support rather than illumination.

LAPHAM Lewis H.
2406
The supply of government exceeds the demand.

LARDNER Ring 1885-1933
2407
They gave each other a smile with a future in it.

2408 *The Young Immigrunts*
Are you lost daddy I arsked tenderly.
Shut up he explained.

LARKIN Philip 1922-1985
2409 *'Annus Mirabilis'*
Sexual intercourse began
In nineteen sixty-three
(Which was rather late for me) -
Between the end of the *Chatterley* ban
And the Beatles' first LP.

2410 *(novel formula)*
A beginning, a muddle, and an end.

2411 *'Study of Reading Habits'*
Don't read too much now: the dude
Who lets the girl down before
The hero arrives, the chap
Who's yellow and keeps the store,
Seem far too familiar. Get stewed:
Books are a load of crap.

2412 *Required Writing*
Deprivation is for me what daffodils were for Wordsworth.

2413 *'Toads'*
Why should I let the toad *work*
Squat on my life?
Can't I use my wit as a pitchfork
And drive the brute off?

Six days of the week it soils
With its sickening poison -
Just for paying a few bills!
That's out of proportion.

2414 *'Toads Revisited'*
Give me your arm, old toad;
Help me down Cemetery Road.

2415 *'This Be The Verse'*
They fuck you up, your mum and dad.
They may not mean to, but they do.
They fill you with the faults they had
And add some extra, just for you.

2416 *'This Be The Verse'*
Man hands on misery to man.
It deepens like a coastal shelf.
Get out as early as you can,
And don't have any kids yourself.

2417 *'The Whitsun Weddings'*
I thought of London spread out in the sun,
Its postal districts packed like squares of wheat.

LAUDER Sir Harry 1870-1950
2418
O! it's nice to get up in the mornin',
But it's nicer to stay in bed.

2419
If y'can say
It's a braw brecht moonlecht necht,
Yer a' recht, ye ken.

LAVER James 1899-1975
2420 *Taste and Fashion*
The same costume will be
Indecent ... 10 years before its time
Shameless ... 5 years before its time
Outré (daring) 1 year before its time
Smart
Dowdy ... 1 year after its time
Hideous ... 10 years after its time
Ridiculous ... 20 years after its time
Amusing ... 30 years after its time
Quaint ... 50 years after its time

Charming ... 70 years after its time
Romantic ... 100 years after its time
Beautiful ... 150 years after its time

LAW Andrew Bonar 1858-1923
2421
If I am a great man, then a good many of
the great men of history are frauds.

LAW Vernon
2422
Experience is the worst teacher; it gives
the test before presenting the lesson.

LAWRENCE D.H. 1885-1930
2423 *'How Beastly the Bourgeois Is'*
How beastly the bourgeois is
Especially the male of the species.

2424 *Letter to Lady Cynthia Asquith*
I like to write when I feel spiteful; it's like
having a good sneeze.

LAWRENSON Helen
2425
You have to go back to the Children's
Crusade in 1212 AD to find as
unfortunate and fatuous an attempt at
manipulated hysteria as the Women's
Liberation Movement.

2426
Whatever else can be said about sex, it
cannot be called a dignified
performance.

LAWSON Sonia 1934-
2427
You're not meant to understand - They're
bloody works of art.

LEACH Jim
2428
Patriotism is when you risk your life not
when you risk your wallet.

LEACH Reggie
2429
Success is not the result of spontaneous
combustion. You must set yourself on
fire.

LEACOCK Stephen 1869-1944
2430
Advertising may be described as the
science of arresting the human

intelligence long enough to get money from it.

2431
The best definition of humour I know is: humour may be defined as the kindly contemplation of the incongruities of life, and the artistic expression thereof. I think this is the best I know because I wrote it myself.

2432
The British are terribly lazy about fighting. They like to get it over and done with and then set up a game of cricket.

2433
You encourage a comic man too much, and he gets silly.

2434
A half truth, like half a brick, is always more forcible as an argument than a whole one. It carries better.

2435
I'm a great believer in luck. I find the harder I work, the more I have of it.

2436 *Here are my Lectures*
I am what is called a *professor emeritus* from the Latin *e*, 'out', and *meritus*, 'so he ought to be'.

2437 *Literary Lapses 'Boarding-House Geometry'*
The landlady of a boarding-house is a parallelogram - that is, an oblong figure, which cannot be described, but which is equal to anything.

2438 *Literary Lapses 'A Manual of Education'*
Electricity is of two kinds, positive and negative. The difference is, I presume, that one comes a little more expensive, but is more durable; the other is a cheaper thing, but the moths get into it.

2439 *Literary Lapses 'Reflections on Riding'*
There are no handles to a horse, but the 1910 model has a string to each side of its face for turning its head when there is anything you want it to see.

2440
The Lord said 'let there be wheat' and Saskatchewan was born.

2441
Any man will admit if need be that his sight is not good, or that he cannot swim or shoots badly with a rifle, but to touch upon his sense of humour is to give him mortal affront.

2442
Many a man in love with a dimple makes the mistake of marrying the whole girl.

2443 *Nonsense Novels 'Gertrude the Governess'*
He flung himself from the room, flung himself upon his horse and rode madly off in all directions.

2444 *My Remarkable Uncle*
A sportsman is a man who, every now and then, simply has to get out and kill something. Not that he's cruel. He wouldn't hurt a fly. It's not big enough.

2445
When actors begin to think, it is time for a change. They are not fitted for it.

2446
Writing is no trouble: you just jot down ideas as they occur to you. The jotting is simplicity itself - it is the occurring which is difficult.

LEAPOR Mary 1722-1746
2447 *'An Essay on Woman'*
Woman, a pleasing but a short-lived flower,
Too soft for business and too weak for power:
A wife in bondage, or neglected maid:
Despised, if ugly; if she's fair, betrayed.

2448 *'Mira to Octavia'*
In spite of all romantic poets sing,
This gold, my dearest, is an useful thing.

LEAR Edward 1812-1888
2449 *A Book of Nonsense*
There was an Old Man with a beard,
Who said, 'It is just as I feared! -
Two Owls and a Hen,

Four Larks and a Wren,
Have all built their nests in my beard!'

2450 *Book of Nonsense*
There was an Old Man in a tree,
Who was horribly bored by a bee;
When they said, 'Does it buzz?'
He replied, 'Yes, it does!
It's a regular brute of a bee!'

2451 *'The Courtship of the Yonghy-Bonghy-Bó*
On the coast of Coromandel
Where the early pumpkins blow,
In the middle of the woods,
Lived the Yonghy-Bonghy-Bó.
Two old chairs, and half a candle;
One old jug without a handle,
These were all his worldly goods.

2452 *'The Dong with a Luminous Nose'*
'The Dong! - the Dong!
The wandering Dong through the forest goes!
The Dong! - the Dong!
The Dong with a Luminous Nose!'

2453 *'The Jumblies'*
Far and few, far and few,
Are the lands were the Jumblies live;
Their heads are green, and their hands are blue,
And they went to sea in a Sieve.

2454 *'The Jumblies'*
They called aloud 'Our Sieve ain't big,
But we don't care a button! We don't care a fig!'

2455 *Nonsense Songs (preface)*
'How pleasant to know Mr Lear!'
Who has written such volumes of stuff!
Some think him ill-tempered and queer,
But a few think him pleasant enough.

2456 *Nonsense Songs (preface)*
He has many friends, laymen and clerical.
Old Foss is the name of his cat:
His body is perfectly spherical,
He weareth a runcible hat.

2457 *'The Owl and the Pussy-Cat'*
The Owl and the Pussy-Cat went to sea
In a beautiful pea-green boat.

They took some honey, and plenty of money,
Wrapped up in a five-pound note.
The Owl looked up to the Stars above
And sang to a small guitar,
'Oh lovely Pussy! O Pussy, my love,
What a beautiful Pussy you are.'

2458 *'The Owl and the Pussy-Cat'*
'Dear Pig, are you willing to sell for one shilling
Your ring?' Said the Piggy, 'I will.'

2459 *'The Owl and the Pussy-Cat'*
They dined on mince, and slices of quince,
Which they ate with a runcible spoon;
And hand in hand, on the edge of the sand,
They danced by the light of the moon.

2460 *'The Pobble Who Has No Toes'*
The Pobble who has no toes
Had once as many as we;
When they said, 'Some day you may lose them all';
He replied, 'Fish fiddle de-dee!'

2461 *'The Pobble Who Has No Toes'*
When boats or ships came near him
He tinkledy-binkledy-winkled a bell.

2462 *'The Quangle-Wangle's Hat'*
'But the longer I live on this Crumpetty Tree
The plainer than ever it seems to me
That very few people come this way
And that life on the whole is far from gay!'
Said the Quangle-Wangle Quee.

2463 *'The Two Old Bachelors'*
And what can we expect if we haven't any dinner,
But to lose our teeth and eyelashes and keep on growing thinner.

LEAVITT Robert Keith
2464
People don't ask for facts in making up their minds. They would rather have one good, soul-satisfying emotion than a dozen facts.

LEBOWITZ Fran 1946-
2465
The best fame is a writer's fame; it's enough to get a table at a good restaurant, but not enough that you get interrupted when you eat.

2466
Ask your child what he wants for dinner only if he is buying.

2467 *Metropolitan Life*
There is no such thing as inner peace. There is only nervousness or death.

2468 *Metropolitan Life*
Life is something to do when you can't sleep.

LEC Stanislaw 1909-1966
2469
I give you bitter pills in sugar coating. The pills are harmless: the poison is in the sugar.

2470 *Unkempt Thoughts*
Is it progress if a cannibal uses knife and fork?

LEDRU-ROLLIN Alexandre
2471
I've got to follow them - I am their leader.

LEE Gypsy Rose 1914-1970
2472 *(attributed)*
God is love, but get it in writing.

LEHRER Tom 1928-
2473 *'We Will All Go Together When We Go'*
Life is like a sewer. What you get out of it depends on what you put into it.

2474
It is a sobering thought, that when Mozart was my age, he had been dead for two years.

LEIGH Fred W. d.1924
2475 *'Waiting at the Church'*
Here's the very note,
This is what he wrote -
'Can't get away to marry you today,
My wife won't let me!'

2476 *'Waiting At The Church'*
There was I, waiting at the church,
Waiting at the church, waiting at the church,
When I found he'd left me in the lurch,
Lor' how it did upset me!...

2477 *'Why Am I Always the Bridesmaid?'*
Why am I always the bridesmaid,
Never the blushing bride?

LEIGH H.S. 1837-1883
2478 *'An Allegory, written in Deep Dejection'*
That loathsome centipede, Remorse,
Invaded with a stealthy tread
My nasal organ.

2479 *Carols of Cockayne*
The rapturous, wild, and ineffable pleasure
Of drinking at somebody else's expense.

2480 *'Only Seven'*
I wondered hugely what she meant,
And said, 'I'm bad at riddles;
But I know where little girls are sent
For telling taradiddles.'

2481 *'The Twins'*
In form and feature, face and limb,
I grew so like my brother
That folks got taking me for him
And each for one another.

2482 *'The Twins'*
For one of us was born a twin
And not a soul knew which.

2483
If you wish to grow thinner, diminish your dinner.

LENIN 1870-1924
2484
Imperialism is the monopoly stage of capitalism.

LENNON John 1940-1980
2485 *(at Royal Variety Performance)*
Will those in the cheap seats clap their hands? All the rest of you, just rattle your jewellery.

LENNON John and McCARTNEY Paul
1940-1980 and 1942-
2486 *'A Day in the Life'*
I heard the news today, oh boy.
Four thousand holes in Blackburn
Lancashire.
And though the holes were rather small,
They had to count them all.
Now they know how many holes it takes
to fill the Albert Hall.
I'd love to turn you on.

2487 *'A Hard Day's Night'*
It's been a hard day's night,
And I've been working like a dog.

2488 *'Happiness is a Warm Gun'*
I know no one can do me no harm
because happiness is a warm gun.

LENO Dan 1860-1904
2489 *Dan Leno Hys Booke*
Ah! What is man? Wherefore does he
why? Whence did he whence? Whither
is he withering?

LENT Edwin
2490
Cats are living adornments.

LERMONTOV Mikhail 1814-1841
2491 *A Hero of our Time*
I am like a man yawning at a ball; the
only reason he does not go home to bed
is that his carriage has not arrived yet.

2492 *A Hero of our Time*
I have always been the essential
character of the fifth act.

2493 *'I'm lonely and sad'*
What is passion? That sickness so sweet,
either early or late,
Will vanish at reason's protesting;
And life, if you ever, attentive and cool,
contemplate,
Is but empty and meaningless jesting.

LERNER Alan Jay 1918-1986
2494 *My Fair Lady 'You Did It'*
Oozing charm from every pore,
He oiled his way around the floor.

2495 *My Fair Lady 'A Hymn to Him'*
Why can't a woman be more like a man?
Men are so honest, so thoroughly square;

Eternally noble, historically fair;
Who, when you win, will always give
your back a pat.
Why can't a woman be like that?

2496 *Gigi 'I Remember it Well'*
We met at nine.
We met at eight.
I was on time.
No, you were late.
Ah yes! I remember it well.

LERNER Max
2497
I have a simple principle for the conduct
of life - never to resist an adequate
temptation.

LESAGE Alain René 1668-1747
2498 *Le Diable boîteux*
They made peace between us; we
embraced, and we have been mortal
enemies ever since.

LESSING Doris 1919-
2499
Growing up is after all only the
understanding that one's unique and
incredible experience is what everyone
shares.

2500 *The Habit of Loving*
Pleasure resorts are like film stars and
royalty ... embarrassed by the figures
they cut in the fantasies of people who
have never met them.

2501
Think wrongly, if you please, but in all
cases think for yourself.

LESSING G.E. 1729-1781
2502 *Emilia Galotti*
A man who does not lose his reason over
certain things has none to lose.

LESTER Richard 1932-
2503
Film-making has become a kind of
hysterical pregnancy.

L'ESTRANGE Sir Roger 1616-1704
2504 *Aesop's Fables*
Though this may be play to you, 'tis
death to us.

LETTE Kathy
2505
As a breastfeeding mother you are basically just meals on heels.

LEVANT Oscar
2506
Epigram: a wisecrack that has played Carnegie Hall.

2507
There is a thin line between genius and insanity. I have erased this line.

LEVERSON Ada 1865-1936
2508 *The Twelfth Hour*
'No hurry, no hurry,' said Sir James, with that air of self-denial that conveys the urgent necessity of intense speed.

LEVIN Bernard 1928-
2509 *The Pendulum Years*
Paul Getty ... had always been vastly, immeasurably wealthy, and yet went about looking like a man who cannot quite remember whether he remembered to turn the gas off before leaving home.

2510 *The Pendulum Years (of Macmillan and Wilson)*
Between them, then, Walrus and Carpenter, they divided up the Sixties.

2511 *The Pendulum Years (of Macmillan)*
The Stag at Bay with the mentality of a fox at large.

LEVINE Ellen
2512
Sexual revolution has allowed us an equal opportunity to ogle.

LEVINSON Sam
2513
Insanity is hereditary - you can get it from your children.

LÉVI-STRAUSS Claude 1908-1990
2514 *La Pensée sauvage*
Language is a form of human reason, and has its reasons which are unknown to man.

LEWES G.H. 1817-1878
2515 *The Physiology of Common Life*
Murder, like talent, seems occasionally to run in families.

2516 *Ranthorpe*
The pen, in our age, weighs heavier in the social scale than the sword of a Norman Baron.

LEWIS C.S. 1898-1963
2517 *The Screwtape Letters*
She's the sort of woman who lives for others - you can always tell the others by their hunted expression.

2518 *'Unreal Estates'*
I'd sooner live among people who don't cheat at cards than among people who are earnest about not cheating at cards.

LEWIS Sir George Cornewall 1806-1863
2519
Life would be tolerable but for its amusements.

LEWIS Joe E.
2520
You only live once - but if you work it right, once is enough.

LEWIS Sinclair 1885-1951
2521 *Babbitt*
His motor car was poetry and tragedy, love and heroism. The office was his pirate ship but the car his perilous excursion ashore.

LEWIS Stephen
2522 *(to Morton Shulman)*
How do you make a million? You start with $900,000.

LIBERACE Wladziu Valentino 1919-1987
2523 *Autobiography*
When the reviews are bad I tell my staff that they can join me as I cry all the way to the bank.

LICHTENBERG G.C. 1742-1799
2524
Barbaric accuracy - whimpering humility.

2525
A book is a mirror: if an ass peers into it, you can't expect an apostle to look out.

2526
Everyone is a genius at least once a year; a real genius has his original ideas closer together.

2527
One can live in this world on soothsaying but not on truth saying.

2528
Most men of education are more superstitious than they admit - nay, than they think.

2529
Sometimes men come by the name of genius in the same way that certain insects come by the name of centipede - not because they have a hundred feet, but because most people can't count above fourteen.

LIEBLING A.J. 1904-1963
2530
Freedom of the press is guaranteed only to those who own one.

2531
I can write better than anyone who can write faster, and I can write faster than anyone who can write better.

LILLIE Beatrice 1894-1989
2532 (to a waiter who had spilled soup down her neck)
Never darken my Dior again!

LINCOLN Abraham 1809-1865
2533 (attributed)
The Lord prefers common-looking people. That is why he makes so many of them.

2534
I feel like the man who was tarred and feathered and ridden out of town on a rail. To the man who asked how he liked it he said: 'If it wasn't for the honour of the thing, I'd rather walk.'

2535
I'm a slow walker, but I never walk back.

2536 (judgement of a book)
People who like this sort of thing will find this the sort of thing they like.

2537
Every man over forty is responsible for his face.

2538
Marriage is neither heaven nor hell; it is simply purgatory.

2539
What kills a skunk is the publicity it gives itself.

2540
When you have got an elephant by the hind leg, and he is trying to run away, it is best to let him run.

2541
A woman is the only thing I am afraid of that I know will not hurt me.

LINDBERGH Anne Morrow 1906-
2542
A simple enough pleasure, surely, to have breakfast alone with one's husband, but how seldom married people in the midst of life achieve it.

LINKLETTER Art 1912-
2543 A Child's Garden of Misinformation
The four stages of man are infancy, childhood, adolescence and obsolescence.

LIPPMANN Walter 1899-1974
2544
Many a time I have wanted to stop talking and find out what I really believed.

LIVINGSTONE Ken 1945-
2545
If voting changed anything they'd abolish it.

LLEWELLYN Karl
2546
Law ... begins when someone takes to doing something someone else does not like.

LLOYD C.F.
2547
God made me on a morning when he had nothing else to do.

LLOYD GEORGE David 1863-1945
2548
A fully-equipped duke costs as much to keep up as two Dreadnoughts; and dukes are just as great a terror and they last longer.

2549
Negotiating with de Valera ... is like trying to pick up mercury with a fork.

2550
A politician was a person with whose politics you did not agree. When you did agree, he was a statesman.

2551
Whenever the Germans found the Canadian Corps coming into the line, they prepared for the worst.

LLOYD Marie 1870-1922
2552
I'm a bit of a ruin that Cromwell knocked about a bit.

2553
A little of what you fancy does you good.

LOCKER-LAMPSON Frederick 1821-1895
2554 *'The Jester's Plea'*
The world's as ugly, ay, as sin,
And almost as delightful.

2555 *'The Jester's Plea'*
And many are afraid of God -
And more of Mrs Grundy.

2556 *'The Jester's Plea'*
Some men are good for righting wrongs,
And some for writing verses.

LOCKHART John Gibson 1794-1854
2557 *Epitaph for Patrick ('Peter'), Lord Robertson*
Here lies that peerless paper peer Lord Peter,
Who broke the laws of God and man and metre.

LODGE David 1935-
2558 *The British Museum is Falling Down*
Literature is mostly about having sex and not much about having children. Life is the other way round.

2559 *Changing Places*
Four times, under our educational rules, the human pack is shuffled and cut - at eleven-plus, sixteen-plus, eighteen-plus and twenty-plus - and happy is he who comes top of the deck on each occasion, but especially the last. This is called Finals, the very name of which implies that nothing of importance can happen after it.

2560 *Small World*
I gave up screwing around a long time ago. I came to the conclusion that sex is a sublimation of the work instinct.

2561 *Small World*
Another law of academic life: *it is impossible to be excessive in flattery of one's peers.*

LODGE Thomas 1558-1625
2562 *'Margarite of America'*
Devils are not so black as they are painted.

LOESSER Frank 1910-1969
2563 *'The King's New Clothes'*
Isn't it grand! Isn't it fine! Look at the cut, the style, thc linc!
The suit of clothes is altogether, but altogether it's altogether
The most remarkable suit of clothes that I have ever seen.

LOEVINGER Lee
2564
Television is a gold goose that lays scrambled eggs; and it is futile and probably fatal to beat it for not laying caviar.

LOGUE Christopher 1926-
2565 *Christopher Logues ABC 'M'*
Said Marx: 'Don't be snobbish, we seek to abolish
The 3rd Class, not the 1st.'

LOLLABRIGIDA Gina
2566
The light is better than a plastic surgeon

LOMBARDI Vince 1913-1970
2567
If you aren't fired with enthusiasm, you'll be fired with enthusiasm.

2568
Winning isn't everything. It is the only thing.

LOMBROSO Cesare 1836-1909
2569 *The Man of Genius*
The ignorant man always adores what he cannot understand.

LONG Huey 1893-1935
2570 *(attributed)*
The time has come for all good men to rise above principle.

2571
Bible's the greatest book ever written. But I sure don't need anybody I can buy for six bits and a chew of tobacco to explain it to me. When I need preachers I buy 'em cheap.

2572 *(to journalists on his political personality)*
Oh hell, say that I am *sui generis* and let it go at that.

LONGFELLOW Henry Wadsworth 1807-1882
2573 *(composed for his second daughter)*
There was a little girl
Who had a little curl
Right in the middle of her forehead,
When she was good
She was very, very good,
But when she was bad she was horrid.

2574 *'Michael Angelo'*
The men that women marry,
And why they marry them, will always be
A marvel and a mystery to the world.

LONGWORTH Alice Roosevelt
2575 *(attributed)*
If you can't say something good about someone, sit right here by me.

2576
I have a simple philosophy. Fill what's empty. Empty what's full. And scratch where it itches.

2577
My speciality is detached malevolence.

LOOS Anita 1893-1981
2578 *Gentlemen Prefer Blondes*
This gentleman said a girl with brains ought to do something with them besides think.

2579 *Gentlemen Prefer Blondes*
She always believed in the old adage, 'Leave them while you're looking good.'

2580 *Gentlemen Prefer Blondes*
Fun is fun but no girl wants to laugh all of the time.

2581 *Gentlemen Prefer Blondes*
Kissing your hand may make you feel very, very good but a diamond and safire bracelet lasts for ever.

2582
I'm furious about Women's Liberationists. They keep getting up on soapboxes and proclaiming that women are brighter than men. That's true, but it should be kept very quiet or it ruins the whole racket.

LORD Peter
2583
Nobody does nothing for nobody for naught.

LORENZ Konrad 1903-1989
2584 *On Agression*
It is a good morning exercise for a research scientist to discard a pet hypothesis every day before breakfast. It keeps him young.

2585
I believe I've found the missing link between animal and civilized man. It is us.

LOUIS Joe 1914-1981
2586
I don't like money actually, but it quiets my nerves.

LOVER Samuel 1797-1868
2587 *Handy Andy*
When once the itch of literature comes over a man, nothing can cure it but the scratching of a pen.

LOW Sir David 1891-1963
2588
I have never met anyone who wasn't against war. Even Hitler and Mussolini were, according to themselves.

LOWE Robert (Viscount Sherbrooke) 1811-1892
2589
The Chancellor of the Exchequer is a man whose duties make him more or less of a taxing machine. He is intrusted with a certain amount of misery which it is his duty to distribute as fairly as he can.

LOWELL A.L. 1856-1943
2590 *(while President of Harvard)*
The freshmen bring a little knowledge in and the seniors take none out, so it accumulates through the years.

LOWELL James Russell 1819-1891
2591 *The Biglow Papers*
An' you've gut to git up airly
Ef you want to take in God.

2592 *The Biglow Papers*
It ain't by princerples nor men
My preudunt course is steadied, -
I scent wich pays the best, an' then
Go into it baldheaded.

2593 *The Biglow Papers*
We've a war, an' a debt, an' a flag; an' ef this
Ain't to be inderpendunt, why, wut on airth is?

2594 *The Biglow Papers*
He's been true to *one* party - an' thet is himself.

2595 *The Biglow Papers*
An' in convartin' public trusts
To very privit uses.

2596 *The Biglow Papers*
I *don't* believe in princerple,
But oh, I *du* in interest.

2597 *The Biglow Papers*
God makes sech nights, all white and still,
Fur'z you can look or listen.

2598 *The Biglow Papers*
All kin' o' smily round the lips,
An' teary round the lashes.

2599 *The Biglow Papers*
My gran'ther's rule was safer 'n 't is to crow:
Don't never prophesy - onless ye know.

2600 *Democracy and other Addresses 'Democracy'*
There is no good in arguing with the inevitable. The only argument available with an east wind is to put on your overcoat.

2601 *Democracy and other Addresses 'Democracy'*
The misfortunes hardest to bear are those which never come.

2602 *'A Fable for Critics'*
There comes Poe with his raven like Barnaby Rudge,
Three-fifths of him genius, and two-fifths sheer fudge.

2603
The foolish and the dead alone never change their opinions.

2604
A ginooine statesman should be on his guard, if he must hev beliefs, not to b'lieve 'em too hard.

2605
God'll send the bill to you.

2606
The pressure of public opinion is like the pressure of the atmosphere; you can't see it - but all the same, it is sixteen pounds to the square inch.

2607
Whatever you may be sure of, be sure of this - that you are dreadfully like other people.

LOWNDES William 1652-1724
2608
Take care of the pence, and the pounds
will take care of themselves.

LUBBOCK John
2609
A poor woman from Manchester, on
being taken to the seaside, is said to have
expressed her delight on seeing for the
first time something of which there was
enough for everybody.

LUCAS E.V. 1868-1938
2610
One of the most adventurous things left
is to go to bed, for no one can lay a hand
on our dreams.

LUCE Clare Booth 1903-1987
2611
Censorship, like charity, should begin at
home; but unlike charity, it should end
there.

2612
Technological man can't believe in
anything that can't be measured, taped,
or put into a computer.

LUCKMAN Charles
2613
Success is that old A B C - ability, breaks
and courage.

LUMLEY Joanna
2614
What sustains the human spirit is
gorgeousness.

LUND Robert S.
2615
Every man of genius is considerably
helped by being dead.

LUTHER Martin 1483-1546
2616 *Tischreden oder Colloquia*
So our Lord God commonly gives riches
to those gross asses to whom He
vouchsafes nothing else.

LYLY John c.1554-1606
2617
It is a blind goose that cometh to the
fox's sermon.

2618 *Campaspe*
Cupid and my Campaspe played
At cards for kisses. Cupid paid.

2619 *Euphues*
It seems to me (said she) that you are in
some brown study.

2620
Where the mind is past hope, the heart is
past shame.

LYND Robert 1879-1949
2621
It may be the games are silly. But, then,
so are human beings.

LYNES Russell
2622
Cynicism - the intellectual cripple's
substitute for intelligence.

2623
The true snob never rests; there is always
a higher goal to attain, and there are, by
the same token, always more and more
people to look down upon.

LYONS Lord
2624
If you're given champagne at lunch,
there's a catch somewhere.

McALPINE Lord 1942-
2625
The party needs a good scrub with a
hard brush.

McARTHUR Peter
2626
A satirist is a man who discovers
unpleasant things about himself and
then says them about other people.

McCARTHY Eugene 1916-
2627
He's like a football coach who's smart
enough to win the game, and dumb
enough to think it's important.

2628
The Senate is the last primitive society in
the world. We still worship the elders of
the tribe and honour the territorial
imperative.

McCARTHY Joseph 19087-1957
2629
McCarthyism is Americanism with its
sleeves rolled.

McCARTHY Mary 1912-1989
2630 *On the Contrary*
The immense popularity of American
movies abroad demonstrates that
Europe is the unfinished negative of
which America is the proof.

2631 *On the Contrary*
If someone tells you he is going to make
a 'realistic decision', you immediately
understand that he has resolved to do
something bad.

2632
Liberty, as it is conceived by current
opinion, has nothing inherent about it; it
is a sort of gift or trust bestowed on the
individual by the state pending good
behaviour.

2633 *(of Lillian Hellmann)*
Every word she writes is a lie, including
'and' and 'the'.

McCARTNEY Paul 1942-
2634 *(on reaching the age of 50)*
Ballads and babies. That's what
happened to me.

McCLENAHAN John L.
2635
It requires a great deal of faith for a man
to be cured by his own placebos.

McCLUNG Nellie 1873-1951
2636 *(to a heckler about women being
elected)*
This proves what a purifying effect
women would have on politics.

2637
Never retract, never explain, never
apologize - get the thing done and let
them howl.

McCLURE Robert 1807-1873
2638
A = r + p (or Adventure equals risk plus
purpose)

McCORD David 1897-
2639 *'Remainders' (epitaph for a waiter)*
By and by
God caught his eye.

MacDIARMID Hugh 1892-1978
2640 *The International Brigade*
It is very rarely that a man loves
And when he does it is nearly always
fatal.

MacDONALD George 1824-1905
2641 *David Elginbrod*
Here lie I, Martin Elginbrodde:
Hae mercy o' my soul, Lord God;
As I wad do, were I Lord God,
And ye were Martin Elginbrodde.

MacDONALD Sir John A. 1815-1891
2642
When Fortune empties her chamberpot
on your head, smile and say 'We are
going to have a summer shower'.

McFEE William 1881-1966
2643
One must choose between Obscurity
with Efficiency, and Fame with its
inevitable collateral of Bluff.

2644
The world belongs to the enthusiast who
keeps cool.

McGEACHY J.B.
2645
We sing about the North, but live as far
south as possible.

McGINLEY Phyllis 1905-
2646
Nothing fails like success; nothing is so
defeated as yesterday's triumphant
cause.

2647
Not reading poetry amounts to a
national pastime here.

McGREGOR Jimmy
2648 *'Football Crazy'*
Oh, he's football crazy, he's football mad
And the football it has robbed him o' the
wee bit sense he had.

McINTYRE Leslie M.
2649
Nobody objects to a woman being a good writer or sculptor or geneticist if at the same time she manages to be a good wife, good mother, good looking, good tempered, well groomed and unaggressive.

MACKENZIE Sir Compton 1883-1972
2650 *Literature in My Time*
Women do not find it difficult nowadays to behave like men, but they often find it extremely difficult to behave like gentlemen.

2651 *Vestal Fire*
You are offered a piece of bread and butter that feels like a damp handkerchief and sometimes, when cucumber is added to it, like a wet one.

MACKENZIE William Lyon 1795-1861
2652
He is ... like many other geniuses, a greater friend to the bottle, than the bottle is to him.

MACKINTOSH Sir James 1765-1832
2653 *Dissertation on the Progress of Ethical Philosophy*
Men are never so good or so bad as their opinions.

MACLAINE Shirley 1934-
2654
The best way to get husbands to do something is to suggest that perhaps they are too old to do it.

2655
When you look back ... on your love affairs ... what you really find out is that the only person you really go to bed with is yourself.

McLAUGHLIN Mignon
2656
No one has ever loved anyone the way everyone wants to be loved.

2657
Every society honours its live conformists and its dead troublemakers.

2658
Our strength is often composed of the weakness that we're damned if we are going to show.

2659
We'd all like a reputation for generosity and we'd all like to buy it cheap.

MacLEISH Archibald 1892-1982
2660
Around, around the sun we go:
The moon goes round the earth.
We do not die of death:
We die of vertigo.

MACLENNAN Hugh 1907-1990
2661
The farmer's way of saving money: to be owed by someone he trusted.

2662
A novel must be exceptionally good to live as long as the average cat.

McLUHAN Marshall 1911-1980
2663
Ads are the cave art of the twentieth century.

2664
Money is the poor people's credit card.

2665
Our sense of identity is our sense of density.

2666
A successful book cannot afford to be more than ten per cent new.

2667 *Understanding Media*
The name of a man is a numbing blow from which he never recovers.

2668 *Understanding Media*
The car has become an article of dress without which we feel uncertain, unclad and incomplete in the urban compound.

MACMILLAN Sir Harold 1894-1986
2669 *(on privatization, summarized as 'Selling off the family silver'*
First of all the Georgian silver goes, and then all that nice furniture that used to be in the saloon. Then the Canalettos go.

2670
You will find the Americans much as the Greeks found the Romans: great, big, vulgar, bustling people more vigorous than we are and also more idle, with more unspoiled virtues but also more corrupt.

2671 *(on the life of a Foreign Secretary)*
Forever poised between a cliché and an indiscretion.

MacNEICE Louis 1907-1963
2672 *'Bagpipe Music'*
It's no go the merry-go-round, it's no go the rickshaw,
All we want is a limousine and a ticket for the peepshow.

2673 *'Bagpipe Music'*
It's no go the Government grants, it's no go the elections,
Sit on your arse for fifty years and hang your hat on a pension.

2674 *'Bagpipe Music'*
It's no go my honey love, it's no go my poppet;
Work your hands from day to day, the winds will blow the profit.
The glass is falling hour by hour, the glass will fall for ever,
But if you break the bloody glass you won't hold up the weather.

McPHEE John
2675
Behind every tennis player there is another tennis player.

McWILLIAM Candia
2676
With the birth of each child you lose two novels.

MACAULAY Baron (Thomas Babington) 1800-1859
2677 *'The Battle of Naseby'*
Obadiah Bind-their-kings-in-chains-and-their-nobles-with-links-of-iron.

2678 *Essays ... 'Lord Clive'*
Every schoolboy knows who imprisoned Montezuma, and who strangled Atahualpa.

2679 *History of England*
There were gentlemen and there were seamen in the navy of Charles the Second. But the seamen were not gentlemen; and the gentlemen were not seamen.

2680
An intellectual is someone whose mind watches itself.

2681 *(of John Dryden)*
His imagination resembled the wings of an ostrich. It enabled him to run, though not to soar.

2682 *Lays of Ancient Rome*
Let no man stop to plunder,
But slay, and slay, and slay;
The Gods who live for ever
Are on our side to-day.

2683 *Lays of Ancient Rome 'Horatius'*
Then none was for a party;
Then all were for the state;
The the great man helped the poor,
And the poor man loved the great:
Then lands were fairly portioned;
The spoils were fairly sold:
The Romans were like brothers
In the brave days of old.

2684 *Lays of Ancient Rome 'Horatius'*
Was none who would be foremost
To lead such dire attack;
But those behind cried 'Forward!'
And those before cried 'Back!'

2685 *Lays of Ancient Rome 'Horatius'*
Oh, Tiber! father Tiber
To whom the Romans pray,
A Roman's life, a Roman's arms,
Take thou in charge this day!

MACAULAY Dame Rose 1889-1958
2686
It was a book to kill time for those who like it better dead.

2687 *Crewe Train*
Gentlemen know that fresh *air* should be kept in its proper place - out of doors - and that, God having given us indoors and out-of-doors, we should not attempt to do away with this distinction.

2688 *Poetry Review*
Poem me no poems.

2689 *The Towers of Trebizond*
'Take my camel, dear,' said my aunt Dot,
as she climbed down from this animal
on her return from High Mass.

MACHLUP Fritz 1902-1983
2690
Let us remember the unfortunate
econometrician who, in one of the major
functions of his system, had to use a
proxy for risk and a dummy for sex.

MADAN Geoffrey 1895-1947
2691
Attractive Etonians who go straight onto
the Stock Exchange missing University
on their fathers' advice: the raw material
of the great bores.

2692
The cat which isn't let out of the bag
often becomes a skeleton in the
cupboard.

2693
Conservative ideal of freedom and
progress: everyone to have an unfettered
opportunity of remaining exactly where
they are.

2694
The great tragedy of the classical
languages is to have been born twins.

2695
King George, passing slowly in a closed
car, looking like a big, rather worn *penny*
in the window.

2696 *Livre sans nom: Twelve Reflections*
The dust of exploded beliefs may make a
fine sunset.

2697
I love drink, so long as it isn't in
moderation.

2698
A marquis is a sort of four-move chess
problem.

2699
Peers: a kind of eye-shade or smoked
glass, to protect us from the full glare of
Royalty.

2700
To say you should treat a duke as an
ordinary man is like telling you to read
the Bible like an ordinary book.

MAGARY James
2701
Computers can figure out all kinds of
problems, except the things in the world
that just don't add up.

MAHLER Gustav 1860-1911
2702 *(on seeing Niagara Falls)*
Fortissimo at last!

MALHERBE François de 1555-1628
2703 *(on his death bed, to a priest)*
Stop, Sir, stop - go away: I cannot bear
your style.

MALONE Dudley Field
2704
I have never in my life learned anything
from any man who agreed with me.

MALRAUX André 1901-1976
2705
Man is a dog's ideal of what God should
be.

MANCROFT Lord 1957-
2706 *Bees in Some Bonnets*
Cricket - a game which the English, not
being a spiritual people, have invented
in order to give themselves some
conception of eternity.

MANDALE W.R.
2707 *'Pop Goes the Weasel'*
Up and down the City Road,
In and out the Eagle,
That's the way the money goes -
Pop goes the weasel!

MANDELSON Peter 1953-
2708
Defeat brings its own humility, which is
not a bad thing for everyone to taste,
especially a politician.

MANION Clarence C.
2709
The average man that I encounter all over the country regards government as a sort of great milk cow, with its head in the clouds eating air, and growing a full teat for everybody on earth.

MANN Horace 1796-1859
2710 *'Lost, Two Golden Hours'*
Lost, yesterday, somewhere between Sunrise and Sunset, two golden hours, each set with sixty diamond minutes. No reward is offered, for they are gone forever.

2711
We put things in order - God does the rest. Lay an iron bar east and west, it is not magnetized. Lay it north and south and it is.

MANSFIELD Katherine 1888-1923
2712 *Journal*
E.M. Forster never gets any further than warming the teapot. He's a rare fine hand at that. Feel this teapot. Is it not beautifully warm? Yes, but there ain't going to be no tea.

MARGOLYES Miriam 1941-
2713
Life, if you're fat, is a minefield - you have to pick your way, otherwise you blow up.

MARIE Queen of Rumania
2714
A woman's virtue ought indeed to be great: since it often has to suffice for two.

2715
Fashion exists for women with no taste, etiquette for people with no breeding.

MARLOWE Christopher 1564-1593
2716 *The Jew of Malta*
BARNARDINE: Thou hast committed-
BARABAS: Fornication? But that was in another
Country: and besides, the wench is dead.

MARQUIS Don 1878-1937
2717 *archy does his part*
boss there is always

a comforting thought
in time of trouble when
it is not our trouble.

2718 *archy and mehitabel*
procrastination is the
art of keeping
up with yesterday.

2719 *archy and mehitabel*
an optimist is a guy
that has never had
much experience.

2720 *archy and mehitabel*
but wotthehell wotthehell
oh i should worry and fret
death and I will coquette
there's a dance in the old dame yet
toujours gai toujours gai.

2721 *archys life of mehitabel*
honesty is a good
thing but
it is not profitable to
its possessor
unless it is
kept under control.

2722 *archys life of mehitabel*
did you ever
notice that when
a politician
does get an idea
he usually
gets it all wrong.

2723 *archys life of mehitabel*
now and then
there is a person born
who is so unlucky
that he runs into accidents
which started to happen
to somebody else.

2724
The art of newspaper paragraphing is to stroke a platitude until it purrs like an epigram.

2725
Happiness comes fleetingly now and then,
To those who have learned to do without

it
And to them only.

2726
Happiness is the interval between periods of unhappiness.

2727
Ours is a world where people don't know what they want and are willing to go through hell to get it.

2728
Pity the meek for they shall inherit the earth.

2729
The successful people are the ones who think up things for the rest of the world to keep busy at.

2730
Writing a book of poetry is like dropping a rose petal down the Grand Canyon and waiting for the echo.

MARRYAT Captain Frederick 1792-1848
2731 *The King's Own*
As savage as a bear with a sore head.

2732 *Mr Midshipman Easy*
All zeal ... all zeal, Mr Easy.

2733 *Mr Midshipman Easy (of an illegitimate baby)*
If you please, ma'am, it was a very little one.

2734 *Settlers in Canada*
Every man paddle his own canoe.

MARSHALL Herbert
2735
There's nothing an economist should fear so much as applause.

MARSHALOV Boris
2736
Congress is so strange. A man gets up to speak and says nothing. Nobody listens, then everybody disagrees.

MARTIAL AD c.40-c.104
2737 *Epigrammata*
I don't love you Sabidius, and I can't tell you why;

All I can tell you is this, that I don't love you.

2730 *Epigrammata*
They praise those works, but read these.

2739
Lawyers are men who hire out their words and anger.

MARTIN Dean 1917-1995
2740
Marriage is not a word but a sentence.

MARTINDELL Jackson
2741
Capital is past savings accumulated for future production.

MARTINEAU Harriet 1802-1876
2742 *Society in America*
Anyone must see at a glance that if men and women marry those whom they do not love, they must love those whom they do not marry.

MARTIN Pete
2743 *(after his Bank's computer had doubled all clients' deposits)*
The hazards of computing are limited only by your imagination.

MARVELL Andrew 1621-1678
2744 *'Upon Appleton House'*
But now the salmon-fishers moist
Their leathern boats begin to hoist;
And, like Antipodes in shoes,
Have shod their heads in their canoes.

2745 *'The Statue in Stocks-Market' (of Charles II)*
For though the whole world cannot show such another,
Yet we'd better by far have him than his brother.

MARX Chico 1891-1961
2746 *(when discovered by his wife with a chorus girl)*
I wasn't kissing her, I was just whispering in her mouth.

MARX Groucho 1895-1977
2747 *(attributed)*
A man is only as old as the woman he feels.

2748
One of the best hearing aids a man can
have is an attentive wife.

2749 *in The Coconuts*
"Your eyes shine like the pants of my
blue serge suit."

2750 *in A Day at the Races*
"Either he's dead, or my watch has
stopped."

2751 *in A Day at the Races*
"I've never been so insulted in my life..."
"Well, it's early yet."

2752 *in Duck Soup*
"Remember, you're fighting for this
woman's honour ... which is probably
more than she ever did."

2753 *in Duck Soup*
"If you can't leave in a taxi you can leave
in a huff. If that's too soon, you can
leave in a minute and a huff."

2754 *Groucho and Me*
Please accept my resignation. I don't
want to belong to any club that will
accept me as a member.

2755
The husband who wants a happy
marriage should learn to keep his mouth
shut and his chequebook open.

2756
I never forget a face, but in your case I'll
make an exception.

2757 *in A Night in Casablanca*
"Send two dozen roses to Room 424 and
put 'Emily, I love you' on the back of the
bill."

2758
Politics doesn't make strange bedfellows,
marriage does.

2759
There is one way to find out if a man is
honest - ask him. If he says 'yes,' you
know he is crooked.

MARY Queen 1867-1953
2760 *(after abdication of her son, King
Edward VIII)*
All *this* thrown away for *that*.

MASARYK Jan 1886-1948
2761
Dictators are rulers who always look
good until the last ten minutes.

MASEFIELD John 1878-1967
2762 *Captain Stratton's Fancy*
Oh some are fond of Spanish wine, and
some are fond of French.

MASSINGER Philip 1583-1640
2763 *The City Madam*
Pray enter
You are learned Europeans and we worse
Than ignorant Americans.

2764
Immature poets imitate: mature poets
steal.

2765 *A New Way to Pay Old Debts*
The devil turned precisian!

MASSON Tom
2766
Hamlet is the tragedy of tackling a family
problem too soon after college.

2767
You can always get someone to love you
- even if you have to do it yourself.

2768
'Be yourself!' is about the worst advice
you can give to some people.

MATHEW Father
2769
Horse-sense is something a horse has
that prevents him betting on people.

MATHEW Sir James 1830-1908
2770
In England, justice is open to all - like
the Ritz Hotel.

MATHEWS Shailer 1863-1941
2771
An epigram is a half-truth so stated as to
irritate the person who believes the
other half.

MATTHEWS Brander 1852-1929
2772
A highbrow is a person educated beyond his intelligence.

MAUGHAM W. Somerset 1874-1965
2773
American women expect to find in their husbands a perfection that English women only hope to find in their butlers.

2774 *The Bread-Winner*
You know, of course, that the Tasmanians, who never committed adultery, are now extinct.

2775 *Cakes and Ale*
Hypocrisy is the most difficult and nerve-racking vice that any man can pursue; it needs an unceasing vigilance and a rare detachment of spirit. It cannot, like adultery or gluttony, be practised at spare moments; it is a whole-time job.

2776 *Cakes and Ale*
From the earliest times the old have rubbed it into the young that they are wiser than they, and before the young had discovered what nonsense this was they were old too, and it profited them to carry on the imposture.

2777 *Cakes and Ale*
Poor Henry [James], he's spending eternity wandering round and round a stately park and the fence is just too high for him to peep over and they're having tea just too far away for him to hear what the countess is saying.

2778 *The Circle*
When married people don't get on they can separate, but if they're not married it's impossible. It's a tie that only death can sever.

2779 *Of Human Bondage*
Money is like a sixth sense without which you cannot make a complete use of the other five.

2780 *The Moon and Sixpence*
Impropriety is the soul of wit.

2781 *The Summing Up*
I would sooner read a time-table or a catalogue than nothing at all ... They are much more entertaining than half the novels that are written.

2782
A Unitarian very earnestly disbelieves what everyone else believes.

2783 *A Writer's Notebook*
Few misfortunes can befall a boy which bring worse consequences than to have a really affectionate mother.

2784 *A Writer's Notebook*
Music-hall songs provide the dull with wit, just as proverbs provide them with wisdom.

MAULDIN Bill 1921-
2785 *(cartoon caption)*
I feel like a fugitive from th' law of averages.

MAURIAC François 1885-1970
2786
Human love is often but the encounter of two weaknesses.

MAUROIS André 1885-1967
2787
Business is a combination of war and sport.

MAXTON James 1885-1946
2788 *(opposing disaffiliation of SILP from Labour)*
All I say is, if you cannot ride two horses you have no right in the circus.

MEANY George 1894-1980
2789
Anybody who has any doubt about the ingenuity or the resourcefulness of a plumber never got a bill from one.

MEARNS Hughes 1875-1965
2790 *The Psycho-ed*
As I was walking up the stair
I met a man who wasn't there.
He wasn't there again today.
I wish, I wish he'd stay away.

MEDICI Cosimo de 1389-1464
2791
We read that we ought to forgive our enemies; but we do not read that we ought to forgive our friends.

MEIR Golda 1898-1978
2792
Don't be so humble. You're not that great.

2793
We Jews have a secret weapon in our struggle with the Arabs - we have no place to go.

MELBOURNE William Lamb 2nd Lord 1779-1848
2794 *(on being dismissed by William IV)*
I have always thought complaints of ill-usage contemptible, whether from a seduced disappointed girl or a turned-out Prime Minister.

2795 *(replying to a politician)*
What I want is men who will support me when I am in the wrong.

MELLON Andrew 1855-1937
2796
Gentlemen prefer bonds.

MELVILLE Herman 1819-1891
2797 *Moby Dick*
A whaleship was my Yale College and my Harvard.

2798 *Moby Dick*
Better sleep with a sober cannibal than a drunken Christian.

MENCKEN H.L. 1880-1956
2799
A man loses his sense of direction after four drinks; a woman loses hers after four kisses.

2800
Bachelors know more about women than married men; if they didn't, they'd be married too.

2801
The basic fact about human existence is not that it is a tragedy, but that it is a bore.

2802
He [Calvin Coolidge] slept more than any other President, whether by day or by night. Nero fiddled, but Coolidge only snored.

2803
A celebrity is one who is known to many persons he is glad he doesn't know.

2804 *Chrestomathy*
Love is the delusion that one woman differs from another.

2805 *Chrestomathy*
Puritanism. The haunting fear that someone, somewhere, may be happy.

2806
Conscience is a mother-in-law whose visit never ends.

2807
A cynic is a man who, when he smells flowers, looks around for a coffin.

2808
Under democracy, one party always devotes its chief energies to trying to prove that the other party is unfit to rule - and both commonly succeed, and are right.

2809
If, after I depart this vale, you ever remember me and have thought to please my ghost, forgive some sinner and wink your eye at some homely girl.

2810
God is a comedian whose audience is afraid to laugh.

2811
I hate all sports as rabidly as a person who likes sports hates common sense.

2812
Injustice is relatively easy to bear; what stings is justice.

2813
I've made it a rule never to drink by daylight and never to refuse a drink after dark.

2814
A judge is a law student who marks his own examination papers.

2815 *A Little Book in C major*
Democracy is the theory that the common people know what they want, and deserve to get it good and hard.

2816 *A Little Book in C major*
Conscience: the inner voice which warns us that someone may be looking.

2817
No matter how happily a woman may be married, it always pleases her to discover that there is a nice man who wishes she were not.

2818
One may no more live in the world without picking up the moral prejudices of the world than one will be able to go to hell without perspiring.

2819
Men have a much better time of it than women. For one thing, they marry later. For another thing, they die earlier.

2820
Nobody ever went broke underestimating the taste of the American public.

2821 *Notebooks*
It is now quite lawful for a Catholic woman to avoid pregnancy by a resort to mathematics, though she is still forbidden to resort to physics and chemistry.

2822
Opera in English is, in the main, just about as sensible as baseball in Italian.

2823
Penetrating so many secrets, we cease to believe in the unknowable. But there it sits nevertheless, calmly licking its chops.

2824 *Prejudices*
Women hate revolutions and revolutionists. They like men who are docile, and well regarded at the bank, and never late at meals.

2825
We must respect the other fellow's religion, but only in the sense and to the extent that we respect his theory that his wife is beautiful and his children smart.

2826
The saddest life is that of a political aspirant under democracy. His failure is ignominious and his success is disgraceful.

2827
Time is a great legalizer, even in the field of morals.

2828
What men value in the world is not rights, but privileges.

2829
Women have simple tastes. They get pleasure out of the conversation of children in arms and men in love.

MENNINGER Karl
2830
Neurotic means he is not as sensible as I am, and psychotic means he's even worse than my brother-in-law.

MENNINGER William 1899-1966
2831
What the world needs is some 'do-give-a-damn' pills.

MERCER Johnny 1909-1976
2832 *'Ac-cent-tchu-ate the Positive'*
You've got to ac-cent-tchu-ate the positive
Elim-my-nate the negative
Latch on to the affirmative
Don't mess with Mister In-between.

2833 *'Jeepers Creepers'*
Jeepers Creepers - where'd you get those peepers?
Jeepers Creepers - where'd get those eyes?

MEREDITH George 1828-1909
2834 *Beauchamp's Career*
Thoughts of heroes were as good as warming-pans.

2835 *One of Our Conquerors*
None of your dam punctilio.

2836 *'Lucifer in Starlight'*
On a starred night Prince Lucifer uprose.
Tired of his dark dominion swung the fiend ...

2837 *Modern Love*
'I play for Seasons; not Eternities!'
Says Nature.

2838 *The Ordeal of Richard Feverel*
Kissing don't last: cookery do!

MERRITT Dixon Lanier 1879-1972
2839
Oh, a wondrous bird is the pelican!
His beak holds more than his belican.
He takes in his beak
Food enough for a week.
But I'll be darned if I know how the helican.

MICHELET Jules 1798-1874
2840
Women are perfectly well aware that the more they seem to obey the more they rule.

MIDDLETON Thomas c.1580-1627
2841 *The Changeling (with William Rowley)*
I could not get the ring without the finger.

2842 *The Witch*
There's no hate lost between us.

2843 *No Wit, No Help, Like a Woman's*
By many a happy accident.

MIKES George 1912-1987
2844 *How to be an Alien*
On the Continent people have good food; in England people have good table manners.

2845 *How to be an Alien*
Continental people have sex life; the English have hot-water bottles.

2846 *How to be an Alien*
An Englishman, even if he is alone, forms an orderly queue of one.

MILL John Stuart 1806-1873
2847
His eminence was due to the flatness of the surrounding landscape.

2848
Unquestionably, it is possible to do without happiness; it is done involuntarily by nineteen-twentieths of mankind.

MILLAY Edna St Vincent 1892-1950
2849
April,
Comes like an idiot, babbling, and strewing flowers.

2850
A person who publishes a book appears willfully in public with his pants down.

2851
With him for a sire, and her for a dam
What should I be, but just what I am?

2852 *'Thursday'*
And if I loved you Wednesday,
Well what is that to you?
I do not love you Thursday -
So much is true.

2853
It is not true that life is one damn thing after another - it's one damn thing over and over.

MILLER Arthur 1915-
2854 *Death of a Salesman*
The world is an oyster, but you don't crack it open on a mattress.

MILLER Harlan
2855
Often the difference between a successful marriage and a mediocre one consists of leaving about three or four things a day unsaid.

MILLER Henry 1891-1980
2856
Destiny is what you are supposed to do

in life. Fate is what kicks you in the ass
to make you do it.

2857
Life, as it is called, is for most of us one
long postponement.

2858
The one thing we can never get enough
of is love. And the one thing we never
give enough of is love.

2859 *Big Sur and the Oranges of
Hieronymus Bosch*
Sex is one of the nine reasons for
reincarnation ... The other eight are
unimportant.

2860 *Tropic of Cancer*
Even before the music begins there is
that bored look on people's faces. A
polite form of self-imposed torture, the
concert.

MILLER Joaquin 1839-1913
2861
The biggest dog has been a pup.

MILLER Jonathan 1934-
2862 *Beyond the Fringe*
In fact, I'm not really a *Jew*. Just Jew-*ish*.
Not the whole hog, you know.

MILLER Max 1895-1963
2863 *The Max Miller Blue Book*
There was a little girl who had a little
curl,
Right in the middle of her forehead;
When she was good she was very very
good,
And when she was bad she was very very
popular.

MILLER Olin
2864
One of the best things people could do
for their decendants would be to sharply
limit the number of them.

MILLIGAN Spike 1918-
2865 *The Goon Show 'Only in the mating
season'*
'Do you come here often?'

2866 *The Last Goon Show of All*
Contraceptives should be used on every
conceivable occasion.

2867 *Puckoon*
Money couldn't buy friends but you got a
better class of enemy.

MILLS Hugh
2868
Nothing unites the English like war.
Nothing divides them like Picasso.

MILLSTEIN Gilbert
2869
He speaks English with the flawless
imperfection of a New Yorker.

MILNE A.A. 1882-1956
2870
One of the advantages of being
disorderly is that one is constantly
making exciting discoveries.

2871 *The House at Pooh Corner*
The more he looked inside the more
Piglet wasn't there.

2872 *The House at Pooh Corner*
'I don't *want* him,' said Rabbit. 'But it's
always useful to know where a friend-
and-relation *is*, whether you want him or
whether you don't.'

2873 *The House at Pooh Corner*
He respects Owl, because you can't help
respecting anybody who can spell
TUESDAY, even if he doesn't spell it
right; but spelling isn't everything. There
are days when spelling Tuesday simply
doesn't count.

2874 *The House at Pooh Corner*
Pooh began to feel a little more
comfortable, because when you are a
Bear of Very Little Brain, and you Think
of Things, you find sometimes that a
Thing which seemed very Thingish
inside you is quite different when it gets
out into the open and has other people
looking at it.

2875 *When We Were Very Young
'Buckingham Palace'*
They're changing guard at Buckingham
Palace -

Christopher Robin went down with Alice.
Alice is marrying one of the guard.
'A soldier's life is terrible hard,'
Says Alice.

2876 *When We Were Very Young*
'Disobedience'
James James
Morrison Morrison
Weatherby George Dupree
Took great
Care of his Mother,
Though he was only three.
James James
Said to his Mother,
'Mother,' he said, said he;
'You must never go down to the end of
the town, if you don't go down with me.'

2877 *When We Were Very Young 'The*
Dormouse ...'
There once was a Dormouse who lived
in a bed
Of delphiniums (blue) and geraniums
(red),
And all the day long he'd a wonderful
view
Of geraniums (red) and delphiniums
(blue)

2878 *When We Were Very Young 'King's*
Breakfast'
The King asked
The Queen, and
The Queen asked
The Dairymaid:
'Could we have some butter for
The Royal slice of bread?'

2879 *When We Were Very Young 'Rice*
Pudding'
What is the matter with Mary Jane?
She's perfectly well and she hasn't a pain,
And it's lovely rice pudding for dinner
again!
What *is* the matter with Mary Jane.

2880 *Winnie-the-Pooh*
Isn't it funny
How a bear likes honey?
Buzz! Buzz! Buzz!
I wonder why he does?

2881 *Winnie-the-Pooh*
How sweet to be a Cloud
Floating in the Blue!
It makes him very proud
To be a little cloud.

2882 *Winnie-the-Pooh*
Time for a little something.

2883 *Winnie-the-Pooh*
My spelling is Wobbly. It's good spelling
but it Wobbles, and the letters get in the
wrong places.

2884 *Winnie-the-Pooh*
Owl hasn't exactly got Brain, but he
Knows Things.

2885 *Winnie-the-Pooh*
I am a Bear of Very Little Brain and long
words Bother me.

2886 *Winnie-the-Pooh*
I have decided to catch a Heffalump.

2887 *Winnie-the-Pooh*
'Pathetic,' he said. 'That's what it is.
Pathetic.'

MILTON John 1608-1674
2888 *Comus*
'Tis chastity, my brother, chastity:
She that has that, is clad in complete
steel.

2889 *'On the Morning of Christ's Nativity'*
Perhaps their loves, or else their sheep,
Was all that did their silly thoughts so
busy keep.

MILVERTON Lord 1930-
2890
The ideal committee is one with me as
chairman, and two other members in
bed with flu.

MISTINGUETT 1874-1956
2891
A kiss can be a comma, a question mark,
or an exclamation point. That's basic
spelling that every woman ought to
know.

MITCHELL Joni 1945-
2892 *'Big Yellow Taxi'*
They paved paradise
And put up a parking lot,

With a pink hotel,
A boutique, and a swinging hot spot.

MITCHELL Langdon
2893
Marriage is three parts love and seven parts forgiveness of sins.

MITCHELL Margaret 1900-1949
2894 *Gone with the Wind*
Death and taxes and childbirth! There's never any convenient time for any of them.

MITFORD Nancy 1904-1973
2895 *Noblesse Oblige*
An aristocracy in a republic is like a chicken whose head has been cut off: it may run about in a lively way, but in fact it is dead.

2896 *The Pursuit of Love*
Wooing, so tiring.

2897 *The Pursuit of Love*
Frogs ... are slightly better than Huns or Wops, but abroad is unutterably bloody and foreigners are fiends.

MITTERAND President François 1916-1996
2898 *(to his adviser)*
You, Attali, are a mere chapter. I am the entire volume.

MIZNER Wilson 1876-1933
2899
The cuckoo who is on to himself is halfway out of the clock.

2900
A fellow who is always declaring he's no fool usually has his suspicions.

2901 *(of Hollywood)*
A trip through a sewer in a glass-bottomed boat.

2902
I've had several years in Hollywood and I still think the movie heroes are in the audience.

2903
Be nice to people on your way up because you'll meet 'em on your way down.

2904
If you steal from one author, it's plagiarism; if you steal from many, it's research.

MOLIÉRE 1622-1673
2905
A doctor wastes no time with patients; and if you have to die, he will put the business through quicker than anybody else.

2906 *Don Juan*
He who lives without tobacco is not worthy to live.

2907 *La Critique de l'école des femmes*
It's an odd job, making decent people laugh.

2908 *Le Dépit amoureux*
One dies only once, and it's for such a long time!

2909 *Les Femmes savantes*
It's good food and not fine words that keeps me alive.

2910 *Les Femmes savantes*
Rags and tatters, if you like: I am fond of my rags and tatters.

2911 *Les Femmes savantes*
A knowledgeable fool is a greater fool than an ignorant fool.

2912 *The Misanthrope*
What's needed in this world is an accommodating sort of virtue.

2913 *The Misanthrope*
Of all human follies there's none could be greater
Than trying to render our fellow-men better.

2914 *The Miser*
Always present your front to the world.

2915
You never see the old austerity
That was the essence of civility;
Young people hereabouts, unbridled, now
Just want.

2916 *The Sicilian*
Assassination is the quickest way.

2917 *Tartuffe*
I am not the less human for being
devout.

2918 *Tartuffe*
God it is true, does some delights
condemn,
But 'tis not hard to come to terms with
Him.

2919 *Tartuffe*
Man, I can assure you, is a nasty
creature.

2920 *The Would-be Gentleman*
Ah, it's a lovely thing, to know a thing or
two.

MONKHOUSE William Cosmo 1840-
1901
2921 *Nonsense Rhymes*
There once was an old man of Lyme
Who married three wives at a time,
When asked 'Why a third?'
He replied, 'One's absurd!
And bigamy, Sir, is a crime!'

MONMOUTH Duke of 1649-1685
2922 *(to his executioner)*
Do not hack me as you did my Lord
Russell.

MONROE Marilyn 1926-1962
2923 *in Gentlemen Prefer Blondes*
"I always say a kiss on the hand might
feel very good, but a diamond tiara lasts
forever."

2924 *(on posing nude)*
It's not true I had nothing on. I had the
radio on.

MONTAGU Ashley 1905-
2925
Today, while the titular head of the
family may still be the father, everyone
knows that he is little more than
chairman, at most, of the entertainment
committee.

2926
In Victorian times the purpose of life was
to develop a personality once and for all
and then stand on it.

MONTAGU Lady Mary Wortley 1689-
1762
2927 *(attributed)*
This world consists of men, women, and
Herveys.

2928 *'Answered, for Lord William
Hamilton'*
But the fruit that can fall without
shaking,
Indeed is too mellow for me.

2929
I give myself, sometimes, admirable
advice, but I am incapable of taking it.

2930 *To the Imitator of the First Satire of
Horace*
Satire should, like a polished razor keen,
Wound with a touch that's scarcely felt or
seen.

2931
People wish their enemies dead - but I
do not; I say give them the gout, give
them the stone!

2932 *The Plain Dealer*
Let this great maxim be my virtue's
guide:
In part she is to blame, who has been
tried,
He comes too near, that comes to be
denied.

2933 *Six Town Eclogues 'The Lover'*
And we meet with champagne and a
chicken at last.

2934 *Six Town Eclogues 'The Lover'*
As Ovid has sweetly in parable told,
We harden like trees, and like rivers grow
cold.

2935 *Summary of Lord Lyttelton's Advice*
Be plain in dress, and sober in your diet;
In short, my deary! kiss me, and be quiet.

MONTAGUE C.E. 1867-1928
2936 *Fiery Particles*
I was born below par to th' extent of two
whiskies.

MONTAIGNE Michel de 1533-1592
2937
The Ancient Mariner said to Neptune
during a great storm, 'O God, you will
save me if you wish, but I am going to go
on holding my tiller straight.'

2938
No doctor takes pleasure in the health
even of his friends.

2939 *Essays*
When I play with my cat, who knows
whether she isn't amusing herself with
me more than I am with her?

2940 *Essays*
Unless a man feels he has a good enough
memory, he should never venture to lie.

2941 *Essays*
A woman who goes to bed with a man
ought to lay aside her modesty with her
skirt, and put it on again with her
petticoat.

2942 *Essays*
A little of everything and nothing
thoroughly.

2943 *Essays*
It [marriage] is like a cage; one sees the
birds outside desperate to get in, and
those inside equally desperate to get out.

2944
I have never seen a greater monster or
miracle in the world than myself.

2945
There never were two opinions alike in
all the world, no more than two hours or
two grains: the most universal quality is
diversity.

2946
I speak the truth, not so much as I
would, but as much as I dare; and I dare
a little more, as I grow older.

2947
A wise man sees as much as he ought,
not as much as he can.

MONTESQUIEU Charles Baron de
1689-1755
2948 *Lettres Persanes*
Men should be bewailed at their birth,
and not at their death.

2949 *Lettres Persanes*
There is a very good saying that if
triangles invented a god, they would
make him three-sided.

2950 *Pensées diverses 'Portrait de
Montesquieu'*
I suffer from the disease of writing books
and being ashamed of them when they
are finished.

2951 *Pensées et fragments inédits*
Great lords have their pleasures, but the
people have fun.

MONTGOMERY Lucy Maud 1874-1942
2952
Worrying helps you some. It seems as if
you are doing something when you're
worrying.

MONTROND Casimir Comte de 1768-
1843
2953 *(attributed)*
If something pleasant happens to you,
don't forget to tell it to your friends, to
make them feel bad.

MOODIE Susanna 1803-1885
2954
When things come to the worst, they
generally mend.

MOODY D.L. 1837-1899
2955
If I take care of my character, my
reputation will take care of itself.

MOORE Brian 1921-
2956
We also serve who only punctuate.

MOORE Edward 1712-1757
2957 *The Foundling*
This is adding insult to injuries.

2958 *The Foundling*
I am rich beyond the dreams of avarice.

MOORE George 1852-1933
2959
No place in England where everyone can go is considered respectable.

2960
Ireland is a fatal disease; fatal to Englishmen and doubly fatal to Irishmen.

2961
A literary movement consists of five or six people who live in the same town and hate each other cordially.

MOORE Marianne 1887-1972
2962
I'm troubled. I'm dissatisfied. I'm Irish.

2963
Poetry is all nouns and verbs.

2964 *'Silence'*
My father used to say,
'Superior people never make long visits, have to be shown Longfellow's grave or the glass flowers at Harvard'.

MOORE Sparkle
2965
The Strip Club is another form of safe sex.

MOORE Thomas 1779-1852
2966 *The Fudge Family in Paris*
Who can help loving the land that has taught us
Six hundred and eighty-five ways to dress eggs?

2967 *The Fudge Family in Paris*
I may, without vanity, hint -
Though an angel should write, still 'tis *devils* must print.

2968 *'The young May moon'*
Then awake! the heavens look bright, my dear;
'Tis never too late for delight, my dear;
And the best of all ways
To lengthen our days
Is to steal a few hours from the night, my dear!

MORDDEN Ethan
2969
For most singers the first half of the career involves extending one's repertoire, the second half trimming it.

MORE Hannah 1745-1833
2970 *Florio*
He liked those literary cooks
Who skim the cream of others' books;
And ruin half an author's graces
By plucking bon-mots from their places.

2971
Going to the opera, like getting drunk, is a sin that carries its own punishment with it and that a very severe one.

MORE Sir Thomas 1478-1535
2972 *(to a friend who had versified a mediocre book)*
Yea, marry, now it is somewhat, for now it is rhyme; before, it was neither rhyme nor reason.

2973 *(on mounting the scaffold)*
I pray you, master Lieutenant, see me safe up, and my coming down let me shift for my self.

MORGAN Augustus de 1806-1871
2974 *A Budget of Paradoxes*
Great fleas have little fleas upon their backs to bite 'em,
And little fleas have lesser fleas, and so *ad infinitum*.

MORGAN J.P. 1837-1913
2975
Well, I don't know as I want a lawyer to tell me what I cannot do. I hire him to tell me how to do what I want to do.

MORGENSTERN Christian
2976
Home is not where you live but where they understand you.

2977
Humour is the contemplation of the finite from the point of view of the infinite.

MORLEY Christopher 1890-1957

2978
The enemies of the future are always the very nicest people.

2979
No man is lonely while eating spaghetti - it requires so much attention.

2980
Any man worth his salt has by the time he is forty-five accumulated a crown of thorns, and the problem is to learn to wear it over one ear.

2981
New York, the nation's thyroid gland.

2982
There are three ingredients in the good life; learning, earning and yearning.

2983 *Thunder on the Left*
Life is a foreign language: all men mispronounce it.

2984
A town that has no ceiling price,
A town of double-talk;
A town so big men name her twice,
Like so; 'N'Yawk, N'Yawk.'

2985
It is unfair to blame man too fiercely for being pugnacious; he learned the habit from nature.

2986
We've had bad luck with our kids - they've all grown up.

MORLEY Lord John 1838-1923

2987
Politics is a field where action is one long second best and where the choice constantly lies between two blunders.

2988
He who hates vice hates men.

MORPHY Countess

2989 *English Recipes*
The tragedy of English cooking is that 'plain' cooking cannot be entrusted to 'plain' cooks.

MORRIS Charles 1745-1838

2990 *The Contrast*
If one must have a villa in summer to dwell,
Oh give me the sweet shady side of Pall Mall!

2991 *'Country and Town'*
But a house is much more to my mind than a tree,
And for groves, O! a good grove of chimneys for me.

MORRIS Desmond 1928-

2992
Life is like a very short visit to a toyshop between birth and death.

MORRIS Robert T.

2993
I hate funerals, and would not attend my own if it could be avoided, but it is well for every man to stop once in a while to think of what sort of a collection of mourners he is training for his final event.

MORROW Dwight 1873-1931

2994
We judge ourselves by our motives and others by their actions.

MORTIMER John 1923-

2995 *(attributed, of himself)*
Champagne socialist.

2996
[Irritable judges] suffer from a bad case of premature adjudication.

2997 *Paradise Postponed*
They do you a decent death on the hunting-field.

2998
Being successful in England is a dangerous occupation.

2999
The virtue of much literature is that it is dangerous and may do you extreme harm.

3000 *A Voyage Round My Father*
At school I never minded the lessons. I just resented having to work terribly hard at playing.

3001 *A Voyage Round My Father*
No brilliance is needed in the law. Nothing but common sense, and relatively clean finger nails.

MOSELY Sir Oswald 1896-1980
3002
Vote Labour: Sleep Tory.

MOSES Ludwig van
3003
Government is the only institution that can take a valuable commodity like paper, and make it worthless by applying ink.

MOSTEL Zero 1915-1977
3004
I wanted to say something about the universe. There's God, angels, plants ... and horseshit.

MOTLEY John Lothrop 1814-1877
3005
Give us the luxuries of life, and we will dispense with its necessities.

MOTTOES and SLOGANS
3006 *(advertising slogan)*
Access, your flexible friend.

3007 *(advertising slogan)*
Beanz meanz Heinz.

3008 *(advertising slogan, British Egg Marketing Bord)*
Go to work on an egg.

3009 *(advertising slogan, British Telecom)*
It's for you-hoo!

3010 *(advertising slogan, Castelmaine lager)*
Australians wouldn't give a XXXX for anything else.

3011 *(advertising slogan, Doan's Backache Kidney Pills)*
Every picture tells a story.

3012 *(advertising slogan, Double Diamond beer)*
I'm only here for the beer.

3013 *(advertising slogan, Esso)*
Put a tiger in your tank.

3014 *(advertising slogan, the Hat Council)*
If you want to get ahead, get a hat.

3015 *(advertising slogan, Milk Marketing Board)*
Drinka Pinta Milka Day.

3016 *(pacifist slogan)*
A bayonet is a weapon with a worker at each end.

3017 *(slogan, 1968)*
Je suis Marxiste - tendance Groucho.
I am a Marxist - of the Groucho tendency.

3018 *(slogan, American life insurance)*
Death [is] nature's way of telling you to slow down.

3019 *(slogan, US Armed Forces)*
The difficult we do immediately - the impossible takes a little longer.

3020 *(slogan, British Rail)*
Let the train take the strain.

3021 *(slogan, World Whores Congress)*
Good girls go to heaven. Bad girls go everywhere.

3022 *(student slogan, 1960s)*
Make love, not war.

MOZART Wolfgang Amadeus 1756-1791
3023
I write as a sow piddles.

MUGABE Robert 1924-
3024
Cricket civilizes people and creates good gentlemen. I want everyone to play cricket in Zimbabwe; I want ours to be a nation of gentlemen.

MUGGERIDGE Malcolm 1903-1990
3025
Good taste and humour are a

contradiction in terms, like a chaste whore.

3026 *The Infernal Grove*
To succeed pre-eminently in English public life it is necessary to conform either to the popular image of a bookie or of a clergyman; Churchill being a perfect example of the former, Halifax of the latter.

3027
Few men of action have been able to make a graceful exit at the appropriate time.

3028
An orgy looks particularly alluring seen through the mists of righteous indignation.

3029 *Tread Softly*
The orgasm has replaced the Cross as the focus of longing and the image of fulfilment.

3030 *Tread Softly (of Sir Anthony Eden)*
He was not only a bore; he bored for England.

MUMFORD Ethel Watts
3031
O wad some power the giftie gie us to see some people before they see us.

MUMFORD Lewis 1895-1990
3032
Our national flower is the concrete cloverleaf.

MUNTHE Axel 1857-1949
3033
Christ - an anarchist who succeeded.

MURRAY Jim
3034 *(on the death of Casey Stengel)*
Well, God is certainly getting an earful tonight.

MUSSELMAN M.M.
3035
One of the best things about marriage is that it gets young people to bed at a decent hour.

NABOKOV Vladimir 1899-1977
3036
Genius is an African who dreams up snow.

NAIPAUL V.S. 1932-
3037
One always writes comedy at the moment of deepest hysteria.

NAITO Fern
3038
When you've got them by their wallets, their hearts and minds will follow.

NAPOLÉON I (Bonaparte) 1769-1821
3039 *(when asked how to deal with the Pope)*
As though he had 200,000 men.

NASH Ogden 1902-1971
3040 *The Canary*
The song of canaries
Never varies,
And when they're moulting
They're pretty revolting.

3041 *'The Cow'*
The cow is of the bovine ilk;
One end is moo, the other, milk.

3042
Ask Daddy, He Won't Know.

3043 *England Expects*
Children aren't happy with nothing to ignore,
And that's what parents were created for.

3044 *'Family Court'*
One would be in less danger
From the wiles of the stranger
If one's own kin and kith
Were more fun to be with.

3045
Another good thing about gossip is that it is within everybody's reach,
And it is much more interesting than any other form of speech.

3046 *'Lather as You Go'*
Beneath this slab
John Brown is stowed.
He watched the ads,
And not the road.

3047 'Lines on Facing Forty'
I have a bone to pick with Fate.
Come here and tell me, girlie,
Do you think my mind is maturing late,
Or simply rotted early?

3048
Middle age: when you're sitting at home
on Saturday night and the telephone
rings and you hope it isn't for you.

3049
Parsley
is gharsley.

3050 'The Perfect Husband'
He tells you when you've got on too
much lipstick,
And helps you with your girdle when
your hips stick.

3051 'Plea for Less Malice Toward None'
Any kiddie in school can love like a fool,
But hating, my boy, is an art.

3052
Poets aren't very useful,
Because they aren't consumeful or very
produceful.

3053
Progress might have been all right once,
but it's gone on too long.

3054
Purity is obscurity.

3055 'Reflections on Ice-breaking'
Candy
Is dandy
But liquor
Is quicker.

3056 'Samson Agonistes'
I test my bath before I sit,
And I'm always moved to wonderment
That what chills the finger not a bit
Is so frigid upon the fundament.

3057
Senescence begins
And middle age ends,
The day your descendants
Outnumber your friends.

3058 'Song of the Open Road'
I think that I shall never see
A billboard lovely as a tree.
Perhaps, unless the billboards fall,
I'll never see a tree at all.

3059 'What's the Use?'
Sure, deck your lower limbs in pants;
Yours are the limbs, my sweeting.
You look divine as you advance -
Have you seen yourself retreating?

3060
In the world of mules there are no rules.

NATHAN George Jean 1882-1958
3061
I drink to make other people interesting.

3062
Love is an emotion experienced by the
many and enjoyed by the few.

3063
Opening night is the night before the
play is ready to open.

NAYLOR James Ball 1860-1945
3064 'King David and King Solomon'
King David and King Solomon
Led merry, merry lives,
With many, many lady friends,
And many, many wives;
But when old age crept over them -
With many, many qualms! -
King Solomon wrote the Proverbs
And King David wrote the Psalms.

NEEDHAM Richard J.
3065
God punishes us mildly by ignoring our
prayers and severely by answering them.

3066
Love is a fever which marriage puts to
bed and cures.

3067
People are like birds - from a distance,
beautiful: from close up, those sharp
beaks, those beady little eyes.

3068
People who are brutally honest get more
satisfaction out of the brutality than out
of the honesty.

3069
When a man tells me he's run out of
steam in the sex department, I'll tell him,
'Count your blessings; you've escaped
from the clutches of a cruel tyrant.
Enjoy!'

NELLIST Dave 1952-
3070
The quickest way to become a left
winger in the Labour Party today is to
stand still for six months.

NELSON John Kirk
3071
More and more these days I find myself
pondering on how to reconcile my net
income with my gross habits.

NEWBOLT Sir Henry 1862-1938
3072 *'Drake's Drum'*
Drake he's in his hammock till the great
Armadas come.
(Capten, art tha sleepin' there below?)

NEWLEY Anthony and BRICUSSE Leslie
1931- and 1931-
3073
Stop the world, I want to get off.

NEWMAN Andrea
3074
Toothache doesn't stop hurting because
someone else has cancer.

NEWMAN Ernest 1868-1959
3075
The good composer is slowly discovered,
the bad composer is slowly found out.

NEWMAN Paul 1925-
3076 *in Butch Cassidy and the Sundance
Kid*
"He'll feel a lot better once we've robbed
a couple of banks."

NEWTON A. Edward
3077
The formula for complete happiness is
to be very busy with the unimportant.

NEWTON Sir Isaac 1642-1727
3078 *(to a dog who destroyed some of his
work)*
O Diamond! Diamond! thou little
knowest the mischief done!

NICHOLAS I 1796-1855
3079 *(attributed)*
Russia has two generals in whom she
can confide - Generals Janvier [January]
and Février [February].

3080
Turkey is a dying man. We may
endeavour to keep him alive, but we
shall not succeed. He will, he must die.

NICHOLSON Jack 1937-
3081
You only lie to two people; your
girlfriend and the police. Everyone else
you tell the truth to.

NICOLSON Sir Harold 1886-1968
3082 *(anticipating the aftermath of World
War 2)*
We shall have to walk and live a
Woolworth life hereafter.

3083
To be a good diarist, one must have a
little snouty, sneaky mind.

3084 *(of King George V)*
For seventeen years he did nothing at all
but kill animals and stick in stamps.

3085
The worst thing, I fear, about being no
longer young, is that one is no longer
young.

NIETZSCHE Friedrich 1844-1900
3086
The abdomen is the reason why man
does not easily take himself for a god.

3087
The advantage of a bad memory is that
one enjoys several times the same good
thing for the first time.

3088 *The Antichrist*
Woman was God's second blunder.

3089 *The Antichrist*
When a man is in love he endures more
than at other times; he submits to
everything.

3090
Ascetic: one who makes a necessity of
virtue.

3091 *Die fröhliche Wissenschaft*
Morality is the herd-instinct in the
individual.

3092 *Die fröhliche Wissenschaft*
Believe me! The secret of reaping the
greatest fruitfulness and the greatest
enjoyment from life is *to live
dangerously!*

3093 *Ecce Homo*
My time has not yet come either; some
are born posthumously.

3094
The historian looks backward. In the
end he also believes backward.

3095 *Jenseits von Gut und Böse*
Is not life a hundred times too short for
us to bore ourselves?

3096
A joke is an epigram on the death of a
feeling.

3097
The lie is a condition of life.

3098
Never to talk of oneself is a form of
hypocrisy.

3099
A politician divides mankind into two
classes: tools and enemies.

3100
Profundity of thought belongs to youth,
clarity of thought to old age.

3101
Sleeping is no mean art. For its sake one
must stay awake all day.

3102
When thou goest to woman, take thy
whip.

3103
A woman may very well form a
friendship with a man, but for this to
endure, it must be assisted by a little
physical antipathy.

3104
Has a woman who knew that she was
well dressed ever caught a cold?

3105
The more you let yourself go, the less
others let you go.

NIGHTINGALE Florence 1820-1910
3106
The very first requirement in a hospital
is that it should do the sick no harm.

3107 *Notes on Nursing*
No *man*, not even a doctor, ever gives
any other definition of what a nurse
should be than this - 'devoted and
obedient'. This definition would do just
as well for a porter. It might even do for
a horse. It would not do for a policeman.

NIXON Richard 1913-1994
3108
Sometimes at the end of the day when
I'm smiling and shaking hands, I want to
kick them.

3109
I welcome this kind of examination
because people have got to know
whether or not their President is a crook.
Well, I'm not a crook.

NIZER Louis 1902-
3110
In cross-examination, as in fishing,
nothing is more ungainly than a
fisherman pulled into the water by his
catch.

NORDEN Dennis
3111 *(dictum on television scripts)*
We don't want it good - we want it
Tuesday.

**NORFOLK Charles Howard, Duke of
1746-1815**
3112
If a man is to go to the devil, he may as
well go thither from the House of Lords
as from any other place on earth.

NORTH Christopher 1785-1854
3113
Such accidents will happen in the best-
regulated families.

3114
Animosities are mortal, but the Humanities live for ever.

3115
Insultin the sun, and quarrellin wi' the equator.

3116
Laws were made to be broken.

3117
I cannot sit still, James, and hear you abuse the shopocracy.

NORTHCLIFFE Lord 1865-1922
3118
When I want a peerage, I shall buy it like an honest man.

NOVALIS 1772-1801
3119
Not only England, but every Englishman is an island.

NYE Bill
3120 *Autobiography*
I have been told that Wagner's music is better than it sounds.

NYE Edgar Wilson
3121
There must be at least 500 million rats in the United States; of course, I am speaking only from memory.

O'BRIEN Flann 1911-1966
3122 *At Swim-Two-Birds*
The conclusion of your syllogism, I said lightly, is fallacious, being based upon licensed premises.

3123 *At Swim-Two-Birds*
A pint of plain is your only man.

O'CASEY Sean 1880-1964
3124 *Juno and the Paycock*
The whole worl's in a state o' chassis!

3125 *Juno and the Paycock*
The Polis as Polis, in this city, is Null an' Void!

3126 *(of P.G. Wodehouse)*
English literature's performing flea.

3127 *The Plough and the Stars*
There's no reason to bring religion into it. I think we ought to have as great a rogard for religion as we can, so as to keep it out of as many things as possible.

3128 *The Plough and the Stars*
It's my rule never to lose me temper till it would be dethrimental to keep it.

O'CONNELL Daniel 1775-1847
3129
The Englishman has all the qualities of a poker except its occasional warmth.

3130
Peel's smile: like the silver plate on a coffin.

O'CONNOR Frank 1903-1966
3131
No man is as anti-feminist as a really feminine woman.

ODETS Clifford 1906-1963
3132
Sex - the poor man's polo.

O'DONNELL Emmett
3133
Retirement: statutory senility.

O'FAOLAIN Sean 1900-
3134
An Irish queer: a fellow who prefers women to drink.

OGBURN Jr. Charleton
3135
Happiness to a dog is what lies on the other side of a door.

OGILVY David 1911-
3136 *(advice to advertising copywriters)*
The consumer is not a moron; she's your wife.

O'KEEFFE John 1747-1833
3137 *The Agreeable Surprise*
Amo, amas, I love a lass,
As a cedar tall and slender;
Sweet cowslip's grace
Is her nom'native case,
And she's of the feminine gender.

3138 *The Irish Mimic*
Fat, fair and forty were all the toasts of the young men.

OLSEN Ken 1926-
3139 *(whilst President of Digital Equipment Corp 1977)*
There is no reason why anyone would want to have a computer in their home.

O'MALLEY Austin
3140
The best blood will sometimes get into a fool or a mosquito.

3141
A hole is nothing at all, but you can break your neck in it.

ONASSIS Aristotle 1906-1975
3142
The secret of business is to know something that nobody else knows.

O'NEIL Max
3143
Flirtation - attention without intention.

OPIE John 1761-1807
3144 *(asked with what he mixed his colours)*
I mix them with my brains, sir.

OPPENHEIMER J. Robert 1904-1967
3145 *(of Albert Einstein)*
Any man whose errors take ten years to correct, is quite a man.

ORBACH Susie 1946-
3146
Fat is a feminist issue.

ORCZY Baroness 1865-1947
3147 *The Scarlet Pimpernel*
We seek him here, we seek him there,
Those Frenchies seek him everywhere.
Is he in heaven? - Is he in hell?
That demmed, elusive Pimpernel?

ORTON Joe 1933-1967
3148 *Entertaining Mr Sloane*
I'd the upbringing a nun would envy ...
Until I was fifteen I was more familiar with Africa than my own body.

3149 *Entertaining Mr. Sloane*
Even if he thee worshipped with his body, his mind would be elsewhere.

3150 *Loot*
Every luxury was lavished on you - atheism, breast-feeding, circumcision.

3151 *Loot*
Policemen, like red squirrels, must be protected.

3152 *Loot*
Reading isn't an occupation we encourage among police officers. We try to keep the paper work down to a minimum.

3153 *What the Butler Saw*
You were born with your legs apart. They'll send you to the grave in a Y-shaped coffin.

ORTON William A.
3154
If you keep your mind sufficiently open, people will throw a lot of rubbish into it.

ORWELL George 1903-1950
3155 *(attributed)*
Advertising is the rattling of a stick inside a swill bucket.

3156 *Animal Farm*
Four legs good, two legs bad.

3157 *Animal Farm*
All animals are equal but some animals are more equal than others.

3158
No doubt alcohol, tobacco, and so forth, are things that a saint must avoid, but sainthood is also a thing that human beings must avoid.

3159
The great enemy of clear language is insincerity. When there is a gap between one's real and one's declared aims, one turns as if it were instinctively to long words and exhausted idioms, like a cuttlefish squirting out ink.

3160
International sport is war without shooting.

3161
Liberal - a power worshipper without power.

3162 *The Road to Wigan Pier*
The typical Socialist is ... a prim little man with a white-collar job, usually a secret teetotaller and often with vegetarian leanings, with a history of Nonconformity behind him, and, above all, with a social position which he has no intention of forfeiting.

3163 *The Road to Wigan Pier*
To the ordinary working man, the sort you would meet in any pub on Saturday night, Socialism does not mean much more than better wages and shorter hours and nobody bossing you about.

3164 *The Road to Wigan Pier*
The high-water mark, so to speak, of Socialist literature is W.H. Auden, a sort of gutless Kipling.

3165 *The Road to Wigan Pier*
We of the sinking middle class ... may sink without further struggles into the working class where we belong, and probably when we get there it will not be so dreadful as we feared, for, after all, we have nothing to lose but our aitches.

3166 *Shooting an Elephant*
Saints should always be judged guilty until they are proved innocent.

OSBORN Robert
3167
America once had the clarity of a pioneer axe.

OSBORNE John 1929-
3168 *The Entertainer*
Don't clap too hard - it's a very old building.

3169 *The Entertainer*
Thank God we're normal,
Yes, this is our finest shower!

3170 *The Entertainer*
But I have a go, lady, don't I? I'ave a go. I do.

3171 *Look Back in Anger*
His knowledge of life and ordinary human beings is so hazy, he really deserves some sort of decoration for it - a medal inscribed 'For Vaguery in the Field'.

3172 *Look Back in Anger*
I don't think one 'comes down' from Jimmy's university. According to him, it's not even red brick, but white tile.

3173 *Look Back in Anger*
They spend their time mostly looking forward to the past.

3174
Monarchy is the gold filling in the mouth of decay.

3175 *Time Present*
She's like the old line about justice - not only must be done, but must be seen to be done.

OSLER Sir William 1849-1919
3176 *Aphorisms from his Bedside Teachings*
One finger in the throat and one in the rectum makes a good diagnostician.

3177
The desire to take medicine is perhaps the greatest feature which distinguishes man from animals.

3178
One of the first duties of the physician is to educate the masses not to take medicine.

3179
Look wise, say nothing, and grunt. Speech was given to conceal thought.

3180 *Science and Immortality*
The natural man has only two primal passions, to get and beget.

3181
The Scots are the backbone of Canada. They are all right in their three vital parts - head, heart and haggis.

OTWAY Thomas 1652-1685
3182 *Venice Preserved*
No praying, it spoils business.

OVERBURY Thomas 1581-1613
3183
The man who has not anything to boast of but his illustrious ancestors is like a potato - the only good belonging to him is underground.

OVID 43 BC-AD c.17
3184 *Ars Amatoria*
It is convenient that there be gods, and, as it is convenient, let us believe that there are.

3185
Whether they give or refuse, women are glad to have been asked.

3186
Judgement of beauty can err, what with the wine and the dark.

3187
A woman is always buying something.

OWEN John c.1563-1622
3188 *Epigrams*
God and the doctor we alike adore
But only when in danger, not before;
The danger o'er, both are alike requited,
God is forgotten, and the Doctor slighted.

OWEN Robert 1771-1858
3189 *(to W. Allen)*
All the world is queer save thee and me, and even thou art a little queer.

PACHET Pierre
3190
Louis Pasteur's theory of germs is ridiculous fiction.

PADEREWSKI Ignacy Jan 1860-1941
3191
Before I was a genius I was a drudge.

PAGE Irvine H.
3192
I came, I saw, I concurred.

PAGE Shebly
3193
The number of agency people required to shoot a commercial on location is in direct proportion to the mean temperature of the location.

PAGNOL Marcel 1895-1974
3194 *Marius*
Honour is like a match, you can only use it once.

PAIGE Satchel 1906-1982
3195
(Airplanes) may kill you, but they ain't likely to hurt you.

3196
Never look behind you. Something may be gaining on you.

3197
If your stomach disputes you, lie down and pacify it with cool thoughts.

PAINE Thomas 1737-1809
3198 *(of Edmund Burke)*
As he rose like a rocket, he fell like the stick.

PALEY William 1743-1805
3199 *Principles of Moral and Political Philosophy*
Who can refute a sneer?

PALMERSTON Lord 1784-1865
3200 *(of Foreign Office handwriting)*
Iron railings leaning out of the perpendicular.

3201 *(last words)*
Die, my dear Doctor, that's the last thing I shall do!

3202 *(attributed, when asked whether English has a word for sensibilité)*
Yes we have. Humbug.

PARKER Dorothy 1893-1967
3203 *(attributed)*
If all the girls attending the Yale Prom were laid end to end, I wouldn't be at all surprised.

3204 *'Ballade of a Great Weariness'*
Scratch a lover, and find a foe.

3205 *'Comment'*
Oh, life is a glorious cycle of song,
A medley of extemporanea;
And love is a thing that can never go wrong;
And I am Marie of Roumania.

3206
It cost me never a stab nor squirm
To tread by chance upon a worm.
'Aha, my little dear' I say,
'Your clan will pay me back one day.'

3207 *'Inventory'*
Four be the things I'd been better
without:
Love, curiosity, freckles, and doubt.

3208 *(of Katherine Hepburn)*
She ran the whole gamut of the
emotions from A to B.

3209 *'Here Lies'*
And I'll stay off Verlaine too; he was
always chasing Rimbauds.

3210 *'Here Lies'*
Sorrow is tranquillity remembered in
emotion.

3211 *'News Item'*
Men seldom make passes
At girls who wear glasses.

3212
He and I had an office so tiny that an
inch smaller and it would have been
adultery.

3213 *'Résumé'*
Poisons pain you;
Rivers are damp;
Acid stains you;
And drugs cause cramp.
Guns aren't lawful;
Nooses give;
Gas smells awful;
You might as well live.

3214
I shall stay the way I am
Because I do not give a damn.

3215 *(suggested epitaph for herself)*
Excuse My Dust.

3216
There's a hell of a distance between
wisecracking and wit. Wit has truth in it;
wisecracking is simply callisthenics with
words.

3217 *'Unfortunate Coincidence'*
By the time you say you're his,
Shivering and sighing
And he vows his passion is
Infinite, undying -
Lady, make a note of this:
One of you is lying.

3218
Where's the man could ease the heart
Like a satin gown?

PARKINSON Northcote 1909-1993
3219 *Parkinson's Law*
Time spent on any item of the agenda
will be in inverse proportion to the sum
involved.

3220 *Parkinson's Law*
The man who is denied the opportunity
of taking decisions of importance begins
to regard as important the decisions he
is allowed to take.

3221 *Parkinson's Law*
Men enter local politics solely as a result
of being unhappily married.

PARNELL Thomas 1679-1718
3222
Let time that makes you homely, make
you sage.

PARR Samuel 1747-1825
3223 *(of Dr Johnson)*
Now that the old lion is dead, every ass
thinks he may kick at him.

PARRIS Matthew 1949-
3224
Being an MP feeds your vanity and
starves your self respect.

PASCAL Blaise 1623-1662
3225
Let is not be said that I have said nothing
new. The arrangement of the material is
new.

3226 *Pensées*
How vain painting is, exciting
admiration by its resemblance to things
of which we do not admire the originals.

3227 *Pensées*
Had Cleopatra's nose been shorter, the whole face of the world would have changed.

PASQUA Charles 1927-
3228
Fear of the policeman is the beginning of wisdom.

PATERSON 'Banjo' 1864-1941
3229 *'Waltzing Matilda'*
Once a jolly swagman camped by a billabong,
Under the shade of a coolibah tree;
And he sang as he watched and waited till his 'Billy' boiled:
'You'll come a waltzing, Matilda, with me.'

PATMORE Coventry 1823-1896
3230 *The Angel in the House*
'I saw you take his kiss!' ''Tis true.'
'O modesty!' ''Twas strictly kept:
He thought me asleep; at least, I knew
He thought I thought he thought I slept.'

3231 *The Angel in the House*
A woman is a foreign land,
Of which, though there he settle young,
A man will ne'er quite understand
The customs, politics and tongue.

3232 *'Olympus'*
Some dish more sharply spiced than this
Milk-soup men call domestic bliss.

PAVESE Cesare
3233
No woman marries for money; they are all clever enough, before marrying a millionaire, to fall in love with him first.

PAXMAN Jeremy 1950-
3234
It's very difficult to remain calm when you're listening to someone talking complete bollocks.

PAYN James 1830-1898
3235
I had never had a piece of toast
Particularly long and wide,
But fell upon the sanded floor,
And always on the buttered side.

PEACOCK Thomas Love 1785-1866
3236 *Melincourt*
Marriage may often be a stormy lake, but celibacy is almost always a muddy horsepond.

3237 *'The Misfortunes of Elphin'*
Not drunk is he who from the floor
Can rise alone and still drink more;
But drunk is he, who prostrate lies,
Without the power to drink or rise.

3238 *'The Misfortunes of Elphin'*
The mountain sheep are sweeter,
But the valley sheep are fatter;
We therefore deemed it meeter
To carry off the latter.

3239 *Nightmare Abbey*
Laughter is pleasant, but the exertion is too much for me.

3240 *Nightmare Abbey*
He was sent, as usual, to a public school, where a little learning was painfully beaten into him, and from thence to the university, where it was carefully taken out of him.

PEARSON Hesketh 1887-1964
3241 *Common Misquotations*
Misquotation is, in fact, the pride and privilege of the learned. A widely-read man never quotes accurately, for the rather obvious reason that he has read too widely.

3242 *The Pilgrim Daughters*
There is no stronger craving in the world than that of the rich for titles, except perhaps that of the titled for riches.

PEARSON Lester 1897-1972
3243 *(defining attitude toward U.S.)*
The situation is one something like living with your wife. Sometimes it is difficult and even irritating to live with her, but it is always impossible to live without her.

PEARSON Maryon
3244
Behind every great man there is a surprised woman.

PEEL Paul
3245
It is no rest to be idle.

PEELE George c.1556-1596
3246 *The Hunting of Cupid*
What thing is love for (well I wot) love is
a thing.
It is a prick, it is a sting,
It is a pretty, pretty thing;
It is a fire, it is a coal
Whose flame creeps in at every hole.

PEMBROKE Henry Herbert, 10th Earl of
1734-1794
3247
Dr Johnson's sayings would not appear
so extraordinary, were it not for his bow-
wow way.

PENDENYS Arthur 1865-1946
3248
A good meal makes a man feel more
charitable toward the whole world than
any sermon.

PENN William 1644-1718
3249
Avoid popularity; it has many snares,
and no real benefit.

3250 *Some Fruits of Solitude*
Men are generally more careful of the
breed of their horses and dogs than of
their children.

PEPYS Samuel 1633-1703
3251 *Diary*
I went out to Charing Cross, to see
Major-general Harrison hanged, drawn,
and quartered; which was done there, he
looking as cheerful as any man could do
in that condition.

3252 *Diary*
If ever I was foxed it was now.

3253 *Diary*
But methought it lessened my esteem of
a king, that he should not be able to
command the rain.

3254 *Diary*
I see it is impossible for the King to have
things done as cheap as other men.

3255 *Diary*
Strange to see how a good dinner and
feasting reconciles everybody.

3256 *Diary*
Strange to say what delight we married
people have to see these poor fools
decoyed into our condition.

PERCIVAL Lloyd
3257
The physically fit can enjoy their vices.

PERELMAN S.J. 1904-1979
3258
There is such a thing as too much couth.

3259 *Quotations for Speakers and Writers*
Love is not the dying moan of a distant
violin - it's the triumphant twang of a
bedspring.

PERRY Jimmy
3260 *'Who do you think you are kidding,
Mister Hitler'*
Who do you think you are kidding,
Mister Hitler?
If you think we're on the run?
We are the boys who will stop your little
game
We are the boys who will make you think
again.

PÉTAIN Henri Philippe 1856-1951
3261
To write one's memoirs is to speak ill of
everybody except oneself.

PETER Irene
3262
Ignorance is no excuse, it's the real thing.

PETER Laurence 1910-1990
3263
The cave-dweller's wife complained that
he hadn't dragged her anywhere in
months.

3264
Early to bed, early to rise, work like hell,
and advertise.

3265 *The Peter Principle*
In a hierarchy every employee tends to
rise to his level of incompetence.

3266
Psychiatry enables us to correct our faults by confessing our parents' shortcomings.

3267
When I want your opinion I'll give it to you.

3268
Work is accomplished by those employees who have not yet reached their level of incompetence.

PETROWSKY Christina
3269
Autumn is the bite of a harvest apple.

PETTITO Anthony J.
3270
The best way to bring up some children is short.

PFIZER Beryl
3271
A little public scandal is good once in a while - takes the tension out of the news.

3272
I wonder what language truck drivers are using, now that everyone is using theirs?

PHELPS Edward John 1822-1900
3273
The man who makes no mistakes does not usually make anything.

PHELPS William Lyon
3274
This is the final test of a gentleman: his respect for those who can be of no possible service to him.

PHILIP Prince, Duke of Edinburgh
1921-
3275
I think our children have all done rather well under very demanding circumstances.

3276
When a man opens the car door for his wife, it's either a new car or a new wife.

PHILLIPS H.I. 1887-1965
3277
Oratory: the art of making deep noises from the chest sound like important messages from the brain.

PHILLIPS Wendell 1811-1884
3278
One on God's side is a majority.

3279
We live under a government of men and morning newspapers.

3280
Every man meets his Waterloo at last.

PICASSO Pablo 1881-1973
3281
God is really only another artist. He invented the giraffe, the elephant, and the cat. He has no real style. He just goes on trying other things.

3282
It takes a long time to become young.

PINERO Sir Arthur Wing 1855-1934
3283
How many 'coming men' has one known? Where on earth do they all go to?

3284 *Second Mrs Tanqueray*
From forty to fifty a man is at heart either a stoic or a satyr.

3285 *Second Mrs Tanqueray*
I love fruit, when it is expensive.

PINTER Harold 1930-
3286 *The Homecoming*
Apart from the known and the unknown, what else is there?

3287
One way of looking at speech is to say it is a constant stratagem to cover nakedness.

3288 *(on being asked what his plays were about)*
The weasel under the cocktail cabinet.

PIRSIG Robert M. 1928-
3289 *Zen and the Art of Motorcycle Maintenance*
That's the classical mind at work, runs fine inside but looks dingy on the surface.

PIUS VII Pope 1742-1823
3290 *(attempting to reach an agreement with Napoleon)*
We are prepared to go to the gates of Hell - but no further.

PLATO 429-347 BC
3291
I have hardly ever known a mathematician who was capable of reasoning.

3292
When the mind is thinking, it is talking to itself.

PLAUTUS c.250-184 BC
3293
Always bring money along with your complaints.

PLOMER William 1903-1973
3294 *'Mews Flat Mona'*
On a sofa upholstered in panther skin
Mona did researches in original sin.

3295 *'Playboy of the Demi-World: 1938'*
A rose-red sissy half as old as time.

PLOMIN Professor Robert
3296 *(on how to have gifted children)*
Marry an intelligent person.

PLUTARCH AD c.46-c.120
3297
It is a hard matter, my fellow citizens, to argue with the belly, since it has no ears.

POGREBIN Letty Cottin
3298
Boys don't make passes at female smart-asses.

3299
No labourer in the world is expected to work for room, board, and love - except the housewife.

POLLARD J.G.
3300
Executive ability is deciding quickly and getting somebody else to do the work.

POLLOCK Channing
3301
A critic is a legless man who teaches running.

3302
Marriage is a great institution, and no family should be without it.

POMERANTZ Hart
3303
To some lawyers, all facts are created equal.

POMFRET John 1667-1702
3304 *'Reason'*
We live and learn, but not the wiser grow.

POPE Alexander 1688-1744
3305
Alive, ridiculous, and dead forgot?

3306 *'Epigram: You beat your pate'*
You beat your pate, and fancy wit will come:
Knock as you please, there's nobody at home.

3307 *'Epigram from the French'*
Sir, I admit your gen'ral rule
That every poet is a fool:
But you yourself may serve to show it,
That every fool is not a poet.

3308 *'An Epistle to Dr Arbuthnot'*
Shut, shut the door, good John! fatigued I said,
Tie up the knocker, say I'm sick, I'm dead,
The dog-star rages!

3309 *Epistles to Several Persons 'To a Lady'*
Still round and round the ghosts of Beauty glide,
And haunt the places where their honour died.
See how the world its veterans rewards!
A youth of frolics, and old age of cards.

3310 *Epistles to Several Persons 'To a Lady'*
And mistress of herself, though china fall.

3311 *Epistles to Several Persons 'To Lord Bathurst'*
Who shall decide, when doctors disagree.

3312 *Epistles to Several Persons 'To Lord Bathurst'*
But thousands die, without or this or that,
Die, and endow a college, or a cat.

3313 *An Essay on Criticism*
As some to church repair,
Not for the doctrine, but the music there.

3314 *An Essay on Criticism*
The bookful blockhead, ignorantly read,
With loads of learned lumber in his head.

3315 *An Essay on Man*
Why has not man a microscopic eye?
For this plain reason, man is not a fly.

3316 *To George, Lord Lyttelton*
Here am I, dying of a hundred good symptoms.

3317 *Imitations of Horace*
Get place and wealth, if possible, with grace;
If not, by any means get wealth and place.

3318 *Imitations of Horace*
The worst of madmen is a saint run mad.

3319 *Imitations of Horace*
But those who cannot write, and those who can,
All rhyme, and scrawl, and scribble, to a man.

3320 *Miscellanies*
To endeavour to work upon the vulgar with fine sense, is like attempting to hew blocks with a razor.

3321 *Miscellanies*
A man should never be ashamed to own he has been in the wrong, which is but saying, in other words, that he is wiser to-day than he was yesterday.

3322 *Miscellanies*
It is with narrow-souled people as with narrow-necked bottles: the less they have in them, the more noise they make in pouring it out.

3323
I never knew any man in my life who could not bear another's misfortunes perfectly like a Christian.

3324 *The Rape of the Lock*
If to her share some female errors fall,
Look on her face, and you'll forget 'em all.

3325 *The Rape of the Lock*
Not louder shrieks to pitying heav'n are cast,
When husbands or when lapdogs breathe their last.

PORTER Cole 1891-1964
3326 *'Anything Goes'*
In olden days a glimpse of stocking
Was looked on as something shocking
Now, heaven knows,
Anything goes.

3327 *'Well, Did You Evah?'*
Have you heard it's in the stars,
Next July we collide with Mars?
Well, did your evah! What a swell party this is.

3328 *'You're the Top'*
You're the top! You're the Coliseum,
You're the top! You're the Louvre Museum,
You're a melody
From a symphony by Strauss,
You're a Bendel bonnet,
A Shakespeare sonnet,
You're Mickey Mouse!

POTTER Beatrix 1866-1943
3329 *The Tailor of Gloucester*
I am worn to a ravelling ... I am undone and worn to a thread-paper, for I have NO MORE TWIST.

3330 *The Tale of the Flopsy Bunnies*
It is said that the effect of eating too much lettuce is 'soporific'.

3331 *The Tale of Peter Rabbit*
Don't go into Mr McGregor's garden: your father had an accident there, he was put into a pie by Mrs McGregor.

POTTER Stephen 1900-1969
3332 *Lifemanship*
How to be one up - how to make the other man feel that something has gone wrong, however slightly.

3333 *One-Upmanship (on wine-tasting)*
A good general rule is to state that the bouquet is better than the taste, and vice versa.

POTTER David E. 1943-
3334
Human beings are not born with a chair stuck to their backsides, and the afterbirth isn't a PC. It is a condition of the human being that he is mobile.

POUND Ezra 1885-1972
3335 *'Ancient Music'*
Winter is icummen in,
Lhude sing Goddamm,
Raineth drop and staineth slop,
And how the wind doth ramm!
Sing: Goddamm.

3336 *'Cino'*
Bah! I have sung women in three cities,
But it is all the same;
And I will sing of the sun.

3337 *Draft of XXX Cantos*
Hang it all, Robert Browning,
There can be but the one 'Sordello'.

POWELL Anthony 1905-
3338 *The Acceptance World*
He fell in love with himself at first sight and it is a passion to which he has always remained faithful.

3339 *The Acceptance World*
Dinner at the Huntercombes' possessed only two dramatic features - the wine was a farce and the food a tragedy.

3340 *A Question of Upbringing*
He's so wet you could shoot snipe off him.

3341 *Temporary Kings*
Growing old is like being increasingly penalised for a crime you haven't committed.

POWELL Enoch 1912-1998
3342
A little nonsense now and then is not a bad thing. Where would we politicians be if we were not allowed to talk it sometimes?

3343
A plumber who has Latin is a better plumber than one who does not.

3344
For a politician to complain about the press is like a ship's captain complaining about the sea.

3345
A politician crystallises what most people mean, even if they don't know it.

PRAED W.M. 1802-1839
3346 *The Chant of the Brazen Head*
I think that nought is worth a thought,
And I'm a fool for thinking.

3347 *Goodnight to the Season*
The ice of her Ladyship's manners,
The ice of his Lordship's champagne.

3348 *'The Talented Man'*
Of science and logic he chatters
As fine and as fast as he can;
Though I am no judge of such matters,
I'm sure he's a talented man.

PRESTON Keith 1884-1927
3349 *'The Liberators'*
Of all the literary scenes
Saddest this sight to me:
The graves of little magazines
Who died to make verse free.

PRÉVERT Jacques 1900-1977
3350 *'Pater Noster'*
Our Father which art in heaven
Stay there
And we will stay on earth
Which is sometimes so pretty.

PRIESTLEY J.B. 1894-1984
3351
I don't like baths. I don't enjoy them in the slightest and, if I could, I'd prefer to go around dirty.

3352
Any fool can be fussy and rid himself of energy all over the place, but a man has to have something in him before he can settle down to do nothing.

3353
God can stand being told by Professor Ayer and Marghanita Laski that He doesn't exist.

3354 *Good Companions*
To say that these men paid their shillings to watch twenty-two hirelings kick a ball is merely to say that a violin is wood and catgut, that *Hamlet* is so much paper and ink. For a shilling the Bruddersford United AFC offered you Conflict and Art.

3355 *Saturn Over the Water*
I can't help feeling wary when I hear anything said about the masses. First you take their faces from 'em by calling 'em the masses and then you accuse 'em of not having any faces.

3356
I sometimes wish they would swagger more now, buy bigger overcoats and wilder hats, and retain those traces of make-up that put them outside respectability and keep them rogues and vagabonds, which is what, at heart - bless 'em - they are.

PRIOR Matthew 1664-1721
3357 *'A Better Answer'*
I court others in verse: but I love thee in prose:
And they have my whimsies, but thou hast my heart.

3358 *'To a Child of Quality of Five Years Old'*
For, as our different ages move,
'Tis so ordained (would Fate but mend it!)
That I shall be past making love,
When she begins to comprehend it.

3359 *'An English Padlock'*
Be to her virtues very kind;
Be to her faults a little blind;
Let all her ways be unconfined;
And clap your padlock - on her mind.

3360 *'Epitaph'*
Nobles and heralds, by your leave,
Here lies what once was Matthew Prior,
The son of Adam and of Eve,
Can Stuart or Nassau go higher?

3361
He's half absolv'd
Who has confess'd.

3362 *'Paolo Purganti and his Wife'*
The doctor understood the call;
But had not always wherewithal.

3363 *'Upon this Passage in Scaligerana'*
They never taste who always drink;
They always talk, who never think.

3364 *'The Remedy Worse than the Disease'*
Cured yesterday of my disease,
I died last night of my physician.

3365 *'Solomon'*
What is a King? - a man condemned to bear
The public burden of the nation's care.

3366 *'A True Maid'*
No, no; for my virginity,
When I lose that, says Rose, I'll die:
Behind the elms last night, cried Dick,
Rose, were you not extremely sick?

PRITCHETT V.S. 1900-1997
3367 *The Living Novel*
The principle of procrastinated rape is said to be the ruling one in all the great best-sellers.

3368
The mark of genius is an incessant activity of mind. Genius is a spiritual greed.

3369
Those mausoleums of inactive masculinity are places for men who prefer armchairs to women.

3370
A natural New Yorker is a native of the present tense.

3371
Queen Victoria - a mixture of national landlady and actress.

3372
The State, that cawing rookery of committees and subcommittees.

PROUST Marcel 1871-1922
3373 *Cities of the Plain*
'Anyhow,' Mme de Cambremer went on, 'I have a horror of sunsets, they're so romantic, so operatic.'

3374
Let us leave pretty women to men without imagination.

3375 *Time Regained*
One of those telegrams of which M. de Guermantes had wittily fixed the formula: 'Cannot come, lie follows'.

PROVERBS and SAYINGS
3376 *African*
When elephants fight it is the grass that suffers.

3377
All would live long, but none would be old.

3378 *American Indian*
Listen or thy tongue will keep thee deaf.

3379 *American Indian*
Never criticize a man until you've walked a mile in his moccasins.

3380 *Arab*
Throw a lucky man into the sea, and he will come up with a fish in his mouth.

3381 *Arab*
The sinning is the best part of repentance.

3382 *Australian Aboriginal*
Hypocrite - mouth one way, belly 'nother way.

3383 *Belgian*
Experience is the comb that Nature gives us when we are bald.

3384 *Chinese*
If heaven made him, earth can find some use for him.

3385 *Chinese*
One dog barks at something, the rest bark at him.

3386 *Chinese*
To be uncertain is to be uncomfortable, but to be certain is to be ridiculous.

3387 *Chinese*
If you don't want anyone to know it, don't do it.

3388 *Colombian*
He who must die must die in the dark, even though he sells candles.

3389 *Czechoslovakian*
When you buy, use your eyes and your mind, not your ears.

3390 *Dutch*
God does not pay weekly, but he pays at the end.

3391 *Dutch*
A handful of patience is worth more than a bushel of brains.

3392 *Dutch*
God made the ocean, but the Dutch made Holland.

3393 *English*
A Scotch mist may wet an Englishman to the skin.

3394 *English*
Affectation is a greater enemy to the face than smallpox.

3395 *English*
We are usually the best men when in the worst health.

3396 *English*
As old as the itch.

3397 *English*
A man of words and not of deeds,
Is like a garden full of weeds.

3398 *English*
One of these days is none of these days.

3399 *English*
There is but an hour a day between a good housewife and a bad one.

3400 *French*
He who can lick can bite.

3401 *French*
The price spoils the pleasure.

3402 *French*
The worst is not always certain but it's very likely.

3403 *French*
A good meal ought to begin with hunger.

3404 *French*
There is no such thing as a pretty good omelette.

3405 *French*
Only great men may have great faults.

3406 *French*
With enough 'ifs' we could put Paris into a bottle.

3407 *French*
There is one who kisses, and the other who offers a cheek.

3408 *French*
A father is a banker provided by nature.

3409 *German*
God gives the nuts, but he does not crack them.

3410 *German*
Old birds are hard to pluck.

3411 *German*
When the fox preaches, look to your geese.

3412 *German*
Invalids live longest.

3413 *German*
The eyes believe themselves; the ears believe other people.

3414 *German*
Better silent than stupid.

3415 *Hindu*
An arch never sleeps.

3416 *Hindu*
If you ask the hungry man how much is two and two, he replies four loaves.

3417 *Hindu*
Dictators ride to and fro upon tigers from which they dare not dismount.

3418 *Hottentot*
Good is when I steal other people's wives and cattle; bad is when they steal mine.

3419
An indecent mind is a perpetual feast.

3420 *Irish*
Better be quarrelling than lonesome.

3421 *Irish*
Every invalid is a physician.

3422 *Irish*
Money swore an oath that nobody who did not love it should ever have it.

3423 *Irish*
A dimple in the chin; a devil within.

3424 *Irish*
Seeing's believing - but feeling is God's own truth.

3425 *Italian*
He that jokes confesses.

3426 *Italian*
Below the navel there is neither religion nor truth.

3427 *Italian*
Since the house is on fire let us warm ourselves.

3428 *Japanese*
The go-between wears out a thousand sandals.

3429 *Japanese*
The nail that sticks out is hammered down.

3430 *Jewish*
Worries go down better with soup than without.

3431 *Jewish*
Make sure to send a lazy man for the Angel of Death.

3432 *Jewish*
The innkeeper loves the drunkard, but not for a son-in-law.

3433 *Jewish*
The poor schlemiel is a man who falls on his back and breaks his nose.

3434 *Jewish*
Good men need no recommendation and bad men it wouldn't help.

3435 *Jewish*
The hardest work is to go idle.

3436 *Jewish*
Truth is the safest lie.

3437 *Jewish*
A half-truth is a whole lie.

3438 *Jewish*
You can't force anyone to love you or to lend you money.

3439 *Jewish*
With money in your pocket, you are wise, and you are handsome, and you sing well too.

3440 *Jewish*
If the rich could hire other people to die for them, the poor would make a wonderful living.

3441 *Jewish*
God could not be everywhere and therefore he made mothers.

3442 *Jewish*
'For example' is not proof.

3443 *Jewish*
Do not make yourself so big. You are not so small.

3444 *Jewish*
Sleep faster, we need the pillows.

3445 *Korean*
Where there are no tigers, a wildcat is very self-important.

3446 *Lancashire*
Shake a bridle over a Yorkshireman's grave, and he'll rise and steal a horse.

3447 *Latvian*
A smiling face is half the meal.

3448 *Malay*
Don't think there are no crocodiles because the water is calm.

3449 *Medieval*
It is better to be than not to be.

3450 *Medieval*
A good man and a good citizen are not the same thing.

3451 *Moroccan*
None but a mule deserves his family.

3452 *Nigerian*
When the mouse laughs at the cat there's a hole nearby.

3453 *Persian*
If fortune turns against you, even jelly breaks your tooth.

3454 *Polish*
Even were a cook to cook a fly, he would keep the breast for himself.

3455 *Polish*
Fish, to taste right, must swim three times - in water, in butter and in wine.

3456 *Polish*
The greater love is a mother's; then comes a dog's; then a sweetheart's.

3457 *Portuguese*
Visits always give pleasure - if not the arrival, the departure.

3458 *Russian*
Don't buy the house; buy the neighbourhood.

3459 *Russian*
If you were born lucky, even your rooster will lay eggs.

3460 *Russian*
Gossip needs no carriage.

3461 *Russian*
The rich would have to eat money, but luckily the poor provide food.

3462 *Scottish*
The Devil's boots don't creak.

3463 *Scottish*
What may be done at any time will be done at no time.

3464 *Siberian*
June's too soon, July's too late - for summer.

3465 *Spanish*
You can't have more bugs than a blanketful.

3466 *Spanish*
Don't offer me advice, give me money.

3467 *Spanish*
Drink nothing without seeing it; sign nothing without reading it.

3468 *Spanish*
Whoever gossips to you will gossip of you.

3469 *Spanish*
How beautiful it is to do nothing, and then rest afterward.

3470 *Spanish*
Tomorrow is often the busiest day of the year.

3471 *Spanish*
Woe to the house where the hen crows and the rooster keeps still.

3472 *Spanish*
An ounce of mother is worth a pound of clergy.

3473 *Spanish*
If I die, I forgive you: if I recover, we shall see.

3474 *Spanish*
When three people call you an ass, put on a bridle.

3475 *Spanish*
Speaking without thinking is shooting without taking aim.

3476
The tongue ever turns to the aching tooth.

3477 *Yiddish*
If you can't bite, don't show your teeth.

3478 *Zen*
A beautiful woman who is pleasing to men is good only for frightening fish when she falls into the water.

PUNCH 1841-1992
3479
Advice to persons about to marry - 'Don't'.

3480
It ain't the 'unting as 'urts 'im, it's the 'ammer, 'ammer, 'ammer along the 'ard 'igh road.

3481
It appears the Americans have taken umbrage.
The deuce they have!
Whereabouts is that?

3482
Botticelli isn't a wine, you Juggins!
Botticelli's a *cheese*!

3483
Go directly - see what she's doing, and tell her she mustn't.

3484
The Half-Way House to Rome, Oxford.

3485
I am not hungry; but thank goodness, I am greedy.

3486
I'm afraid you've got a bad egg, Mr Jones.
Oh no, my Lord, I assure you! Parts of it are excellent!

3487
Look here, Steward, if this is coffee, I want tea; but if this is tea, then I wish for coffee.

3488
Nearly all our best men are dead! Carlyle, Tennyson, Browning, George Eliot! - I'm not feeling very well myself.

3489
I never read books - I *write* them.

3490
Never do today what you can put off till tomorrow.

3491
Nothink for nothink 'ere, and precious little for sixpence.

3492
There was an old owl lived in an oak
The more he heard, the less he spoke;
The less he spoke, the more he heard
O, if men were all like that wise bird!

3493
You pays your money and you takes your choice.

3494
I used your soap two years ago; since then I have used no other.

3495
Sometimes I sits and thinks, and then again I just sits.

3496
What is Matter? - Never mind.
What is Mind? - No matter.

3497
What is better than presence of mind in a railway accident? Absence of body.

3498
What sort of a doctor is he?
Oh well, I don't know very much about his ability; but he's got a very good bedside manner!

3499
It's worse than wicked, my dear, it's vulgar.

PYM Barbara 1913-1980
3500 *Jane and Prudence*
It is better taste somehow that a man should be unfaithful to his wife away from home.

3501 *Less than Angels*
She experienced all the cosiness and irritation which can come from living with thoroughly nice people with whom one has nothing in common.

QUILLER-COUCH Sir Arthur (Q) 1863-1944
3502 *'Lady Jane. Sapphics'*
Simple this tale! - but delicately perfumed

As the sweet roadside honeysuckle.
That's why,
Difficult though its metre was to tackle,
I'm glad I wrote it.

QUINE W.V.O. 1908-
3503 *Theories and Things*
Students of the heavens are separable into astronomers and astrologers as readily as are the minor domestic ruminants into sheep and goats, but the separation of philosophers into sages and cranks seems to be more sensitive to frames of reference.

QUINTILIAN AD 42-118
3504
A liar should have a good memory.

3505
The obscurity of a writer is generally in proportion to his incapacity.

RABELAIS François c.1494-c.1553
3506 *Gargantua*
The appetite grows by eating.

3507 *Gargantua*
I drink for the thirst to come.

3508 *(attributed last words)*
I am going to seek a great perhaps ...
Bring down the curtain, the farce is played out.

3509
I never sleep in comfort save when I am hearing a sermon or praying to God.

3510
There are more old drunkards than old physicians.

RADFORD Arthur William 1896-1973
3511
A decision is the action an executive must take when he has information so incomplete that the answer does not suggest itself.

RADNER Gilda
3512
I can always be distracted by love, but eventually I get horny for my creativity.

RAE Bob
3513
Forgiving is all; forgetting is another
thing.

RALEGH Sir Walter 1552-1618
3514 *(on feeling the edge of the axe at his
execution)*
'Tis a sharp remedy, but a sure one for all
ills.

RALEIGH Sir Walter Alexander 1861-
1922
3515 *'Stans Puer ad Mensam'*
Eat slowly: only men in rags
And gluttons old in sin
Mistake themselves for carpet bags
And tumble victuals in.

3516 *'Wishes of an Elderly Man'*
I wish I loved the Human Race;
I wish I loved its silly face;
I wish I liked the way it walks;
I wish I liked the way it talks;
And when I'm introduced to one
I wish I thought *What Jolly Fun!*

RANDALL Stanley J.
3517
The closest to perfection a person ever
comes is when he fills out a job
application form.

RANKIN Ruth
3518
The government is concerned about the
population explosion, and the
population is concerned about the
government explosion.

RANSOM John Crowe 1888-1974
3519 *'Here Lies a Lady'*
Here lies a lady of beauty and high
degree.
Of chills and fever she died, of fever and
chills,
The delight of her husband, her aunts,
an infant of three,
And of medicos marvelling sweetly on
her ills.

RAPHAEL Frederic 1931-
3520 *Darling*
Your idea of fidelity is not having more
than one man in bed at the same time.

3521
Truth may be stranger than fiction, but
fiction is truer.

RAPSON Ralph
3522
Develop an infallible technique and then
place yourself at the mercy of
inspiration.

RATNER Gerald 1949-
3523
We even sell a pair of earrings for under
£1, which is cheaper than a prawn
sandwich from Marks & Spencers. But I
have to say the earrings probably won't
last as long.

RATTIGAN Terence 1911-1977
3524 *Separate Tables*
You can be in the Horseguards and still
be common, dear.

RAVERAT Gwen 1885-1957
3525 *Period Piece*
Ladies were ladies in those days; they did
not do things themselves.

RAY John 1628-1705
3526
The honester the man, the worse luck.

RAYBURN Sam 1882-1961
3527
Any jackass can kick down a barn, but it
takes a good carpenter to build one.

RAYMOND F.J.
3528
Next to being shot at and missed,
nothing is quite as satisfying as an
income tax refund.

REAGAN Ronald 1911-
3529
Middle age is when you're faced with two
temptations and you choose the one that
will get you home by nine o'clock.

3530
Politics is supposed to be the second
oldest profession. I have come to realize
that it bears a very close resemblance to
the first.

3531
You can tell a lot about a fellow's character by his way of eating jellybeans.

REED Henry 1914-1986
3532 *Emily Butler*
I think it may justly be said that English women in general are very common diatonic little numbers.

3533 *A Very Great Man Indeed*
Modest? My word no ... He was an all-the-lights-on man.

3534 *A Very Great Man Indeed*
I have known her pass the whole evening without mentioning a single book, or *in fact anything unpleasant*, at all.

3535 *Private Life of Hilda Tablet*
And the sooner the tea's out of the way, the sooner we can get out the gin, eh?

REED Rex
3536
In Hollywood, if you don't have happiness, you send out for it.

REEVE Christopher
3537 *in Superman*
"I never drink when I fly."

REGER Max 1873-1916
3538
I am sitting in the smallest room in my house. I have your review in front of me. Soon it will be behind me.

REIK Theodor 1888-1969
3539
Even the wisest men make fools of themselves about women, and even the most foolish women are wise about men.

REINHARDT Adina
3540
Art disease is caused by a hardening of the categories.

REINHARDT Gottfried
3541
Money is good for bribing yourself through the inconveniences of life.

RENARD Jules 1864-1910
3542
I am afraid I shall not find Him, but I shall still look for Him. If He exists, He may be appreciative of my efforts.

3543
A cold in the head causes less suffering than an idea.

3544
Failure is not our only punishment for laziness: there is also the success of others.

3545
Les bourgeois, ce sont les autres.
The bourgeois are other people.

3546
I have a remarkable memory; I forget everything. It is wonderfully convenient. It is as though the world were constantly renewing itself for me.

RENOIR Pierre Auguste 1841-1919
3547 *(attributed)*
I paint with my prick. (possibly an inversion of 'It's with my brush, that I make love')

3548
A painter who has the feel of breasts and buttocks is saved.

RICE Tim 1944-
3549 *Jesus Christ Superstar 'Herod's Song'*
Prove to me that you're no fool,
Walk across my swimming pool.

RICHARDS Rebecca
3550
Oh, to be only half as wonderful as my child thought I was when he was small, and only half as stupid as my teenager now thinks I am.

RICHARDSON Justin
3551
If only I hadn't had sisters
How much more romantic I'd be
But my sisters were such little blisters
That all women are sisters to me.

RICHLER Mordecai 1931-
3552
Listen your Lordship, I'm a respecter of institutions. Even in Paris, I remained a

Canadian. I puffed hashish, but I didn't inhale.

3553
There are ten commandments, right? Well, it's like an exam. You get eight out of ten, you're just about top of the class.

3554
Wherever I travel, I'm too late. The orgy has moved elsewhere.

RICHTER Hans 1843-1916
3555 *(attributed)*
Up with your damned nonsense will I put twice, or perhaps once, but sometimes always, by God, never.

RICHTER Jean Paul 1763-1825
3556
Sleep, riches and health to be truly enjoyed must be interrupted.

3557
A variety of nothing is superior to a monotony of something.

RIDDING George 1828-1904
3558
I feel a feeling which I feel you all feel.

RIIS Sharon
3559
Basically, I'm interested in friendship, sex and death.

RIMBAUD Arthur 1854-1891
3560 *'Ma Bohème'*
I was walking along, hands in holey pockets; my overcoat also was entering the realms of the ideal.

RIVAROL Antoine de 1753-1801
3561
What is not clear is not French.

ROADE W. Winwood
3562
Men prefer to believe that they are degenerated angels, rather than elevated apes.

ROBBINS Leonard H.
3563
How a minority,
Reaching majority,
Seizing authority,
Hates a minority!

ROBINSON James Harvey 1863-1935
3564
We find it hard to believe that other people's thoughts are as silly as our own, but they probably are.

ROCHE Sir Boyle 1743-1807
3565 *(attributed)*
Mr Speaker, I smell a rat; I see him forming in the air and darkening the sky; but I'll nip him in the bud.

ROCHESTER John Wilmot, Earl of 1647-1680
3566 *'The King's Epitaph' (Charles II)*
Here lies a great and mighty king
Whose promise none relies on;
He never said a foolish thing,
Nor ever did a wise one.

ROCKNE Knute 1888-1931
3567
Show me a good and gracious loser, and I'll show you a failure.

ROGERS Samuel 1763-1855
3568 *(attributed)*
A man who attempts to read all the new productions must do as the fleas do - skip.

3569 *Table Talk*
Sheridan was listened to with such attention that you might have heard a pin drop.

3570 *Table Talk*
It doesn't much signify whom one marries, for one is sure to find next morning that it was someone else.

ROGERS Thorold 1823-1890
3571
See, ladling butter from alternate tubs
Stubbs butters Freeman, Freeman butters Stubbs.

ROGERS Will 1879-1935
3572
We are all here for a spell, get all the good laughs you can.

3573
Well, all I know is what I read in the papers.

3574 *Autobiography*
There is only one thing that can kill the movies, and that is education.

3575
You can't say civilization don't advance, however, for in every war they kill you in a new way.

3576
A difference of opinion is what makes horse racing and missionaries.

3577
Don't gamble; take all your savings and buy some good stock and hold it till it goes up, then sell it. If it don't go up, don't buy it.

3578
Everybody is ignorant, only on different subjects.

3579
Half our life is spent trying to find something to do with the time we have rushed through life trying to save.

3580
This thing of being a hero, about the main thing to it is to know when to die.

3581
Being a hero is about the shortest-lived profession on earth.

3582
A holding company is the people you give your money to while you're being searched.

3583 *The Illiterate Digest*
The more you read and observe about this Politics thing, you got to admit that each party is worse than the other.

3584 *The Illiterate Digest*
Everthing is funny as long as it is happening to Somebody Else.

3585
I'm not a member of any organized party, I'm a Democrat.

3586
The income tax has made more liars out of the American people than golf has. Even when you make a tax form out on the level, you don't know when it's through, if you are a crook or a martyr.

3587
If you ever injected truth into politics you would have no politics.

3588
Invest in inflation. It's the only thing going up.

3589
More men have been elected between Sundown and Sun-up than ever were elected between Sun-up and Sundown.

3590
Politics has got so expensive that it takes lots of money to even get beat with.

3591
One revolution is like one cocktail, it just gets you organized for the next.

3592
The schools ain't what they used to be and never was.

3593
Be thankful we're not getting all the government we're paying for.

3594 *Weekly Articles*
Communism is like prohibition, it's a good idea but it won't work.

3595
It isn't what we don't know that gives us trouble, it's what we know that ain't so.

3596
When you put down the good things you ought to have done, and leave out the bad things you did do - well, that's memoirs.

ROHE Mies Van der 1886-1969
3597
Architecture begins when you place two bricks *carefully* together.

ROONEY Mickey
3598
You always pass failure on the way to success.

ROOSEVELT Eleanor 1884-1962
3599
No one can make you feel inferior without your consent.

ROOSEVELT Franklin D. 1882-1945
3600
I have no expectation of making a hit every time I come to bat.

3601
I think we consider too much the good luck of the early bird, and not enough the bad luck of the early worm.

ROOSEVELT Theodore 1858-1919
3602
I am only an average man, but, by George, I work harder at it than the average man.

3603
There is no room in this country for hyphenated Americanism.

3604
The most successful politician is he who says what everybody is thinking most often and in the loudest voice.

ROSE Billy 1899-1966
3605
Never invest your money in anything that eats or needs repairing.

ROSENBERG Leo
3606
First you forget names, then you forget faces, then you forget to pull your zipper up, then you forget to pull your zipper down.

ROSSETTI Dante Gabriel 1828-1882
3607
The worst moment for the atheist is when he is really thankful, and has nobody to thank.

ROSSINI Gioacchino 1792-1868
3608
Give me a laundry-list and I'll set it to music.

3609
How wonderful opera would be if there were no singers.

3610
One cannot judge 'Lohengrin' from a first hearing, and I certainly do not intend to hear it a second time.

3611
Wagner has lovely moments but awful quarters of an hour.

ROSTAND Edmond 1868-1918
3612 *Cyrano de Bergerac*
A large nose is in fact the sign of an affable man, good, courteous, witty, liberal, courageous, such as I am.

ROSTAND Jean 1894-1977
3613 *Le Mariage*
A married couple are well suited when both partners usually feel the need for a quarrel at the same time.

3614 *Pensées d'un biologiste*
Kill a man, and you are an assassin. Kill millions of men, and you are a conqueror. Kill everyone, and you are a god.

3615
My pessimism goes to the point of suspecting the sincerity of the pessimists.

ROSTEN Leo 1908-
3616 *(of W.C. Fields)*
Any man who hates dogs and babies can't be all bad.

ROTH Philip 1933-
3617 *Portnoy's Complaint*
A Jewish man with parents alive is a fifteen-year-old boy, and will remain a fifteen-year-old boy until *they die!*

3618 *Portnoy's Complaint*
Doctor, my doctor, what do you say, LET'S PUT THE ID BACK IN YID!

ROTHSCHILD Baron 1840-1915
3619
It isn't enough for you to love money - it's also necessary that money should love you.

ROTSTEIN Abraham
3620
Every dogma has its day.

ROTTEN Johnny
3621
Love is two minutes and fifty seconds of squelching.

ROUPELL Charles
3622 *(attributed)*
To play billiards well is a sign of an ill-spent youth.

ROUSSEAU Jean-Jacques 1712-1778
3623
Happiness: a good bank account, a good cook and a good digestion.

ROUTH Martin Joseph 1755-1854
3624 *(attributed)*
You will find it a very good practice always to verify your references, sir!

ROUX Joseph
3625
Science is for those who learn; poetry for those who know.

ROWAN Carl T. 1925-
3626
A minority group has 'arrived' only when it has the right to produce some fools and scoundrels without the entire group paying for it.

ROWE Nicholas 1674-1718
3627 *The Fair Penitent*
Is this that haughty, gallant, gay Lothario?

ROWLAND Helen 1875-1950
3628
Failing to be there when a man wants her is a woman's greatest sin, except to be there when he doesn't want her.

3629 *A Guide to Men*
A husband is what is left of a lover, after the nerve has been extracted.

3630 *A Guide to Men*
Somehow a bachelor never quite gets over the idea that he is a thing of beauty and a boy forever.

3631 *A Guide to Men*
The follies which a man regrets most in his life, are those which he didn't commit when he had the opportunity.

3632
In olden times, sacrifices were made at the altar, a practice which is still very much practised.

3633 *Reflections of a Bachelor Girl*
When you see what some girls marry, you realize how much they must hate to work for a living.

3634 *The Rubaiyat of a Bachelor*
Never trust a husband too far, nor a bachelor too near.

3635
When a girl marries, she exchanges the attentions of many men for the inattention of one.

3636 *The Wit of Women*
Before marriage, a man will lie awake thinking about something you said; after marriage, he'll fall asleep before you finish saying it.

ROWLAND Richard c.1881-1947
3637 *(of the take-over of United Artists)*
The lunatics have taken charge of the asylum.

ROYDE-SMITH Naomi c.1875-1964
3638 *Weekend Book*
I know two things about the horse
And one of them is rather coarse.

RUBENS Paul Alfred 1875-1917
3639 *'Your King and Country Want You'*
Oh! we don't want to lose you but we think you ought to go
For your King and your Country both need you so.

RUBINSTEIN Artur 1888-1982
3640
When I was young, I used to have successes with women because I was

young. Now I have successes with women because I am old. Middle age was the hardest part.

RUBINSTEIN Helena 1871-1965
3641
There are no ugly women, only lazy ones.

RUNES Dagobert
3642
Happy the man who gains sagacity in youth, but thrice happy he who retains the fervour of youth in age.

RUNYON Damon 1884-1946
3643 *'A Very Honourable Guy'*
Always try to rub up against money, for if you rub up against money long enough, some of it may rub off on you.

3644 *'The Idyll of Miss Sarah Brown'*
At such an hour the sinners are still in bed resting up from their sinning of the night before, so they will be in good shape for more sinning a little later on.

3645 *'A Nice Price'*
I long ago came to the conclusion that all life is 6 to 5 against.

3646
Much as he is opposed to lawbreaking, he is not bigoted about it.

3647
The race is not always to the swift nor the battle to the strong - but that's the way to bet.

RUSHTON Willie 1937-1996
3648 *(to a guest who had spilt red wine on his white dinner jacket)*
I always dress to match the colour of the food.

RUSK Dean 1909-1994
3649
One of the best ways to persuade others is with your ears.

3650 *(of the Cuban missile crisis)*
We're eyeball to eyeball, and I think the other fellow just blinked.

3651
One third of the people of the world are asleep at any given moment. The other two thirds are awake and probably stirring up trouble somewhere.

RUSKIN John 1819-1900
3652 *Sesame and Lilies*
We call ourselves a rich nation, and we are filthy and foolish enough to thumb each other's books out of circulating libraries!

3653 *On Whistler's Nocturne in Black and Gold*
I have seen, and heard, much of Cockney impudence before now; but never expected to hear a coxcomb ask two hundred guineas for flinging a pot of paint in the public's face.

RUSSELL Bertrand 1872-1970
3654
If we were all given by magic the power to read each other's thoughts, I suppose the first effect would be to dissolve all friendships.

3655
The average man's opinions are much less foolish than they would be if he thought for himself.

3656 *The Conquest of Happiness*
Men who are unhappy, like men who sleep badly, are always proud of the fact.

3657 *The Conquest of Happiness*
One of the symptoms of approaching nervous breakdown is the belief that one's work is terribly important, and that to take a holiday would bring all kinds of disaster.

3658 *The Conquest of Happiness*
One should as a rule respect public opinion in so far as is necessary to avoid starvation and to keep out of prison, but anything that goes beyond this is voluntary submission to an unnecessary tyranny.

3659 *The Conquest of Happiness*
A sense of duty is useful in work, but offensive in personal relations. People

wish to be liked, not to be endured with patient resignation.

3000 *The Conquest of Happiness*
Of all forms of caution, caution in love is perhaps the most fatal to true happiness.

3661
I do not believe that any peacock envies another peacock his tail, because every peacock is persuaded that his own tail is the finest in the world. The consequence of this is that peacocks are peaceable birds.

3662
The fundamental defect of fathers is that they want their children to be a credit to them.

3663
The good life, as I conceive it, is a happy life. I do not mean that if you are good you will be happy - I mean that if you are happy you will be good.

3664 *Marriage and Morals*
To fear love is to fear life, and those who fear life are already three parts dead.

3665
Many people would die sooner than think; in fact, they do.

3666 *Sceptical Essays*
We have two kinds of morality side by side: one which we preach but do not practice, and the other which we practice but seldom preach.

3667 *Sceptical Essays*
It is obvious that 'obscenity' is not a term capable of exact legal definition; in the practice of the Courts, it means 'anything that shocks the magistrate'.

3668
Simpson succeeded in proving that there was no harm in giving anaesthetics to men, because God put Adam into a deep sleep when He extracted his rib. But male ecclesiastics remained unconvinced as regards the sufferings of women, at any rate in childbirth.

RUSSELL Foster Meharny
3669
Every story has three sides to it - yours, mine and the facts.

RUSSELL Lord John 1792-1878
3670 *(attributed)*
A proverb is one man's wit and all men's wisdom.

RUTHERFORD Lord 1871-1937
3671 *(attributed)*
All science is either physics or stamp collecting.

3672 *(attributed)*
We haven't got the money, so we've got to think!

3673 *(in 1937)*
The energy produced by the breaking down of the atom is a very poor kind of thing. Anyone who expects a source of power from the transformation of these atoms is talking moonshine.

RYAN Joe
3674
A committee of one gets things done.

SACKLER Howard 1929-
3675 *Good-bye Fidel*
Affairs, like revolutions, should only have beginnings.

SAGAN Françoise 1935-1994
3676
I like men to behave like men. I like them strong and childish.

SAINT-EXUPÉRY Antoine de 1900-1944
3677 *Le Petit Prince*
Grownups never understand anything for themselves, and it is tiresome for children to be always and forever explaining things to them.

SAKI (Hector Hugh Monro) 1870-1916
3678 *Chronicles of Clovis*
All decent people live beyond their incomes nowadays, and those who aren't respectable live beyond other peoples'.

3679
The clock struck eleven with the respectful unobtrusiveness of one whose mission in life is to be ignored.

3680
Hating anything in the way of ill-natured gossip ourselves, we are always grateful to those who do it for us and do it well.

3681
Oysters are more beautiful than any religion ... there's nothing in Christianity or Buddhism that quite matches the sympathetic unselfishness of an oyster.

3682 *Reginald*
The cook was a good cook, as cooks go; and as good cooks go, she went.

3683 *Reginald*
I always say beauty is only sin deep.

3684 *Reginald in Russia*
Good gracious, you've got to educate him first. You can't expect a boy to be vicious till he's been to a good school.

3685 *Reginald in Russia*
Addresses are given to us to conceal our whereabouts.

3686 *The Square Egg*
A little inaccuracy sometimes saves tons of explanation.

3687 *Toys of Peace and Other Papers*
Children with Hyacinth's temperament don't know better as they grow older; they merely know more.

3688 *The Unbearable Bassington*
We all know that Prime Ministers are wedded to the truth, but like other married couples they sometimes live apart.

SALISBURY Lord 1830-1903
3689 *Letter to Lord Lytton*
English policy is to float lazily downstream, occasionally putting out a diplomatic boathook to avoid collisions.

SALMON Andrew
3690
There is only one truth, steadfast, healing, salutary, and that is the absurd.

SAMPSON Anthony 1926-
3691 *Anatomy of Britain*
Members [of civil service orders] rise from CMG (known sometimes in Whitehall as 'Call Me God') to the KCMG ('Kindly Call Me God') to - for a select few governors and super-ambassadors - the GCMG ('God Calls Me God').

SAMUEL Lord 1870-1963
3692 *A Book of Quotations*
A library is thought in cold storage.

3693 *Book of Quotations*
It takes two to make a marriage a success and only one to make it a failure.

3694
Equality of opportunity is an equal opportunity to prove unequal talents.

SANDBURG Carl 1878-1967
3695 *'Prairie'*
I tell you the past is a bucket of ashes.

3696
Slang is a language that rolls up its sleeves, spits on its hands and goes to work.

3697
Sometime they'll give a war and nobody will come.

SANDERS Henry 'Red'
3698
Sure, winning isn't everything. It's the only thing.

SANTAYANA George 1863-1952
3699
Art is a delayed echo.

3700
An artist may visit a museum but only a pedant can live there.

3701
Friendship is almost always the union of a part of one mind with a part of another; people are friends in spots.

3702 *The Life of Reason*
Fanaticism consists in redoubling your effort when you have forgotten your aim.

3703 *The Life of Reason*
Those who cannot remember the past are condemned to repeat it.

3704 *The Life of Reason*
An artist is a dreamer consenting to dream of the actual world.

3705
Man is as full of potentiality as he is of impotence.

3706
By nature's kindly disposition, most questions which it is beyond man's power to answer do not occur to him at all.

3707
Real unselfishness consists in sharing the interests of others.

3708 *Soliloquies in England*
There is no cure for birth and death save to enjoy the interval.

3709 *Soliloquies in England, 'The British Character'*
England is the paradise of individuality, eccentricity, heresy, anomalies, hobbies, and humours.

3710 *The Unknowable*
It is a great advantage for a system of philosophy to be substantially true.

SAPHIR Moritz G.
3711
Love makes of the wisest man a fool, and of the most foolish woman, a sage.

3712
The mirror is the conscience of women; they never do a thing without first consulting it.

SAPHIR Morty
3713
Man's attitude toward great qualities in others is often the same as toward high mountains - he admires them but he prefers to walk around them.

SARAH 1st Duchess of Marlborough
1660-1744
3714

The Duke returned from the wars today and did pleasure me in his top-boots.

SARAH Duchess of York 1959-
3715 *(as spokesperson for US Weightwatchers)*
Free your mind and your bottom will follow.

3716
I don't know where the money went - it just went. I don't even like shopping.

SARGENT John Singer 1856-1925
3717
A portrait is a painting with something wrong with the mouth.

3718
Every time I paint a portrait I lose a friend.

SARONY Leslie 1897-1985
3719
Ain't it grand to be blooming well dead?

SAROYAN William 1908-1981
3720
Every man in the world is better than someone else. And not as good as some one else.

SARTRE Jean-Paul 1905-1980
3721 *Words*
There is no good father, that's the rule. Don't lay the blame on men but on the bond of paternity, which is rotten. To beget children, nothing better; to *have* them, what iniquity!

3722 *Words*
The poor don't know that their function in life is to exercise our generosity.

3723 *Words*
She believed in nothing; only her scepticism kept her from being an atheist.

SASSOON Vidal
3724
Hair is another name for sex.

SAVILE George 1633-1695
3725 *Political, Moral, and Miscellaneous Thoughts and Reflections*

Malice is of a low stature, but it hath very long arms.

SCHERER Paul 1933-
3726
Love is a spendthrift, leaves its arithmetic at home, is always 'in the red'.

SCHIFF Leonard
3727
Electric clocks reveal to you
Precisely when your fuses blew.

SCHILLER Friedrich von 1759-1805
3728
I am better than my reputation.

SCHNABEL Artur 1882-1951
3729 *My Life and Music*
I know two kinds of audiences only - one coughing, and one not coughing.

3730 *(of Mozart's sonatas)*
Too easy for children, and too difficult for artists.

3731
The notes I handle no better than many pianists. But the pauses between the notes - ah, that is where the art resides!

SCHOPENHAUER Arthur 1788-1860
3732
The fly ought to be used as the symbol of impertinence and audacity; for whilst all other animals shun man more than anything else, and run away even before he comes near them, the fly lights upon his very nose.

3733
A man never feels the want of what it never occurs to him to ask for.

3734
Money is human happiness in the abstract.

3735
Pride is the direct appreciation of oneself.

3736
Not to go to the theatre is like making one's toilet without a mirror.

3737
If you want to know your true opinion of someone, watch the effect produced in you by the first sight of a letter from him.

SCHUDSON Michael
3738
Buy me and you will overcome the anxieties I have just reminded you of.

SCHULLER Robert
3739
Someone once said to me, 'Reverend Schuller, I hope you live to see all your dreams fulfilled'. I replied, 'I hope not, because if I live and all my dreams are fulfilled, I'm dead'. It's unfulfilled dreams that keep you alive.

SCHULZ Charles M. 1922-
3740
I've developed a new philosophy - I only dread one day at a time.

3741
Jogging is very beneficial. It's good for your legs and your feet. It's also very good for the ground. It makes it feel needed.

3742
My life has no purpose, no direction, no aim, no meaning, and yet I'm happy. I can't figure it out. What am I doing right?

SCHWEITZER Albert 1875-1965
3743
A great secret of success is to go through life as a man who never gets used up.

3744
Happiness? That's nothing more than health and a poor memory.

3745
A man does not have to be an angel in order to be a saint.

SCOTT C.P. 1846-1932
3746
Television? The word is half Latin and half Greek. No good can come of it.

SCOTT Howard
3747
A criminal is a person with predatory instincts who has not sufficient capital to form a corporation.

SCOTT Robert 1868-1912
3748 *(of the South Pole)*
Great God! this is an awful place.

SCOTT Sir Walter 1771-1832
3749 *The Bride of Lammermoor*
I live by twa trades ... fiddle, sir, and spade; filling the world, and emptying of it.

3750 *Redgauntlet*
The ae half of the warld thinks the tither daft.

SCOTT William 1745-1836
3751
A dinner lubricates business.

SCOTT-MAXWELL Florida
3752
No matter how old a mother is, she watches her middle-aged children for signs of improvement.

SEDLEY Sir Charles c.1639-1701
3753 *'Phyllis Knotting'*
Phyllis, without frown or smile,
Sat and knotted all the while.

SÉGUR Sophie Rostopchine
3754
God keeps the wicked to give them time to repent.

SELDEN John 1584-1654
3755 *Table Talk 'Friends'*
Old friends are best. King James used to call for his old shoes; they were easiest for his feet.

3756 *Table Talk 'Humility'*
'Tis not the drinking that is to be blamed, but the excess.

3757 *Table Talk 'Of a King'*
A king is a thing men have made for their own sakes, for quietness' sake. Just as in a family one man is appointed to buy the meat.

3758 *Table Talk 'Libels'*
Take a straw and throw it up into the air, you shall see by that which way the wind io.

3759 *Table Talk 'Marriage'*
Marriage is nothing but a civil contract.

3760 *Table Talk 'Parson'*
There never was a merry world since the fairies left off dancing, and the Parson left conjuring.

3761 *Table Talk 'Pleasure'*
Pleasure is nothing else but the intermission of pain.

3762 *Table Talk 'Preaching'*
Preachers say, Do as I say, not as I do.

SELDON Arthur 1584-1654
3763 *Capitalism*
Government of the busy by the bossy for the bully.

SELLAR W.C. and YEATMAN R.J. 1898-1951 and 1898-1968
3764 *1066 and All That*
The Roman Conquest was, however, a *Good Thing*, since the Britons were only natives at the time.

3765 *1066 and All That*
The Cavaliers (Wrong but Wromatic) and the Roundheads (Right but Repulsive).

3766 *1066 and All That*
The National Debt is a very Good Thing and it would be dangerous to pay it off, for fear of Political Economy.

3767 *1066 and All That*
Napoleon's armies always used to march on their stomachs shouting: 'Vive l'Intérieur!'

3768 *1066 and All That 'Compulsory Preface'*
History is not what you thought. *It is what you can remember.*

3769 *And Now All This*
For every person who wants to teach there are approximately thirty who don't want to learn - much.

SENECA c.4 BC-AD 65
3770
A great step toward independence is a good-humoured stomach.

3771
When I think over what I have said, I envy dumb people.

SENN J.P.
3772
Let us respect grey hairs, especially our own.

SERVICE Robert 1874-1958
3773
It isn't the mountain ahead that wears you out - it's the grain of sand in your shoe.

SÉVIGNÉ Mme de 1626-1692
3774 *(attributed)*
The more I see of men, the more I admire dogs.

SHAFFER Ivan
3775
A man isn't a man until he has to meet a payroll.

SHAFFER Peter 1926-
3776 *Equus*
All my wife has ever taken from the Mediterranean - from that whole vast intuitive culture - are four bottles of Chianti to make into lamps.

SHAKESPEARE William 1564-1616
3777 *As You Like It*
Do you not know I am a woman? when I think, I must speak.

3778 *As You Like It*
I do desire we may be better strangers.

3779 *As You Like It*
Your 'if' is the only peace-maker; much virtue in 'if'.

3780 *Much Ado About Nothing*
When I said I would die a bachelor, I did not think I should live till I were married.

3781 *Much Ado About Nothing*
I thank God, I am as honest as any man living, that is an old man and no honester than I.

3782 *Much Ado About Nothing*
Comparisons are odorous.

3783 *Much Ado About Nothing*
There was never yet philosopher
That could endure the toothache patiently.

3784 *Antony and Cleopatra*
O excellent! I love long life better than figs.

3785 *Antony and Cleopatra*
Indeed the tears live in an onion that should water this sorrow.

3786 *Henry IV, Part 1*
Thou hast the most unsavoury similies.

3787 *Henry IV, Part 1*
Go hang thyself in thine own heir-apparent garters!

3788 *Henry IV, Part 1*
If sack and sugar be a fault, God help the wicked!

3789 *Henry IV, Part 1*
Honour pricks me on. Yea, but how if honour prick me off when I come on? how then? Can honour set-to a leg? No. Or an arm? No. Or take away the grief of a wound? No. Honour hath no skill in surgery, then? No. What is honour? A word. What is that word, honour? Air.

3790 *Henry IV, Part 2*
I am as poor as Job, my lord, but not so patient.

3791 *Henry IV, Part 2*
Doth it not show vilely in me to desire small beer?

3792 *Henry IV, Part 2*
Is it not strange that desire should so many years outlive performance?

3793 *King Lear*
Thou whoreson zed! thou unnecessary letter!

3794 *King Lear*
There was never yet fair woman but she made mouths in a glass.

3795 *King Lear*
Get thee glass eyes;
And, like a scurvy politician, seem
To see the things thou dost not.

3796 *Love's Labour's Lost*
He hath not fed of the dainties that are
bred in a book; he hath not eat paper, as
it were; he hath not drunk ink.

3797 *Love's Labour's Lost*
He draweth out the thread of his
verbosity finer than the staple of his
argument.

3798 *Measure for Measure*
Thou hast nor youth nor age;
But, as it were, an after-dinner's sleep,
Dreaming on both.

3799 *The Merchant of Venice*
God made him, and therefore let him
pass for a man.

3800 *The Merchant of Venice*
There is not one among them but I dote
on his very absence.

3801 *The Merchant of Venice*
My daughter! O my ducats! O my
daughter!
Fled with a Christian! O my Christian
ducats!
Justice! the law! my ducats, and my
daughter!

3802 *The Merchant of Venice*
A light wife doth make a heavy husband.

3803 *The Merry Wives of Windsor*
O, what a world of vile ill-favoured faults
Looks handsome in three hundred
pounds a year!

3804 *A Midsummer Night's Dream*
A lion among ladies, is a most dreadful
thing; for there is not a more fearful
wild-fowl than your lion living.

3805 *Richard II*
Grace me no grace, nor uncle me no
uncle.

3806 *Twelfth Night*
Not to be a-bed after midnight is to be
up betimes.

3807 *Twelfth Night*
My purpose is, indeed, a horse of that
colour.

3808 *Twelfth Night*
Some men are born great, some achieve
greatness, and some have greatness
thrust upon them.

3809 *Twelfth Night*
Still you keep o' the windy side of the
law.

3810 *The Two Gentlemen of Verona*
He was more than over shoes in love.

3811 *The Two Gentlemen of Verona*
I have no other but a woman's reason:
I think him so, because I think him so.

3812 *The Winter's Tale*
Though I am not naturally honest, I am
so sometimes by chance.

3813 *The Winter's Tale (stage direction)*
Exit, pursued by a bear.

SHANKLY Bill 1914-1981
3814
Some people think football is a matter of
life and death ... I can assure them it is
much more serious than that.

SHAW George Bernard 1856-1950
3815 *(attributed)*
England and America are two countries
divided by a common language.

3816 *Annajanska*
All great truths begin as blasphemies.

3817
I believe in the discipline of silence and
could talk for hours about it.

3818
Beware of the man whose God is in the
skies.

3819 *Candida*
I'm only a beer teetotaller, not a
champagne teetotaller.

3820
Christianity might be a good thing if
anyone ever tried it.

3821
[Dancing is] a perpendicular expression of a horizontal desire.

3822 *The Devil's Disciple*
Martyrdom ... the only way in which a man can become famous without ability.

3823 *The Devil's Disciple*
I never expect a soldier to think.

3824 *The Devil's Disciple*
SWINDON: What will history say?
BURGOYNE: History, sir, will tell lies as usual.

3825 *The Devil's Disciple*
The British soldier can stand up to anything except the British War Office.

3826
Do not do unto others as you would that they should do unto you. Their tastes may not be the same.

3827 *Everybody's Political What's What?*
A government which robs Peter to pay Paul can always depend on the support of Paul.

3828 *Fanny's First Play*
It's all that the young can do for the old, to shock them and keep them up to date.

3829
Fashions, after all, are only induced epidemics.

3830 *Getting Married*
What God hath joined together no man ever shall put asunder: God will take care of that.

3831 *John Bull's Other Island*
An Irishman's heart is nothing but his imagination.

3832
She had lost the art of conversation, but not, unfortunately, the power of speech.

3833
Love is a gross exaggeration of the difference between one person and everybody else.

3834 *Major Barbara*
I am a Millionaire. That is my religion.

3835 *Major Barbara*
Wot prawce Selvytion nah?

3836 *Major Barbara*
Alcohol is a very necessary article ... It enables Parliament to do things at eleven at night that no sane person would do at eleven in the morning.

3837 *Major Barbara*
He knows nothing; and he thinks he knows everything. That points clearly to a political career.

3838 *Man and Superman*
But a lifetime of happiness! No man alive could bear it: it would be hell on earth.

3839 *Man and Superman*
An Englishman thinks he is moral when he is only uncomfortable.

3840 *Man and Superman*
When the military man approaches, the world locks up its spoons and packs off its womankind.

3841 *Man and Superman*
What is virtue but the Trade Unionism of the married?

3842 *Man and Superman*
It is a woman's business to get married as soon as possible, and a man's to keep unmarried as long as he can.

3843 *Man and Superman*
There are two tragedies in life. One is to lose your heart's desire. The other is to gain it.

3844 *Man and Superman 'Maxims: Education'*
He who can, does. He who cannot, teaches.

3845 *Man and Superman 'Maxims: Marriage'*
Marriage is popular because it combines the maximum of temptation with the maximum of opportunity.

3846 *Man and Superman 'Maxims: Stray Sayings'*
Every man over forty is a scoundrel.

3847 *Man and Superman 'The Revolutionist's Handbook'*
Revolutions have never lightened the burden of tyranny: they have only shifted it to another shoulder.

3848 *Back to Methuselah*
I enjoy convalescence. It is the part that makes illness worthwhile.

3849
My only policy is to profess evil and do good.

3850
A perpetual holiday is a good working definition of hell.

3851 *The Philanderer*
The fickleness of the women I love is only equalled by the infernal constancy of the women who love me.

3852 *Pygmalion*
PICKERING: Have you no morals, man?
DOOLITTLE: Can't afford them, Governor.

3853
I often quote myself. It adds spice to my conversation.

3854
Reformers have the idea that change can be achieved by brute sanity.

3855 *Saint Joan*
If ever I utter an oath again may my soul be blasted to eternal damnation!

3856 *Saint Joan*
How can what an Englishman believes be heresy? It is a contradiction in terms.

3857
I was taught when I was young that if people would only love one another, all would be well with the world. This seemed simple and very nice; but I found when I tried to put it in practice not only that other people were seldom lovable, but that I was not very lovable myself.

3858
The test of a man or woman's breeding is how they behave in a quarrel.

3859
When I was a young man I observed that nine out of ten things I did were failures. I didn't want to be a failure, so I did ten times more work.

3860
I work as my father drank.

SHAW Henry Wheeler (Josh Billings)
1818-1885
3861 *Josh Billings, his Sayings*
Thrice is he armed that hath his quarrel just,
But four times he who gets his blow in fust.

3862 *Proverb*
It is better to know nothing than to know what ain't so.

SHAY R.E.
3863
Depend on the rabbit's foot if you will, but remember it didn't work for the rabbit!

SHEEHY Gail
3864
When men reach their sixties and retire, they go to pieces. Women just go right on cooking.

SHELLEY Percy Bysshe 1792-1822
3865 *'Letter to Maria Gisborne'*
Have you not heard
When a man marries, dies or turns Hindoo,
His best friends hear no more of him?

SHERIDAN Richard Brinsley 1751-1816
3866 *'Clio's Protest'*
You write with ease, to show your breeding,
But easy writing's vile hard reading.

3867 *The Critic*
I wish sir, you would practise this without me. I can't stay dying here all night.

3868 *The Critic*
An oyster may be crossed in love!

3869 *The Duenna*
I was struck all of a heap.

3870 *The Duenna*
Conscience has no more to do with
gallantry than it has with politics.

3871
The Right Honourable gentleman is
indebted to his memory for his jests and
to his imagination for his facts.

3872 *The Rivals*
Illiterate him, I say, quite from your
memory.

3873 *The Rivals*
'Tis safest in matrimony to begin with a
little aversion.

3874 *The Rivals*
He is the very pineapple of politeness!

3875 *The Rivals*
An aspersion upon my parts of speech!
was ever such a brute! Sure, if I
reprehend anything in this world, it is
the use of my oracular tongue, and a
nice derangement of epitaphs!

3876 *The School for Scandal*
You had no taste when you married me.

3877 *The School for Scandal*
Here is the whole set! a character dead at
every word.

3878 *The School for Scandal*
An unforgiving eye, and a damned
disinheriting countenance!

SHIPLEY Sir Arthur 1861-1927
3879 *Life 'Ere you were Queen of Sheba'*
When we were a soft amoeba, in ages
past and gone,
Ere you were Queen of Sheba, or I King
Solomon,
Alone and undivided, we lived a life of
sloth,
Whatever you did, I did; one dinner
served for both.
Anon came separation, by fission and
divorce,

A lonely pseudopodium I wandered on
my course.

SHORT Clare 1946-
3880
I fear I will carry on irritating some
people because some people are very
irritable.

SHRINER Herb
3881
Our doctor would never really operate
unless it was necessary. He was just that
way. If he didn't need the money, he
wouldn't lay a hand on you.

SICKERT Walter 1860-1942
3882 *'The Language of Art'*
Nothing knits man to man, ... like the
frequent passage from hand to hand of
cash.

SIDNEY Algernon 1622-1683
3883 *Discourses concerning Government*
Liars ought to have good memories.

3884 *Discourses concerning Government*
Men lived like fishes; the great ones
devoured the small.

SIDNEY Sir Philip 1554-1586
3885 *Arcadia*
Who shoots at the mid-day sun, though
he be sure he shall never hit the mark;
yet as sure he is he shall shoot higher
than who aims but at a bush.

SIFTON Clifford Sir 1861-1929
3886
I think a stalwart peasant in a sheepskin
coat, born on the soil, whose forefathers
have been farmers for ten generations,
with a stout wife and a half-dozen
chickens, is good quality.

SIGISMUND Emperor 1361-1437
3887 *(to prelate who had criticized his
Latin)*
I am the Roman Emperor, and am above
grammar.

SIMPSON N.F. 1919-
3888 *A Resounding Tinkle*
A problem left to itself dries up or goes
rotten. But fertilize a problem with a
solution - you'll hatch out dozens.

SIMS Sylvia
3889
You can have your face lifted but there comes a time when you are still going to be offered the Nurse, not Juliet.

SINCLAIR Gordon John
3890 *in Gregory's Girl*
"It doesn't look nice. If women were meant to play football they'd have their tits somewhere else."

SINGER Isaac Bashevis 1904-1991
3891
The waste basket is a writer's best friend.

SISSON C.H. 1914-
3892 *In The London Zoo*
Here lies a civil servant. He was civil
To everyone, and servant to the devil.

SITWELL Dame Edith 1887-1964
3893
A great many people now reading and writing would be better employed in keeping rabbits.

3894
I have often wished I had time to cultivate modesty ... But I am too busy thinking about myself.

SITWELL Sir Osbert 1892-1969
3895 *'On the Coast of Coromandel'*
On the coast of Coromandel
Dance they to the tunes of Handel.

3896 *At the House of Mrs Kinfoot*
The British Bourgeoisie
Is not born,
And does not die,
But, if it is ill,
It has a frightened look in its eyes.

3897 *'Milordo Inglese'*
In reality, killing time
Is only the name for another of the multifarious ways
By which Time kills us.

SKELTON John c.1460-1529
3898 *Magnificence*
I blunder, I bluster, I blow, and I blother,
I make on the one day, and I mar on the other.

Busy, busy, and ever busy,
I dance up and down till I am dizzy.

SKINNER B.F. 1904-1990
3899
Education is what survives when what has been learnt has been forgotten.

SKINNER Cornelia Otis 1901-1979
3900
Women keep a special corner of their hearts for sins they have never committed.

SMILES Samuel 1812-1904
3901 *Thrift*
A place for everything, and everything in its place.

SMITH Adam 1723-1790
3902
Man, an animal that makes bargains.

SMITH A.W. 1937-
3903
Where there is one Englishman there is a garden. Where there are two Englishmen there will be a club. But this does not mean any falling off in the number of gardens. There will be three. The club will have one too.

SMITH Charles Merrill
3904
The cocktail party - a device for paying off obligations to people you don't want to invite to dinner.

SMITH Sir Cyril 1928-
3905 *(of the House of Commons)*
The longest running farce in the West End.

SMITH Edgar 1857-1938
3906 *'Heaven Will Protect the Working-Girl'*
You may tempt the upper classes
With your villainous demi-tasses,
But; Heaven will protect a working-girl!

SMITH F.E. 1872-1930
3907 *Law, Life and Letters*
Nature has no cure for this sort of madness [Bolshevism], though I have known a legacy from a rich relative work wonders.

SMITH Horace 1779-1849
3908
Inconsistency is the only thing in which
men are consistent.

SMITH John 1938-1995
3909 *(of John Major)*
I sometimes think that when the Prime
Minister tries to select a weapon it is the
boomerang he finds most effective.

SMITH Logan Pearsall 1865-1946
3910 *Afterthoughts 'Age and Death'*
There is more felicity on the far side of
baldness than young men can possibly
imagine.

3911 *Afterthoughts 'Age and Death'*
The denunciation of the young is a
necessary part of the hygiene of older
people, and greatly assists the circulation
of their blood.

3912 *Afterthoughts 'All Trivia'*
What I like in a good author is not what
he says, but what he whispers.

3913 *Afterthoughts 'Art and Letters'*
A best-seller is the gilded tomb of a
mediocre talent.

3914 *Afterthoughts 'Life and Human
Nature'*
An improper mind is a perpetual feast.

3915 *Afterthoughts 'Myself'*
People say that life is the thing, but I
prefer reading.

3916 *Afterthoughts 'Other People'*
Those who set out to serve both God and
Mammon soon discover that there is no
God.

3917 *Afterthoughts 'Other People'*
Most people sell their souls, and live
with a good conscience on the proceeds.

3918 *Afterthoughts 'In the World'*
To suppose, as we all suppose, that we
could be rich and not behave as the rich
behave, is like supposing that we could
drink all day and keep absolutely sober.

3919
Don't tell your friends their social faults;
they will cure the fault and never forgive
you.

3920
How it infuriates a bigot, when he is
forced to drag out his dark convictions!

3921
How can they say my life isn't a success?
Have I not for more than sixty years got
enough to eat and escaped being eaten?

3922
There are few sorrows, however
poignant, in which a good income is of
no avail.

SMITH Stevie 1902-1971
3923 *'This Englishwoman'*
This Englishwoman is so refined
She has no bosom and no behind.

3924 *'The Past'*
People who are always praising the past
And especially the times of faith as best
Ought to go and live in the Middle Ages
And be burnt at the stake as witches and
sages.

SMITH Sydney 1771-1845
3925
Death must be distinguished from dying,
with which it is often confused.

3926
My definition of marriage ... it resembles
a pair of shears, so joined that they
cannot be separated; often moving in
opposite directions, yet always
punishing anyone who comes between
them.

3927
As the French say, there are three sexes -
men, women, and clergymen.

3928
No furniture so charming as books.

3929
Heat, ma'am! It was so dreadful here
that I found there was nothing left for it
but to take off my flesh and sit in my
bones.

3930
How can a bishop marry? How can he flirt? The most he can say is, 'I will see you in the vestry after service'

3931
I am just going to pray for you at St Paul's, but with no very lively hope of success.

3932 *Letter to Miss G. Harcourt*
I have no relish for the country; it is a kind of healthy grave.

3933 *(of Macaulay)*
He not only overflowed with learning, but stood in the slop.

3934 *(of Macauley)*
He has occasional flashes of silence, that make his conversation perfectly delightful.

3935
I never read a book before reviewing it; it prejudices a man so.

3936
Oh, don't tell me of facts - I never believe in facts; you know Canning said nothing was so fallacious as facts, except figures.

3937
Poverty is no disgrace to a man, but it is confoundedly inconvenient.

3938 *'Receipt for a Salad'*
Let onion atoms lurk within the bowl, And, scarce-suspected, animate the whole.

3939 *'Receipt for a Salad'*
Serenely full, the epicure would say, Fate cannot harm me, I have dined to-day.

3940
It requires a surgical operation to get a joke well into a Scotch understanding.

3941
He has returned from Italy a greater bore than ever; he bores on architecture, painting, statuary and music.

3942 *Sketches of Moral Philosophy*
I never could find any man who could think for two minutes together.

3943
What you don't know would make a great book.

3944
What a pity it is that we have no amusements in England but vice and religion!

3945
What two ideas are more inseparable than Beer and Britannia?

3946 *(of Whewell)*
Science is his forte, and omniscience his foible.

SMITH Willie ('The Lion') 1897-
3947
Romance without finance is no good.

SMOLLETT Tobias 1721-1771
3948 *The Adventures of Sir Launcelot Greaves*
I think for my part one half of the nation is mad - and the other not very sound.

3949 *Humphry Clinker*
I am pent up in frowzy lodgings, where there is not room enough to swing a cat.

SMYTH Harley S.
3950 *(medical maxim)*
When you hear hoofbeats, think of horses before zebras.

SOCRATES 469-399 BC
3951 *(looking at multitude of wares exposed for sale)*
How many things I can do without!

SONDHEIM Stephen 1930-
3952 *Gypsy*
Everything's coming up roses.

3953 *West Side Story*
I like to be in America!
O.K. by me in America!
Ev'rything free in America
For a small fee in America!

SOPER Baron 1903-
3954 *(on the quality of debate in the House of Lords)*
It is, I think, good evidence of life after death.

SOPHOCLES c.496-406
3955
Most gladly indeed am I rid of it all [sex], as though I had escaped from a mad and savage master.

SOUTHEY Robert 1774-1843
3956 *'The Battle of Blenheim'*
'And everybody praise the Duke,
Who this great fight did win.'
'But what good came of it at last?'
Quoth little Peterkin.
'Why that I cannot tell,' said he,
'But 'twas a famous victory.'

3957 *'The Battle of Blenheim'*
He came to ask what he had found,
That was so large, and smooth, and round.

3958 *'The Battle of Blenheim'*
But what they fought each other for,
I could not well make out.

3959 *Colloquies on the Progress ... of Society*
The arts babblative and scribblative.

3960 *The Curse of Kehama (motto)*
Curses are like young chickens, they always come home to roost.

3961 *'The Devil's Walk' (written with Coleridge)*
From his brimstone bed, at break of day
A walking the Devil is gone,
To look at his little snug farm of the World,
And see how his stock went on.

3962 *'The March to Moscow'*
And last of all an Admiral came,
A terrible man with a terrible name -
A name which you all know by sight very well,
But which no one can speak, and no one can spell.

3963
It has been more wittily than charitably said that hell is paved with good intentions. They have their place in heaven also.

SPARK Muriel 1918-
3964 *The Prime of Miss Jean Brodie*
I am putting old heads on your young shoulders ... all my pupils are the crème de la crème.

3965 *The Prime of Miss Jean Brodie*
One's prime is elusive. You little girls, when you grow up, must be on the alert to recognize your prime at whatever time of your life it may occur.

3966 *The Prime of Miss Jean Brodie*
To me education is a leading out of what is already there in the pupil's soul. To Miss Mackay it is a putting in of something that is not there, and that is not what I call education, I call it intrusion.

3967 *The Wit of Women*
Do you think it pleases a man when he looks into a woman's eyes and sees a reflection of the British Museum Reading Room?

SPARROW John 1906-1992
3968 *Epitaph for Maurice Bowra*
Without you, Heaven would be too dull to bear,
And Hell would not be Hell if you are there.

3969
That indefatigable and unsavoury engine of pollution, the dog.

SPENCER Herbert 1820-1903
3970 *Definitions*
Time: That which man is always trying to kill, but which ends in killing him.

3971 *Education*
People are beginning to see that the first requisite to success in life is to be a good animal.

3972
It was remarked to me ... that to play billiards was the sign of an ill-spent youth.

SPENSER Edmund c.1552-1599
3973 *The Faerie Queen*
A gentle knight was pricking on the plain.

SPETTIGUE Doug
3974
Husbands don't really count ... in the miracle of birth.

SPINOZA Baruch 1632-1677
3975 *Ethics*
Man is a social animal.

SPOCK Dr. Benjamin 1903-1998
3976
There are only two things a child will share willingly - communicable diseases and his mother's age.

SPOONER Rev. W.A. 1844-1930
3977 *(attributed)*
I remember your name perfectly, but I just can't think of your face.

3978 *(attributed)*
Let us drink to the queer old Dean.

3979 *(attributed)*
Sir, you have tasted two whole worms; you have hissed all my mystery lectures and been caught fighting a liar in the quad; you will leave Oxford by the next town drain.

3980 *(announcing the hymn in New College Chapel)*
Kinquering Congs their titles take.

3981
You will find as you grow older that the weight of rages will press harder and harder upon the employer.

SPRING-RICE Sir Cecil 1859-1918
3982 *(of American politics)*
Dullness, occasionally relieved by rascality.

3983 *The Masque of Balliol*
I am the Dean of Christ Church, Sir:
There's my wife; look well at her.

She's the Broad and I'm the High;
We are the University.

SPURGEON Charles Haddon 1834-1992
3984
Learn to say 'No'; it will be of more use to you than to be able to read Latin.

SQUIRE Sir J.C. 1884-1958
3985 *'Ballade of Soporific Absorption'*
But I'm not so think as you drunk I am.

3986 *'In continuation of Pope on Newton'*
It did not last: the Devil howling 'Ho!
Let Einstein be!' restored the status quo.

STANLEY Sir Henry Morton 1841-1904
3987
Dr Livingstone, I presume?

STARK Freya 1893-1993
3988
Absence is one of the most useful ingredients of family life, and to do it rightly is an art like any other.

STARR Roger
3989
Money is the most egalitarian force in society. It confers power on whoever holds it.

STAËL Mme de 1766-1817
3990 *(attributed, asked what she talked of with lover)*
Speech happens not to be his language.

STEAD Christina 1902-1983
3991 *House of All Nations*
A self-made man is one who believes in luck and sends his son to Oxford.

STEELE Sir Richard 1672-1729
3992
The insupportable labour of doing nothing.

3993 *(of Lady E. Hastings)*
To love her is a liberal education.

3994
Reading is to the mind what exercise is to the body.

3995 *(of The Tatler)*
It is to be noted that when any part of
this paper appears dull there is a design
in it.

3996
There are so few who can grow old with
a good grace.

3997
A woman seldom writes her mind but in
her postscript.

STEIN Gertrude 1874-1946
3998
The central theme of the novel is that
they were glad to see each other.

3999
Everybody gets so much common
information all day long that they lose
their common sense.

4000
You have to learn to do everything, even
to die.

4001
Money is always there but the pockets
change; it is not in the same pockets
after a change, and that is all there is to
say about money.

4002 *Sacred Emily*
Rose is a rose is a rose is a rose, is a rose.

4003 *Four Saints in Three Acts*
Pigeons on the grass alas.

4004
I understand you undertake to
overthrow my undertaking.

4005
When you get there, there isn't any there
there.

4006
I write for myself and strangers. The
strangers, dear Readers, are an
afterthought.

STEINEM Gloria 1934-
4007
We are becoming the men we wanted to
marry.

4008
Outrageous acts and everyday rebellions.

4009
A woman without a man is like a fish
without a bicycle.

STENDHAL 1783-1842
4010
The first qualification for a historian is to
have no ability to invent.

STENGEL Casey 1889-1975
4011
Going to bed with a woman never hurt a
ball player. It's staying up all night
looking for them that does you in.

STEPHEN J.K. 1859-1892
4012 *'To R.K.'*
Will there never come a season
Which shall rid us from the curse
Of a prose which knows no reason
And an unmelodious verse ...

4013 *'To R.K.'*
When the Rudyards cease from kipling
And the Haggards ride no more.

4014 *'A Sonnet' (parodying Wordsworth)*
.. an old half-witted sheep
Which bleats articulate monotony,
And indicates that two and one are three.

STEPHEN Leslie 1832-1904
4015
Every man who says frankly and fully
what he thinks is doing a public service.

STEPHENS James 1882-1950
4016 *The Crock of Gold*
Finality is death. Perfection is finality.
Nothing is perfect. There are lumps in it.

STERN Gil
4017
Man is a complex being: he makes
deserts bloom and lakes die.

STERNE Laurence 1713-1768
4018
A man cannot dress, without his ideas
get clothed at the same time.

4019
Philosophy has a fine saying for
everything - for Death it has an entire
set.

4020 *A Sentimental Journey*
If ever I do a mean action, it must be in
some interval betwixt one passion and
another.

4021 *A Sentimental Journey*
There are worse occupations in this
world than feeling a woman's pulse.

4022 *Tristram Shandy*
I wish either my father or my mother, or
indeed both of them, as they were in
duty both equally bound to it, had
minded what they were about when they
begot me.

4023 *Tristram Shandy*
As we jog on, either laugh with me, or at
me, or in short do anything - only keep
your temper.

4024 *Tristram Shandy*
'Tis known by the name of perseverance
in a good cause - and of obstinacy in a
bad one.

4025 *Tristram Shandy*
Digressions, incontestably, are the
sunshine; they are the life, the soul of
reading; take them out of this book for
instance, you might as well take the book
along with them.

4026 *Tristram Shandy*
Writing, when properly managed (as you
may be sure I think mine is) is but a
different name for conversation.

4027 *Tristram Shandy*
Whenever a man talks loudly against
religion, always suspect that it is not his
reason, but his passions which have got
the better of his creed.

4028 *Tristram Shandy*
'Our armies swore terribly in Flanders,'
cried my uncle Toby, 'but nothing to
this.'

4029 *Tristram Shandy*
Of all the cants which are canted in this
canting world, though the cant of
hypocrites may be the worst, the cant of
criticism is the most tormenting!

4030 *Tristram Shandy*
My brother Toby, quoth she, is going to
be married to Mrs Wadman.
Then he will never, quoth my father, lie
diagonally in his bed again as long as he
lives.

4031 *Tristram Shandy*
A man should know something of his
own country too, before he goes abroad.

4032 *Tristram Shandy*
And who are you? said he. Don't puzzle
me, said I.

4033 *Tristram Shandy*
'-d!' said my mother, 'what is all this
story about?'
'A Cock and a Bull', said Yorick.

4034 *Tristram Shandy*
The nonsense of the old women (of both
sexes).

STEVENS Wallace 1879-1955
4035 *'Bantams in Pine Woods'*
Chieftain Iffucan of Azcan in caftan
Of tan with henna hackles, halt!

4036
Frogs Eat Butterflies. Snakes Eat Frogs.
Hogs Eat Snakes. Men Eat Hogs.

STEVENSON Adlai 1900-1965
4037
In America, any boy may become
president, and I suppose it's just one of
the risks he takes.

4038
My definition of a free society is a society
where it is safe to be unpopular.

4039
It is often easier to fight for principles
than to live up to them.

4040
A funny thing happened to me on the
way to the White House.

4041
We hear the Secretary of State [John Foster Dulles] boasting of his brinkmanship - the art of bringing us to the edge of the abyss.

4042
A hungry man is not a free man.

4043
It is not the years in your life but the life in your years that counts.

4044
Some people approach every problem with an open mouth.

4045
If they [the Republicans] will stop telling lies about the Democrats, we will stop telling the truth about them.

4046
I suppose flattery hurts no one, that is, if you don't inhale.

4047
What a man knows at fifty that he did not know at twenty is for the most part incommunicable.

4048
It is said that a wise man who stands firm is a statesman, and a foolish man who stands firm is a catastrophe.

STEVENSON Robert Louis 1850-1894
4049 *A Child's Garden of Verses 'Whole Duty ...'*
A child should always say what's true,
And speak when he is spoken to,
And behave mannerly at table:
At least as far as he is able.

4050
For God's sake give me the young man who has brains enough to make a fool of himself.

4051
Marriage is one long conversation checkered by disputes.

4052 *New Arabian Nights 'The Rajah's Diamond'*
I regard you with an indifference closely bordering on aversion.

4053 *New Arabian Nights 'The Suicide Club'*
The devil, depend upon it, can sometimes do a very gentlemanly thing.

4054 *Treasure Island*
Many's the long night I've dreamed of cheese - toasted, mostly.

4055 *Virginibus Puerisque*
In marriage, a man becomes slack and selfish, and undergoes a fatty degeneration of his moral being.

4056 *Virginibus Puerisque 'An Apology for Idlers'*
He sows hurry and reaps indigestion.

4057 *The Wrong Box (with Lloyd Osborne)*
What hangs people ... is the unfortunate circumstance of guilt.

STILL John
4058
The memories of men are too frail a thread to hang history from.

STING
4059
Cocaine is God's way of telling you you've got too much money.

STINNETT Caskie 1911-
4060 *Out of the Red*
A diplomat ... is a person who can tell you to go to hell in such a way that you actually look forward to the trip.

4061
The trouble with being a hypochondriac these days is that antibiotics have cured all the good diseases.

STIPE Michael
4062
I believe in the theory that anyone can get laid, it's just a matter of lowering your standards!

STOCKDALE Edmund
4063
Money isn't everything - but it's a long way ahead of what comes next.

STONE I.F. 1907-1989
4064
Every government is run by liars and
nothing they say should be believed.

STOPPARD Tom 1937-
4065
Age is a high price to pay for maturity.

4066 *Jumpers*
It's not the voting that's democracy, it's
the counting.

4067 *Lord Malquist and Mr Moon (c/f
Kipling of Max Aitken)*
The House of Lords, an illusion to which
I have never been able to subscribe -
responsibility without power, the
prerogative of the eunuch throughout
the ages.

4068 *Night and Day*
The media. It sounds like a convention
of spiritualists.

4069 *Night and Day*
I'm with you on the free press. It's the
newspapers I can't stand.

4070 *Night and Day*
Comment is free but facts are on
expenses.

4071
It's better to be quotable than to be
honest.

4072 *Rosencrantz and Guildenstern are
Dead*
You're familiar with the tragedies of
antiquity, are you? The great homicidal
classics?

4073 *Rosencrantz and Guildenstern are
Dead*
Eternity's a terrible thought. I mean,
where's it all going to end?

4074 *Rosencrantz and Guildenstern are
Dead*
Life is a gamble at terrible odds - if it was
a bet, you wouldn't take it.

4075
You could say you'd seen the future after
visiting America. I don't think you could
add: 'and it works'.

STOREY Wilbur F.
4076
It is a newspaper's duty to print the news
and raise hell

STOWE Harriet Beecher 1811-1896
4077 *Uncle Tom's Cabin*
'Never was born!' persisted Topsy ...
'never had no father, nor mother, nor
nothin'. I was raised by a speculator,
with lots of others.'

4078 *Uncle Tom's Cabin*
I s'pect I growed. Don't think nobody
never made me.

STRACHEY Lionel
4079
A brilliant epigram is a solemn platitude
gone to a masquerade ball.

STRACHEY Lytton 1880-1932
4080 *(on his deathbed)*
If this is dying, then I don't think much
of it.

4081
Discretion is not the better part of
biography.

4082 *Eminent Victorians 'Cardinal
Manning'*
The time was out of joint, and he was
only too delighted to have been born to
set it right.

4083 *Eminent Victorians 'Florence
Nightingale'*
Her conception of God was certainly not
orthodox. She felt towards Him as she
might have felt towards a glorified
sanitary engineer; and in some of her
speculations she seems hardly to
distinguish between the Deity and the
Drains.

4084
Happiness is the perpetual possession of
being well deceived.

4085 *Pope*
The verses, when they were written,
resembled nothing so much as spoonfuls
of boiling oil, ladled out by a fiendish
monkey at an upstairs window upon

such passers-by whom the wretch had a grudge against.

STRAVINSKY Igor 1882-1971
4086
Childhood - a period of waiting for the moment when I could send everyone and everything connected with it to hell.

4087
Conformism is so hot on the heels of the mass-produced avant garde that the 'ins' and the 'outs' change places with the speed of mach 3.

STREETER Edward
4088
Travel is ninety per cent anticipation and ten per cent recollection.

STREISAND Barbra 1942-
4089 *(of Bill Clinton, in 1998)*
We elected a President, not a Pope.

STRINDBERG Johan August 1849-1912
4090
Growing old - it's not nice, but it's interesting.

STRINGER Arthur 1922-
4091
Society, my dear, is like salt water, good to swim in but hard to swallow.

STRUNSKY Simeon 1879-1948
4092
Once a man would spend a week patiently waiting if he missed a stage coach, but now he rages if he misses the first section of a revolving door.

4093
If you want to understand democracy, spend less time in the library with Plato, and more time in the buses with people.

STUBBS John Heath 1918-
4094
Its always good to remember that people find it easier to name 10 artists from any century than 10 politicians.

STUDDERT KENNEDY G.A. 1883-1929
4095
It is much easier to do and die than it is to reason why.

4096 *Peace Rhymes of a Padre*
'Indifference'
When Jesus came to Birmingham they simply passed Him by,
They never hurt a hair of Him, they only let Him die.

SUCKLING Sir John 1609-1642
4097 *Aglaura 'Song'*
If of herself she will not love,
Nothing can make her:
The devil take her!

4098 *'A Ballad upon a Wedding'*
Her feet beneath her petticoat,
Like little mice, stole in and out,
As if they feared the light.

4099 *'Against Fruition'*
Women enjoyed (whatsoe'er before they've been)
Are like romances read, or sights once seen: ...
'Tis expectation makes a blessing dear;
It were not heaven, if we knew what it were.

4100 *'Love's Offence'*
Love is the fart
Of every heart:
It pains a man when 'tis kept close,
And others doth offend, when 'tis let loose.

SULZBERGER Arthur Hays 1891-1968
4101 *(on journalism)*
We tell the public which way the cat is jumping. The public will take care of the cat.

SURTEES R.S. 1805-1864
4102 *Mr Facey Romford's Hounds*
Life would be very pleasant if it were not for its enjoyments.

4103 *Mr Facey Romford's Hounds*
Everyone knows that the real business of a ball is either to look out for a wife, to look after a wife, or to look after somebody else's wife

4104 *Handley Cross*
I'll fill hup the chinks wi' cheese.

4105 *Handley Cross*
It ar'n't that I loves the fox less, but that I loves the 'ound more.

4106 *Hillingdon Hall*
Three things I never lends - my 'oss, my wife, and my name.

4107 *Jorrocks's Jaunts and Jollities*
Champagne certainly gives one werry gentlemanly ideas, but for a continuance, I don't know but I should prefer mild hale.

4108 *Ask Mamma*
The only infallible rule we know is, that the man who is always talking about being a gentleman never is one.

4109 *Mr Sponge's Sporting Tour*
The young ladies entered the drawing-room in the full fervour of sisterly animosity.

4110 *Mr Sponge's Sporting Tour*
He was a gentleman who was generally spoken of as having nothing a-year, paid quarterly.

SWANSON Gloria 1897-1983
4111 *(of her passport photo)*
If I look like this, I need the trip.

SWIFT Jonathan 1667-1745
4112 *The Battle of the Books*
Satire is a sort of glass, wherein beholders do generally discover everybody's face but their own.

4113
He was a bold man that first ate an oyster.

4114 *The Drapier's Letters*
I have heard of a man who had a mind to sell his house, and therefore carried a piece of brick in his pocket, which he shewed as a pattern to encourage purchasers.

4115 *Journal to Stella*
We were to do more business after dinner; but after dinner is after dinner - an old saying and a true, 'much drinking, little thinking'.

4116 *Journal to Stella*
We are so fond of one another, because our ailments are the same.

4117 *Journal to Stella*
I love good creditable acquaintance; I love to be the worst of the company.

4118 *Letter to Miss Vanhomrigh*
If Heaven had looked upon riches to be a valuable thing, it would not have given them to such a scoundrel.

4119 *Letter to Pope*
Principally I hate and detest that animal called man; although I heartily love John, Peter, Thomas, and so forth.

4120 *'A Pastoral Dialogue between Richmond Lodge ...'*
Walls have tongues, and hedges ears.

4121 *'On Poetry'*
So, naturalists observe, a flea
Hath smaller fleas that on him prey;
And these have smaller fleas to bite 'em,
And so proceed *ad infinitum*.
Thus every poet, in his kind,
Is bit by him that comes behind.

4122 *Polite Conversation*
Faith, that's as well said, as if I had said it myself.

4123 *Polite Conversation*
Promises and pie-crust are made to be broken.

4124 *Polite Conversation*
Bachelor's fare; bread and cheese, and kisses.

4125 *Polite Conversation*
'Tis happy for him, that his father was before him.

4126 *Polite Conversation*
Why, everyone one as they like; as the good woman said when she kissed her cow.

4127 *A Tale of a Tub*
Last week I saw a woman flayed, and you will hardly believe, how much it altered her person for the worse.

4128
'Tis an old maxim in the schools,
That flattery's the food of fools;
Yet now and then your men of wit
Will condescend to take a bit.

4129
What some invent, the rest enlarge.

SWINBURNE Algernon Charles 1837-1909
4130 *The Heptalogia 'The Higher Pantheism ...'*
Fiddle, we know, is diddle: and diddle, we take it, is dee.

SWOPE Herbert Bayard
4131
I cannot give you the formula for success, but I can give you the formula for failure, which is - try to please everybody.

SYMS Rev Richard
4132
An actor and a priest both require similar skills - dressing up and talking in a loud voice.

SYNGE John Millington 1871-1909
4133 *The Aran Islands*
We do be afraid of the sea, and we do only be drownded now and again.

4134 *The Playboy of the Western World*
Oh my grief, I've lost him surely. I've lost the only Playboy of the Western World.

SYRUS Publilius 1st Century BC
4135
There are some remedies worse than the disease.

SZASZ Thomas 1920-
4136 *The Second Sin 'Education'*
A teacher should have maximal authority and minimal power.

4137 *The Second Sin 'Emotions'*
Happiness is an imaginary condition, formerly often attributed by the living to the dead, now usually attributed by adults to children, and by children to adults.

4138 *The Second Sin 'Personal Conduct'*
The stupid neither forgive nor forget; the naïve forgive and forget; the wise forgive but do not forget.

4139 *The Second Sin 'Science and Scientism'*
Formerly, when religion was strong and science weak, men mistook magic for medicine; now, when science is strong and religion weak, men mistake medicine for magic.

4140 *The Second Sin 'Sex'*
Masturbation: the primary sexual activity of mankind. In the nineteenth century, it was a disease; in the twentieth, it's a cure.

4141 *The Second Sin 'Social Relations'*
Two wrongs don't make a right, but they make a good excuse.

4142
If you talk to God, you are praying; if God talks to you, you have schizophrenia.

SZELL George 1897-1970
4143
Conductors must give unmistakable and suggestive signals to the orchestra, not choreography to the audience.

SZENT-GYÖRGYI Albert von 1893-1986
4144
Discovery consists of seeing what everybody has seen and thinking what nobody has thought.

TAINE Hippolyte 1828-1893
4145
There are four varieties in society; the lovers, the ambitious, observers, and fools. The fools are the happiest.

TALLEYRAND Charles Maurice de 1754-1838
4146 *(of Mme. de Staël)*
She is such a good friend that she would throw all her acquaintances into the water for the pleasure of fishing them out.

The TALMUD
4147
Three things are good in little measure and evil in large: yeast, salt and hesitation.

TANFIELD Elizabeth Lady c.1565-1628
4148 *(epitaph for her husband)*
Love made me poet,
And this I writ;
My heart did do it,
And not my wit.

TARKINGTON Booth 1869-1946
4149 *(attributed)*
An ideal wife is any woman who has an ideal husband.

4150 *Penrod*
There are two things that will be believed of any man whatsoever, and one of them is that he has taken to drink.

TAWNEY R.H. 1880-1962
4151 *(declining the offer of a peerage)*
What harm have I ever done to the Labour Party?

TAYLOR A.J.P. 1906-1990
4152 *English History 1914-45*
History gets thicker as it approaches recent times.

4153 *Rumours of Wars*
Crimea: The War That Would Not Boil.

TAYLOR Bert Leston 1866-1921
4154
A bore is a man who, when you ask him how he is, tells you.

TAYLOR Bishop Jeremy 1613-1667
4155 *The Rule and Exercise of Holy Dying*
As our life is very short, so it is very miserable, and therefore it is well it is short.

TAYLOR Joe
4156
It takes time to save time.

TAYLOR W.M.
4157
Temptation rarely comes in working hours. It is in their leisure time that men are made or marred.

TEBBIT Norman 1931-
4158
It is a mistake to judge people by their friends. Judge them by their enemies. I am very proud of my enemies.

TEMPLE William 1881-1944
4159 *(attributed)*
Personally, I have always looked on cricket as organized loafing.

TENNYSON Alfred Lord 1809-1892
4160 *'Locksley Hall'*
He will hold thee, when his passion shall have spent its novel force,
Something better than his dog, a little dearer than his horse.

4161 *'Locksley Hall'*
Like a dog, he hunts in dreams.

4162 *'Locksley Hall'*
But the jingling of the guinea helps the hurt that Honour feels.

4163 *'Northern Farmer. New Style'*
'Doänt thou marry for munny, but goä wheer munny is!'

TERENCE c.190-159 BC
4164
My closest relation is myself.

4165 *Eunuchus - prologue*
Nothing has yet been said that's not been said before.

4166
Of my friends I am the only one I have left.

4167
I know the nature of women;
When you want to, they don't want to;
And when you don't want to, they desire exceedingly.

TESSIER Josephine
4168
Anything that comes easy, comes wrong.

THACKERAY William Makepeace 1811-1863
4169
Charlotte, having seen his body borne before her on a shutter, like a well

conducted person, went on cutting bread and butter.

4170 *Pendennis*
Yes, I am a fatal man, Madame Frisbi. To inspire hopeless passion is my destiny.

4171 *Pendennis*
Remember, it is as easy to marry a rich woman as a poor woman.

4172 *Pendennis*
For a slashing article, sir, there's nobody like the Capting.

4173 *Vanity Fair*
A woman with fair opportunities and without a positive hump, may marry whom she likes.

4174 *Vanity Fair*
Whenever he met a great man he grovelled before him, and my-lorded him as only a free-born Briton can do.

4175 *Vanity Fair*
If a man's character is to be abused, say what you will, there's nobody like a relation to do the business.

4176 *Vanity Fair*
Nothing like blood, sir, in hosses, dawgs, and men.

4177 *Vanity Fair*
I think I could be a good woman if I had five thousand a year.

THATCHER Margaret 1925-
4178 *(after John Major's appointment)*
I shan't be pulling the levers there but I shall be a very good back-seat driver.

4179
The lady's not for turning.

4180
I think sometimes the Prime Minister should be intimidating. There's not much point being a weak, floppy thing in the chair, is there?

THOMAS Brandon 1856-1914
4181 *Charley's Aunt*
I'm Charley's aunt from Brazil - where the nuts come from.

THOMAS Dylan 1914-1953
4182 *(defining an alcoholic)*
A man you don't like who drinks as much as you do.

4183 *Under Milk Wood*
Before you let the sun in, mind it wipes its shoes.

4184 *Under Milk Wood*
Oh, isn't life a terrible thing, thank God?

4185 *Under Milk Wood*
Nothing grows in our garden, only washing. And babies.

4186 *Under Milk Wood*
Seventeen and never been sweet in the grass ho ho.

4187 *(of Wales)*
The land of my fathers. My fathers can have it.

THOMAS Irene
4188
Protestant women may take the pill. Roman Catholic women must keep taking The Tablet.

THOMAS Lewis
4189
Cats - a standing rebuke to behavioural scientists ... least human of all creatures.

4190
Most things get better by themselves. Most things, in fact, are better by morning.

THOMPSON Kent
4191
If you're on the merry-go-round, you have to go round.

THOMPSON William Hepworth 1810-1886
4192 *(of Sir Richard Jebb)*
What time he can spare from the adornment of his person he devotes to the neglect of his duties.

THOMSON James 1700-1748
4193 *'Epitaph on Solomon Mendez'*
Here lies a man who never lived,
Yet still from death was flying;

Who, if not sick, was never well;
And died - for fear of dying!

THOMSON Roy (Baron Thomson of Fleet) 1894-1976
4194
I'm frank, brutally frank. And even when I'm not frank, I look frank.

4195
If people knew what they had to do to be successful, most people wouldn't.

4196 *(on the profitability of commercial TV in Britain)*
Like having your own licence to print money.

THOREAU Henry David 1817-1862
4197
Beware all enterprises that require new clothes.

4198
Some circumstantial evidence is very strong, as when you find a trout in the milk.

4199
Do not be too moral. You may cheat yourself out of much life. So aim above morality. Be not simply good; be good for something.

4200
The eye is the jewel of the body.

4201
How vain it is to sit down to write when you have not stood up to live.

4202
If I knew ... that a man was coming to my house with the conscious design of doing me good, I should run for my life.

4203
Politics is the gizzard of society, full of gut and gravel.

4204
You cannot receive a shock unless you have an electric affinity for that which shocks you.

4205
'Tis healthy to be sick sometimes.

4206 *Walden 'Economy'*
As for Doing-good, that is one of the professions which are full.

4207 *Walden 'Sounds'*
The three-o'clock in the morning courage, which Bonaparte thought was the rarest.

4208 *Walden 'Where I Lived, and What I Lived For'*
Time is but the stream I go a-fishing in.

4209
To know that we know what we know, and that we do not know what we do not know, that is true knowledge.

4210
What recommends commerce to me is its enterprise and bravery. It does not clasp its hands and pray to Jupiter.

4211
The youth gets together this material to build a bridge to the moon, or perchance, a palace or temple on earth, and at length, the middle-aged man concludes to build a woodshed with them.

THOREAU Marshall
4212
A man is rich in proportion to the things he can afford to let alone.

THORPE Jeremy 1929-
4213 *(on Macmillan sacking seven of his Cabinet)*
Greater love hath no man than this, that he lay down his friends for his life.

THURBER James 1894-1961
4214
We all have flaws, and mine is being wicked.

4215 *'The Bear Who Let It Alone'*
You might as well fall flat on your face as lean over too far backward.

4216
I am not a dog-lover. To me, a dog-lover is a dog who is in love with another dog.

4217
Humour is emotional chaos remembered in tranquillity.

4218
A lady of forty-seven who has been married twenty-seven years and has six children knows what love really is and once described it for me like this: 'Love is what you've been through with somebody.'

4219 *My Life and Hard Times*
Her own mother lived the latter years of her life in the horrible suspicion that electricity was dripping invisibly all over the house.

4220
Man is flying too fast for a world that is round. Soon he will catch up with himself in a great rear-end collision and Man will never know that what hit him from behind was Man.

4221
It's a naive domestic burgundy without any breeding, but I think you'll be amused by its presumption.

4222
Though statisticians in our time
Have never kept the score
Man wants a great deal here below
And Woman even more.

4223
Woman's place is in the wrong.

4224
Well, if I called the wrong number, why did you answer the phone?

THURLOW Edward 1731-1806
4225 *(attributed)*
Did you ever expect a corporation to have a conscience, when it has no soul to be damned, and no body to be kicked.

TICHNOR Don
4226
To convert an hourly wage to an approximate yearly salary, double the wage and change the decimal to a comma.

TICKELL Thomas 1686-1740
4227
Boredom is rage spread thin.

TILLICH Paul 1886-1965
4228 *The Courage To Be*
Neurosis is the way of avoiding non-being by avoiding being.

TOFFLER Alvin 1928-
4229
Parenthood remains the greatest single preserve of the amateur.

TOLKIEN J.R.R. 1892-1973
4230 *The Hobbit*
Never laugh at live dragons.

TOMLIN Lily
4231
We're all in this together - by ourselves.

4232
If love is the answer, could you rephrase the question?

TOSCANINI Arturo 1867-1957
4233
When I was very young, I kissed my first woman, and smoked my first cigarette on the same day. Believe me, never since have I wasted any more time on tobacco.

TOUSSENEL A.
4234 *L'Esprit des bêtes*
The more one gets to know of men, the more one values dogs.

TOYNBEE Arnold 1889-1975
4235
We have been God-like in our planned breeding of our domestic plants and animals, but rabbit-like in our unplanned breeding of ourselves.

TRAILL Henry Duff 1842-1900
4236 *'After Dilettante Concetti'*
Look in my face. My name is Used-to-was;
I am also called Played-out and Done-to-death,
And It-will-wash-no-more.

TRAPP Joseph 1679-1747
4237 *(of George I's donation of Library to Cambridge)*
The King, observing with judicious eyes
The state of both his universities,
To Oxford sent a troop of horse, and why?
That learned body wanted loyalty;
To Cambridge books, as very well discerning
How much that loyal body wanted learning.

TREE Sir Herbert Beerbohm 1852-1917
4238 *(to females assembled to play ladies-in-waiting)*
Ladies, just a little more virginity, if you don't mind.

4239 *(of Israel Zangwill)*
He is an old bore. Even the grave yawns for him.

4240 *(pressed by gramophone company for testimonial)*
Sirs, I have tested your machine. It adds a new terror to life and makes death a long-felt want.

TREVELYAN G.M. 1876-1962
4241 *English Social History*
If the French noblesse had been capable of playing cricket with their peasants, their chateaux would never have been burnt.

TREVOR William 1928-
4242 *(of the troubles in Northern Ireland)*
A disease in the family that is never mentioned.

TRILLIN Calvin
4243 *(attributed)*
The shelf life of the modern hardback writer is somewhere between the milk and the yoghurt.

TRINDER Tommy 1909-1989
4244 *(of American troops in Britain during World War 2)*
Overpaid, overfed, oversexed, and over here.

TROLLOPE Anthony 1815-1882
4245 *Autobiography*
He must have known me had he seen me as he was wont to see me, for he was in the habit of flogging me constantly. Perhaps he did not recognize me by my face.

4246 *The Small House at Allington*
I doubt whether any girl would be satisfied with her lover's mind if she knew the whole of it.

4247
There is no villainy to which education cannot reconcile us.

TRONCHIN Théodore 1709-1781
4248
In medicine, sins of commission are mortal, sins of omission venial.

TRUDELL Dennis
4249
Sloppy, raggedy-assed old life. I love it. I never want to die.

TRUMAN Harry S. 1884-1972
4250 *(attributed)*
Always be sincere, even if you don't mean it.

4251
Within the first few months I discovered that being a president is like riding a tiger. A man has to keep riding or be swallowed.

4252 *Letter to his sister*
All the President is, is a glorified public relations man who spends his time flattering, kissing and kicking people to get them to do what they are supposed to do anyway.

4253
I never give them [the public] hell. I just tell the truth, and they think it is hell.

4254
A politician is a man who understands government, and it takes a politician to run a government.
A statesman is a politician who's been dead 10 or 15 years.

4255
It's a recession when your neighbour loses his job; it's a depression when you lose yours.

4256
Well, I wouldn't say that I was in the 'great' class, but I had a great time while I was trying to be great.

TUCKER Sophie 1884-1966
4257
From birth to 18 a girl needs good parents. From 18 to 35, she needs good looks. From 35 to 55, good personality. From 55 on, she needs good cash.

TUER A.W. 1838-1900
4258 *(title of Portuguese-English conversational guide)*
English as she is Spoke.

TURGENEV Ivan 1818-1823
4259 *Fathers and Sons*
Just try and set death aside. It sets you aside, and that's the end of it!

4260 *Fathers and Sons*
Whatever a man prays for, he prays for a miracle. Every prayer reduces itself to this: Great God, grant that twice two be not four.

TUSSER Thomas c.1524-1580
4261 *Five Hundred Points of Good Husbandry*
Who goeth a-borrowing
Goeth a-sorrowing.
Few lend (but fools)
Their working tools.

4262 *Five Hundred Points of Good Husbandry*
In doing of either, let wit bear a stroke,
For buying or selling of pig in a poke.

TWAIN Mark 1835-1910
4263 *The Adventures of Huckleberry Finn*
There was things which he stretched, but mainly he told the truth.

4264 *The Adventures of Huckleberry Finn*
All kings is mostly rapscallions.

4265 *The Adventures of Huckleberry Finn*
Hain't we got all the fools in town on our side? and ain't that a big enough majority in any town.

4266
Put all thine eggs in one basket and - watch that basket.

4267
It isn't so astonishing, the number of things that I can remember, as the number of things I can remember that aren't so.

4268
Biographies are but the clothes and buttons of the man - the biography of the man himself cannot be written.

4269
I was born modest; not all over, but in spots.

4270
We should be careful to get out of an experience only the wisdom that is in it - and stop there, lest we be like the cat that sits down on a hot stove-lid. She will never sit down on a hot stove-lid again - and that is well; but also she will never sit down on a cold one anymore.

4271
In certain trying circumstances, urgent circumstances, desperate circumstances, profanity furnishes a relief denied even to prayer.

4272
We are chameleons, and our partialities and prejudices change places with an easy and blessed facility.

4273
Consider well the proportion of things. It is better to be a young June bug, than an old bird of paradise.

4274 *A Curious Dream 'Facts concerning...'*
Soap and education are not as sudden as a massacre, but they are more deadly in the long run.

4275 *A Curious Dream 'A Mysterious Visit'*
Barring that natural expression of
villainy which we all have, the man
looked honest enough.

4276 *Following the Equator*
Truth is the most valuable thing we have.
Let us economize it.

4277 *Following the Equator*
It is by the goodness of God that in our
country we have those three
unspeakably precious things: freedom of
speech, freedom of conscience, and the
prudence never to practise either of
them.

4278 *Following the Equator*
Man is the Only Animal that Blushes. Or
needs to.

4279 *Following the Equator*
It takes your enemy and your friend,
working together, to hurt you to the
heart: the one to slander you and the
other to get the news to you.

4280
Ethical man - a Christian holding four
aces.

4281
Get your facts first, and then you can
distort 'em as much as you please.

4282
Fewer things are harder to put up with
than the annoyance of a good example.

4283
Golf is a good walk spoiled.

4284
The human race is a race of cowards;
and I am not only marching in that
procession but carrying a banner.

4285 *The Innocents Abroad*
They spell it Vinci and pronounce it
Vinchy; foreigners always spell better
than they pronounce.

4286
That kind of so-called housekeeping
where they have six Bibles and no cork-
screw.

4287
Life would be infinitely happier if we
could only be born at the age of eighty
and gradually approach eighteen.

4288
I can live for two months on a good
compliment.

4289
We may not pay Satan reverence, for that
would be indiscreet, but we can at least
respect his talents.

4290
Make money and the whole world will
conspire to call you a gentleman.

4291
Noise proves nothing. Often a hen who
has merely laid an egg cackles as if she
had laid an asteroid.

4292 *Notebooks*
Familiarity breeds contempt - and
children.

4293 *Notebooks*
Good breeding consists in concealing
how much we think of ourselves and
how little we think of the other person.

4294
I am opposed to millionaires, but it
would be dangerous to offer me the
position.

4295
In Paris they simply stared when I spoke
to them in French; I never did succeed in
making those idiots understand their
own language.

4296
In prayer we call ourselves 'worms of the
dust', but it is only on a sort of tacit
understanding that the remark shall not
be taken at par.

4297 *Pudd'nhead Wilson*
Cauliflower is nothing but cabbage with
a college education.

4298 *Pudd'nhead Wilson*
When angry, count four; when very
angry, swear.

4299 *Pudd'nhead Wilson*
As to the Adjective: when in doubt, strike it out.

4300
The reports of my death are greatly exaggerated.

4301
Richard Wagner, a musician who wrote music which is better than it sounds.

4302
If I cannot smoke cigars in heaven, I shall not go.

4303
Let us be thankful for the fools. But for them the rest of us could not succeed.

4304
Tomorrow night I appear for the first time before a Boston audience - 4000 critics.

4305
Travel is fatal to prejudice, bigotry and narrow-mindedness.

4306
There is no unhappiness like the misery of sighting land again after a cheerful, careless voyage.

4307
What a good thing Adam had - when he said a good thing, he knew nobody had said it before.

4308
When I was a boy of fourteen, my father was so ignorant I could hardly stand to have the old man around. But when I got to be twenty-one, I was astonished at how much the old man had learned in seven years.

4309
When we remember that we are all mad, the mysteries disappear and life stands explained.

4310
When I was younger, I could remember anything, whether it had happened or not.

4311
I wish to become rich, so that I can instruct the people and glorify honest poverty a little, like those kind-hearted, fat, benevolent people do.

4312
Wit is the sudden marriage of ideas which, before their union, were not perceived to have any relation.

TYNAN Kenneth 1927-1980
4313
A critic is a man who knows the way but can't drive the car.

4314 *Curtains (of Noel Coward)*
Forty years ago he was Slightly in *Peter Pan,* and you might say that he has been wholly in *Peter Pan* ever since.

4315
A neurosis is a secret you don't know you're keeping.

4316 *Tynan Right and Left*
Drama criticism ... [is] a self-knowing account of the way in which one's consciousness has been modified during an evening in the theatre.

4317
The unique thing about Margaret Rutherford is that she can act with her chin alone. Among its many moods I especially cherish the chin commanding, the chin in doubt, and the chin at bay.

UDALL Steward
4318
Gross National Product is our Holy Grail.

UDKOFF Bob
4319
Hate is such a luxurious emotion, it can only be spent on one we love.

UPDIKE John 1932-
4320 *Assorted Prose 'Confessions of a Wild Bore'*
A healthy male adult bore consumes *each year* one and a half times his own weight in other people's patience.

4321
The Englishman is under no
constitutional obligation to believe that
all men are created equal. The American
agony is therefore scarcely intelligible,
like a saint's self-flagellation viewed by
an atheist.

4322 *Picked Up Pieces (of England)*
A soggy little island huffing and puffing
to keep up with Western Europe.

4323 *Problems 'How to love America ...'*
America is a vast conspiracy to make you
happy.

4324
Russia is the only country of the world
you can be homesick for while you're still
in it.

USTINOV Sir Peter 1921-
4325
If Botticelli were alive today he'd be
working for *Vogue*.

4326
Comedy is simply a funny way of being
serious.

4327 *Dear Me*
Laughter ... the most civilized music in
the world.

4328 *Dear Me*
I do not believe that friends are
necessarily the people you like best, they
are merely the people who got there first.

4329 *(on imitating Harold Macmillan -
attributed)*
Talk as though you have a cathedral in
your mouth.

4330
By increasing the size of the keyhole,
today's playwrights are in danger of
doing away with the door.

4331
Laughter would be bereaved if snobbery
died.

4332
Parents are the bones on which children
cut their teeth.

4333 *Romanoff and Juliet*
At the age of four with paper hats and
wooden swords we're all Generals. Only
some of us never grow out of it.

4334 *Romanoff and Juliet*
This is a free country, madam. We have a
right to share your privacy in a public
place.

VALENTINE Alan
4335
Whenever science makes a discovery, the
devil grabs it while the angels are
debating the best way to use it.

VALERIUS MAXIMUS fl. AD c.15
4336 *Facta et Dicta Memorabilia*
I appeal from Philip drunk to Philip
sober.

VALÉRY Paul 1871-1945
4337
A businessman is a hybrid of a dancer
and a calculator.

4338
If some great catastrophe is not
announced every morning, we feel a
certain void. 'Nothing in the paper
today,' we sigh.

4339
To penetrate one's being, one must go
armed to the teeth.

4340 *Tel Quel 1 'Moralités'*
God created man and, finding him not
sufficiently alone, gave him a companion
to make him feel his solitude more
keenly.

4341 *Tel Quel 2 'Rhumbs'*
Politics is the art of preventing people
from taking part in affairs which
properly concern them.

VANBRUGH Sir John 1664-1726
4342 *The Provoked Husband*
Much of a muchness.

4343 *The Relapse*
When once a woman has given you her
heart, you can never get rid of the rest of
her body.

4344 *The Relapse*
In matters of love men's eyes are always bigger than their bellies. They have violent appetites, 'tis true; but they have soon dined.

4345
The want of a thing is perplexing enough, but the possession of it is intolerable.

VAUGHAN Bill
4346
Occasionally we sigh for an earlier day when we could just look at the stars without worrying whether they were theirs or ours.

4347
One trouble with growing older is that it gets progressively tougher to find a famous historical figure who didn't amount to much when he was your age.

VAUGHAN Harry
4348
If you can't stand the heat, get out of the kitchen.

VAUGHAN Henry 1622-1695
4349
Caesar had perished from the world of men
Had not his sword been rescued by his pen.

VAUVENARGUES Marquis de 1715-1747
4350
All men are born truthful, and die liars.

4351
The lazy are always wanting to do something.

4352
The mind reaches great heights only by spurts.

4353
When we are sick our virtues and our vices are in abeyance.

VESPASIAN AD 9-79
4354 *(replying to objection to tax public lavatories)*
Money has no smell.

4355 *(when fatally ill)*
Woe is me, I think I am becoming a god.

VICTORIA Queen 1819-1901
4356 *(attributed)*
We are not amused.

4357 *(of Gladstone)*
He speaks to me as if I was a public meeting.

4358
The important thing is not what they think of me, it is what I think of them.

VIDAL Gore 1925-
4359
[Commercialism is] doing well that which should not be done at all.

4360
I'm all for bringing back the birch, but only between consenting adults.

4361 *(of Ronald Regan)*
A triumph of the embalmer's art.

4362
Whenever a friend succeeds, a little something in me dies.

VIERA GALLO José Antonio 1943-
4363
Socialism can only arrive by bicycle.

VILLARS Marshall de 1653-1734
4364
God save me from my friends - I can protect myself from my enemies.

VILLIERS George 1628-1687
4365 *The Rehearsal*
Ay, now the plot thickens very much upon us.

VILLIERS DE L'ISLE-ADAM Philippe-Auguste 1838-1889
4366 *Axël*
Living? The servants will do that for us.

VINCENT Field Marshall Sir Richard 1931-
4367
The first principle of war is: For God's sake decide what you're trying to achieve before you go out and start doing it.

VOLTAIRE 1694-1778
4368
I advise you to go on living solely to enrage those who are paying your annuities. It is the only pleasure I have left.

4369
I know I am among civilized men because they are fighting so savagely.

4370
The best government is a benevolent tyranny tempered by an occasional assassination.

4371 *Candide*
In this country [England] it is thought well to kill an admiral from time to time to encourage the others.

4372
England has forty-two religions and only two sauces.

4373
If God made us in his image, we have certainly returned the compliment.

4374 *Le Mondain*
The superfluous, a very necessary thing.

4375 *L'Enfant prodigue*
All styles are good except the tiresome kind.

4376
Never having been able to succeed in the world, he took his revenge by speaking ill of it.

4377
I never was ruined but twice - once when I lost a lawsuit, and once when I gained one.

4378 *The Piccini Notebooks*
Governments need both shepherds and butchers.

4379 *The Piccini Notebooks*
God is on the side not of the heavy battalions, but of the best shots.

4380 *Thoughts of a Philosopher*
Marriage is the only adventure open to the cowardly.

4381
Ask a toad what is beauty? ... a female with two great round eyes coming out of her little head, a large flat mouth, a yellow belly and a brown back.

4382
When it is a question of money, everybody is of the same religion.

4383 *(when asked to renounce the Devil, on deathbed)*
This is no time for making new enemies.

VONNEGUT Kurt 1922-
4384
Educating a beautiful woman is like pouring honey into a fine Swiss watch: everything stops.

VORSE Mary Heaton
4385
(Writing) - the art of applying the seat of the pants to the seat of the chair.

VOZNESENKSY Andrei 1933-
4386
The times spat at me. I spit back at the times.

WAGNER Robert 1930-
4387
As a parent you just hang on for the ride.

WALKER James J.
4388
A reformer is a guy who rides through a sewer in a glass-bottomed boat.

WALL Max 1908-1990
4389
Show business is like sex. When it's wonderful, it's wonderful. But when it isn't very good, it's still all right.

WALLACE Edgar 1875-1932
4390
What is a highbrow? He is a man who has found something more interesting than women.

WALLACE Joe
4391
Ours is a sovereign nation
Bows to no foreign will

But whenever they cough in Washington
They spit on Parliament Hill.

WALLAS Graham 1858-1932
4392 *The Art of Thought*
The little girl had the making of a poet in
her who, being told to be sure of her
meaning before she spoke, said, 'How
can I know what I think till I see what I
say?'

WALPOLE Horace 1717-1797
4393 *Letter to Hon. Henry Conway*
But, thank God! the Thames is between
me and the Duchess of Queensberry.

4394 *Letter to Revd. William Cole*
The way to ensure summer in England is
to have it framed and glazed in a
comfortable room.

4395
I am in a moment of pretty wellness.

4396
Virtue knows to a farthing what it has
lost by not having been vice.

WALPOLE Sir Robert 1676-1745
4397
I always tell a young man not to use the
word `always'.

WALTERS Barbara
4398
I can get a better grasp of what is going
on in the world from one good
Washington dinner party than from all
the background information NBC piles
on my desk.

WALTERS Maryanne
4399
The point of therapy is to get unhooked,
not to thrash around on how you got
hooked.

WALTON Izaak 1593-1683
4400 *The Compleat Angler*
An excellent angler, and now with God.

4401 *The Compleat Angler*
The dish of meat is too good for any but
anglers, or very honest men.

4402 *The Compleat Angler 'Epistle to the
Reader'*
Angling may be said to be so like the
mathematics, that it can never be fully
learnt.

4403 *The Compleat Angler 'Epistle to the
Reader'*
As no man is born an artist, so no man is
born an angler.

WARBURTON William 1698-1779
4404 *(to Lord Sandwich)*
Orthodoxy is my doxy; heterodoxy is
another man's doxy.

WARD Artemus 1834-1867
4405 *Artemus Ward His Book 'Fourth of
July Oration'*
I'm not a politician and my other habits
are good.

4406 *Artemus Ward His Book 'The
Showman's Courtship'*
I wish thar was winders to my Sole, sed I,
so that you could see some of my feelins.

4407 *Artemus Ward His Book 'A Visit to
Brigham Young'*
I girdid up my Lions & fled the Seen.

4408 *Artemus Ward His Book 'Woman's
Rights'*
The female woman is one of the greatest
institooshuns of which this land can
boste.

4409 *Artemus Ward in London*
It is a pity that Chawcer, who had
geneyus, was so unedicated. He's the
wuss speller I know of.

4410 *Artemus Ward in London*
Let us all be happy, and live within our
means, even if we have to borrer the
money to do it with.

4411 *Artemus Ward's Lecture*
Why is this thus? What is the reason of
this thusness?

4412 *Artemus Ward's Lecture 'Brigham
Young's...'*
He is dreadfully married. He's the most
married man I ever saw in my life.

4413
Why don't you show us a statesman who can rise up to the emergency, and cave in the emergency's head?

WARNER H.M.
4414 *(of talking pictures - in 1927)*
Who the hell wants to hear actors talk?

WASHINGTON Ned 1901-1976
4415 *(song from the film Pinocchio)*
Hi diddle dee dee (an actor's life for me).

WATKYNS Richard
4416
When I was born I did lament and cry
And now each day doth shew the reason why.

WATSON Arthur K. 1867-1947
4417
Show me a man with both feet on the ground and I'll show you a man who can't put his pants on.

WATTS Isaac 1674-1748
4418 *Divine Songs for Children 'The Sluggard'*
'Tis the voice of the sluggard; I heard him complain,
'You have waked me too soon, I must slumber again'.
As the door on its hinges, so he on his bed,
Turns his sides and his shoulders and his heavy head.

WAUGH Evelyn 1903-1966
4419 *Decline and Fall*
I haven't been to sleep for over a year. That's why I go to bed early. One needs more rest if one doesn't sleep.

4420 *Decline and Fall*
Very hard for a man with a wig to keep order.

4421 *Decline and Fall*
That's the public-school system all over. They may kick you out, but they never let you down.

4422 *The Loved One*
You never find an Englishman among the under-dogs - except in England, of course.

4423
Manners are especially the need of the plain. The pretty can get away with anything.

4424 *'An Open Letter'*
Impotence and sodomy are socially O.K. but birth control is flagrantly middle-class.

4425
Perhaps host and guest is really the happiest relation for father and son.

4426
Punctuality is the virtue of the bored.

4427 *Scoop*
I will not stand for being called a woman in my own house.

4428 *Scoop*
Other nations use 'force'; we Britons alone use 'Might'.

4429 *Vile Bodies*
All this fuss about sleeping together. For physical pleasure I'd sooner go to my dentist any day.

4430 *(asked what he did for his college)*
I drink for it.

4431
Winston Churchill is always expecting rabbits to come out of an empty hat.

WAVELL Lord 1883-1950
4432 *(attributed)*
(Love) is like a cigar. If it goes out, you can light it again but it never tastes quite the same.

WEBB Sidney (Baron Passfield) 1859-1947
4433
Marriage is the waste-paper basket of the emotions.

WEBSTER John c.1580-c.1625
4434 *The Duchess of Malfi*
Unequal nature, to place women's hearts
So far upon the left side.

4435 *The Duchess of Malfi*
We are merely the stars' tennis-balls,
struck and bandied
Which way please them.

4436 *The White Devil*
Fortune's a right whore:
If she give aught, she deals it in small
parcels,
That she may take away all at one
swoop.

4437 *The White Devil*
I have caught
An everlasting cold; I have lost my voice
Most irrecoverably.

WEISSMULLER Johnny 1904-1984
4438 *(summing up his role in Tarzan)*
Me Tarzan, you Jane.

WEIZMANN Chaim 1874-1952
4439
Miracles sometimes occur, but one has
to work terribly hard for them.

WELDON Fay 1931-
4440
Hell is not other people, hell is no other
people.

WELLINGTON Duke of 1769-1852
4441
Possible? Is anything impossible? Read
the newspapers.

4442 *(attributed, on reviewing his troops)*
I don't know what effect these men will
have on the enemy, but by God, they
frighten *me*.

4443 *(on seeing the first Reformed
Parliament)*
I never saw so many shocking bad hats
in my life.

4444 *(of steam locomotives)*
I see no reason to suppose that these
machines will ever force themselves into
general use.

WELLS Carolyn 1869-1942
4445
We should live and learn; but by the time
we've learned, it's too late to live.

WELLS C.M. 1908-
4446
All port tastes the same after lunch.

WELLS H.G. 1866-1946
4447
Advertising is legalized lying.

4448 *The History of Mr Polly*
I'll make a gory mess of you. I'll cut bits
orf you.

4449 *Kipps*
'I'm a Norfan, both sides,' he would
explain, with the air of one who had seen
trouble.

4450 *Select Conversations with an Uncle*
Bah! the thing is not a nose at all, but a
bit of primordial chaos clapped on to my
face.

4451
I want to go ahead of Father Time with a
scythe of my own.

4452 *The Wife of Sir Isaac Harman*
Moral indignation is jealousy with a halo.

WESKER Arnold 1932-
4453 *Chips with Everything*
It said 'Chips with everything'. Chips
with every damn thing. You breed
babies and you eat chips with
everything.

WESLEY John 1703-1791
4454 *Letter to Miss March*
Though I am always in haste, I am never
in a hurry.

WEST Mae 1892-1980
4455 *(attributed)*
When I'm good, I'm very good, but when
I'm bad, I'm better.

4456 *in Belle of the Nineties*
"A man in the house is worth two in the
street."

4457 *in Every Day's a Holiday*
"I always say, keep a diary and some day
it'll keep you."

4458
I generally avoid temptation unless I
can't resist it.

4459
Too much of a good thing can be wonderful.

4460 *in I'm No Angel*
"It's not the men in my life that counts - it's the life in my men."

4461 *in Klondike Annie*
"Give a man a free hand and he'll try to put it all over you."

4462 *in My Little Chickadee*
"Is that a gun in your pocket, or are you just glad to see me?"

4463
Marriage is a great institution, but I am not ready for an institution.

4464
I used to be snow-white ... but I drifted.

4465
When choosing between two evils, I always like to take the one I've never tried before.

4466 *The Wit and Wisdom of Mae West*
When women go wrong, men go right after them.

4467 *in She Done Him Wrong*
"Why don't you come up sometime, and see me?" [usually quoted: 'Why don't you come up and see me sometime?']

WEST Rebecca 1892-1983
4468 *(of Michael Arlen)*
Every other inch a gentleman.

4469 *The Salt of the Earth*
The point is that nobody likes having salt rubbed into their wounds, even if it is the salt of the earth.

WESTCOTT Edward Noyes 1846-1898
4470
The only man who can change his mind is the man who's got one.

4471
I reckon there's as much human nature in some folks as there is in others, if not more.

4472
They say a reasonable amount o' fleas is good for a dog - it keeps him from broodin' over bein' a dog mebbe.

WESTON R.P. and LEE Bert 1878-1936 and 1880-1947
4473 *'Good-bye-ee!'*
Good-bye-ee! - Good-bye-ee!
Wipe the tear, baby dear, from your eye-ee.
Tho' it's hard to part, I know,
I'll be tickled to death to go.
Don't cry-ee - don't sigh-ee!
There's a silver lining in the sky-ee!
Bonsoir, old thing! cheerio! chin-chin!
Nahpoo! Toodle-oo! Good-bye-ee!

WHARTON Edith 1862-1937
4474 *Xingu and Other Stories 'Xingu'*
Mrs Ballinger is one of the ladies who pursue Culture in bands, as though it were dangerous to meet it alone.

WHATELY Richard 1787-1863
4475 *Apophthegms*
Happiness is no laughing matter.

4476 *Apophthegms*
It is a folly to expect men to do all that they may reasonably be expected to do.

4477 *Apophthegms*
Honesty is the best policy; but he who is governed by that maxim is not an honest man.

WHISTLER James McNeill 1834-1903
4478 *(in his case against Ruskin)*
[Replying to the question 'For two days' labour, you ask two hundred guineas?']
No, I ask it for the knowledge of a lifetime.

4479 *The Gentle Art of Making Enemies*
I am not arguing with you - I am telling you.

4480 *(to a lady reminded of his work by a 'haze')*
Yes madam, Nature is creeping up.

4481
Nature is usually wrong.

4482 *Mr Whistler's 'Ten O'Clock'*
Art is upon the Town!

WHITE E.B. 1899-1985
4483 *'The Commuter'*
Commuter - one who spends his life
In riding to and from his wife;
A man who shaves and takes a train,
And then rides back to shave again.

4484
The first day of spring was once the time
for taking the young virgins into the
fields, there in dalliance to set an
example in fertility for Nature to follow.
Now we just set the clock an hour ahead
and change the oil in the crankcase.

WHITE John
4485
There are three kinds of people in the
world: those who can't stand Picasso,
those who can't stand Raphael and those
who've never heard of either of them.

WHITE William Allen 1868-1944
4486 *(when Roosevelt retired from
Presidential campaign)*
All dressed up, with nowhere to go.

WHITEFIELD George
4487
It is better to wear out than to rust out.

WHITEHEAD Alfred North 1861-1947
4488
Ideas won't keep: something must be
done about them.

WHITEHORN Katharine 1926-
4489 *Roundabout 'The Office Party'*
Bringing down the mighty from their
seats is an agreeable and necessary
pastime, but no one supposes that the
mighty, having struggled so hard to get
seated, will enjoy the dethronement.

4490 *Shouts and Murmurs 'Hats'*
Hats divide generally into three classes:
offensive hats, defensive hats, and
shrapnel.

4491 *Sunday Best 'Decoding the West'*
I wouldn't say when you've seen one
Western you've seen the lot; but when

you've seen the lot you get the feeling
you've seen one.

WHITMAN Walt 1819-1892
4492
I am as bad as the worst, but, thank God,
I am as good as the best.

4493
The dirtiest book of all is the expurgated
book.

WHITTIER John Greenleaf 1807-1892
4494 *'Barbara Frietchie'*
'Shoot, if you must, this old grey head,
But spare your country's flag,' she said.

WHITTON Charlotte 1896-1975
4495
Whatever women do they must do twice
as well as men to be thought half as
good. Luckily, this is not difficult.

WHUR Cornelius
4496 *'The Female Friend'*
While lasting joys the man attend
Who has a faithful female friend.

WHYTE-MELVILLE George John 1821-
1878
4497 *'The Good Grey Mare'*
But I freely admit that the best of my fun
I owe it to horse and hound.

WICKHAM Anna 1884-1947
4498 *'The Affinity'*
It is well within the order of things
That man should listen when his mate
sings;
But the true male never yet walked
Who liked to listen when his mate
talked.

WIGGAN A.E.
4499
Intelligence appears to be the thing that
enables a man to get along without
education. Education appears to be the
thing that enables a man to get along
without the use of his intelligence.

WILBERFORCE Samuel 1805-1873
4500 *Impromptu verse (attributed)*
If I were a cassowary
On the plains of Timbuctoo,

I would eat a missionary,
Cassock, band, and hymn-book too.

4501 *(to T.H. Huxley)*
Was it through his grandfather or his
grandmother that he claimed his descent
from a monkey?

WILBUR Richard 1921-
4502 *'Epistemology'*
We milk the cow of the world, and as we
do
We whisper in her ear, 'You are not true'.

WILDE Oscar 1854-1900
4503
Anybody can be good in the country.
There are no temptations there.

4504
Arguments are to be avoided - they are
always vulgar and often convincing.

4505 *(of Bernard Shaw)*
He hasn't an enemy in the world, and
none of his friends like him.

4506
English conversationalists have a
miraculous power of turning wine into
water.

4507
I hope you have not been leading a
double life, pretending to be wicked and
being really good all the time. That
would be hypocrisy.

4508 *The Importance of Being Earnest*
Really, if the lower orders don't set us a
good example, what on earth is the use
of them?

4509 *The Importance of Being Earnest*
To lose one parent, Mr Worthing, may be
regarded as a misfortune; to lose both
looks like carelessness.

4510 *The Importance of Being Earnest*
In married life three is company and two
none.

4511 *The Importance of Being Earnest*
The good ended happily, and the bad
unhappily. That is what fiction means.

4512 *The Importance of Being Earnest*
None of us are perfect. I myself am
peculiarly susceptible to draughts.

4513 *The Importance of Being Earnest*
I never travel without my diary. One
should always have something
sensational to read in the train.

4514 *The Importance of Being Earnest*
This suspense is terrible. I hope it will
last.

4515 *Impressions of America 'Leadville'*
Please do not shoot the pianist. He is
doing his best.

4516 *Intentions 'The Critic as Artist'*
Every great man nowadays has his
disciples, and it is always Judas who
writes the biography.

4517 *Intentions 'The Critic as Artist'*
The one duty we owe to history is to
rewrite it.

4518 *Intentions 'The Critic as Artist'*
A little sincerity is a dangerous thing,
and a great deal of it is absolutely fatal.

4519
I've put my genius into my life; I've only
put my talent into my works.

4520 *Lady Windermere's Fan*
I can resist everything except
temptation.

4521 *Lady Windermere's Fan*
We are all in the gutter, but some of us
are looking at the stars.

4522 *Lady Windermere's Fan*
What is a cynic?
A man who knows the price of
everything and the value of nothing.

4523 *Lady Windermere's Fan*
Experience is the name every one gives
to their mistakes.

4524 *(to Mrs Leverson on his release from
prison)*
My dear, you're the only woman in the
world who'd have known the right hat to
wear on an occasion like this.

4525
I have nothing to declare except my genius.

4526
Nothing that is worth knowing can be taught.

4527
The only thing to do with good advice is to pass it on. It is never any use to oneself.

4528
It is only shallow people who do not judge by appearances. The true mystery of the world is the visible, not the invisible.

4529
The only way to get rid of a temptation is to yield to it. Resist it, and your soul grows sick with longing for the things it has forbidden to itself.

4530
She is a peacock in everything but beauty.

4531
Pessimist - one who, when he has the choice of two evils, chooses both.

4532 *The Picture of Dorian Gray*
There is only one thing in the world worse than being talked about, and that is not being talked about.

4533 *The Picture of Dorian Gray*
A cigarette is the perfect type of a perfect pleasure. It is exquisite, and it leaves one unsatisfied. What more can one want?

4534
I played with an idea, and grew wilful; tossed it into the air and transformed it; let it escape and recaptured it; made it iridescent with fancy, and winged it with paradox.

4535
The public is wonderfully tolerant. It forgives everything except genius.

4536
Success is a science. If you have the conditions, you get the result.

4537
The tragedy of old age is not that one is old, but that one is young.

4538
A true gentleman is one who is never unintentionally rude.

4539 *(when told of huge fee for surgical operation)*
Ah, well, then, I suppose that I shall have to die beyond my means.

4540 *A Woman of No Importance*
The English country gentleman galloping after a fox - the unspeakable in full pursuit of the uneatable.

4541 *A Woman of No Importance*
One should never trust a woman who tells one her real age. A woman who would tell one that, would tell one anything.

4542 *A Woman of No Importance*
The Book of Life begins with a man and a woman in a garden.
It ends with Revelations.

4543 *A Woman of No Importance*
Children begin by loving their parents; after a time they judge them; rarely, if ever, do they forgive them.

4544 *A Woman of No Importance*
You should study the Peerage, Gerald ... It is the best thing in fiction the English have ever done.

4545 *A Woman of No Importance*
Twenty years of romance make a woman look like a ruin; but twenty years of marriage make her something like a public building.

4546
Work is the curse of the drinking classes.

WILDER Billy 1906-
4547
Hindsight is always twenty-twenty.

WILDER Thornton 1897-1975
4548
If a man has no vices, he's in great danger of making vices about his virtues, and there's a spectacle.

4549 *The Merchant of Yonkers*
Marriage is a bribe to make a
housekeeper think she's a householder.

4550 *The Merchant of Yonkers*
The fights are the best part of married
life. The rest is merely so-so.

4551
Many plays, certainly mine, are like
blank cheques. The actors and directors
put their own signatures on them.

WILENSKY Robert
4552
We've all heard that a million monkeys
banging on a million typewriters will
eventually reproduce the entire works of
Shakespeare. Now, thanks to the
Internet, we know this is not true.

WILLIAMS Heathcote
4553
Reason is an emotion for the sexless.

WILLIAMS Nigel
4554
This is the BBC - we are not making
programmes for the glitterati or the
literati of any kindy of arty.

WILLIAMS Tennessee 1911-1983
4555
A vacuum is a hell of a lot better than
some of the stuff that nature replaces it
with.

WILLIAMS William Carlos 1883-1963
4556 'To Ford Madox Ford in Heaven'
Is it any better in heaven, my friend
Ford,
Than you found it in Provence?

4557 'Paterson'
No woman is virtuous
who does not give herself to her lover
- forthwith.

WILLS Garry
4558
Politicians make good company for a
while just as children do - their self-
enjoyment is contagious. But they soon
exhaust their favourite subjects -
themselves.

WILSON Earl
4559
Gossip is when you hear something you
like about someone you don't.

WILSON Ethel 1890-
4560
Dullness is a misdemeanour.

WILSON Sir Harold 1916-1995
4561
The office of president requires the
constitution of an athlete, the patience
of a mother, the endurance of an early
Christian.

WILSON Sandy 1924-
4562 *The Boyfriend*
We've got to have
We plot to have
For it's so dreary not to have
That certain thing called the Boy Friend.

4563 *The Boy Friend*
But it's nicer, much nicer in Nice.

WILSON Woodrow 1856-1924
4564
A friend of mine says that every man
who takes office in Washington either
grows or swells, and when I give a man
an office, I watch him carefully to see
whether he is swelling or growing.

4565
I'm a vague, conjunctured personality,
more made up of opinions and
academic prepossessions than of human
traits and red corpuscles.

4566
I used to be a lawyer, but now I am a
reformed character.

4567
No man ever saw a government. I live in
the midst of the Government of the
United States, but I never saw the
Government of the United States.

4568
A man's rootage is more important than
his leafage.

4569
Nothing was ever done so systematically as nothing is being done now.

4570
I not only use all the brains I have, but all I can borrow.

WINCHELL Walter 1897-1972
4571
Gossip is the art of saying nothing in a way that leaves practically nothing unsaid.

WISE Dennis
4572
We've signed five foreigners over the summer but I'll be on hand to learn them a bit of English.

WODEHOUSE P.G. 1881-1975
4573 *The Adventures of Sally*
When you marry, Sally, grab a chump. Tap his forehead first, and if it rings solid, don't hesitate. All the unhappy marriages come from the husbands having brains.

4574
The butler entered the room, a solemn procession of one.

4575 *The Code of the Woosters*
He spoke with a certain what-is-it in his voice, and I could see that, if not actually disgruntled, he was far from being gruntled.

4576 *The Code of the Woosters*
Slice him where you like, a hellhound is always a hellhound.

4577 *The Inimitable Jeeves*
It was my Uncle George who discovered that alcohol was a food well in advance of medical thought.

4578 *My Man Jeeves 'Rallying Round Old George'*
What a queer thing Life is! So unlike anything else, don't you know, if you see what I mean.

4579
Why don't you get a haircut; you look like a chrysanthemum.

WOLFE Humbert 1886-1940
4580 *'Over the Fire'*
You cannot hope
to bribe or twist,
thank God! the
British journalist.
But, seeing what
the man will do
unbribed, there's
no occasion to.

WOLFE Thomas 1900-1938
4581 *Look Homeward, Angel*
Most of the time we think we're sick, it's all in the mind.

WOLFENDEN John
4582
Schoolmasters and parents exist to be grown out of.

WOMBAT R.T.
4583
The lazy man gets round the sun as quickly as the busy one.

WOOD Mrs Henry 1814-1887
4584 *East Lynne*
Dead! and ... never called me mother.

WOODS Harry
4585 *'Side by Side'*
Oh we ain't got a barrel of money,
Maybe we're ragged and funny,
But we'll travel along
Singin' a song,
Side by side.

WOOLF Virginia 1882-1941
4586 *The Common Reader 'Lady Dorothy Nevill'*
In one of those comfortably padded lunatic asylums which are known, euphemistically, as the stately homes of England.

4587
Money dignifies what is frivolous if unpaid for.

4588
Have you any notion how many books are written about women in the course of one year? Have you any notion how many are written by men? Are you aware

that you are, perhaps, the most discussed animal in the universe?

WOOLLCOTT Alexander 1887-1943
4589
All the things I really like to do are either immoral, illegal or fattening.

4590
A broker is a man who takes your fortune and runs it into a shoestring.

4591
The English have an extraordinary ability for flying into a great calm.

4592
I must get out of these wet clothes and into a dry Martini.

WOOTON Sir Henry 1568-1639
4593
An ambassador is an honest man sent to lie abroad for the good of his country.

4594
Critics are like brushers of noblemen's clothes.

4595 *'Upon the Death of Sir Albertus Moreton's Wife'*
He first deceased; she for a little tried
To live without him: liked it not, and died.

WORDSWORTH Dame Elizabeth 1840-1932
4596 *'Good and Clever'*
If all the good people were clever,
And all clever people were good,
The world would be nicer than ever
We thought that it possibly could.

WORK H.C. 1832-1884
4597 *'Grandfather's Clock'*
But it stopped short - never to go again -
When the old man died.

WRIGHT Frank Lloyd 1867-1959
4598 *Autobiography*
The necessities were going by default to save the luxuries until I hardly knew which were necessities and which luxuries.

4599
A doctor can bury his mistakes, but an architect can only advise his clients to plant vines.

4600
Early in life I had to choose between arrogance and hypocritical humility. I chose honest arrogance and have seen no occasion to change.

4601
I hate intellectuals. They are from the top down. I am from the bottom up.

4602
An idea is salvation by imagination.

4603
Pictures deface walls oftener than they decorate them.

4604
Television is chewing gum for the eyes.

WRIGHT Ronald 1908-
4605
Societies that do not eat people are fascinated by those that do.

WRIGHT Steven
4606
The older you get, the more you learn to see what you've been taught to see. When you're a kid, you see what's there.

WRIGLEY Jr. William 1861-1932
4607
When two men in business always agree, one of them is unnecessary.

WYBROW Bob
4608
We have three sexes: men, women who are housewives, and other women.

WYCHERLEY William c.1640-1716
4609 *The Country Wife*
A mistress should be like a little country retreat near the town, not to dwell in constantly, but only for a night and away.

4610 *The Country Wife*
Go to your business, I say, pleasure, whilst I go to my pleasure, business.

YATES Douglas
4611
No scientific theory achieves public acceptance until it has been thoroughly discredited.

YATES John 1925-
4612
There is a lot to be said in the Decade of Evangelism for believing more and more in less and less.

YBARRA Thomas Russell 1880-
4613 *'The Christian'*
A Christian is a man who feels
Repentance on a Sunday
For what he did on Saturday
And is going to do on Monday.

YEATS William Butler 1865-1939
4614 *'Politics'*
How can I, that girl standing there,
My attention fix
On Roman or on Russian
Or on Spanish politics?

4615
A statesman is an easy man,
He tells his lies by rote;
A journalist makes up his lies
And takes you by the throat;
So stay at home and drink your beer
And let the neighbours vote.

YEATS-BROWN Francis 1888-1944
4616
To me the charm of an encyclopedia is that it knows - and I needn't.

YESENIN Sergei 1895-1925
4617 *'Pleasure's for the Bad'*
It's always the good feel rotten.
Pleasure's for those who are bad.

YOUNG Arthur
4618
There is a great difference between a good physician and a bad one; yet very little between a good one and none at all.

YOUNG Edward 1683-1765
4619 *The Love of Fame*
Be wise with speed;
A fool at forty is a fool indeed.

4620 *The Love of Fame*
With skill she vibrates her eternal tongue,
For ever most divinely in the wrong.

4621 *Night Thoughts 'Night 1'*
At thirty a man suspects himself a fool;
Knows it at forty, and reforms his plan;
At fifty chides his infamous delay,
Pushes his prudent purpose to resolve;
In all the magnanimity of thought
Resolves; and re-resolves; then dies the same.

YOUNG Jock
4622
The person by far the most likely to kill you is yourself.

YUTANG Lin 1895-1976
4623
All women's dresses are merely variations on the eternal struggle between the admitted desire to dress and the unadmitted desire to undress.

ZANGWILL Israel 1864-1926
4624
In how many lives does Love really play a dominant part? The average taxpayer is no more capable of a 'grand passion' than of a grand opera.

ZAPPA Frank 1940-
4625
Rock journalism is people who can't write interviewing people who can't talk for people who can't read.

ZINGERS 'Smile'
4626
The first sign of maturity is the discovery that the volume knob also turns to the left.

The ZOHAR
4627
It is the way of a dog that if he is hit by a stone, he bites a fellow dog.

Keyword Index

a b c
2613 is that old A B C - ability,

a-smokin'
2295 her first a-smokin' of a

abandonment
2259 involve abandonment of the

abdomen
3086 The abdomen is the reason why

abducted
1740 Léonie Abducted by a

abduction
1789 ready for a possible abduction.

abeyance
4353 and our vices are in abeyance.

abilities
1723 suits one's abilities, plain

ability
1400 Ability will never catch up
2613 old A B C - ability, breaks
3300 Executive ability is deciding
3498 about his ability; but he's
3822 become famous without ability.

able
4049 at able: At least

abolish
2545 anything they'd abolish it.
2565 we seek to abolish The 3rd

abomination
128 An abomination unto the Lord, but

abortion
2248 pregnant, abortion would be a

abridgement
1690 who can, An abridgement of all

abroad
1263 Abroad', that large home of
1567 Abroad is bloody.
2897 Wops, but abroad is
4031 too, before he goes abroad.
4593 sent to lie abroad for the

absence
454 in my absence and
824 nature is the absence of man.
3497 accident? Absence of body.
3800 I dote on his very absence.
3988 Absence is one of the most

absent
1101 The absent are always in the

absent-minded
721 be getting absent-minded. Whenever
892 I am not absent-minded. It is the

absents
2377 I often say, endear Absents.

absolutely
1061 corrupts absolutely, where

absolutism
170 ours is absolutism moderated

absolve
681 It seems to absolve us.
3361 He's half absolv'd Who has

abstain
1260 to say, abstains from

abstinence
1192 made almost a sin of abstinence.
2115 Abstinence is as easy for me as

abstract
3734 happiness in the abstract.

absurd
689 A scientific faith's absurd.
941 nothing so absurd but some
2921 'One's absurd! And
3690 and that is the absurd.

absurdities
716 to talk of errors and absurdities.

abuse
991 when he abuses his horse
1529 only offer abuse as a
1975 Abuse a man unjustly, and
3117 hear you abuse the

abused
4175 is to be abused, say what

abyss
4041 us to the edge of the abyss.

academic
2561 law of academic life: it

acceptance
4611 public acceptance until it

accepted
2071 an idea is accepted it is time

accident
15 Accident counts for much in
258 of an auto accident it makes
347 a profession; it's an accident.
1743 been an accident,' they
2081 out by accident, so I now
2843 By many a happy accident.
3331 had an accident there, he
3497 a railway accident? Absence

accidents
486 of habitual accidents .. is to
2723 runs into accidents which
3113 Such accidents will happen in

accommodating
2912 world is an accommodating sort of

accomplish
1976 some men accomplish in life is

account
1024 like a bank account. You put
3623 a good bank account, a good

accounted
860 have accounted to God for

accumulated
1167 he has accumulated during the

accuracy
1033 We are dying of accuracy.
2524 Barbaric accuracy - whimpering

accurately
3241 quotes accurately, for the

accusations
1496 doubtful accusations leave a

accuse
3355 then you accuse 'em of not

aces
4280 holding four aces.

achieve
627 great, some achieve greatness,
1855 some men achieve
4367 trying to achieve before you

achievement
1836 of every achievement is a proud

achievements
559 we pay to achievements that
1204 most of the achievements from the

acquaintance
556 Acquaintance, n: a person whom we
1139 A new acquaintance is like a
4117 creditable acquaintance; I love to

act
1419 and to act in an
1527 courage and act on
2492 cha acter of the
4317 she can act with her

acting
396 Acting consists of the
1692 he was off he was acting.
1781 Acting is happy agony.
1842 as when he is acting a part.
1868 do half your acting for you.

action
869 In action, be primitive; in
2987 field where action is one
3027 Few men of action have been
4020 I do a mean action, it must

actions
771 Great actions are not always
2994 and others by their actions.

activity
1720 important ongoing activity.

actor
259 A good actor must never be
664 An actor's a guy who, if
841 who tell an actor he is not
4132 An actor and a priest both
4415 dee dee (an actor's life for

actor-manager
2090 Actor-manager - one to whom the

actors
1398 The best actors do not let
1837 Actors are the only honest
4414 wants to hear actors talk?
4551 The actors and

actress
1880 Actresses will happen in the
3371 national landlady and actress.

acts
1390 no second acts in

ad infinitum
2974 fleas, and so ad infinitum.
4121 so proceed ad infinitum . Thus

adage
2579 in the old adage, 'Leave

adam
190 Adam Had'em.
242 Whilst Adam slept, Eve
642 I wish Adam had died with
645 When Adam and Eve were
1955 then That Adam was not
4307 good thing Adam had - when

addresses
3685 Addresses are given to us to

adjective
123 as if they were adjectives.
4299 As to the Adjective: when in

adjudication
2996 bad case of premature adjudication.

administrative
2251 three major administrative problems

admiral
3962 of all an Admiral came, A

admire
44 admire any man
619 a greater fool to admire him.

admired
1983 is usually admired - if

admires
3713 - he admires them but

admiring
2253 you've been admiring for a long

admit
1511 never admit it, but I

adorable
635 are most adorable when they

adore
2019 does not adore his
3188 we alike adore But only

adornment
2490 Cats are living adornments.
4192 from the adornment of his

ads
2663 Ads are the cave art of
3046 watched the ads, And not

adulterer
1076 able to find a happy adulterer.

adultery
782 and gods adultery, Is much
784 Not quite adultery, but
846 committed adultery in my
848 commit adultery at one end

960 Do not adultery commit;
2774 committed adultery, are now
3212 it would have been adultery.

adults
1107 is not that adults produce
4137 by adults to
4360 between consenting adults.

advance
81 things advance; nine
3575 don't advance, however,

advantage
960 commit; Advantage rarely
1094 when sex gave her an advantage.
1259 that takes advantage that gets
3087 The advantage of a bad memory

adventure
1258 temptation to foreign adventure.
2638 = r + p (or Adventure equals
4380 is the only adventure open to

adventures
1705 All our adventures were by the

adventurous
2610 of the most adventurous things

adversity
580 Adversity has the same effect

advertise
3264 work like hell, and advertise.

advertising
1005 Advertising is what you do when
2430 Advertising may be described as
3155 Advertising is the rattling of a
4447 Advertising is legalized lying.

advice
21 seldom asks advice until she
581 My advice to those who are
598 to me for advice, I find
980 To ask advice is in nine
1981 to a man than good advice.
2075 "Take my advice, there's
2361 nothing so freely as advice.
2768 the worst advice you can
2929 admirable advice, but I am
3466 offer me advice, give me
3479 Advice to persons about to
4527 with good advice is to pass

advise
489 Flooded. Please advise.

aesthetic
1629 in the high aesthetic line as a

aestheticism
157 Aestheticism is the last resort of

affable
3612 sign of an affable man, good,

affairs
2655 your love affairs .. what
3675 Affairs, like revolutions,
4341 part in affairs which

affectation
3394 Affectation is a greater enemy to

affection
330 show more affection than she

affectionate
2783 have a really affectionate mother.

affections
1261 a great strain on the affections.

affinity
4204 an electric affinity for that

afflict
1215 Comfort the afflicted and

afford
1557 we can afford it or no,
3852 Can't afford them,
4212 he can afford to let

afghanistan
2309 and left on Afghanistan's plains

afraid
68 I'm not afraid to die. I
1480 nothing I'm afraid of like
2555 many are afraid of God -
4133 We do be afraid of the sea,

africa
2277 over Africa - (Boots -
3148 with Africa than my

african
3036 is an African who dreams

after
780 soda-water the day after.
4466 men go right after them.

after-dinner
3798 it were, an after-dinner's sleep,

afternoon
1952 a beautiful afternoon with

afterthought
4006 dear Readers, are an afterthought.

afterwards
97 together afterwards that is
1425 anyone may have them afterwards.

against
736 and against little
1736 Time and I against any two.

age
828 at your age, it is
844 I feel age like an icicle
909 Old age is not so bad
943 Old age is by nature
1084 Middle age is youth
1199 in such an age, When no
1217 when age has
1309 Old age brings along with
1332 knew; if age was able.
1643 a woman's age in half a
1669 don't let age get you
3100 of thought to old age.

3642 fervour of youth in age.
4065 Age is a high price to
4541 her real age. A woman

aged
778 means Certainly aged.

agenda
3219 item of the agenda will be in

ages
3358 different ages move, 'Tis

agnostic
1464 Don't be agnostic - be

agony
1781 Acting is happy agony.

agree
602 that you agree to a thing
984 not always agree to die
1147 idea of an agreeable person
2366 to those who agree with us.
2550 you did not agree. When you
4607 always agree, one of

agreeable
329 to be very agreeable, as it
705 tolerably agreeable if it were
1147 idea of an agreeable person is
2352 of life along an agreeable road.

agreed
2704 any man who agreed with me.

agreement
953 Too much agreement kills a

ahead
3014 want to get ahead, get a
4063 a long way ahead of what

aid
1838 Without the aid of

ailments
4116 because our ailments are the

aim
3702 have forgotten your aim.

aims
2299 about the Aims of Art,
3885 than who aims but at a

air
20 with the air of a man
2687 that fresh air should be
3758 up into the air, you shall
3789 that word, honour? Air.

airplanes
1397 Airplanes are interesting toys
3195 Airplanes) may kill you, but

aitches
3165 to lose but our aitches.

alarm
715 A little alarm now and then

alas
1161 say? Ah no! Alas, Time

albert
1142 to take a message to Albert.'

albert hall
2486 to fill the Albert Hall. I'd love

alcohol
213 caused by lack of alcohol.
866 Alcohol is like love: the
3158 No doubt alcohol, tobacco,
3836 Alcohol is a very necessary
4577 that alcohol was a food

aldershot
540 by Aldershot sun, What

alexander
1134 Alexander .. asked him if he

alibi
1274 has an alibi, and one

alice
2875 down with Alice. Alice is

alike
1925 come to look alike at last.
2274 everyone is alike and no one

alimony
96 Alimony: the cash surrender
1881 and the expense of alimony.

alive
514 no longer alive. There is
535 Half dead and half alive!
793 Industry is alive and well
959 Officiously to keep alive.
1098 I'm still alive. I'd
1714 were alive he'd turn
2909 words that keeps me alive.
3080 to keep him alive, but we
3305 Alive, ridiculous, and dead
3739 dreams that keep you alive.

all
167 wife, all things to
295 beneath me. All women do.

allotted
1606 a few are allotted to you,

allowed
3220 he is allowed to take.

alluring
3028 alluring seen

almighty
2069 by the Lord Almighty and not by

alone
1313 you let it alone, it will
1865 they are alone, they'd
2076 never dine alone. When they
2846 if he is alone, forms an
4340 alone, gave him

altar
647 A high altar on the move.
2197 threw our altars to the
3632 made at the altar, a

altered
4127 how much it altered her person

alternation
2104 a perpetual alternation between

alternative
933 no superior alternative has yet

alternatives
909 when you consider the alternatives.

altogether
2563 clothes is altogether, but

always
4397 I always tell a young man

amateur
1749 sport, the amateur status
4229 preserve of the amateur.

amateurs
2230 Amateurs hope. Professionals

amazed
710 constantly amazed when I

amazing
2105 got this amazing thing.."

ambassador
1581 Ambassadors cropped up like hay,
4593 An ambassador is an honest man

ambition
2164 life, an ambition to be a

america
61 America - the best poor man's
407 minds of America had better
488 In America there are two
1095 called America before the
1568 The true America is the
1729 order. In America I think
1732 North America ought to
2630 of American movies
3167 America once had the clarity
3953 to be in America! O.K. by
4037 In America, any boy may
4075 visiting America. I don't
4323 America is a vast conspiracy

american
901 matter with Americans except
1453 Part of the American dream is
2773 American women expect to find
2820 taste of the American public.
4321 equal. The American agony is

americanism
2629 is Americanism with its
3603 for hyphenated Americanism.

americans
269 Good Americans, when they die,
730 Americans have a special horror
1529 amazes Americans, who do
2089 To Americans, English manners
2670 find the Americans much as
2763 worse Than ignorant Americans.
3481 appears the Americans have taken

ammunition
1405 the Lord and pass the ammunition.

amoeba
1782 Amoebas at the start were
3879 were a soft amoeba, in ages

amorous
152 quite so amorous Over

amount to
4347 who didn't amount to much when

amphibious
1087 From this amphibious ill-born

amused
4356 We are not amused.

amusements
705 it were not for its amusements.
2519 tolerable but for its amusements.
3944 we have no amusements in England

amuses
1139 Anybody amuses me for once.

amusing
716 vastly more amusing to talk of
2939 she isn't amusing herself

anaesthetics
3668 in giving anaesthetics to men,

analysis
1971 analysis is not the

anarchist
500 up a small anarchist community,
3033 Christ - an anarchist who

anarchy
438 next to anarchy, is

anatomy
382 has studied anatomy and

ancestors
42 had begotten their ancestors.
934 from rich ancestors after the
1149 when the ancestors of the
1924 all our ancestors ride, and
3183 illustrious ancestors is like a

ancestry
1608 trace my ancestry back to a

anchor
1518 have a firm anchor in

anecdotage
1152 into his anecdotage it was a

angel
2967 - Though an angel should
3431 man for the Angel of Death.
3745 to be an angel in order

angels
3562 degenerated angels, rather
4335 while the angels are

anger
349 Anger makes dull men witty,
613 degree of anger, fear and
1801 Anger raiseth invention,

angler
4400 excellent angler, and now
4401 for any but anglers, or very
4403 so no man is born an angler.

anglican
1313 for the Anglican Church is

angling
2157 but angling or float
4402 Angling may be said to be so

anglo-irishman
453 He was an Anglo-Irishman. MEG: In

angry
4298 When angry, count four;

anguish
1831 perish with anguish could they

animal
1809 than a reasonable animal.
3902 Man, an animal that makes
3975 Man is a social animal.

animals
416 us from the other animals.
3084 but kill animals and stick
3157 All animals are equal but
3177 man from animals.

animate
3938 animate the whole.

animosities
3114 Animosities are mortal, but the

animosity
4109 fervour of sisterly animosity.

anno domini
1898 him - only anno domini, but

annoyance
4282 than the annoyance of a good

annoys
1042 whose scent the fair annoys.

annuities
4368 paying your annuities. It is

annuity
339 An annuity is a very serious

annulled
578 universe be annulled in behalf

annus
1286 to be an annus

anomalies
3709 heresy, anomalies, hobbies,

another
2481 him And each for one another.

answer
8 The Answer to the great
70 Love is the answer, but while
804 getting the answer yes
1485 are the hardest to answer.
2332 a riddle out of an answer.
3511 that the answer does not
3706 power to answer do not
4224 why did you answer the phone?
4232 love is the answer, could you

answered
2061 prayers have not been answered.

answering
3065 and severely by answering them.

anthropomorphic
2326 erstwhile anthropomorphic view of

anti-feminist
3131 man is as anti-feminist as a

antibiotics
4061 is that antibiotics have cured

anticipation
4088 per cent anticipation and ten

antipathy
3103 by a little physical antipathy.

antipodes
2744 And, like Antipodes in shoes,

antiquarian
2125 A mere antiquarian is a rugged

antiquity
2386 I will write for Antiquity!'

anxieties
3738 the anxieties I have

anxiety
1602 taboo'd by anxiety, I
2264 Anxiety is the dizziness of

anxious
1629 If you're anxious for to

anybody
1062 to find anybody who'll
1366 vote for anybody. I always
1582 Then no one's anybody.
4503 Anybody can be good in the

anything
1808 for nothing fall for anything.
3010 give a XXXX for anything else.
3326 heaven knows, Anything goes.

anywhere
554 and go anywhere I damn

apart
3286 Apart from the known and
3688 they sometimes live apart.

ape
1823 story of an ape playing

apes
2193 varlet; And apes are apes,
3562 rather than elevated apes.

apologize
557 Apologize, v: to lay the
2637 never apologize - get the

apology
1319 person ever made an apology.
1920 Apology - a desperate habit,
1921 Apology is only egotism wrong
2273 God's apology for relations.

apostle
1631 rank as an apostle in the

appeal
1214 An appeal is when ye ask wan
4336 I appeal from Philip drunk

2663 the cave art of the
2718 is the art of keeping
3101 is no mean art. For its
3540 Art disease is caused by
3699 Art is a delayed echo.
3988 is an art like any
4482 Art is upon the Town!

artist
1348 An artist is a creature
3281 another artist. He
3700 An artist may visit a museum
3704 An artist is a dreamer
4403 is born an artist, so no man

artistic
1623 to give artistic

artists
4094 to name 10 artists from any

ascetic
3090 Ascetic: one who makes a

ashamed
940 I am not ashamed to confess
2950 and being ashamed of them
3321 never be ashamed to own he

ashes
1744 nice new ashes, Fell in
3695 past is a bucket of ashes.

ashore
2521 perilous excursion ashore.

aside
4259 set death aside. It sets

ask
3733 occurs to him to ask for.

asked
3185 are glad to have been asked.

asleep
3636 he'll fall asleep before you
3651 world are asleep at any

asparagus
1581 Grew like asparagus in May,

aspersion
3875 An aspersion upon my parts of

ass
1020 a solemn ass as a
1491 If an ass goes
2343 greatest ass of the
3223 dead, every ass thinks he
3474 call you an ass, put on a

assassin
3614 you are an assassin. Kill

assassination
170 moderated by assassination'.
2916 Assassination is the quickest way.
4370 by an occasional assassination.

asses
2616 those gross asses to whom He

asset
891 greatest asset in the

assumed
1774 had always assumed that

assumption
2274 on the assumption that

asteroid
4291 as if she had laid an asteroid.

astonishing
4267 It isn't so astonishing, the

astray
2282 who've gone astray,

astrologers
3503 and astrologers as readily

astute
2291 the small 'Stute Fish said

asunder
3830 shall put asunder: God will

asylum
3637 taken charge of the asylum.
4586 lunatic asylums which are

atahualpa
2678 and who strangled Atahualpa.

atari
2105 We went to Atari and said

atheism
3150 on you - atheism,

atheist
696 An atheist is a man who has
708 to God, I am still an atheist.
3607 for the atheist is when he
3723 her from being an atheist.

atlantic
254 across the Atlantic, and more

atom
662 of the atom, and
3673 down of the atom is a very

attack
322 for an unforeseen attack.
1331 until after the first attack.
2324 Frontal attack never works,

attacking
547 in attacking the

attend
86 did not attend was

attendance
1154 in his attendance at the

attention
507 their entire attention to it.
981 pays most attention to those
1523 and holding attention. But it
2979 - it requires so much attention.
3143 - attention without
3569 with such attention that you
4614 there, My attention fix On

attentions
3635 the attentions of many

attentive
2748 can have is an attentive wife.

attorney
1586 boy to an Attorney's firm. I
1604 find your attorney (who
1652 with a rich attorney's Elderly

attract
1353 kind, you attract a lot of
1632 magnet ever Attract a Silver

attributed
4137 often attributed by the

auden
3164 is W.H. Auden, a sort of

audible
246 Audible at five miles,

audience
396 to keep an audience from
2902 heroes are in the audience.
4143 choreography to the audience.

audiences
1868 If you give audiences a chance
3729 kinds of audiences only - one

aunt
1742 Aunt Jane observed, the
4181 Charley's aunt from

aunts
1585 and his aunts! His

austerity
2915 see the old austerity That was

australia
2096 Australia is so kind that, just

australians
3010 Australians wouldn't give a XXXX

author
1272 tell the author his
1436 of an author, to
3912 in a good author is not

authority
4136 maximal authority and

authors
1930 her authors, contrived

auto-eroticism
1487 it is fundamentally auto-eroticism.

autobiography
473 intolerable, so with autobiography.

automatic
818 Automatic simply means that you

autumn
2036 the ape Or Autumn sunsets
3269 Autumn is the bite of a

avail
3922 good income is of no avail.

avant garde
4087 avant garde that the

avarice
2958 beyond the dreams of avarice.

average
1128 The average man is more
3602 am only an average man, but,

aversion
3873 begin with a little aversion.
4052 closely bordering on aversion.

avoid
3158 saint must avoid, but

avoided
34 that could have been avoided.
4504 are to be avoided - they are

avoiding
1881 one way of avoiding the

awake
1606 to you, you awake with a
2968 Then awake! the heavens
3101 one must stay awake all day.
3651 thirds are awake and

away
1548 the hills and far away.
3500 to his wife away from home.

awe
1446 The awe and dread with
2196 Invented to awe fools.

awful
3611 moments but awful quarters
3748 God! this is an awful place.

awkward
729 let the awkward squad fire

axe
183 took an axe And gave
3167 clarity of a pioneer axe.

axiom
1250 I simply ignored axiom.

babblative
3959 The arts babblative and

babies
1884 Babies are such a nice way
2634 Ballads and babies. That's
3616 dogs and babies can't be
4185 only washing. And babies.
4453 You breed babies and you

baby
2252 having a baby is that
2321 The baby doesn't

bacchus
1538 Bacchus has drowned more men

bach
1619 'ops' By Bach,

bachelor
3630 Somehow a bachelor never quite
3634 far, nor a bachelor too near.
3780 would die a bachelor, I did not
4124 Bachelor's fare; bread and

bachelors
1268 reasons for bachelors to go out.
2800 Bachelors know more about women

back
447 put gently back at Oxford
843 to have me back So I could

1984 behind your back is your
2270 Nowhere to come but back.
2535 but I never walk back.
2684 those before cried Back!'

back-seat
4178 be a very good back-seat driver.

backbone
2280 But the backbone of the
3181 are the backbone of Canada.

backside
3334 to their backsides, and the

backward
3094 looks backward. In the
4215 as lean over too far backward.

backwards
2265 understood backwards; but it

bad
155 and so much bad in the
448 will come to a bad end.
660 is bad it must be
759 part like bad sixpences
797 good or as bad as it
1118 were no bad people,
1294 were bad speakers
1445 I feel bad that I don't
1803 to the bad - for
2145 It is as bad as bad can
2631 to do something bad.
3021 to heaven. Bad girls go
3418 and cattle; bad is when
3434 and bad men it
3486 got a bad egg, Mr
3616 babies can't be all bad.
4455 when I'm bad, I'm
4492 I am as bad as the worst,
4511 and the bad unhappily.

badder
2229 say 'bigger and badder'.

badly
906 it is worth doing badly.

bag
2068 a paper bag, You
2692 out of the bag often

balance
1339 a little mental balance.

bald
361 is either bald or dead or
634 between two bald men over a
3383 gives us when we are bald.

baldheaded
2592 an' then Go into it baldheaded.

baldness
1886 thing about baldness - it's
3910 far side of baldness than young

ball
2491 at a ball; the only
4103 of a ball is either

ballads
1607 patches. Of ballads, songs and
2634 Ballads and babies. That's

balliol
460 Balliol made me, Balliol fed

balls
402 can hear my balls clank.

banalities
873 The banalities of a great man

bandage
1066 makes best is the bandage.

bandied
4435 struck and bandied Which way

bang
115 A bigger bang for a buck.

bank
72 in my name at a Swiss bank.
1024 is like a bank account.
1960 A bank is a place that
2523 all the way to the bank.
3076 robbed a couple of banks."

banker
3408 father is a banker provided

bankruptcy
17 Bankruptcy is a legal proceeding

banks
1578 who banks with

banner
4284 but carrying a banner.

baptism
2064 With soap baptism is a good

baptist
147 John the Baptist pretending

bargain
2180 Bargain: something you can't

bargains
3902 an animal that makes bargains.

bark
2139 out as I do, and bark .
3385 One dog barks at

barking
122 you cannot keep from barking.

barn
3527 kick down a barn, but it

baseball
252 those of a baseball player.
407 had better learn baseball.
2822 sensible as baseball in

basingstoke
1648 hidden meaning - like Basingstoke.

basket
4266 eggs in one basket and -

bastard
1535 to be a bastard to be a
1896 we knocked the bastard off!

bat
3600 every time I come to bat.

bath
3056 I test my bath before I

bathing
1603 a large bathing machine

bathroom
615 goes to the bathroom, with the

baths
3351 don't like baths. I don't

battalions
4379 the heavy battalions, but of

battle
838 to one in a battle - to get
2049 go out to battle for
3647 nor the battle to the

bayonet
3016 A bayonet is a weapon with a

bbc
4554 This is the BBC - we are

beach
2099 upon it - from the beach.

beachy head
903 Birmingham by way of Beachy Head.

beak
2839 His beak holds more

beans
3007 Beanz meanz Heinz.

bear
2703 I cannot bear your
2731 savage as a bear with a
2874 you are a Bear of Very
2885 I am a Bear of Very Little
3813 Exit, pursued by a bear.
3838 alive could bear it: it

bearable
1222 makin' life bearable. A little

beard
2449 Man with a beard, Who said,

bearing
2213 I seen him bearing down on me

bears
1909 dogs and bears, And
2068 wandering bears might come

beastie
150 beasties And

beat
135 his wife can beat him at.
829 boy, And beat him when

beaten
3240 painfully beaten into him,

beatles
2409 ban And the Beatles' first LP.

beats
891 world. It beats money and

beautiful
1128 any woman - with beautiful legs.
1412 right until it is beautiful.
1734 A beautiful woman should break
1829 says, she is not beautiful.
2420 its time Beautiful .. 150
3067 a distance, beautiful: from

beauty
103 rather have beauty than
702 the hundredth with a beauty.
1068 Female beauty is an
1335 As a beauty I am not a star,
1344 can be a beauty without a
1637 A thing of beauty, Would she
2036 Beauty for some provides
2305 'Tisn't beauty, so to speak,
3186 of beauty can err,
3309 ghosts of Beauty glide, And
3630 a thing of beauty and a boy
3683 always say beauty is only
4381 what is beauty? .. a
4530 in everything but beauty.

becoming
4007 We are becoming the men we
4355 I think I am becoming a god.

bed
43 is not a bed to be made
52 Never go to bed with a
84 get out of bed for it;
88 to stay in bed with
108 never go to bed alone.
486 to stay in bed all day.
505 years in bed and over
1132 Never go to bed mad. Stay
2418 it's nicer to stay in bed.
2491 go home to bed is that
2655 go to bed with is
2941 who goes to bed with a man
3035 people to bed at a
3520 one man in bed at the
4011 Going to bed with a woman
4418 he on his bed, Turns his

bedchamber
1897 calls on my bedchamber less

bedfellows
2758 strange bedfellows, marriage

bedroom
800 do in the bedroom as long as

bedside
3498 a very good bedside manner!

bedspring
3259 triumphant twang of a bedspring.

bee
54 sting like a bee.
1123 concern the bee; A clover,
2450 bored by a bee; When

been
93 Been there, done that, got

bequests
845 two lasting bequests we can

bereaved
4331 would be bereaved if

best
10 now is the best time of
1056 gave the best years of
1297 is always a best way of
1340 run is always the best.
1461 The best things and best
3395 usually the best men when
4379 but of the best shots.
4515 He is doing his best.

best man
158 not marrying the best man.

best-loved
1831 The best-loved man or maid in

best-seller
628 A best-seller was a book which
3913 A best-seller is the gilded tomb

best-sellers
3367 one in all the great best-sellers.

bet
3647 but that's the way to bet.
4074 if it was a bet, you

betimes
3806 midnight is to be up betimes.

betray
1550 those who betray their
1707 that men betray, What

betraying
1407 between betraying my country

better
340 `He is not better, he is
368 knows of a better 'ole, go
805 who are better than
880 What is bettre than
1230 be feeling better. I really
1272 writing is better than it
1499 good, where better is
2010 world gets better every day
2286 You're a better man than I
2342 are either better or worse
2531 I can write better than
2745 Yet we'd better by far
2913 render our fellow-men better.
3076 feel a lot better once we've
3449 It is better to be than not
3687 don't know better as they
3720 world is better than
3728 I am better than my
4190 things get better by
4455 but when I'm bad, I'm better.

betting
2769 him betting on people.

between
3926 anyone who comes between them.
4393 Thames is between me and the

bewailed
2948 should be bewailed at their

beware
3818 Beware of the man whose God
4197 Beware all enterprises that

bias
1833 minds, a bias recognized

bible
105 The bible tells us to
176 page of the Bible and it's
2571 Bible's the greatest book
2700 to read the Bible like an

bibles
4286 have six Bibles and no

bicycle
4009 like a fish without a bicycle.
4363 can only arrive by bicycle.

big
1584 I never use a big, big D -
3443 yourself so big. You are

bigamy
106 Bigamy is having one husband
1881 Bigamy is one way of
2921 absurd! And bigamy, Sir, is a

bigger
107 The bigger they are, the
2229 people say bigger and

bigness
2178 if some bigness is good,

bigot
1942 mind of a bigot is like
3920 a bigot, when he

bigoted
3646 he is not bigoted about it.

bill
2605 send the bill to you.
2757 on the back of the bill."

billabong
3229 camped by a billabong, Under the

billboard
3058 never see A billboard lovely as

billiard
1620 The billiard sharp whom any

billiards
3622 To play billiards well is a
3972 to play billiards was the

billowy
1627 into the billowy wave, And

bills
265 she sends in terrific bills.
776 of his weekly bills.
2413 a few bills! That's

billy
1744 Billy, in one of his nice
3229 till his Billy' boiled:

bind
2677 Obadiah Bind-their-

binomial
1639 About binomial theorem I'm

biographies
4268 Biographies are but the clothes

biography
515 The Art of Biography Is
1141 nothing but biography, for that
4081 the better part of biography.
4516 Judas who writes the biography.

biology
2333 a matter of biology, if

birch
4360 back the birch, but only

bird
1917 gives every bird its food,
3601 the early bird, and not

birds
376 others - birds, wild
2068 unobservant birds Have never
2943 sees the birds outside
3067 are like birds - from a
3410 Old birds are hard to

birmingham
4096 came to Birmingham they

birth
1280 Birth, and copulation, and
2284 was at the birth of Man -
2676 With the birth of each
2948 at their birth, and not
3974 .. in the miracle of birth.
4257 From birth to 18 a girl

birth control
4424 O.K. but birth control is

birthday
1027 your wife's birthday is to

bishop
3930 How can a bishop marry? How

bishopric
2203 should refuse a bishopric.

bit
1684 Went mad and bit the man.

bite
1563 he will bite some of
2974 backs to bite 'em, And
3400 He who can lick can bite.
3477 you can't bite, don't
4121 fleas to bite 'em, And

bites
1754 A dead woman bites not.
2333 something bites you it is
4627 a stone, he bites a fellow

biting
1716 always biting the hand

black
843 how well you look in black.
1403 - so long as it's black.
2187 within, black as her pan
2562 are not so black as they

blackburn
2486 holes in Blackburn

blame
1674 Don't blame the mirror if
2932 she is to blame, who has
2985 unfair to blame man too

blancmange
2320 Of cold blancmange and

bland
1862 Bland as a Jesuit, sober as

blank
1413 at the blank sheet of

blanketful
3465 have more bugs than a blanketful.

blasphemies
3816 great truths begin as blasphemies.

blazer
366 to make them wear a blazer.

blessed
323 no man so blessed that some
1260 Blessed is the man who,

blessing
4099 makes a blessing dear; It

blessings
3069 'Count your blessings; you've

blind
197 judge - Too blind the
650 of a blind man in a
975 a deaf man to a blind woman.

blinding
1002 for blinding people to

blindness
2279 in 'is blindness bows down

blinked
3650 the other fellow just blinked.

bliss
1282 promise of pneumatic bliss.
3232 men call domestic bliss.

blisters
3551 such little blisters That all

block
1614 on a big black block.

blockhead
2123 man but a blockhead ever
3314 The bookful blockhead,

blood
875 strong wyn, reed as blood.
1413 drops of blood form on
3140 The best blood will
4176 like blood, sir, in

bloody
1567 Abroad is bloody.

bloom
400 a sort of bloom on a
4017 deserts bloom and lakes

blotted
2194 he never blotted out a

blow
1645 it, And blow your own
2713 way, otherwise you blow up.
3861 who gets his blow in fust.

blows
205 that nobody blows good.

bluebottles
948 are like bluebottles. Some are

blunder
516 At so grotesque a blunder.
589 than with making a blunder.
728 frae mony a blunder free us,
3088 was God's second blunder.
3898 I blunder, I bluster, I blow,

blunders
590 makes any blunders; when she
1040 of Nature's agreeable blunders.
2987 lies between two blunders.

blurring
925 a line without blurring it.

blushes
4278 Animal that Blushes. Or needs

board
1874 wasn't any Board, and now

boast
3183 anything to boast of but his

boathook
3689 diplomatic boathook to avoid

boats
1747 messing about in boats.
2461 When boats or ships came

bodies
136 it had worn out two bodies.
2353 our minds than in our bodies.

body
422 use of my body I would
984 Body and mind, like man
1034 My body has certainly
3148 Africa than my own body.
3149 with his body, his mind
3994 exercise is to the body.
4169 seen his body borne
4225 and no body to be
4343 of the rest of her body.

bognor
1566 Bugger Bognor.

boil
1297 be only to boil an egg.
4153 War That Would Not Boil.

boiling
1622 with boiling oil in it,
4085 of boiling oil,

bold
4113 He was a bold man that

bollocks
3234 talking complete bollocks.

bombs
539 friendly bombs, and fall

bon-mots
2970 By plucking bon-mots from their

bonaparte
4207 which Bonaparte thought

bonds
2796 Gentlemen prefer bonds.

bone
569 hope of retaining his bone.
3047 I have a bone to pick with

bones
3929 flesh and sit in my bones.
4332 are the bones on which

bonnet
3328 a Bendel bonnet, A

bonsoir
4473 the sky-ee! Bonsoir, old

book
108 Book lovers never go to
548 when he can read the book?
826 use of a book' thought
1139 like a new book. I prefer
1867 square book! Always
2374 afterwards - over a book.
2666 successful book cannot
2686 It was a book to kill time
3534 a single book, or in
3796 bred in a book; he hath
3935 read a book before
3943 would make a great book.
4025 out of this book for
4493 dirtiest book of all is
4542 The Book of Life begins

bookie
3026 image of a bookie or of a

books
36 of good books, the point
352 Some books are to be
923 man to read books of
1420 Never lend books - nobody
1890 Do give books - religious
1935 of the hundred best books.
2383 of books - those
2411 Get stewed: Books are a load
2950 of writing books and being
3652 other's books out of
3928 so charming as books.
4588 how many books are

booksellers
1968 nor even booksellers have put

bookstore
437 so weak as in the bookstore?

boomerang
3909 it is the boomerang he finds

boots
1578 who cleans the boots.

1175 his little brain attic
1249 his own brain too little
1599 they've a brain and
2884 exactly got Brain, but he
2885 Very Little Brain and long
3277 messages from the brain.

brains
288 his brains go to his
1483 It takes brains to see the
1660 you can do without brains.
2578 a girl with brains ought to
3144 mix them with my brains, sir.
3391 more than a bushel of brains.
4050 man who has brains enough to
4570 use all the brains I have,
4573 the husbands having brains.

branch
2078 A branch of the sin of

brandy
1565 get me a glass of brandy.
2127 (smiling) must drink brandy.
2392 drink cold brandy and water.

brassiere
391 is not a brassiere. At

bravery
4210 and bravery. It does

braw
2419 say It's a braw brecht

brazil
4181 aunt from Brazil - where

bread
98 trees were bread and cheese
1030 Eat bread at pleasure,
1958 God! that bread should be
2651 a piece of bread and butter
2878 The Royal slice of bread?'
4124 fare; bread and

break
506 on the shoe, but not break.
1368 give a sucker an even break.
3141 but you can break your neck

breakdown
3657 nervous breakdown is the

breakfast
358 is a good breakfast, but it is
1794 on a leisurely breakfast.
2542 to have breakfast alone with

breakfast-time
1875 in matrimony is breakfast-time.

breaks
325 every party breaks up the
3433 his back and breaks his nose.

breast
3454 keep the breast for

breast-beaters
679 amuse the breast-beaters. By the

breastfeeding
2505 As a breastfeeding mother you are

breasts
3548 the feel of breasts and

breathe
223 students to breathe for one
2269 Nothing to breathe but air,
3325 lapdogs breathe their

breed
3250 of the breed of their

breeding
1360 of gaiety and good breeding.
2715 for people with no breeding.
3858 or woman's breeding is how
3866 show your breeding, But easy
4221 without any breeding, but I
4235 our planned breeding of our
4293 Good breeding consists in

breezy
1292 Droppy, Breezy, Sneezy,

brewery
139 me to a brewery And leave

bribe
4549 is a bribe to make a
4580 hope to bribe or twist,

bribing
3541 is good for bribing yourself

brick
2434 like half a brick, is always
3597 place two bricks
4114 a piece of brick in his

bride
158 day for the bride as she
2477 always the bridesmaid,

bridesmaid
2477 always the bridesmaid, Never the

bridge
471 and Bridge) Broke -
536 through the bridge? And
2261 to build a bridge even when
4211 to build a bridge to the

bridle
3446 Shake a bridle over a
3474 you an ass, put on a bridle.

brigands
739 Brigands demand your money or

bright
159 are what makes a man bright.
703 lady named Bright, Whose

brilliance
3001 No brilliance is needed in the

brilliant
294 He has a brilliant mind until

brillig
831 'Twas brillig, and the slithy

brimstone
3961 From his brimstone bed, at

bring up
582 To bring up a child in the way
3270 best way to bring up some

brinkmanship
4041 of his brinkmanship - the art

britannia
3945 than Beer and Britannia?

british
302 I think the British have the
1529 rude as the British, which
2267 is the British tourist.
2432 The British are terribly lazy
3825 The British soldier can stand

britons
3764 , since the Britons were only

broadminded
1473 a man too broadminded to take

broke
471 and Bridge) Broke - and
2281 - for you broke a British
2397 If it ain't broke, don't fix
2557 Peter, Who broke the laws
2820 ever went broke

broken
3116 Laws were made to be broken.
4123 are made to be broken.

broken-hearted
1835 There's a broken-hearted woman

broker
4590 A broker is a man who takes

bronchitis
45 unless he or she has bronchitis.

brooding
1271 is always brooding on a

brother
178 it been his brother, Still
472 Strong brother in God and
1701 Still to my brother turns with
2481 so like my brother That folks
2745 far have him than his brother.

brown
2619 you are in some brown study.

brush
2625 scrub with a hard brush.
3547 with my brush, that I

brushers
4594 are like brushers of

brutally
3068 who are brutally honest get
4194 I'm frank, brutally frank.

brute
1698 such a cross-grained brute?
2450 a regular brute of a bee!'

brutes
1688 Brutes never meet in bloody

bubble
685 to tattoo soap bubbles.
1191 Honour but an empty bubble.

buck
115 A bigger bang for a buck.

bucket
3695 past is a bucket of ashes.

buckingham
2875 guard at Buckingham Palace -

buddhism
3681 or Buddhism that quite

buffoon
1188 statesman, and buffoon.

bug
1433 snug As a bug In as rug.

bugs
492 all the bugs off a
3465 have more bugs than a

build
682 Men build bridges and throw

built
344 I have built her up.
2449 Have all built their

bullshit
1213 silence: The bullshit stops.

bully
3763 by the bossy for the bully.

bump
150 that go bump in the

bumpy
1071 going to be a bumpy night."

bunk
1404 is more or less bunk.

burden
3365 The public burden of the

burglar
1901 a burglar busily at

burglary
1218 embezzlement an' burglary.

burgled
261 is never burgled, and the

burgundy
4221 domestic burgundy without

burial
1933 of the burial service

buried
991 and the other to be buried.
2302 Who was buried in snow to

burned
468 and the House, were Burned.

burning
478 A smell of burning fills the

burnt
3924 Ages And be burnt at the

bus
1665 be a Motor Bus? Yes, the

buses
4093 time in the buses with

busiest
3470 often the busiest day of the

business
9 over, and Business is
29 had attended business college.
326 Business, you know, may bring
480 It is the business of the
850 in the language of business.
888 quality for business; many a
1208 Business? It's quite simple.
1350 clean, quite solvent business.
1853 pardon me. It's his business.
1863 to do with it is a business.
2787 Business is a combination of
3142 secret of business is to know
3182 No praying, it spoils business.
3751 A dinner lubricates business.
3842 a woman's business to get
4115 to do more business after
4607 two men in business always
4610 Go to your business, I say,

businessman
1709 is no businessman - all he
4337 A businessman is a hybrid of a

busy
1348 usually too busy to wonder
1423 While I am busy with
2002 can look so busy doing
2729 the world to keep busy at.
2889 thoughts so busy keep.
3763 of the busy by the
3894 I am too busy thinking
3898 the other. Busy, busy, and
4583 as quickly as the busy one.

but
435 qualifies it with a but'.

butchers
4378 both shepherds and butchers.

butler
4574 The butler entered the room,

butlers
466 my opinion, Butlers ought To
2773 hope to find in their butlers.

butter
1666 We have no butter .. but I
2878 have some butter for The
3455 water, in butter and in
3571 ladling butter from
4169 on cutting bread and butter.

buttered
3235 always on the buttered side.

butterfly
54 like a butterfly, sting
1768 what's a butterfly? At best,

buttocks
2036 gorgeous buttocks of the ape
3548 breasts and buttocks is saved.

button
1410 can press a button to get
2454 care a button! We don't

buttons
387 to sew buttons on a
682 don't have to sew buttons.

buy
2221 you have to buy it
2571 I can buy for six
3118 I shall buy it like an
3389 When you buy, use your
3458 Don't buy the house; buy
3738 Buy me and you will

buying
2466 dinner only if he is buying.
3187 is always buying something.
4262 stroke, For buying or selling

buys
243 Who buys has need of two

bystanders
1316 but the bystanders are

cabbage
832 wax - Of cabbages - and
4297 nothing but cabbage with a

cabots
638 talk to the Cabots And the

cactus
2110 between a cactus and a

caesar
167 Like Caesar's wife, all
4349 Caesar had perished from the

caftan
4035 of Azcan in caftan Of tan

cage
2943 is like a cage; one sees

cake
291 lies to ice a wedding cake.

calculator
4337 of a dancer and a calculator.

calculus
1638 calculus, I know

california
815 In California everyone goes to a

call
3362 the call; But had
3691 as Call Me God')

called
4224 Well, if I called the wrong
4236 I am also called Played-out

calling
1938 Every calling is great when

callisthenics
3216 is simply callisthenics with

cars
404 think that cars today are

case
1624 to do with the case.

cash
3882 from hand to hand of cash.
4257 55 on, she needs good cash.

cassowary
4500 If I were a cassowary On the

castrate
1323 you would castrate the

cat
1023 and a cat that comes
1274 never was a Cat of such
2456 name of his cat: His body
2662 long as the average cat.
2692 The cat which isn't let
2939 with my cat, who knows
3452 at the cat there's a
3949 enough to swing a cat.
4101 way the cat is

cataclysm
2035 of their cataclysm but one

catalogue
1417 delightful than a catalogue.

catastrophe
4048 who stands firm is a catastrophe.
4338 some great catastrophe is not

catch
861 sir, to catch old birds
2624 there's a catch somewhere.
2886 decided to catch a
3110 into the water by his catch.

catching
458 Come away; poverty's catching.
1863 Catching a fly ball is a

categories
3540 by a hardening of the categories.

caterpillar
1768 He's but a caterpillar, drest.

cathedral
404 Gothic cathedrals: I mean
4329 you have a cathedral in your

catholic
86 did not attend was Catholic.
2821 for a Catholic woman to
4188 Roman Catholic women must

cato
125 to Cato, and

cats
2334 Cats seem to go on the
2490 Cats are living
4189 Cats - a standing rebuke

cattle
3418 wives and cattle; bad is

caucus
2110 and a caucus>? A cactus

caught
1059 wouldn't be caught dead
1772 but caught my foot in

cauliflower
4297 Cauliflower is nothing but

cause
2646 triumphant cause.

caution
3660 forms of caution, caution

cavaliers
3765 The Cavaliers (Wrong but

cave-dweller
3263 The cave-dweller's wife complained

caviar
2564 it for not laying caviar.

cease
4013 Rudyards cease from

celebrate
2098 just to celebrate the event.

celebrity
629 A sign of a celebrity is often
2803 A celebrity is one who is known

celibacy
1103 Celibacy is the worst form of
3236 lake, but celibacy is almost

cemetery
2414 Help me down Cemetery Road.

censorship
2611 Censorship, like charity, should

cent
1470 he did with every cent.

centipede
2478 loathsome centipede, Remorse,

certain
778 lady of a certain age',
1434 said to be certain, except
2284 four things certain since
3402 not always certain but it's

cesspool
1177 that great cesspool into which

chaff
861 catch old birds with chaff.
1997 from the chaff, and to

chain
1701 remove a lengthening chain.

chains
2677 chains-and-their-

chair
2137 nothing. He fills a chair.
3334 born with a chair stuck to
4385 to the seat of the chair.

chairman
2890 with me as chairman, and two
2925 more than chairman, at most,

chaise-longue
801 hurly-burly of the chaise-longue.

chamber
114 In his chamber, weak and
chambermaid
2126 arms of a chambermaid as of a
chamberpot
2642 empties her chamberpot on your
chameleons
4272 We are chameleons, and our
champagne
2624 given champagne at lunch,
2933 meet with champagne and a
2995 Champagne socialist.
3347 ice of his Lordship's champagne.
3819 not a champagne
4107 Champagne certainly gives one
chance
761 that one will chance it.
1043 and then be right by chance.
1080 the efficient use of chance.
1159 being ready for the chance.
1416 Chance is the pseudonym of
1645 me, you haven't a chance.
3812 I am so sometimes by chance.
chancellor
2121 by the Lord Chancellor, upon a
2589 The Chancellor of the Exchequer
change
146 but an abhorrence of change.
926 who can't change his mind
1127 to try to change a man -
2445 time for a change. They are
3854 idea that change can be
4001 the pockets change; it is not
4087 the 'outs' change places
4272 prejudices change places
changed
2545 If voting changed anything
changes
1220 see gr-reat changes takin'
chaos
4217 emotional chaos remembered
4450 primordial chaos clapped on
chaperone
2015 Her face was her chaperone.
chaplin
1709 Chaplin is no businessman -
chaps
515 Biography is about Chaps.
chapter
2898 are a mere chapter. I am the
character
1298 Character is that which can do
2492 essential character of the
2955 care of my character, my
3531 a fellow's character by his way
3877 set! a character dead at
4175 If a man's character is to be

characters
727 Who have characters to lose.
2121 of characters and
2202 whose characters are above
2228 has three characters - that
charge
2336 serious charge which can
2685 Take thou in charge this day!
charing cross
3251 went out to Charing Cross, to see
charitable
3248 feel more charitable toward the
charity
278 living need charity more than
1961 haven't any charity in your
2611 like charity, should
charm
804 Charm is a way of getting
1707 What charm can soothe
2494 Oozing charm from every
charmer
1551 t'other dear charmer away!
charming
1008 All charming people have
charms
1050 flocks have charms, For him
chartreuse
193 pot calls the kettle chartreuse.
chassis
3124 worl's in a state o' chassis!
chaste
1633 If I pronounce it chaste!
2350 are few chaste women who
3025 terms, like a chaste whore.
chastity
320 Give me chastity and
847 book where chastity really
1731 the most peculiar is chastity.
2888 'Tis chastity, my brother,
chat
953 agreement kills a chat.
chateaux
4241 their chateaux would
chattanooga
1725 is that the Chattanooga Choo-choo,
chatter
1630 only idle chatter of a
chatterley
2409 end of the Chatterley ban And
chaucer
4409 a pity that Chawcer, who had
cheap
1958 flesh and blood so cheap!
2485 in the cheap seats clap
2659 all like to buy it cheap.
3254 done as cheap as other

cheaper
2438 other is a cheaper thing, but
3523 which is cheaper than a

cheat
640 he may cheat at cards
961 it's so lucrative to cheat.
1492 Cheat me in the price but
2518 who don't cheat at cards
4199 You may cheat yourself

cheating
574 a period of cheating between

cheats
856 every man cheats in his

cheek
3407 other who offers a cheek.

cheerful
3251 looking as cheerful as any man

cheerfully
910 sets forth cheerfully towards

cheerfulness
1239 know how, cheerfulness was always

cheerio
536 And cheerioh' or
4473 old thing! cheerio!

cheers
1408 So Two cheers for Democracy:

cheese
670 hole when the cheese is gone?
1090 has 246 varieties of cheese?
1338 Cheese - milk's leap toward
3482 Botticelli's a cheese !
4054 dreamed of cheese - toasted,
4104 hup the chinks wi' cheese.

cheesed
501 soon had me cheesed off.

chemistry
603 a matter of chemistry. That must

cheque
4551 like blank cheques. The

chequebook
2755 shut and his chequebook open.

cheroot
2295 white cheroot, An'

cherry-stones
2143 not carve heads upon cherry-stones.

cheshire
2040 smile of a cosmic Cheshire cat.

chess
2698 of four-move chess problem.

chest
3277 from the chest sound like

chew
2111 fart and chew gum at the

chianti
3776 bottles of Chianti to make

chicken
1877 The chicken is the country's,

chickens
40 count your chickens before
3960 like young chickens, they

chieftain
4035 Chieftain Iffucan of Azcan in

child
582 bring up a child in the way
1429 A child thinks twenty
2466 Ask your child what he
3976 things a child will share
4049 A child should always say

childbirth
2894 taxes and childbirth! There's
3668 women, at any rate in childbirth.

childhood
409 Genius is childhood recaptured.
1389 go from one childhood to
4086 Childhood - a period of waiting

childish
135 a silly, childish game, it's
3676 like them strong and childish.

children
1 for their children - clean,
101 now learn from their children.
211 the world is done by children.
372 Children have never been very
488 first class, and with children.
1026 allow their children to come
1107 produce children but that
1236 parents obey their children.
1425 Give me the children until they
1667 If children grew up according
2399 want your children to listen,
2513 can get it from your children.
2558 having children. Life is
3043 Children aren't happy with
3250 dogs than of their children.
3270 up some children is short.
3275 I think our children have all
3662 want their children to be a
3677 for children to be
3687 Children with Hyacinth's
3752 middle-aged children for signs
4137 adults to children, and by
4292 breeds contempt - and children.
4332 on which children cut their
4543 Children begin by loving their

chills
3056 That what chills the finger

chilly
1744 room grows chilly, I haven't

chimneys
2991 good grove of chimneys for me.

chin
3423 in the chin; a devil
4317 with her chin alone.

china
3310 herself, though china fall.

chinese
1089 will be united by the Chinese.

chintzy
535 Oh! Chintzy, Chintzy

chips
4453 It said Chips with

chivalry
1780 Chivalry is the most delicate

chocolate
817 box of chocolate liqueurs

choice
2121 having any choice in the
2987 where the choice constantly
3493 and you takes your choice.
4531 he has the choice of two

choo-choo
1725 Chattanooga Choo-choo, Track

choose
655 have to choose between
2643 One must choose between

choosing
4465 When choosing between two

chopper
1614 and chippy chopper on a big

chops
2823 calmly licking its chops.

chorus
1391 a dozen are only a chorus.

chose
1704 I .. chose my wife, as she

christ
3033 Christ - an anarchist who

christian
905 The Christian ideal has not
1178 do As little as a Christian can.
2798 than a drunken Christian.
3323 perfectly like a Christian.
3801 Fled with a Christian! O my
4280 man - a Christian holding
4613 A Christian is a man who feels

christianity
195 Muscular Christianity.
3681 nothing in Christianity or
3820 Christianity might be a good thing

christians
341 like good Christians.

christmas
9 Christmas is over, and Business
23 well that Christmas should
1773 insulting Christmas card I
1890 - for Christmas. They're

chrysanthemum
4579 you look like a chrysanthemum.

chump
4573 grab a chump. Tap his

church
117 The Church of England is the
1977 you go to church, and like
2092 but the Church has driven
2476 at the church, waiting
3313 As some to church repair,

churchill
303 Winston Churchill - fifty per
3026 clergyman; Churchill being a
4431 Winston Churchill is always

churchman
615 the British churchman, he goes

churchyard
2205 taste, than in a churchyard.

cicero
125 terrible to Cicero, desirable

cigar
13 five-cent cigars in the
704 A good cigar is as great a
722 A good cigar, a good
2276 but a good cigar is a
4432 is like a cigar. If it

cigarette
4533 A cigarette is the perfect type

cigars
4302 smoke cigars in heaven,

circulation
3911 assists the circulation of their

circumcision
3150 breast-feeding, circumcision.

circumstances
1543 I am I plus my circumstances.
2081 by circumstances beyond
3275 under very demanding circumstances.
4271 trying circumstances, urgent

circus
2788 have no right in the circus.

cistern
496 loud the cistern, As I read

cities
39 hell to men, hell to cities.
3336 in three cities, But it is

citizen
3450 and a good citizen are not

city
1877 but the city eats it.
2707 down the City Road, In

civil
3759 but a civil contract.
3892 Here lies a civil servant.

civility
2915 essence of civility; Young

civilization
1679 the great rewards of civilization.
3575 can't say civilization don't

civilize
2017 you would civilize a man,

civilized
2585 animal and civilized man. It
4369 I am among civilized men

civilizes
3024 Cricket civilizes people and

clad
2888 that, is clad in

clan
3206 say, 'Your clan will pay

clap
3168 Don't clap too hard - it's

claret
1328 with more claret than
2127 Claret is the liquor for

clarity
3100 to youth, clarity of thought
3167 had the clarity of a

class
665 coulda had class and been
2565 The 3rd Class, not the

classes
863 two great classes: those
3099 into two classes: tools and
3906 the upper classes With your

classic
1139 it, even if bad, to a classic.

classical
1619 At classical Monday
3289 That's the classical mind at

classics
4072 The great homicidal classics?

clatter
1778 cheerful clatter of Sir

claws
827 spreads his claws, And

cleaned
1586 firm. I cleaned the

clear
2199 that they do not make clear.
3561 What is not clear is not

cleopatra
3227 Had Cleopatra's nose been

clergy
3472 is worth a pound of clergy.

clergyman
2203 No married clergyman should
3026 or of a clergyman; Churchill

clergymen
1178 have with clergymen to do As
3927 - men, women, and clergymen.

clerks
2047 clearly built for clerks.

clever
288 He's very clever, but
1226 always a clever thing to
4596 people were clever, And all

cleverest
118 The cleverest woman finds a

cleverness
2355 height of cleverness is to be

clich,
1774 that cliché was a

client
1554 bend to favour ev'ry client.

climate
315 but a whole climate of
671 the climate, the
782 where the climate's sultry.

climbed
91 curiosity, one climbed on.
1140 I have climbed to the top of

clive
514 like about Clive Is that he

cloak
1504 often borrows her cloak.

clock
293 and his eye on the clock.
2266 setting a clock half an
2268 as to stop the church clock.
2899 is halfway out of the clock.
3679 The clock struck eleven
4484 set the clock an hour

clocks
3727 Electric clocks reveal to

close
85 man trying to close in.
343 ugly head, close your eyes
1897 on my bed, close my eyes,

closed
1367 but it was closed.

closer
605 Pope be any closer to God
2526 ideas closer together.

closet
985 own hearts in their closet.

cloth
380 wearing a cloth coat. The

clothed
4018 ideas get clothed at the

clothes
431 Clothes and manners do not
866 take the girl's clothes off.
1157 away with their clothes.
1354 can have with your clothes on.
1888 of her clothes. Next,
2563 The suit of clothes is
4197 that require new clothes.
4268 are but the clothes and
4592 these wet clothes and into a

clothing
920 A sheep in sheep's clothing.

cloud
2881 to be a Cloud Floating

cloverleaf
3032 is the concrete cloverleaf.

club
581 hand and a club in the
2754 to any club that will
3903 will be a club. But this

cluttered
119 If a cluttered desk is an

coach
2627 a football coach who's
4092 a stage coach, but now

coal
549 mainly of coal and

coarse
3638 one of them is rather coarse.

coat
251 a mink coat but a
1700 and my coat from the

cocaine
4059 Cocaine is God's way of

cock
4033 about?' 'A Cock and a

cocktail
3288 under the cocktail cabinet.
3591 is like one cocktail, it just
3904 The cocktail party - a device

cocktails
152 over cocktails That

codfish
494 out of it. That and codfish.

coffee
120 Coffee in England is just
3487 if this is coffee, I want

coffin
57 won't fit into my coffin.
2807 looks around for a coffin.
3130 the silver plate on a coffin.
3153 grave in a Y-shaped coffin.

cold
346 the common cold, And gives
1507 cat fears even cold water.
2302 call this cold in
2934 and like rivers grow cold.
3104 dressed ever caught a cold?
3543 A cold in the head causes
4437 everlasting cold; I have

cold storage
3692 library is thought in cold storage.

coliseum
3328 You're the Coliseum, You're

collections
2383 of collections, spoilers

college
937 is what a college becomes
1861 sons to college either

2105 got through college yet."
2231 asked what college I
2766 too soon after college.

collide
3327 July we collide with Mars?

collision
4220 rear-end collision and Man

collisions
1775 collisions between
3689 boathook to avoid collisions.

colossus
2143 could cut a Colossus from a

colour
1403 Any colour - so long as it's
3648 match the colour of the

columbus
1568 West, and Columbus discovered
1676 If Columbus had had an

column
1927 and the column of

comatose
946 lachrymose and comatose.

comb
634 two bald men over a comb.
3383 is the comb that

combination
1106 there is a combination, but the

combustion
2429 spontaneous combustion. You must

come
1248 future. It comes soon
1564 We are come for your good,
2031 want to come, nothing
2865 'Do you come here often?'
3697 a war and nobody will come.
4467 don't you come up

comedian
1879 A comedian is a fellow who
2810 God is a comedian whose

comedy
714 Comedy is tragedy - plus
3037 writes comedy at the
4326 Comedy is simply a funny way

comfort
335 at home for real comfort.
704 as great a comfort to a man
1215 Comfort the afflicted and

comfortable
1342 to make you comfortable. It is
1824 into something more comfortable."

comforting
2717 is always a comforting thought in

comic
2433 encourage a comic man too

comical
1598 think it's comical How Nature

computers
144 Computers in the future will
2701 Computers can figure out all

computing
2743 hazards of computing are

conceal
1008 to conceal, usually
2355 is to be able to conceal it.
3685 to us to conceal our

concealing
4293 consists in concealing how much

conceivable
2866 on every conceivable occasion.

conceived
404 of an era, conceived with

concentrates
2176 it concentrates his mind

conception
4083 Her conception of God was

concern
4341 which properly concern them.

concert
2860 torture, the concert.

conclusion
612 A conclusion is the place where
3645 came to the conclusion that all

concrete
3032 is the concrete

concurred
3192 I came, I saw, I concurred.

condemn
2918 delights condemn, But 'tis

condescend
4128 of wit Will condescend to take a

condition
3256 decoyed into our condition.

conditions
4536 have the conditions, you get

conductors
430 foreign conductors around -
4143 Conductors must give

conference
1387 born in a conference, but a lot

confess
2365 We only confess our little
3361 absolv'd Who has confess'd.
3425 He that jokes confesses.

confessing
3266 faults by confessing our

confession
902 is confession without

confide
805 We seldom confide in those

confirmation
121 Confirmation at Eton: like a huge

conflict
3354 offered you Conflict and Art.

conflicts
1971 inner conflicts. Life

conform
3026 to conform either to

conformism
4087 Conformism is so hot on the

conformists
2657 its live conformists and its

confound
1163 Confound those who have said

confused
3925 which it is often confused.

confusing
1537 looks confusing and messy,

congregation
1086 has the largest congregation.

congress
2736 Congress is so strange. A man

conjugation
2060 nature is a conjugation of the

conquer
1854 had time to conquer the world

conqueror
3614 you are a conqueror. Kill

conscience
122 Conscience is a cur that will
745 Conscience is thoroughly
2806 Conscience is a mother-in-law
2816 Conscience: the inner voice
3712 is the conscience of women;
3870 Conscience has no more to do
3917 with a good conscience on the
4225 to have a conscience, when it

consciousness
4316 which one's consciousness has been

consent
783 will ne'er consent' -
3599 inferior without your consent.

consenting
4360 only between consenting adults.

consequences
46 to take all the consequences.

conservative
1477 make me conservative when old.
1598 Or else a little Conservative!
1912 while marriage is conservative.
2097 A Conservative is a man who will
2693 Conservative ideal of freedom and

conservatives
1301 Men are conservatives when they are

considerable
2118 to appear considerable in his

consistency
522 Consistency requires you to be as

corner
502 bit in the corner you can't
2139 into a corner, and who

coromandel
2451 coast of Coromandel Where the
3895 coast of Coromandel Dance they

corporation
3747 capital to form a corporation.
4225 expect a corporation to have a

corps
2551 Canadian Corps coming

corpuscles
4565 human traits and red corpuscles.

correct
1357 to seek to correct the
1883 will correct these
2107 great deal: correct a little.
3145 years to correct, is quite

corroborative
1623 Merely corroborative detail,

corrugated
427 on a corrugated tin roof.

corrupt
2670 virtues but also more corrupt.

corrupts
1061 power corrupts

cosiness
3501 all the cosiness and

cosmos
899 the cosmos, but never

cost
2005 on account of the cost.

costs
238 What costs nothing is worth
262 you get free costs too much.

costume
2420 The same costume will be

cotton
189 to' don't pick no cotton.

cough
4391 they cough in

coughing
396 keep an audience from coughing.
3729 only - one coughing, and one

count
40 Don't count your chickens
2486 They had to count them all.
2529 can't count above
4298 When angry, count four; when

counterfeiting
1430 a good man and counterfeiting him.

countess
2777 what the countess is saying.

counting
4066 democracy, it's the counting.

countries
3815 are two countries divided by

country
719 to run the country are busy
1179 not a bad country .. It's
1407 my country and
1610 and every country but his
1844 had in the country, or, if
1899 is a country where they
3639 and your Country both need
3932 for the country; it is a
4031 of his own country too,
4503 good in the country. There
4593 for the good of his country.

counts
1257 What counts is not

coupled
915 and wife, Coupled together

courage
530 Courage - fear that has said
985 the rarest courage; since
1493 if we had courage enough.
1549 us With courage, love and
4207 the morning courage, which

courageous
3612 liberal, courageous, such as I

course
2592 My preudunt course is

court
1219 the Supreme Court follows
3357 I court others in verse:

courted
802 Better be courted and jilted

courts
3667 of the Courts, it means

cousins
1585 and his cousins and his

couth
3258 a thing as too much couth.

covet
2271 as ever coveted his

cow
418 till the cow comes
2709 great milk cow, with its
3041 The cow is of the bovine
4126 when she kissed her cow.
4502 We milk the cow of the

coward
1013 often be a coward, but for

cowardice
1471 engaging cowardice. With it
2070 it too far, and it's cowardice.

cowardly
4380 adventure open to the cowardly.

cowards
1493 We could be cowards, if we had
4284 a race of cowards; and I am

coxcomb
3653 to hear a coxcomb ask two

crack
1300 There is a crack in
3409 but he does not crack them.

craved
1654 and who craved no crumb,

craving
3242 no stronger craving in the

crazy
141 to have a crazy person
206 and find oil? You're crazy.
679 one to be crazy and amuse

creak
3462 Devil's boots don't creak.

cream
1461 I want the cream to rise.
1589 milk masquerades as cream.
2970 skim the cream of others'

created
822 never created a man half

creativity
3512 I get horny for my creativity.

creatures
1026 the only creatures on earth

credit
1590 to his credit, That he
2664 poor people's credit card.
3662 to be a credit to them.

creditors
17 your coat to your creditors.

creed
1178 His creed no parson ever
4027 got the better of his creed.

creeping
4480 madam, Nature is creeping up.

cremated
1828 should be cremated, not

cricket
2432 then set up a game of cricket.
2706 Cricket - a game which the
3024 Cricket civilizes people and
4159 looked on cricket as
4241 of playing cricket with their

crime
979 that crime does not
1221 It isn't a crime exactly.
1618 fit the crime - The
3341 for a crime you

crimea
4153 Crimea: The War That Would

crimes
1345 Crimes, like virtues, are

criminal
3747 A criminal is a person with

critic
1203 A critic at best is a waiter

2393 English critic is a don
3301 A critic is a legless man
4313 A critic is a man who knows

criticism
613 of anger, fear and criticism.
685 dramatic criticism must seem
1408 because it permits criticism.
1989 To escape criticism - do
4029 the cant of criticism is the
4316 Drama criticism .. [is] a

criticize
932 never to criticize or attack
1532 fool can criticize, and many
3379 Never criticize a man until

critics
451 Critics are like eunuchs in a
1930 to make critics out of the
4304 audience - 4000 critics.
4594 Critics are like brushers of

crocodile
919 who feeds a crocodile - hoping
2288 to the Crocodile's musky,

crocodiles
2039 female crocodiles continue
3448 are no crocodiles because

cromwell
425 a ruin that Cromwell knocked
2197 They set up Cromwell and his
2552 a ruin that Cromwell knocked

crook
3109 is a crook. Well,
3586 you are a crook or a

crooked
608 but the crooked roads
2759 'yes,' you know he is crooked.

cross
3029 the Cross as the

cross-grained
1698 ever such a cross-grained brute?

crossed
337 likes to be crossed in love a

crosses
2197 down the crosses. They set

crow
876 and thenk upon the crowe.
2599 'n 't is to crow: Don't

crowd
395 Every crowd has a silver
443 you can make a crowd of men.
2331 of the crowd will not

crowing
48 silly cock crowing on its own

crown
546 have the crown of thorns
2980 a crown of thorns,

crumbs
2068 the bags to hold the crumbs.

crumpetty
2462 on this Crumpetty Tree The

crusade
2425 Children's Crusade in 1212 AD

cry
704 as a good cry is to a
2165 cries, Cry not when
2523 me as I cry all the
4416 lament and cry And now

crystal
548 read the crystal when he

crystallises
3345 politician crystallises what most

cuckold
1326 to cuckold' for

cuckoo
2899 The cuckoo who is on to

cucumber
2146 are but cucumbers after
2651 when cucumber is added

cue
1620 a twisted cue And

cult
77 What's a cult? It just

culture
457 who leaves culture to his
1486 the popular culture of the
1629 line as a man of culture rare.
4474 who pursue Culture in bands,

cupid
2618 Cupid and my Campaspe

cupidons
717 away all the little cupidons.

cur
122 is a cur that will

curable
570 often curable by

curate
1375 the average curate at home as
1651 was a pale young curate then.

curates
675 shower of curates has fallen

cure
2 The best cure for
464 is no Cure for this
2290 The cure for this ill is
3708 There is no cure for birth
3907 has no cure for this
4140 the twentieth, it's a cure.

cured
1920 one that is rarely cured.
2635 a man to be cured by his own
3364 Cured yesterday of my

cures
3066 puts to bed and cures.

curiosity
91 of general curiosity, one

curl
2573 a little curl Right in
2863 a little curl, Right in

curse
4012 us from the curse Of a prose
4546 Work is the curse of the

curses
3960 Curses are like young

curtain
3508 down the curtain, the farce

curve
224 smile is a curve that can

custom
2079 A custom loathsome to the

cut
2200 Never cut what you can
2563 Look at the cut, the
4448 you. I'll cut bits orf

cuttlefish
3159 like a cuttlefish squirting

cynic
560 Cynic, n: a blackguard
2807 A cynic is a man who, when
4522 What is a cynic? A man who

cynical
456 Irish are cynical. It's

cynicism
2622 Cynicism - the intellectual

daddy
3042 Ask Daddy, He Won't Know.

daffodils
2412 for me what daffodils were for

daft
3750 thinks the tither daft.

daintily
537 have things daintily served.
538 Pardon's Daintily alights

dainty
1887 my Julia's dainty leg, Which

dairy
2190 doth nightly rob the dairy.

dairymaid
2878 asked The Dairymaid: 'Could we

daisies
1630 upon the daisies and

dam
2851 her for a dam What

dammed
1956 only saved by being dammed.

damn
220 give a damn, I wish I
2386 exclaimed, Damn the age; I
2853 life is one damn thing
3214 I do not give a damn.

damnation
3855 be blasted to eternal damnation!

damned
1697 It's a damned long, dark,
1995 is just one damned thing
2282 the spree, Damned from here

damning
770 to, By damning those they

dance
725 the ae best dance e'er cam
2720 there's a dance in the old
3895 Coromandel Dance they to

danced
2459 sand, They danced by the

dancer
4337 hybrid of a dancer and a

dancing
3821 Dancing is] a perpendicular

danger
2041 is dangerous, where
2345 me out of danger. You can
3044 be in less danger From the
3188 when in danger, not

dangerous
1697 boggy, dirty, dangerous way.
2041 is dangerous, where is
2079 the brain, dangerous to the
2244 none is so dangerous as the
2998 is a dangerous
2999 that it is dangerous and may do
4474 it were dangerous to meet it
4518 is a dangerous thing, and

dangerously
3092 life is to live dangerously !

dare
2946 much as I dare; and I

dark
877 Derk was the nyght as
1864 to go home in the dark.
3388 die in the dark, even

darken
2532 Never darken my Dior again!

darkest
1758 The darkest hour of any man's

darkness
788 between his Darkness and his

darling
392 to call you darling after sex.

darwinian
1576 Darwinian Man, though

date
499 out of date.

daughter
3801 My daughter! O my ducats! O my

daughters
273 one of her daughters - any one

david
3064 King David and King Solomon

day
806 It happens every day.
1220 place ivry day, but no
3620 Every dogma has its day.

day-to-day
883 - it's this day-to-day living

days
79 the bad old days, there
2968 our days Is to
3398 of these days is none of

dead
124 A dead man Who never
178 and is dead: Had it
278 charity more than the dead.
463 When I am dead, I hope it
480 struck him dead: And serve
514 to be said For being dead.
1109 - the quick, and the dead.
1144 I am dead; dead, but in
1168 when I am dead And
1571 before he is dead.
1686 she was dead, Her last
1754 A dead woman bites not.
1951 a composer is to be dead.
2474 he had been dead for two
2603 and the dead alone
2615 helped by being dead.
2686 who like it better dead.
2716 besides, the wench is dead.
2750 he's dead, or my
2895 but in fact it is dead.
3488 men are dead! Carlyle,
3664 already three parts dead.
3719 to be blooming well dead?
4254 who's been dead 10 or 15
4584 Dead! and .. never

deadly
4274 are more deadly in the

deaf
975 union of a deaf man to a
3378 tongue will keep thee deaf.

dealing
1506 men, must leave off dealing.

dean
1156 Mr. Dean, no dogma,
3978 to the queer old Dean.
3983 I am the Dean of Christ

dearer
4160 a little dearer than his

death
84 Death has got something to
125 Death is terrible to
196 thing to death in life Is
225 O Death, where is thy
362 for the death of a
539 a cow. Swarm over, Death!
755 then so neither must death.
1280 and death. That's
1365 presence of death lurks with

1434 except death and taxes.
1954 His death, which happened
2467 only nervousness or death.
2504 to you, 'tis death to us.
2660 not die of death· We die of
2894 Death and taxes and
2948 and not at their death.
2997 a decent death on the
3018 Death [is] nature's way of
3431 man for the Angel of Death.
3559 friendship, sex and death.
3925 Death must be distinguished
4016 Finality is death.
4019 - for Death it has an
4193 still from death was
4240 and makes death a
4259 try and set death aside. It
4300 of my death are

deathbed
323 by his deathbed won't hail

debatable
1967 Hunger is not debatable.

debauch
640 a man may debauch his

debauche
562 Debauche, n: one who has so

debt
767 He'd run in debt by
3766 National Debt is a very

decay
1923 of mild decay, But
3174 in the mouth of decay.

decayed
1628 you are sufficiently decayed?

deceased
2297 of the late deceased, And the
4595 He first deceased; she for a

deceitfulness
1274 Cat of such deceitfulness and

deceived
4084 of being well deceived.

december
397 might have roses in December.

decendants
2864 for their decendants would be

decent
2997 do you a decent death on
3678 All decent people live

decentralized
1834 means decentralized planning

decide
2335 cannot decide what it
3311 Who shall decide, when
4367 God's sake decide what

decision
3220 of taking decisions of
3511 A decision is the action an

declare
4525 nothing to declare except my

declaring
2900 is always declaring he's no

decorate
4603 than they decorate them.

decoration
3171 sort of decoration for it - a

decorum
727 cant about DECORUM, Who have

dee
4130 we take it, is dee.

deed
680 No good deed ever goes

deeds
3397 and not of deeds, Is like a

deep
127 Deep down he is shallow.
1691 Who, too deep for his

deface
4603 Pictures deface walls

defeat
910 towards sure defeat.
2307 we should defeat you, we
2708 Defeat brings its own

defeated
2646 is so defeated as

defect
3662 fundamental defect of fathers

defence
672 no adequate defence, except
678 another defence against

defiance
1702 their port, defiance in their

definition
3107 any other definition of what a
3667 exact legal definition; in the
3850 good working definition of hell.

deformity
289 modesty amounts to deformity.

defunct
871 hand of the defunct must not

degeneration
4055 a fatty degeneration of his

deity
4083 between the Deity and the

delay
204 To avoid delay, please have

delegate
630 in trouble, delegate. (3) When

delight
323 the occasion with delight.
2609 her delight on seeing
2968 late for delight, my dear;
3519 chills, The delight of her

delightful
2554 as sin, And almost as delightful.

delights
2918 does some delights condemn,

delinquencies
1270 indulge in a few delinquencies.

deliver
150 night, Good Lord, deliver us!

delphiniums
2877 in a bed Of delphiniums (blue) and

delusion
2804 Love is the delusion that one

demand
595 been in excess of the demand.
1400 up with the demand for it.
2108 by popular demand, sometimes
2406 exceeds the demand.

democracy
301 Democracy means government by
896 Democracy means government by
921 said that Democracy is the
1408 cheers for Democracy: one
2808 Under democracy, one party
2815 Democracy is the theory that
4066 that's democracy, it's the
4093 understand democracy, spend

democrat
3585 party, I'm a Democrat.

democratic
1223 an' votes th' Dimmycratic Ticket.

democrats
4045 about the Democrats, we will

demolished
521 No man is demolished but by

demons
1348 driven by demons. He

denied
2932 that comes to be denied.
3220 man who is denied the

density
2665 is our sense of density.

dentist
4429 go to my dentist any day.

denunciation
3911 The denunciation of the young is a

depart
2320 the kings depart, And we
2809 If, after I depart this vale,

department
1458 it is a big department store,

departure
1143 Departure should be sudden.
3457 not the arrival, the departure.

depend
3863 Depend on the rabbit's foot

dependence
1008 their total dependence on the

deposit
72 a large deposit in my name

depraved
2223 ever suddenly became depraved.

depression
4255 job; it's a depression when you

deprivation
2412 Deprivation is for me what

descendants
3057 day your descendants Outnumber

descended
2401 the Fourth descended God be

deserve
1465 have to deserve your
1657 - and how little I deserve it.
1748 of the men who deserve them.
2021 when they do not deserve it.
2815 want, and deserve to get it
3451 but a mule deserves his

design
3995 dull there is a design in it.
4202 conscious design of doing

designing
513 Say I am designing St.

desire
663 man, the desire for
757 innate desire on the
977 The man's desire is for the
1363 namely the desire of
1668 From desire I plunge to its
3778 I do desire we may be better
3791 in me to desire small
3792 that desire should so
3843 heart's desire. The
4167 to, they desire
4623 admitted desire to dress

desired
1767 leave much to be desired.

desirous
1549 ought else on earth desirous?

desk
1588 to your desks and never

despair
1748 a girl, I'd despair. The
2378 the experiment of despair.

despairing
1606 awake with a shudder despairing.

desperate
2943 outside desperate to get in,

despise
1510 Never despise what it says in

despised
2447 maid: Despised, if ugly;

dessert
113 uncertain - eat dessert first

destination
1724 way of travel - not a destination.

destiny
561 Destiny, n: a tyrant's
1346 you know, go by Destiny.
1893 Wedding is destiny, and
2856 Destiny is what you are
4170 passion is my destiny.

destroy
825 but it will destroy him with a

destroyed
2234 you do is destroyed, laid

destroying
1872 the rain is destroying his grain

destroys
2337 wantonly destroys a work of

destruction
1468 that for destruction ice Is
1525 complete destruction rather

determined
2038 extent determined by the

detest
785 but they detest at

dethronement
4489 will enjoy the dethronement.

detrimental
3128 it would be dethrimental to keep

devil
161 He'd give the devil ulcers.
725 Was, the deil's awa wi'
741 for the Devil - it must
1086 prayer, The Devil always
1494 The Devil himself is good
1847 that the devil can throw
1895 why the devil should
2278 But the Devil whoops, as
2321 and the Devil knows
2765 The devil turned precisian!
3112 go to the devil, he may as
3423 in the chin; a devil within.
3462 The Devil's boots don't
3892 and servant to the devil.
3961 walking the Devil is gone,
3986 last: the Devil howling
4053 The devil, depend upon it,
4097 her: The devil take her!
4335 the devil grabs it

devils
2562 Devils are not so black as
2967 still 'tis devils must

devon
645 west, 'Twas Devon, glorious

devoted
3107 this - devoted and

devotion
1617 Matrimonial devotion Doesn't

devoured
3884 great ones devoured the small.

devout
2917 less human for being devout.

diagnostician
3176 rectum makes a good diagnostician.

diagonally
4030 lie diagonally in his

diamond
2581 good but a diamond and safire
2923 good, but a diamond tiara
3078 O Diamond! Diamond! thou

diamonds
1516 to give him his diamonds back.

diarist
3083 be a good diarist, one must

diary
4457 say, keep a diary and some
4513 without my diary. One

diatonic
3532 very common diatonic little

dice
1243 God plays dice with the

dickens
501 were put to Dickens as

dictators
924 Dictators ride to and fro on
2761 Dictators are rulers who always
3417 Dictators ride to and fro upon

dictatorship
1899 A dictatorship is a country where

dictionaries
2148 To make dictionaries is dull
2149 A writer of dictionaries, a

dictionary
965 is only a dictionary out of

diddle
1633 'High diddle diddle' Will
4130 we know, is diddle: and

die
53 when you die. You want
124 others to die Seldom
139 And leave me there to die.
269 when they die, go to
285 in case you don't die.
694 liable to die and are
766 to do is to die at once.
984 agree to die together.
1316 hope that he will die.
1453 live long and die young.
1520 More die in the United
1882 Only the young die good.
1947 before I die about
2048 better to die on your
2160 rich than to die rich.
2384 do any thing but die.
2819 thing, they die earlier.
2905 you have to die, he will
3080 He will, he must die.
3201 Die, my dear Doctor,
3312 thousands die, without
3366 Rose, I'll die: Behind

3388 He who must die must die
3440 people to die for them,
3473 If I die, I forgive you:
3580 it is to know when to die.
3617 boy until they die!
3665 would die sooner
4000 everything, even to die.
4017 bloom and lakes die.
4095 to do and die than it is
4096 they only let Him die.
4249 it. I never want to die.
4539 have to die beyond my

died
1552 was scorned and died.
1685 The dog it was that died.
3364 disease, I died last night
3519 fever she died, of fever
4595 liked it not, and died.
4597 - When the old man died.

dies
2908 One dies only once, and
4362 something in me dies.
4621 then dies the same.

diet
2935 in your diet; In short,

difference
997 is more difference within the
1843 by the difference between
2085 very little difference between
2110 What's the difference between a
3833 of the difference between
4618 is a great difference between a

different
209 How different, how very
1035 the same with different hats on.
1385 They are different from you
2874 is quite different when it

differs
2804 one woman differs from

difficult
97 afterwards that is difficult.
591 the most difficult thing to
905 been found difficult; and left
2650 not find it difficult nowadays
3019 The difficult we do immediately
3730 and too difficult for
4495 Luckily, this is not difficult.

dig
2290 also, And dig till you

digest
133 is human, to digest, divine.

digested
352 few to be chewed and digested.

digestion
3623 good cook and a good digestion.

dignified
2426 be called a dignified

dignifies
4587 Money dignifies what is

dignity
1772 with silent dignity, but
2136 to write trifles with dignity.

digressions
4025 Digressions, incontestably, are

dimensions
1928 back to its original dimensions.

dimple
2442 love with a dimple makes the
3423 A dimple in the chin; a

dine
255 her to dine; Private
513 am going to dine with some
2076 Women never dine alone.
2098 to meet and dine somewhere

dined
654 a man more dined against
3939 me, I have dined to-day.

diner
1725 in the diner nothing

dingy
3289 but looks dingy on the

dining
1691 thought of dining; Though

dinner
194 to get your dinner, and you
1966 an old friend for dinner."
2162 has a good dinner upon his
2463 haven't any dinner, But to
2466 wants for dinner only if he
2483 diminish your dinner.
3255 how a good dinner and
3339 Dinner at the Huntercombes'
3751 A dinner lubricates
3904 want to invite to dinner.
4115 after dinner; but after

dinner party
1792 for a dinner party is two -
4398 Washington dinner party than from

dinner-knives
2283 paths with broken dinner-knives.

dinners
863 have more dinners than

dinosaur
2178 The dinosaur's eloquent lesson

dior
2532 Never darken my Dior again!

diplomacy
852 Diplomacy; the art of saying
1678 Diplomacy is to do and say The

diplomat
130 diplomat could hold
1088 Diplomats are useful only in
4060 A diplomat .. is a person who

direction
2443 madly off in all directions.
2799 sense of direction after four
director
1716 with these directors, they're
dirt
1497 that flings dirt at another
1519 thicker will be the dirt.
1753 Dirt is only matter out of
dirtiest
4493 The dirtiest book of all is
dirty
3351 prefer to go around dirty.
disadvantage
2151 One of the disadvantages of wine
2161 to his own disadvantage. People
disagrees
2736 then everybody disagrees.
disappointed
467 you have disappointed us! We had
disappointing
406 he'll be the least disappointing.
disappointment
1828 Disappointments should be cremated,
disaster
3657 bring all kinds of disaster.
disbelieves
2782 earnestly disbelieves what
disciples
4516 has his disciples, and it is
discipline
3817 in the discipline of silence
discover
803 those we discover after all
discovered
11 ago we discovered the exact
3075 is slowly discovered, the bad
discoveries
2870 making exciting discoveries.
discovery
4144 Discovery consists of seeing
4335 makes a discovery, the devil
discredited
4611 has been thoroughly discredited.
discretion
4081 Discretion is not the better
discussed
4588 the most discussed animal in
discussion
301 by discussion, but it is
disease
156 sexually transmitted disease.
257 youth is a disease from which
1940 a chronic disease and taking
2239 In disease Medical Men guess:
2950 from the disease of writing
2960 is a fatal disease; fatal to

4135 worse than the disease.
4140 it was a disease; in the
4242 A disease in the family that
diseases
3976 diseases and his
4061 cured all the good diseases.
disgrace
1221 but it's a kind iv a disgrace.
3937 is no disgrace to a man,
disgruntled
4575 actually disgruntled, he was
disguise
1360 through the disguise of gaiety
dish
3232 Some dish more sharply
dishes
855 pass the dishes again.
dishonest
1550 be reckoned dishonest, because,
disinheriting
3878 a damned disinheriting
dislike
1826 able to dislike someone
dismiss
1969 Dismiss the old horse in good
dismount
924 dare not dismount. And the
3417 which they dare not dismount.
disorderly
2870 of being disorderly is that
dispossessed
645 Eve were dispossessed Of the
disputes
4051 checkered by disputes.
disregard
1535 but a disregard for others
dissected
382 anatomy and dissected at least
dissolve
3654 would be to dissolve all
distance
631 shortest distance between
distinguish
416 there is to distinguish us from
distinguishes
3177 which distinguishes man from
distort
4281 you can distort 'em as
distracted
3512 always be distracted by love,
distribute
2589 his duty to distribute as fairly
disturb
870 world to disturb nothing
diversity
2945 universal quality is diversity.

divided
2325 one million divided by one
2510 they divided up the
3815 countries divided by a

divine
133 is human, to digest, divine.
3059 You look divine as you

divine service
215 it being Sunday, had Divine Service.

divinest
2029 The two divinest things this

divorce
1513 I get a divorce, I keep
1881 of divorce and the

divorced
2254 Being divorced is like being

dizziness
2264 is the dizziness of

dizzy
1394 going at a dizzy rate. We
3898 up and down till I am dizzy.

do
2387 and what I do to be
3525 did not do things
3579 to do with the
3762 say, Do as I say,
3826 Do not do unto others as
4095 easier to do and die

dock
1676 still be at the dock.

doctor
3 Doctor, feel my purse.
270 training to become a doctor.
544 in front of the doctor.
1431 and the doctor takes the
1545 go to the doctor when they
1686 The doctor found, when she
1902 Wherever a doctor cannot do
2905 A doctor wastes no time with
2938 No doctor takes pleasure in
3107 not even a doctor, ever
3188 God and the doctor we alike
3362 The doctor understood the
3498 sort of a doctor is he? Oh
3618 Doctor, my doctor, what do
3881 Our doctor would never
4599 A doctor can bury his

doctors
3311 decide, when doctors disagree.

doctrine
772 makes all doctrines plain and
3313 Not for the doctrine, but the

does
385 A gentleman does things no

dog
433 The dog is the god of
749 of a dog is that
1023 I have a dog that

1257 size of the dog in the
1440 and old dog, and ready
1684 The dog, to gain some
1685 bite, The dog it was
2033 To his dog, every man is
2191 the very flea of his dog.
2284 That the Dog returns to
2301 heart to a dog to tear.
2705 Man is a dog's ideal of
2861 The biggest dog has been a
3135 to a dog is what
3385 One dog barks at
3456 comes a dog's; then a
3969 of pollution, the dog.
4160 than his dog, a little
4161 Like a dog, he hunts in
4216 I am not a dog-lover. To
4472 good for a dog - it keeps
4627 way of a dog that if he

dog-star
3308 I'm dead, The dog-star rages!

dogma
1156 Mr. Dean, no dogma, no Dean.
1776 will serve to beat a dogma.
3620 Every dogma has its day.

dogs
3616 who hates dogs and babies
3774 the more I admire dogs.
4234 the more one values dogs.

doing
80 Doing easily what others
364 in life is doing what
485 to be doing at that
666 is when I'm doing what I
1906 It is always doing or dying.
2952 if you are doing something
3483 what she's doing, and tell
4359 is] doing well that

doing-good
4206 As for Doing-good, that is one

dollar
585 of a dollar with a

domestic
3232 men call domestic bliss.

dominant
566 always been dominant and

dominion
2836 of his dark dominion swung the

don
1664 the typical Don, and of

done
451 how it's done, they've
1183 and are never done.
1441 a thing done, go - if
3175 must be done, but must
3463 What may be done at any
3674 of one gets things done.

4359 should not be done at all.
4488 must be done about
4569 was ever done so

dong
2462 'The Dong! the Dong! The

donkey
1762 where the donkey finally

donne
1165 John Donne, Anne Donne,
2080 Dr Donne's verses are like

doom
1755 of their doom, The

door
3135 the other side of a door.
3308 shut the door, good
4092 of a revolving door.
4330 doing away with the door.

dormouse
2877 once was a Dormouse who lived

dote
3800 them but I dote on his

double life
4507 leading a double life,

double-bed
801 of the double-bed after the

doubled
1082 to have your trouble doubled.

doubt
462 never doubt What
1577 manner of doubt - No
2317 enabled to doubt Thee, Help
2328 or doubt
4299 when in doubt, strike it

down
1466 a fence down until you
2623 people to look down upon.
2903 meet 'em on your way down.
2973 my coming down let me

dozens
1585 up by dozens, And his

dragged
3263 he hadn't dragged her

dragon
2233 a damn big dragon. You kick

dragons
4230 Never laugh at live dragons.

drain
3979 by the next town drain.

drains
4083 the Deity and the Drains.

drake
3072 Drake he's in his hammock

drama
1904 Drama is life with the dull

drank
3860 I work as my father drank.

draughts
4512 susceptible to draughts.

dread
542 The dread of beatings!
3740 - I only dread one day at

dreadfully
4412 He is dreadfully married. He's

dreading
776 Dreading that climax of all

dreadnoughts
2548 up as two Dreadnoughts; and dukes

dream
131 To dream of the person you
1603 For you dream you are
1908 ever have a boring dream?

dreamed
4054 night I've dreamed of cheese

dreamer
3704 artist is a dreamer consenting

dreaming
3798 sleep, Dreaming on both.

dreams
2610 can lay a hand on our dreams.
2958 beyond the dreams of
3739 all your dreams
4161 a dog, he hunts in dreams.

dress
849 and a hundred in dress.
1122 I dress for women - and I
2668 article of dress without
3648 I always dress to match the
4018 man cannot dress, without

dressed
3104 was well dressed ever
4486 All dressed up, with nowhere

dresses
4623 All women's dresses are merely

dressing up
4132 skills - dressing up and

drifted
4464 snow-white .. but I drifted.

drill
206 Drill for oil? You mean

drink
98 What should we do for drink?
151 a duck a drink if he
875 And for to drynken strong
1371 drove me to drink - and, you
1878 Drink not the third glass -
2073 reason why I never drink it.
2195 Our drink shall be prepared
2697 I love drink, so long as it
2813 never to drink by
3015 Drinka Pinta Milka Day.
3061 I drink to make other
3134 who prefers women to drink.
3467 Drink nothing without
3507 I drink for the thirst to

3537 "I never drink when I fly."
3918 we could drink all day
3978 Let us drink to the queer
4150 that he has taken to drink.
4430 I drink for it.

drinking
416 Drinking when we are not
1365 too much drinking. That
3756 not the drinking that is to
4115 true, 'much drinking, little
4546 curse of the drinking classes.

drinks
244 He who drinketh by the inch
618 is about three drinks behind.
2799 after four drinks; a woman
4182 like who drinks as much as

drive
254 time to drive to the
4313 way but can't drive the car.

driver
420 he was in the driver's seat.

drop
2131 well to drop, but would

dropout
1536 the term dropout' to mean a

dropped
2131 not wish to be dropped by.

drown
712 a rat may drown a nation.
1088 rains, they drown in every

drowned
1538 Bacchus has drowned more men
2175 the chance of being drowned.
4133 do only be drownded now and

drowning
1355 death by drowning, a really

drowns
1241 Whisky drowns some troubles

drudge
2149 a harmless drudge.
3191 was a genius I was a drudge.

drugs
3213 you; And drugs cause

drunk
640 he gets drunk; but most
787 and then drunk.
2128 the art of getting drunk.
2971 getting drunk, is a sin
3237 Not drunk is he who from
3985 so think as you drunk I am.
4336 from Philip drunk to Philip

drunkard
903 English drunkard made the
3432 loves the drunkard, but not

drunkards
3510 more old drunkards than old

drunkenness
2078 the sin of drunkenness, which is

ducats
3801 O my ducats! O my

duck
151 give a duck a drink if
1096 I just forgot to duck.

duke
1048 enough who knows a duke.
2700 treat a duke as an
3714 The Duke returned from the

dukes
1581 in May, And dukes were three
2548 and dukes are just

dull
5 is that he be dull.
2148 Dull. To make
3968 be too dull to bear,
3995 appears dull there is a

dullness
3982 Dullness, occasionally
4560 Dullness is a misdemeanour.

dumb
2111 So dumb he can't fart and
2627 game, and dumb enough to
3771 said, I envy dumb people.

dunce
1044 How much a dunce that has

dungeon
1620 - In a dungeon cell On a

dunghill
48 crowing on its own dunghill.

durable
667 are too durable, that's

dusk
1653 In the dusk with a

dust
1383 into the dust descend;
2696 The dust of exploded
3215 Excuse My Dust.

dutch
813 of the Dutch Is
3392 but the Dutch made

duties
3178 the first duties of the
4192 to the neglect of his duties.

duty
1570 he had a duty to
1637 as keen A sense of duty?
3659 A sense of duty is useful
4022 were in duty both
4517 The one duty we owe to

dwarf
2195 : and my dwarf shall

dwell
4609 not to dwell in

dying
51 I am dying with the help of
641 Smoking is a dying habit.

1033 We are dying of accuracy.
1365 of people dying from too
1906 It is always doing or dying.
3316 Here am I, dying of a
3007 can't stay dying here all
3925 from dying, with
4080 If this is dying, then I

dyke
712 through a dyke, even a

eagle
2012 fly like an eagle with the
2707 and out the Eagle, That's

ear
310 The ear tends to be lazy,
2980 is to earn to wear

earful
3034 getting an earful tonight.

earl
1578 be, The Earl, the

early
1978 time to get an early start.
2591 to git up airly Ef you
2751 "Well, it's early yet."
3264 Early to bed, early to

earn
648 thee surely will earn it.
1746 be set to earn their

earnest
2518 who are earnest about not

earning
1758 get money without earning it.

earrings
3523 a pair of earrings for under

ears
1325 but two ears, that we
2344 hungry stomach has no ears.
3297 since it has no ears.
3413 the ears believe
3649 others is with your ears.
4120 tongues, and hedges ears.

earth
153 lived on earth, people
306 all here on earth to help
1026 on earth that allow
1489 Spaceship Earth, and that
3283 Where on earth do they
3350 stay on earth Which is
3384 made him, earth can find
4469 it is the salt of the earth.

earthquake
2098 If an earthquake were to engulf
2330 which no earthquake is a

easiest
3755 they were easiest for his

easy
2732 zeal .. all zeal, Mr Easy.
3730 Too easy for children, and
4168 that comes easy, comes

eat
52 Never eat at a place
94 Eat British Lamb: 50,000
113 uncertain - eat dessert
133 To eat is human, to
317 that he eat than that
919 it will eat him last.
2060 the verb to eat, in the
3515 Eat slowly: only men in
4036 Frogs Eat Butterflies.
4605 that do not eat people are

eaten
2234 waste or eaten within

eating
505 over three years in eating.
817 is like eating an entire
2028 the subject of eating.
3506 The appetite grows by eating.

eats
3605 that eats or needs

eccentricity
3709 eccentricity, heresy,

echo
2730 and waiting for the echo.
3699 Art is a delayed echo.

eclipse
1580 anon, In a merciful eclipse.

ecology
996 law of ecology is that

econometrician
2690 unfortunate econometrician who, in

economical
277 was being economical with the

economics
60 A study of economics usually
1521 In economics, the majority is
2257 more about economics than my

economies
1352 The petty economies of the rich

economist
2735 nothing an economist should

economize
4276 we have. Let us economize it.

economy
1959 Economy is going without
3766 for fear of Political Economy.

edge
4041 us to the edge of the

editor
1272 An editor should tell the
1997 An editor - a person

editors
1279 some editors are failed

educate
1051 Educate a man and you educate
3178 is to educate the masses
3684 got to educate him first.

educated
862 must be educated, the thumb

educating
4384 Educating a beautiful woman is

education
563 Education, n: that which
621 you think education is
1195 By education most have been
1467 Education is the ability to
1767 A good education should leave
2528 Most men of education are more
3574 movies, and that is education.
3899 Education is what survives when
3966 To me education is a leading
3993 love her is a liberal education.
4247 to which education cannot
4274 Soap and education are not as
4297 with a college education.
4499 without education.

educational
2559 under our educational rules, the

effect
564 have a retroactive effect.
3330 that the effect of eating
3737 watch the effect produced

effects
2073 and its effects - and that
2323 to. It's the after effects.

efficient
2009 hard to be efficient without

efficiently
1181 as doing efficiently that which

effort
490 mental effort would be
1536 up serious effort to meet

efforts
3542 be appreciative of my efforts.

egg
751 is only an egg's way of
1045 the fatal egg by
1887 and hairless as an egg.
2303 eating an egg without
3008 Go to work on an egg.
3486 got a bad egg, Mr Jones.
4291 laid an egg cackles as

eggs
2039 to lay eggs into their
2966 ways to dress eggs?
3459 your rooster will lay eggs.
4266 all thine eggs in one

ego
899 never the ego; the self

egoism
1763 husband's egoism in order

egotism
1323 Take egotism out, and you
1921 is only egotism wrong side

egypt
2014 would still be in Egypt.

eiffel tower
134 The Eiffel Tower is the Empire

eight
3553 You get eight out of

eighty
73 up is eighty percent of
849 A man of eighty has outlived
4287 the age of eighty and

einstein
3986 'Ho! Let Einstein be!'

elderly
1941 to all his elderly

elders
1935 of the elders to young

elected
1136 1. Get elected. 2. Get
3589 have been elected between

election
1262 An election is coming.

elections
12 Elections are won by men and
2673 no go the elections, Sit on

electric
480 to mend the Electric Light
4204 you have an electric affinity

electrician
478 Air - The Electrician is no

electricity
2438 Electricity is of two kinds,
4219 that electricity was

elegant
1295 be so elegant as to have

elephant
610 A herd of elephant .. pacing
2540 have got an elephant by the

elephants
1372 are like elephants. They are
3376 When elephants fight it is the

eleven
1604 tells you he's only eleven.
3836 things at eleven at night

elopement
28 an elopement would be

eloquent
599 fails to be eloquent and often

else
3720 someone else. And not

elsewhere
3149 his mind would be elsewhere.

elusive
3965 prime is elusive. You

elvis
1230 I'd be seeing Elvis soon.

elysian
1144 but in the Elysian fields.

elysium
538 our lost Elysium - rural

embalmer
4361 triumph of the embalmer's art.

embarrassed
2500 royalty .. embarrassed by the

embarrasses
1924 his head out and embarrasses us.

embarrassment
497 us in our place is embarrassment.

embody
1595 I, my Lords, embody the Law.

embraced
2498 us; we embraced, and we

emergency
4413 up to the emergency, and cave

emeritus
2436 professor emeritus from the

eminence
2847 His eminence was due to the

emotion
2464 emotion than a
3062 Love is an emotion
3210 remembered in emotion.
4319 a luxurious emotion, it can
4553 is an emotion for the

emotions
1108 an ocean of emotions entirely
3208 of the emotions from A to
4433 basket of the emotions.

emperor
3887 the Roman Emperor, and am

empire
134 is the Empire State
1162 old Glasgow Empire on a
1177 of the Empire are

employed
1502 that might be better employed.

employee
3265 every employee tends to

employees
3268 by those employees who have

employer
3981 and harder upon the employer.

employment
480 man To give employment to the
1550 indeed, our employment may be

empties
1435 If a man empties his purse

empty
119 indicated by an empty desk?
1531 man with an empty stomach
2576 Fill what's empty. Empty

emptying
3749 the world, and emptying of it.

encores
203 don't respond with encores.

encountered
373 I even encountered myself.

encourage
4371 to time to encourage the

encumbers
2172 ground, encumbers him with

encyclopedia
4616 charm of an encyclopedia is that it

end
1663 and an end,'
2410 a muddle, and an end.
2611 it should end there.
3016 with a worker at each end.
3390 but he pays at the end.
4073 it all going to end?
4259 and that's the end of it!

endow
3312 Die, and endow a college,

ends
445 and loose ends.

endurance
4561 mother, the endurance of an

endure
1897 is, I now endure but two

endured
3659 not to be endured with

endures
3089 in love he endures more than

enemies
105 forgive our enemies; not our
897 we make our enemies; but God
1815 with my enemies. I can
2498 been mortal enemies ever
2791 forgive our enemies; but we do
2931 wish their enemies dead - but
2978 The enemies of the future are
3099 classes: tools and enemies.
4158 by their enemies. I am
4364 myself from my enemies.
4383 time for making new enemies.

enemy
985 bitterest enemy in the
1009 more sombre enemy of good
1334 of an old enemy down on
2867 got a better class of enemy.
3159 The great enemy of clear
3394 a greater enemy to the
4279 takes your enemy and your
4442 have on the enemy, but by
4505 hasn't an enemy in the

energy
2208 deal of energy will long
3352 himself of energy all over
3673 The energy produced by the

engels
2259 of Marx, Engels and Lenin

engineer
4083 sanitary engineer; and in

england
120 Coffee in England is just
964 England to me was always the
1179 England's not a bad country
1396 England is the paradise of
1729 In England I would rather be
1897 my legs, and think of England.
2101 France and England is - the
2117 that leads him to England.
2171 which in England is
2844 food; in England people
2959 No place in England where
3030 a bore; he bored for England.
3119 Not only England, but every
3709 England is the paradise of
4372 England has forty-two
4586 the stately homes of England.

english
44 The English instinctively
429 The English may not like
658 The English have the most
786 The English winter - ending
798 telling the English some
925 The English never draw a line
931 the sort of English up with
1201 of our English nation,
1805 The English never smash in a
1807 of the English gentleman,
2098 the English would
2339 in any language but English.
2706 which the English, not being
2822 Opera in English is, in the
2869 He speaks English with the
3532 said that English women in
4258 English as she is Spoke.
4572 learn them a bit of English.
4591 The English have an

englishman
1087 ill-natured thing, an Englishman.
1590 He is an Englishman! For he
1591 He remains an Englishman!
1642 No Englishman unmoved that
2130 or not; an Englishman is content
2271 thorough an Englishman as ever
2846 An Englishman, even if he is
3129 The Englishman has all the
3393 may wet an Englishman to the
3856 can what an Englishman believes
3903 is one Englishman there is a
4321 The Englishman is under no
4422 find an Englishman among the

englishmen
601 trust all Englishmen except
2114 atrophied Englishmen, lacking
2155 When two Englishmen meet, their

englishwoman
656 lover. The Englishwoman simply
3923 This Englishwoman is so refined

enjoy
848 other, and enjoy both
889 Many people enjoy the
1950 To really enjoy the better
2094 to enjoy idling
3351 I don't enjoy them in
3708 save to enjoy the

enjoyed
2025 I've rather enjoyed them.
3062 many and enjoyed by the
3556 to be truly enjoyed must be
4099 Women enjoyed (whatsoe'er

enjoyment
1720 Enjoyment is not a goal, it is
2100 with a great deal of enjoyment.
2159 not from enjoyment to
3092 greatest enjoyment from life
4102 it were not for its enjoyments.

enjoys
3087 is that one enjoys several

enlarge
4129 some invent, the rest enlarge.

enormity
2189 very womb and bed of enormity.

enough
699 cared enough, everybody
1544 ought to be enough for
2609 there was enough for
2858 never get enough of is

enrage
4368 solely to enrage those who

enterprise
1182 criterion of the enterprise.
4210 me is its enterprise and

entertain
1459 you to be entertained in your
2007 only way to entertain some folks

entertaining
2781 much more entertaining than half

enthusiasm
377 that enthusiasm moves the
891 Enthusiasm is the greatest asset
1421 errors of enthusiasm to the
2393 'Above all no enthusiasm'.
2567 fired with enthusiasm, you'll be

enthusiast
2644 to the enthusiast who keeps

enthusiastic
1610 with enthusiastic tone, All

envies
3661 any peacock envies another

environment
709 is nothing but stored environment.
1245 The environment is everything

envy
448 dullard's envy of

epicure
3939 full, the epicure would say,

epidemics
3829 all, are only induced epidemics.

epigram
2606 Epigram: a wisecrack that has
2771 An epigram is a half-truth so
3096 joke is an epigram on the
4079 A brilliant epigram is a

epitaph
564 Epitaph, n: an inscription on
2297 And the epitaph drear: 'A

epitaphs
3875 a nice derangement of epitaphs!

epitaphy
1098 the taffy than the epitaphy.

epitome
1188 mankind's epitome. Stiff in

equal
1290 For equal division
1578 All shall equal be, The
1691 Though equal to all
2150 at equal distances,
2437 which is equal to
3157 animals are equal but some
3303 all facts are created equal.
4321 are created equal. The

equality
1094 settle for equality when sex
3694 Equality of opportunity is an

equalled
3851 is only equalled by the

equator
3115 quarrellin wi' the equator.

equity
650 hear of an equity' in a case

erased
2507 I have erased this line.

erection
99 gives a judge an erection.

erotic
1574 the erotic and the

errands
1579 on little errands for the

error
947 and made the error double.
1449 From error to error one

errors
252 your errors were
555 weapon: the errors of those
1270 Errors look so very ugly in
1436 certain errors of the
2045 harmful than reasoned errors.
3145 man whose errors take ten

escaped
3921 to eat and escaped being
3955 I had escaped from a mad

eskimo
1130 about an Eskimo hunter who

esquires
1733 We are all esquires now, and

esse
18 In esse I am nothing; in

essential
2492 been the essential character

estate
1189 and they had his estate.

esteem
3253 lessened my esteem of a king,

estimation
583 him in his estimation, and yours

eternal
3855 blasted to eternal damnation!

eternity
2282 here to Eternity, God ha'
2706 some conception of eternity.
4073 Eternity's a terrible thought.

ethical
4280 Ethical man - a Christian

etiquette
1057 Etiquette means behaving
2715 no taste, etiquette for people

eton
240 who didn't go to Eton.

etonians
2318 him like Etonians, without a
2691 Attractive Etonians who go

eunuch
1375 between a eunuch and a
4067 of the eunuch throughout

eunuchs
451 are like eunuchs in a

europe
373 people in Europe. I even
1089 not be any European
1568 at all except another Europe.
2630 that Europe is the
4322 keep up with Western Europe.

europeans
2763 are learned Europeans and we

evangelism
4612 Decade of Evangelism for

eve
1955 When Eve upon the first

even
1136 Don't get mad, get even.

evening
3534 the whole evening without

events
565 false, of events, mostly

ever
1583 What, ever? No, never!

everybody
1738 Everybody has a little bit of

everyone
958 And almost everyone when age,
2499 is what everyone shares.
2656 the way everyone wants to
3272 now that everyone is using

everything
249 only two Everything they say,
1245 is everything that isn't
2568 isn't everything. It is
2942 A little of everything and
3837 he knows everything. That
3901 A place for everything, and
3952 Everything's coming up roses.
4453 'Chips with everything'. Chips

evidence
1223 weighs th' ividence an' th'
1260 us wordy evidence of the
3954 think, good evidence of life
4198 evidence is very

evil
3849 to profess evil and do

evils
1204 Most of the evils of the
4465 between two evils, I always
4531 of two evils, chooses

ex-patriotism
552 example (of ex-patriotism) is James

ex-wife
1011 like an ex-wife searching

exaggerate
1240 Never exaggerate your faults;

exaggerated
4300 my death are greatly exaggerated.

exaggeration
592 addicted to exaggeration that they
3833 is a gross exaggeration of the

exam
3553 like an exam. You get

examination
2814 marks his own examination papers.
3109 kind of examination because

examiners
2257 economics than my examiners.

example
552 favourite example (of
3442 'For example' is not proof.
4282 annoyance of a good example.
4508 us a good example, what on

excellent
1595 that's excellent. It has no
3486 you! Parts of it are excellent!

exception
2756 case I'll make an exception.

excess
192 to be practised to excess.
3756 to be blamed, but the excess.

exchanges
3635 she exchanges the

excited
886 get all excited about
1093 his public excited and

excuse
3215 Excuse My Dust.
3262 is no excuse, it's the
4141 but they make a good excuse.

executive
3300 Executive ability is deciding
3511 action an executive must take

exercise
1194 cure, on exercise depend;
3994 mind what exercise is to the

exertion
3239 but the exertion is too

exhaust
1869 they soon exhaust their

exhausted
1158 a range of exhausted volcanoes.
1710 I'm exhausted from not talking.

exhibits
2228 which he exhibits, that

exist
1104 he need not exist in order
3353 Laski that He doesn't exist.

existence
2801 about human existence is not

exit
3027 a graceful exit at the
3813 Exit, pursued by a bear.

expectation
3600 I have no expectation of making a
4099 .. 'Tis expectation makes a

expected
4476 reasonably be expected to do.

expense
2479 at somebody else's expense.

expenses
1108 surrounded by expenses.
4070 free but facts are on expenses.

expensive
2438 little more expensive, but is
3285 fruit, when it is expensive.
3590 has got so expensive that it

experience
154 comes from experience, and
265 Experience is a good teacher,
414 every experience once,
1401 a lot of experience with
1456 we don't have to experience it.
2141 triumph of hope over experience.
2422 Experience is the worst teacher;
2719 has never had much experience.
3383 Experience is the comb that
4270 out of an experience only the
4523 Experience is the name every one

experienced
181 of the i experienced giving
1950 first have experienced the things
3062 an emotion experienced by the

experimentation
1246 amount of experimentation can ever

expert
738 An expert is one who knows

explain
2571 tobacco to explain it to me.

explained
2335 ever yet explained away the
4309 and life stands explained.

explaining
3677 and forever explaining things to

explanation
615 and with no explanation if he can
3686 saves tons of explanation.

exploitation
307 of mutual exploitation, a mental

explosion
3518 population explosion, and the

exposes
2128 A man who exposes himself

exposing
573 weather and exposing them to

express
390 content to express itself

expressing
2037 nearest to expressing the

expression
1330 quizzical expression of the
1457 the highest expression of
4275 natural expression of

expurgated
4493 of all is the expurgated book.

extemporanea
3205 A medley of extemporanea; And love

extinct
2774 adultery, are now extinct.

extraordinary
3247 appear so extraordinary, were it

extravagance
1352 the silly extravagances of the
2182 An extravagance is anything you

extremes
915 The two extremes appear like
1303 Extremes meet, and there is no
2342 run to extremes; they are

eye
293 and his eye on the
310 the eye, on the
1067 The eye sees only what
2639 and by God caught his eye.
3315 microscopic eye? For this
4200 The eye is the jewel of

eye-shade
2699 a kind of eye-shade or smoked

eyeball
3650 We're eyeball to eyeball, and

eyeballs
87 to move his eyeballs again.

eyebrows
1661 above 'A' with her eyebrows.

eyeglasses
2199 Words, like eyeglasses, blur

eyes
1029 takes his eyes off his
1321 daily bread of the eyes.
1530 One's eyes are what one
1580 sparkling eyes, Hidden,
2749 "Your eyes shine like the
3389 use your eyes and your
3413 The eyes believe
3967 a woman's eyes and sees a
4344 love men's eyes are always

eyewitness
258 heard two eyewitness accounts

face
136 Her face looks as if it
305 My face looks like a
711 to be young - not her face.
1694 Am I in face to-day?
2015 Her face was her
3227 the whole face of the
3324 Look on her face, and
3394 to the face than
3447 A smiling face is half the
3653 paint in the public's face.
3889 have your face lifted but
3977 can't think of your face.
4112 everybody's face but their
4245 recognize me by my face.
4450 clapped on to my face.

faces
3355 take their faces from 'em
3606 you forget faces, then you

fact
2043 hypothesis by an ugly fact.

facts
37 is full of facts but it
1448 the full facts of life
2258 is belief in facts.
2464 ask for facts in making
3669 - yours, mine and the facts.
3936 tell me of facts - I never
4070 is free but facts are on
4281 Get your facts first, and

faculty
937 when the faculty loses
2251 and parking for the faculty.

fail
507 husbands fail. They
1969 lest he fail in the

fails
2646 Nothing fails like success;

failure
644 We learn only from failure.
1037 utterly unspoiled by failure!
2826 His failure is
3544 Failure is not our only
3567 and I'll show you a failure.
3598 always pass failure on the way
3693 only one to make it a failure.
4131 formula for failure, which is

failures
7 has made failures of many
1820 Half the failures in life
3859 I did were failures. I didn't

fair
503 remained at 'set fair'.
1088 only in fair weather.
2495 fair; Who, when

fairies
3760 since the fairies left off

fairy
2190 Mistress Fairy That doth

faith
86 was of the faith chiefly in
689 A scientific faith's absurd.
794 through faith, hardly
2635 deal of faith for a man
3924 times of faith as best
4122 Faith, that's as well said,

faith-healer
138 There was a faith-healer from Deal

faithful
1785 who remains faithful to you but

faked
701 else did - faked it.

falklands
634 The Falklands thing was a fight

fall
3233 to fall in love
4215 as well fall flat on

fall out
23 should fall out in the
486 chance that you will fall out.

fallacious
3122 lightly, is fallacious, being
3936 was so fallacious as facts,

fallen
675 curates has fallen upon the

falls
3433 a man who falls on his

false
772 Prove false again?
1254 is false. The

fame
141 test of fame is to have
297 Fame means absolutely
1160 Fame is a food that dead

1937 Fame usually comes to
2465 The best fame is a
2643 and Fame with its

familiar
2411 far too familiar. Get

familiarity
4292 Familiarity breeds contempt - and

families
1880 in the best regulated families.
2515 to run in families.
3113 in the best-regulated families.

family
228 a wonderful family called
684 the family of last
933 does the family start? It
1051 and you educate a family.
1721 The family is the American
2925 head of the family may still
3302 and no family should be
3451 a mule deserves his family.
3988 of family life, and

famous
487 that time I was too famous.
3822 can become famous without

fan
2331 of becoming his own fan.

fan club
841 A fan club is a group of

fanatic
926 A fanatic is one who can't

fanaticism
3702 Fanaticism consists in

fancy
1973 keep your fancy free.' But
2553 of what you fancy does you

fantasies
2500 cut in the fantasies of people

far
1116 Mexico, so far from God

farce
3508 the farce is played
3905 running farce in the

farm
3961 little snug farm of the

farmer
1872 The Farmer will never be
1978 Even if a farmer intends to
2661 The farmer's way of saving

farmers
1979 Farmers worry only during the
3886 have been farmers for ten

farming
79 and farming the most

farms
1050 gazes or for him that farms.

farrow
2214 old sow that eats her farrow.

fart
1283 I had forgot the fart.
2111 he can't fart and chew
4100 Love is the fart Of every

fascinated
4605 people are fascinated by those

fascinating
1869 - the very fascinating ones try

fascination
1621 elbow has a fascination that few
1628 There's a fascination frantic In

fascism
1721 is the American fascism.

fashion
851 does not go out of fashion.
890 is once in fashion, all he
2715 Fashion exists for women with

fashions
3829 Fashions, after all, are only

fast
2103 you run fast. It makes

faster
703 was far faster than
2531 can write faster, and I can

fasting
1437 upon hope will die fasting.

fat
85 every fat man there
1010 in every fat man a thin
1016 'til the fat lady
1392 A few more fat, old bald
1662 but fat people are
2144 'Who drives fat oxen
2713 if you're fat, is a
3138 Fat, fair and forty were
3146 Fat is a feminist issue.

fatal
1443 is more fatal to health
2564 probably fatal to beat it
2640 it is nearly always fatal.
2960 is a fatal disease;
4170 Yes, I am a fatal man,
4305 Travel is fatal to
4518 of it is absolutely fatal.

fate
1932 Fate tried to conceal him
2856 in life. Fate is what
3047 pick with Fate. Come here

fates
1650 See how the Fates their

father
183 gave her father forty-one!
234 knew my father, My father
734 To become a father is not
1448 was 17. My father [Sigmund
2165 when his father dies, 'Tis
2218 the limp father of
2925 be the father, everyone

2964 My father used to say,
3350 Our Father which art in
3408 A father is a banker
3721 is no good father, that's
3860 I work as my father drank.
4022 either my father or my
4125 that his father was before
4308 my father was so
4425 relation for father and son.

fathers
1861 Fathers send their sons to
2019 There are fathers who do not
2691 on their fathers' advice:
3662 defect of fathers is that
4187 land of my fathers. My

fatigued
3308 good John! fatigued I said,

fattening
4589 immoral, illegal or fattening.

fatter
3238 sheep are fatter; We

fatuous
2425 and fatuous an attempt

fault
674 is my own fault. Verdi is
1269 to find fault with but
2312 they think it's their fault.
2367 long if the fault was only
3788 sugar be a fault, God help

faults
186 they had no faults at all.
249 have their faults Men have
744 all thy faults I love
1079 the faults in a
1240 your faults; your
1642 all our faults, we love
1910 I may have faults but being
2357 we had no faults we should
2365 our little faults to
2402 greater faults than
2415 with the faults they had
3266 correct our faults by
3359 Be to her faults a little
3405 men may have great faults.
3803 faults Looks
3919 social faults; they will

faulty
1674 if your face is faulty.

favourite
74 It's my second favourite organ.

fear
76 For fear of little
261 lives with fear of
1174 Fear can be headier than
1347 we call it fear of
2211 till the fear of the
2805 haunting fear that

3228 Fear of the policeman is
3664 To fear love is to fear
4193 died - for fear of dying!

feared
2449 just as I feared! - Two
2449 just as I feared! - Two

fearful
3804 not a more fearful wild-fowl

feast
3419 mind is a perpetual feast.

feather
2385 ear; not a feather to tickle

feature
324 please, every feature works.

february
2336 is not Puritanism but February.

fed
3796 He hath not fed of the

feel
138 what I fancy I feel'.
2038 think and feel and are is
3558 I feel a feeling which I

feeling
982 old as he's feeling. A woman
1508 but feeling's the
1720 it is a feeling that
2205 more true feeling, and
3096 on the death of a feeling.
3424 - but feeling is God's
3558 I feel a feeling which I feel

feelings
4406 could see some of my feelins.

feels
2747 old as the woman he feels.

fees
464 took their Fees, 'There is
1431 the doctor takes the fees.

feet
182 much work for the feet.
859 carry the feet, not the
2213 over his feet, humbly
4098 Her feet beneath her
4417 with both feet on the

felicity
3910 is more felicity on the far

fell
686 Doctor Fell, The

fellow-men
2913 to render our fellow-men better.

felon
175 the great felon loose Who

female
2333 you it is probably female.
2339 Female empowerment is such
3324 share some female errors
4496 has a faithful female friend.

feminine
1451 into the feminine soul, is
3131 as a really feminine woman.
3137 she's of the feminine gender.

feminist
1804 by feminists is making
3146 Fat is a feminist issue.

fence
1466 ever take a fence down until

fences
1474 Good fences make good

fertility
4484 example in fertility for Nature

fertilize
3888 But fertilize a problem

fervour
3642 retains the fervour of youth
4109 in the full fervour of

festivals
637 of holidays and festivals.

fever
3066 Love is a fever which
3519 chills and fever she died,

few
377 that so few
3062 and enjoyed by the few.

fickleness
3851 The fickleness of the women I

fiction
3190 germs is ridiculous fiction.
3521 than fiction, but
4511 That is what fiction means.
4544 thing in fiction the

fiddle
492 He could fiddle all the bugs
2158 learned to fiddle, I should
4130 Fiddle, we know, is diddle:

fidelity
3520 idea of fidelity is not

fifteen
405 is always fifteen years

fifth
2219 And he came fifth and lost

fifty
2020 of youth; fifty is the
4047 knows at fifty that he

fig
483 over a fig leaf yet
2454 We don't care a fig!'
3784 life better than figs.

fight
634 thing was a fight between
1132 bed mad. Stay up and fight.
1257 dog in the fight - it's the
1488 Don't fight forces; use
2247 is hard to fight an enemy

3376 elephants fight it is the
3956 this great fight did win.'
4039 easier to fight for

fighting
574 two periods of fighting.
580 him to his fighting weight.
2281 first-class fightin' man; An'
2432 lazy about fighting. They
2752 you're fighting for this
3979 been caught fighting a liar in
4369 they are fighting so

fights
140 He that fights and runs
4550 The fights are the best part

figures
123 He uses figures as if they
3936 as facts, except figures.

fill
2576 Fill what's
4104 I'll fill hup the chinks

filled
1611 can be, Filled to the

filling
3174 is the gold filling in the
3749 and spade; filling the world,

film
793 The British Film Industry

film-making
2503 Film-making has become a kind of

films
1718 and see bad films when they

filthy
3652 and we are filthy and

finality
4016 Finality is death. Perfection

finals
2559 is called Finals, the very

finance
3947 without finance is no

financial
69 if only for financial reasons.

find
830 if you can only find it.
1076 able to find a happy
1169 To find a friend one must
3542 I shall not find Him, but I
3942 never could find any man

fine
3289 work, runs fine inside but

finest
3661 tail is the finest in the

finger
2841 the ring without the finger.
3176 One finger in the throat and

fingers
862 The fingers must be educated,

finish
426 and finish together.

finished
1515 married. Then he's finished
2950 of them when they are finished.

finite
2977 of the finite from the

fire
198 water, the fire next time.
468 shouted Fire!' They
729 awkward squad fire over me.
1468 will end in fire, Some say
1744 Fell in the fire and was
1825 k'n hide de fier, but what
2429 must set yourself on fire.
3246 It is a fire, it is a
3427 house is on fire let us

fired
2567 you aren't fired with

fires
1512 are like fires. They go

firm
4048 who stands firm is a

first
702 to be first with an
1340 One's first book, kiss,
1730 the first kiss after
2103 It makes you run first.
3338 himself at first sight and
4328 people who got there first.

fish
549 by fish. Only an
860 I have my own fish to fry.
3380 up with a fish in his
3455 Fish, to taste right, must
4009 is like a fish without a

fish-knives
537 for the fish-knives, Norman As

fisherman
3110 than a fisherman pulled

fishes
2381 muteness of fishes.
3884 lived like fishes; the great

fishing
4146 pleasure of fishing them out.

fit
3257 physically fit can enjoy

five-cent
13 of good five-cent cigars in

five-pound
2457 up in a five-pound note. The

fix
2397 ain't broke, don't fix it.

flag
4494 country's flag,' she

flame
3246 coal Whose flame creeps in

flanders
4028 terribly in Flanders,' cried my

flatter
2369 us, we flatter ourselves

flattering
4252 his time flattering, kissing

flatters
2170 Nothing flatters a man as much

flattery
980 of ten to tout for flattery.
2364 Flattery is false coin that is
2561 in flattery of one's
4046 I suppose flattery hurts no
4128 That flattery's the food

flavour
1923 A general flavour of mild

flaw
4214 We all have flaws, and mine

flayed
4127 saw a woman flayed, and you

flea
2142 between a louse and a flea.
2191 the very flea of his
3126 performing flea.
4121 observe, a flea Hath

fleas
2404 Fleas know not whether they
2974 Great fleas have little
3568 do as the fleas do - skip.
4472 amount o' fleas is good

fled
4407 my Lions & fled the Seen.

fleetingly
2725 comes fleetingly now and

flesh
268 is the east wind made flesh.
408 The more flesh you show,
1363 delicate white human flesh.
1958 dear, And flesh and blood
3929 take off my flesh and sit in

flexible
3006 Access, your flexible friend.

flies
142 If it flies, floats or

flinging
3653 guineas for flinging a pot of

flings
1497 He that flings dirt at

flint
633 Flint must be an extremely

flirt
3930 How can he flirt? The most

flirtation
784 innocent flirtation. Not quite
3143 Flirtation - attention without

float
3689 is to float lazily

floating
2218 of his bush floating, floating
2881 be a Cloud Floating in the

floats
1241 and floats a lot

flock
443 standing a flock of sheep

flogging
4245 habit of flogging me

flood
777 at the flood, leads -

flooded
489 Streets Flooded. Please

floor
3235 the sanded floor, And

floppy
4180 a weak, floppy thing in

florida
1769 Florida: God's waiting room.

flower
2218 a languid floating flower.
3032 national flower is the

flowering
1296 The flowering of geometry.

flowers
1624 The flowers that bloom in the
2807 he smells flowers, looks
2849 and strewing flowers.

flu
2890 members in bed with flu.

flung
2443 He flung himself from the

flushpots
2210 The flushpots of Euston and the

fly
173 be able to fly over
254 time to fly across the
2154 A fly, Sir, may sting a
2157 Fly fishing may be a very
2444 hurt a fly. It's not
3315 reason, man is not a fly.
3454 to cook a fly, he would
3537 never drink when I fly."
3732 The fly ought to be used

flying
2246 flying machines
4220 Man is flying too fast for a
4591 ability for flying into a

focus
3029 as the focus of longing

foe
812 and manly foe, Bold I
1664 wrong the foe, Good, and
3204 a lover, and find a foe.

fog
1148 subject to fogs and with

folk
274 music is folk music, I
2394 with a folk song is

folks
4471 in some folks as there

follies
588 man has his follies - and
2913 all human follies there's
3631 The follies which a man

follow
732 pack, and follow at
2057 it does not follow that most
2471 I've got to follow them - I
3038 hearts and minds will follow.

followers
299 at least two or three followers.

folly
571 funniest folly of the
1281 stoops to folly and Paces
1357 no greater folly than to
1757 bliss 'Tis folly to be
2370 without folly is not as
4476 It is a folly to expect men

fond
2910 like: I am fond of my rags
4116 We are so fond of one

font
2315 second-hand font, would

food
668 Food comes first, then
1063 age where food has taken
1164 problem is food. When you
1520 of too much food than of
1531 empty stomach food is god.
2844 have good food; in
2909 It's good food and not
3339 and the food a tragedy.
3461 the poor provide food.
3648 the colour of the food.
4577 was a food well in

fool
143 Any fool can make a rule,
266 A fool bolts pleasure,
303 fifty per cent bloody fool.
561 crime and a fool's excuse
590 she makes a fool she means
619 A fool can always find a
749 may make a fool of
1043 A fool must now and then
1173 a lie. A fool had better
1190 yet, but was a fool.
1196 that is not fool is rogue.
1349 shouldn't fool with booze
1424 man than a fool who holds
1532 Any fool can criticize,
1672 here, poor fool, with all
1802 A busy fool is fitter to
1991 is a damn fool for at
2157 end and a fool at the

2169 None but a fool worries
2284 the burnt Fool's bandaged
2297 drear: 'A fool lies here
2306 A fool there was and he
2900 he's no fool usually
2911 fool is a
3140 get into a fool or a
3307 poet is a fool: But you
3346 And I'm a fool for
3352 Any fool can be fussy and
3549 you're no fool, Walk
3711 man a fool, and of
4050 to make a fool of
4619 speed; A fool at forty
4621 himself a fool; Knows it

foolish
118 a need for foolish admirers.
563 from the foolish their lack
1418 say a foolish thing, it
2603 The foolish and the dead
3539 the most foolish women are
3566 said a foolish thing, Nor
3655 much less foolish than they
4048 and a foolish man who

fools
256 old men fools and old
351 is the virtue of fools.
2058 kinds of fools: one says,
2372 hath more fools in it than
3256 these poor fools decoyed
4128 the food of fools; Yet now
4145 and fools. The
4265 got all the fools in town on
4303 for the fools. But for

foot
413 to put your foot tactfully
1379 is 12 inches to a foot.
2277 Foot - foot - foot - foot
3863 rabbit's foot if you

football
614 is like football - it
1575 Pro football is like nuclear
2648 Oh, he's football crazy, he's
3814 think football is a
3890 to play football they'd

footmen
1846 But of all footmen the lowest

forbidden
4529 it has forbidden to itself.

force
3438 You can't force anyone to
3989 egalitarian force in
4428 use force'; we

forced
2146 They are forced plants,

forcible
2434 always more forcible as an

forebears
681 in our forebears. It seems

forehead
2573 of her forehead, When she
2863 of her forehead; When she

foreign
550 Britain's Foreign Secretary
3231 woman is a foreign land, Of

foreigners
2897 bloody and foreigners are
4285 it Vinchy; foreigners always
4572 signed five foreigners over the

foremost
2684 would be foremost To lead

foreplay
498 all .. No foreplay. No

foresight
869 in foresight, a

forest
2147 clipped hedge is to a forest.
2452 through the forest goes! The

forever
857 the wicked, but not forever.
2710 for they are gone forever.
2923 diamond tiara lasts forever."

forfeiting
3162 has no intention of forfeiting.

forge
1428 been forged in cases
1647 a man can't forge his own

forget
721 I always forget to include
835 never forget!' 'You
874 is the thing you forget with.
981 whom it will soonest forget.
1027 is to forget it once.
1926 before he can forget it.
2756 I never forget a face, but
3324 and you'll forget 'em all.
3546 memory; I forget
3606 First you forget names, then
4138 forgive nor forget; the naïve

forgetting
3513 is all; forgetting is another

forgive
583 job to forgive a man,
1462 Forgive, O Lord, my little
2351 We often forgive those who
2791 we ought to forgive our
2809 my ghost, forgive some
3473 If I die, I forgive you: if I
3919 fault and never forgive you.
4138 neither forgive nor
4543 if ever, do they forgive them.

forgiven
1205 What is forgiven is usually

forgiveness
2893 seven parts forgiveness of sins.

forgives
846 - and God forgives me for it.

forgiving
1478 To be social is to be forgiving.
3513 Forgiving is all; forgetting is

forgot
1096 Honey, I just forgot to duck.
3305 ridiculous, and dead forgot?

forgotten
1730 men have forgotten the last.
3702 you have forgotten your aim.
3899 been learnt has been forgotten.

fork
2549 up mercury with a fork.

form
2481 In form and feature, face

formalities
717 in the formalities of the

formidable
1807 and equally formidable on both

formula
3077 The formula for complete
3375 fixed the formula: 'Cannot
4131 you the formula for

fornicated
807 man: he fornicated and read

fornication
2716 BARABAS: Fornication? But that

forte
3946 is his forte, and

forth
2219 Come forth, Lazarus! And

fortissimo
2702 Fortissimo at last!

fortune
1270 people of fortune may
1344 be a beauty without a fortune.
1756 method of making a fortune.
2356 to bear good fortune than bad.
2642 When Fortune empties her
3453 If fortune turns against you,
4436 Fortune's a right whore: If
4590 takes your fortune and runs

forty
263 you are forty, half of
711 woman past forty should
1197 young till forty, and then
1946 than to be forty years old.
2020 Forty is the old age of
3138 fair and forty were all
3284 From forty to fifty a man
3846 man over forty is a

forty-five
2980 time he is forty-five

forty-three
1653 pass for forty-three In the

forty-two
8 and Everything..is Forty-two.

forward
2684 cried Forward!' And
3173 looking forward to the
4060 look forward to the

forwards
2265 but it must be lived forwards.

fought
3958 what they fought each other

found
2052 just before he is found out.
2207 perhaps found it. But
3075 is slowly found out.
3957 what he had found, That was

founding
669 compared with founding a bank?

fountains
2024 in the fountains of

four
3156 Four legs good, two legs
3207 Four be the things I'd
4333 the age of four with paper

fox
2511 of a fox at large.
2617 to the fox's sermon.
3411 When the fox preaches,
4105 I loves the fox less, but
4540 after a fox - the

foxed
3252 ever I was foxed it was

foxes
94 50,000 foxes can't be
1503 Old foxes want no tutors.

fragile
1291 so fragile, so easy

frail
4058 men are too frail a thread

framed
4394 to have it framed and glazed

france
216 they love France itself but
2101 between France and

frank
4194 I'm frank, brutally frank.

frankly
4015 who says frankly and fully

frauds
2421 men of history are frauds.

freckles
3207 curiosity, freckles, and

fred
178 Here lies Fred, Who was

free
84 They bring it to you, free.
227 such thing as a free lunch.
262 you get free costs too
1422 and sex for free is that
3953 Ev'rything free in America

4038 of a free society is
4042 man is not a free man.
4334 This is a free country,

free press
4069 you on the free press. It's the

free-born
4174 as only a free-born Briton can

free-will
543 This free-will business is a

freedom
655 between freedom and
723 Freedom and Whisky gan
1561 O Freedom, what liberties are
2264 is the dizziness of freedom.
2530 Freedom of the press is
2693 ideal of freedom and
4277 things: freedom of speech,

freely
2361 nothing so freely as advice.

freemasonry
449 have a kind of bitter freemasonry.

french
146 The French have a passion
174 no more French, No more
216 that the French didn't
356 The French are wiser than
601 those who speak French.
656 A French woman, when
813 much. The French are with
1732 to speak French, not
1740 by a French Marquis!
2762 and some are fond of French.
3561 is not clear is not French.
3927 As the French say, there are
4241 If the French noblesse had
4295 to them in French; I never

frenchies
3147 Those Frenchies seek him

frenchman
2130 A Frenchman must be always

fresh air
284 fond of fresh air and

freshmen
2590 The freshmen bring a little

freud
1162 Freud's theory was that

friend
16 A friend in power is a
477 luncheon with a city friend.
812 me from the candid friend!
991 with your friend when he
1407 my friend, I hope I
1901 doorway.   Friend' he said,
1966 an old friend for
1980 If a friend is in trouble,
2003 A friend that ain't in need
2348 himself a friend, but only
2872 where a friend-and-relati

3006 Access, your flexible friend.
3718 a portrait I lose a friend.
4146 such a good friend that she
4362 Whenever a friend succeeds,

friendless
707 no man so friendless but what

friends
105 our enemies; not our friends.
889 of their best friends.
897 We make our friends; we make
1240 your friends will
1440 faithful friends: an old
1815 But my damn friends, my
1831 that their friends say in the
1975 you will make friends for him.
2133 few of his friends' houses
2456 He has many friends, laymen
2791 ought to forgive our friends.
2867 buy friends but you
2953 it to your friends, to make
3057 Outnumber your friends.
3755 Old friends are best. King
3865 His best friends hear no
3919 tell your friends their
4158 by their friends. Judge
4166 Of my friends I am the only
4213 down his friends for his
4328 that friends are
4364 me from my friends - I can
4505 none of his friends like him.

friendship
326 money, but friendship hardly
1558 Who friendship with a knave hath
2358 like hatred than like friendship.
3103 well form a friendship with a
3559 in friendship, sex and
3701 Friendship is almost always the

friendships
3654 be to dissolve all friendships.

frighten
635 why they frighten so easily.
800 street and frighten the
4442 but by God, they frighten me.

frightened
3896 It has a frightened look in

frightening
2089 far more frightening than none
3478 only for frightening fish when

frigid
3056 a bit Is so frigid upon the

frivolous
4587 what is frivolous if unpaid

frogs
2897 Frogs .. are slightly
4036 Frogs Eat Butterflies.

front
78 bet as to what is out front.
2914 your front to the

frown
3753 without frown or smile,

frowzy
3949 pent up in frowzy lodgings,

fruit
2928 But the fruit that can fall
3285 I love fruit, when it is

fuck
498 And fuck all in
2415 They fuck you up, your mum

fucks
142 floats or fucks...don't

fudge
2602 and two-fifths sheer fudge.

fuel
1974 a wonderful fuel for

fugitive
2785 feel like a fugitive from th'

fulfilled
3739 your dreams fulfilled'. I

fulfilment
1668 to its fulfilment, where I
3029 and the image of fulfilment.

full
724 I wasna fou, but just had
3939 Serenely full, the epicure

fully-equipped
2548 A fully-equipped duke costs as much

fun
63 the most fun I ever had
1354 is the most fun you can
2185 is all the fun you think
2207 But have we had any fun?
2225 time, Ain't we got fun.
2580 Fun is fun but no girl
2951 but the people have fun.
3044 Were more fun to be
4497 best of my fun I owe it

function
1110 They only function when they
3722 that their function in life is

functions
2690 the major functions of his

fundament
3056 Is so frigid upon the fundament.

funeral
2388 mis-behaved once at a funeral.

funerals
2993 I hate funerals, and would not

funny
1373 "It's a funny old world - a
1830 you mean, funny?
2880 Isn't it funny How a bear
3584 is funny as long as
4040 A funny thing happened to
4585 ragged and funny, But we'll

furniture
1175 all the furniture that he is
2669 that nice furniture that used
3928 No furniture so charming as

further
107 are, the further they fall.
2346 did not see further than his
3290 of Hell - but no further.

fury
1011 There is no fury like an

fuse
3727 when your fuses blew.

fuss
615 minimum of fuss and with

future
144 in the future will weigh
1248 of the future. It comes
2256 is in the future because I
2284 be in the future, it was at
2407 a smile with a future in it.
4075 seen the future after

fuzzy-wuzzy
2281 to you, Fuzzy-Wuzzy, at your

gain
3843 The other is to gain it.

gained
4377 and once when I gained one.

gaining
3196 may be gaining on you.

gallantry
782 men call gallantry, and gods
3870 to do with gallantry than it

gallery
1635 Grosvenor Gallery,

gallon
199 buys his ink by the gallon.

gallop
733 and he will ride a gallop.

gamble
3577 Don't gamble; take all your
4074 Life is a gamble at terrible

gambling
1080 organize gambling are some

game
135 childish game, it's
532 The game isn't over until
3260 your little game We are the

games
542 of all, the dread of games!
2621 may be the games are silly.

gamut
3208 the whole gamut of the

gap
964 endless gap between

garden
645 Of the garden hard by
2283 is a garden, and such

garden (cont.)
3397 Is like a garden full of
3903 there is a garden. Where
4542 woman in a garden. It ends

garlic
179 thing as a little garlic.
875 loved he garleek, oynons,

garrick
1689 Our Garrick's a salad; for in
1690 lies David Garrick, describe

gas
2509 to turn the gas off before
3213 give; Gas smells

gates
3290 go to the gates of Hell -

gathered
313 See us gathered on behalf

geese
3411 look to your geese.

gender
3137 she's of the feminine gender.

genealogist
148 A genealogist is one who traces

general
4444 themselves into general use.

generals
3079 has two generals in whom
4333 we're all Generals. Only

generation
178 the whole generation, Still
440 to the generation that says
1131 history, generation follows

generis
2572 I am sui generis and let

generosity
2659 for generosity and we'd
3722 is to exercise our generosity.

genesis
102 rewrites the Book of Genesis.

genius
80 for talent is genius.
303 per cent genius, fifty per
409 Genius is childhood
523 We define genius as the
608 are roads of genius.
1237 Men of genius are the worst
1384 is the feminine of genius.
1535 to be a genius, but a
1699 Gives genius a better
1849 of human genius, we should
2063 mediocrity, genius is
2083 Genius, in truth, means
2192 Ramp up my genius, be not
2507 between genius and
2526 is a genius at least
2529 the name of genius in the
2602 of him genius, and
2615 man of genius is
3036 Genius is an African who

3191 I was a genius I was a
3368 The mark of genius is an
4519 I've put my genius into my
4525 to declare except my genius.
4535 everything except genius.

geniuses
311 Geniuses are the luckiest of
1667 have nothing but geniuses.
2652 many other geniuses, a greater

genteel
640 is not genteel when he

gentility
934 Gentility is what is left over

gentle
1264 be they gentle or simple,

gentleman
58 (A gentleman) is any man who
149 Gentleman: one who never hurts
362 English gentleman, in his
375 what a gentleman is to a
385 A gentleman does things no
1807 the English gentleman, the
3274 test of a gentleman: his
3871 Honourable gentleman is
4108 being a gentleman never is
4110 He was a gentleman who was
4290 to call you a gentleman.
4468 Every other inch a gentleman.
4538 A true gentleman is one who is
4540 country gentleman galloping

gentlemanly
4053 do a very gentlemanly thing.
4107 one werry gentlemanly ideas, but

gentlemen
1713 Gentlemen, include me out.
1733 none of us gentlemen any more.
2173 of conversation among gentlemen.
2650 to behave like gentlemen.
2679 There were gentlemen and there
2796 Gentlemen prefer bonds.
3024 good gentlemen. I want

geography
515 from Geography. Geography

geometry
1296 The flowering of geometry.

george
516 George the Third Ought never
2401 George the First was always

georgian
2669 of all the Georgian silver

geraniums
2877 (blue) and geraniums (red), And

germans
1559 The Germans, if this
2551 the Germans found the

germs
3190 theory of germs is

get
1926 A man must get a thing

gharsley
3049 Parsley is gharsley.

ghosts
3309 round the ghosts of Beauty

ghoulies
150 From ghoulies to ghosties and

giant
2404 body of a giant or upon

gibbon
1867 scribble! Eh! Mr. Gibbon?

gift
35 skin is a gift from God.
625 Guilt: the gift that goes
1859 essential gift for a good
2632 a sort of gift or trust

giftie
728 Pow'r the giftie gie us To
3031 power the giftie gie us to

gimble
831 gyre and gimble in the

gin
946 never drink gin. It makes
3535 can get out the gin, eh?

girdle
3050 with your girdle when your

girl
103 The average girl would
541 is the girl of my
885 that a girl will wait
1351 Claus to a girl of twenty.
1748 If I were a girl, I'd
2573 a little girl Who had a
2578 said a girl with
2580 fun but no girl wants to
2863 a little girl who had a
4246 whether any girl would be
4392 The little girl had the
4614 can I, that girl standing

girlfriend
948 All girlfriends are like
3081 your girlfriend and the

girls
935 looking at girls and
1810 American girls turn into
3021 Good girls go to heaven.
3203 If all the girls attending

give
1062 a matter of give and take,
2858 we never give enough of
3185 they give or refuse,
3267 I'll give it to you.

gives
389 those to whom he gives it.
2361 One gives nothing so freely

giving
1457 Giving is the highest

gizzard
4203 is the gizzard of

glad
690 soon made glad, Too

glances
152 The glances over cocktails

glands
2038 ductless glands and our

glass
476 the Sound of Broken Glass
2674 profit. The glass is falling
4112 a sort of glass, wherein

glass eye
3795 Get thee glass eyes; And, like

glass-bottomed
2901 a sewer in a glass-bottomed boat.
4388 a sewer in a glass-bottomed boat.

glasses
3211 At girls who wear glasses.

glen
76 the rushy glen, We

glitterati
4554 for the glitterati or the

glittering
1888 O how that glittering taketh me!

gloomy
196 that gloomy shell He

glorified
4252 is, is a glorified public

glorious
1636 is, it is a glorious thing To

glossy
1704 for a fine glossy surface,

glow-worm
918 believe that I am a glow-worm.

glutton
1797 is just a glutton with

gluttons
3515 in rags And gluttons old in sin

gnawing
712 By gnawing through a dyke,

go
1441 thing done, go - if not,
2703 Sir, stop - go away: I
3170 I have a go, lady,

go-between
3428 The go-between wears out a

goal
1029 his eyes off his goal.
2623 a higher goal to attain,

goals
1723 very modest goals for
2287 muddied oafs at the goals.

goat
474 hairy goat With an

god
71 is there no God, but try
72 If only God would give me
102 April, God rewrites
153 If God lived on earth,
176 all give God a great
239 ask of God when they
386 God has been replaced, as
389 the Lord God thinks of
393 you're .. God? EARL OF
397 God gave us memories that
433 dog is the god of frolic.
638 Cabots talk only to God.
708 Thanks to God, I am still
736 God is usually on the
741 the case. God has
748 that though God cannot
822 God Almighty never
857 God bears with the
958 there is a God, Or
1061 where does that leave God?
1075 deal of God. He
1086 Wherever God erects a
1130 know about God and sin,
1300 everything God has made.
1410 God is not a cosmic
1416 of God when he
1431 God heals, and the doctor
1531 empty stomach food is god.
1769 Florida: God's waiting
1807 between God and a goat
1990 God will not look you
2040 God is
2313 God and I both knew what
2472 God is love, but get it
2547 God made me on a morning
2591 you want to take in God.
2639 By and by God caught his
2705 of what God should be.
2711 in order - God does the
2810 God is a comedian whose
2918 God it is true, does some
2949 invented a god, they
3004 There's God, angels,
3034 Well, God is certainly
3065 God punishes us mildly by
3086 take himself for a god.
3188 God and the doctor we
3278 One on God's side is a
3281 God is really only
3353 God can stand being told
3390 God does not pay weekly,
3392 God made the ocean, but
3441 God could not be
3614 and you are a god.
3668 because God put Adam
3691 as 'Call Me God') to the
3754 God keeps the wicked to
3799 God made him, and
3818 man whose God is in the
3830 What God hath joined

3916 serve both God and Mammon
4142 you talk to God, you are
4340 God created man and,
4379 God is on the side not of
4400 angler, and now with God.

god-like
4235 have been God-like in our

goddamm
3335 Lhude sing Goddamm, Raineth

gods
1968 Not gods, nor men, nor
2682 slay; The Gods who live
3184 there be gods, and, as

goethe
1060 Goethe said there would be

going
2250 When the going gets tough,

gold
2448 sing, This gold, my

golden
763 that is golden, not
1716 that lays the golden egg.

golf
11 to take up golf and too
1277 thousand lost golf balls.'
1965 you work at it, it's golf.
4283 Golf is a good walk

gone
1129 love is gone? If you

good
155 is so much good in the
165 But what..is it good for?
482 is only as good as what he
587 of feeling good all over,
797 as good or as bad
907 The word good' has many
1170 is too good for some
1494 himself is good when he is
1499 Good is not good, where
1500 Great and good are seldom
1564 for your good, for all
1771 What's the good of a home
1803 The good should be
1858 anything as good as
1885 who feels good about it.
1902 cannot do good, he must
2166 is both good and
2570 for all good men to
2573 she was good She was
2575 something good about
2579 while you're looking good.'
2649 being a good writer or
2653 never so good or so bad
2863 she was good she was
3418 Good is when I steal other
3434 Good men need no
3450 A good man and a good
3596 down the good things you
3663 The good life, as I

3682 cook was a good cook, as
3720 And not as good as some
3746 Greek. No good can come
3849 profess evil and do good.
3971 is to be a good animal.
4177 could be a good woman if I
4199 not simply good; be good
4202 of doing me good, I should
4455 When I'm good, I'm very
4492 I am as good as the
4503 can be good in the
4511 The good ended happily,
4596 If all the good people
4617 always the good feel

goodbye
440 that says goodbye at the
4473 Good-bye-ee! - Good-bye-ee! Wipe

goodness
4277 is by the goodness of God

goods
2451 were all his worldly goods.

goolies
1727 Party by the goolies.

goose
2564 is a gold goose that lays
2617 is a blind goose that

gored
639 tossed and gored several

gorgeousness
2614 the human spirit is gorgeousness.

gory
4448 I'll make a gory mess of

gossip
2004 Gossip is vice enjoyed
3045 thing about gossip is that it
3460 Gossip needs no carriage.
3680 ill-natured gossip ourselves,
4559 Gossip is when you hear
4571 Gossip is the art of saying

gossips
3468 Whoever gossips to you will

gotten
1817 mess you've gotten me into."

goulash
2262 better to have good goulash?'

gourmet
1797 A gourmet is just a glutton

gout
2931 them the gout, give them

govern
467 Go out and govern New South
1090 How can you govern a country

governed
4477 he who is governed by that

governess
676 Be a governess! Better be a

government
438 next to anarchy, is government.
684 The government is becoming the
916 support the government, the
921 form of government except all
932 attack the government of my own
974 what the government gives, it
979 pay, the government should
1856 to see the government get out of
1903 toppled the government? Swift
2673 no go the Government grants,
2709 regards government as a sort
3003 Government is the only
3279 under a government of men and
3518 The government is concerned
3593 all the government we're
3763 Government of the busy by the
3827 A government which robs Peter to
4064 Every government is run by liars
4254 understands government, and it
4370 The best government is a
4567 ever saw a government. I live

governments
524 Governments last as long as the
4378 Governments need both shepherds

gown
3218 heart Like a satin gown?

grace
403 thing to the grace of God.
957 Grace is given of God, but
2317 all by Thy grace To
3317 with grace; If not,
3805 Grace me no grace, nor
3996 grow old with a good grace.

gracehoper
2212 The Gracehoper was always

grail
4318 Product is our Holy Grail.

grammar
1155 posterity talking bad grammar.
2018 bows to success, even grammar.
3887 Emperor, and am above grammar.

grammatical
930 with a grammatical ending -

grand
2563 Isn't it grand! Isn't it
3719 Ain't it grand to be

grand canyon
2730 down the Grand Canyon and

grandfather
4501 through his grandfather or his

grandmother
2017 a man, begin with his grandmother.

grandson
2019 does not adore his grandson.

grant
652 knows who's in Grant's tomb.
4260 Great God, grant that twice

grasp
4398 a better grasp of what is

grass
??? this grass will
539 There isn't grass to graze a
3376 it is the grass that
4003 Pigeons on the grass alas.

grateful
3680 are always grateful to those

gratification
790 is accepting deferred gratification.
1811 the maximum gratification of the

gratuitous
1266 prophecy is the most gratuitous.

grave
225 O grave, thy
843 And by my grave you'd pray
1714 he'd turn in his grave.
2100 if I was a grave digger, or
3932 is a kind of healthy grave.
4239 Even the grave yawns for

graves
3349 to me: The graves of little

greasy
1140 the top of the greasy pole.

great
55 you're as great as I am,
292 is not a great man, he
697 Its a great life if you
1341 - the great ones who
1500 Great and good are seldom
1722 Few great men could pass
1938 calling is great when
2402 Great men too often have
2421 If I am a great man, then a
2683 The the great man helped
2714 to be great: since it
2792 You're not that great.
3244 every great man there
3405 Only great men may have
4256 was in the great' class,

greater
2913 could be greater Than
4213 Greater love hath no man than

greatest
1819 The greatest truths are the

greatness
286 Greatness is a zigzag streak of
3808 achieve greatness, and some

greed
699 enough for everyone's greed.
3368 Genius is a spiritual greed.

greedy
3485 thank goodness, I am greedy.

greek
775 loving, natural, and Greek.
2162 when his wife talks Greek.
3746 and half Greek. No good

green
726 Green grow the rashes, O,

greenery
1635 A greenery-yallery, Grosvenor
2260 There is no greenery. It would

grey
2338 Nature prematurely grey.
3772 us respect grey hairs,

griefs
945 keep his griefs in their

grin
827 he seems to grin, How

grope
1247 How do I work? I grope.

gross
3071 income with my gross habits.
4318 Gross National Product is

groucho
3017 - tendance Groucho. I am a

ground
53 here on the ground while
3741 for the ground. It makes
4417 feet on the ground and I'll

group
56 - a group of men who
775 they form a group that's

grove
2991 And for groves, O! a

grovelled
4174 man he grovelled before

grow
421 We grow neither better nor
1759 man, and grow up with
4333 of us never grow out of it.

growed
4078 I s'pect I growed. Don't

growing
2499 Growing up is after all only

growl
2139 sit and growl ; let him

grown
1389 Grown up, and that is a
2986 kids - they've all grown up.
4582 exist to be grown out of.

grownups
3677 Grownups never understand

grows
1210 from the soil he grows in.
4185 Nothing grows in our
4564 either grows or swells,

grubbing
2283 lives At grubbing weeds from

grudge
197 or too fresh the grudge.
4085 wretch had a grudge against.

grundy
2555 God - And more of Mrs Grundy.

grunt
3179 and grunt. Speech

guard
2604 be on his guard, if he
2875 changing guard at

guess
2239 Medical Men guess: if they

guest
1075 guest in a

guests
442 classes: hosts and guests.

guide
2932 my virtue's guide: In part

guidelines
630 Guidelines for bureaucrats: (1)

guilt
625 Guilt: the gift that goes
1707 art can wash her guilt away?
1915 they don't feel guilt.
4057 circumstance of guilt.

guiltless
597 only are guiltless

guilty
1001 to be guilty of it.
3166 be judged guilty until they

guinea
4162 of the guinea helps the

guitar
126 sound, and guitar music is

gum
4604 is chewing gum for the

gun
475 The Maxim Gun, and they
2488 happiness is a warm gun.
4462 "Is that a gun in your

gunga din
2286 better man than I am, Gunga Din!

gunpowder
821 Gunpowder, Printing,

guns
1666 butter or guns? ..

gunshot
1471 in play far out of gunshot.

gut
4203 full of gut and

gutless
3164 a sort of gutless Kipling.

guts
859 The guts carry the feet,

gutter
4521 all in the gutter, but some

habit
1920 a desperate habit, and one

habits
1167 but the habits he has
3071 income with my gross habits.
4405 and my other habits are good.

hack
2922 Do not hack me as you did

hackles
4035 tan with henna hackles, halt!

haggis
3181 - head, heart and haggis.

hair
3724 Hair is another name for

haircut
4579 you get a haircut; you look

hairy
91 a small hairy individual

hale
4107 I should prefer mild hale.

half
535 cheeriness, Half dead and
1065 The first half of our
1167 the second half of a man's

half-a-crown
1818 bar is, Or help to half-a-crown.

half-mental
534 cent of this game is half-mental.

half-truth
2771 is a half-truth so stated
3437 A half-truth is a whole lie.

half-way
3484 The Half-Way House to Rome,

half-witted
4014 . an old half-witted sheep Which

ham'n eggs
1725 have your ham'n eggs in

hamlet
402 want him (Hamlet') to be so
1813 said that Hamlet is the
2766 Hamlet is the tragedy of

hammer
3480 it's the 'ammer, 'ammer,

hammered
3429 sticks out is hammered down.

hamsters
579 tigress surrounded by hamsters.

hand
2459 spoon; And hand in hand,
3882 from hand to hand of
4461 man a free hand and he'll

handel
3895 they to the tunes of Handel.

handkerchief
2651 like a damp handkerchief and

handle
210 Some people handle the truth
722 happiness you can handle.

handles
2439 are no handles to a

handmaid
350 are a good handmaid, but the

hands
2373 what hands you would
3108 and shaking hands, I want to

handsome
1335 others more handsome by far,
3803 Looks handsome in three

hang
1439 indeed all hang together,
3337 Hang it all, Robert
3787 Go hang thyself in thine

hanged
2176 he is to be hanged in a
3251 Harrison hanged, drawn,

hanging
1346 Hanging and marriage, you
1893 destiny, and hanging likewise.
2210 and the hanging garments

hangman
2100 or even a hangman, there are

hangs
4057 What hangs people .. is

happen
730 things happen their own
1883 few things happen at the

happened
2066 things after they've happened.
4040 funny thing happened to me on
4310 whether it had happened or not.

happens
2953 pleasant happens to you,

happier
2053 are often happier than the
4287 infinitely happier if we

happiest
585 The happiest time in any man's
4145 The fools are the happiest.

happily
632 He was happily married -
2817 matter how happily a woman

happiness
332 recipe for happiness I ever
370 Happiness is a small and
447 owe their happiness chiefly to
718 ruin of all happiness! There's
722 Happiness? A good cigar, a
1469 Happiness makes up in height
1724 that happiness is a way
1794 All happiness depends on a
2036 Who gain a happiness in eyeing
2120 so much happiness is
2170 much as the happiness of his
2488 because happiness is a warm
2725 Happiness comes fleetingly now
2726 Happiness is the interval

2848 do without happiness; it is
3077 complete happiness is to be
3135 Happiness to a dog is what lies
3536 don't have happiness, you send
3623 Happiness: a good bank account,
3660 most fatal to true happiness.
3734 is human happiness in the
3744 Happiness? That's nothing more
3838 lifetime of happiness! No man
4084 Happiness is the perpetual
4137 Happiness is an imaginary
4475 Happiness is no laughing

happy
1551 How happy could I be with
1640 lot is not a happy one.
1650 For A is happy - B is
1872 never be happy again; He
2112 one's wife happy. One is
2126 would be as happy in the
2755 who wants a happy marriage
2805 somewhere, may be happy.
3663 it, is a happy life. I
3742 and yet I'm happy. I can't
4125 'Tis happy for him, that
4323 to make you happy.
4410 us all be happy, and live

hard
734 is not hard, To be a
750 It is hard to come down
1800 is awfully hard to get it
2487 It's been a hard day's

harden
2934 told, We harden like

hardships
1460 his son the hardships that made

hardware
1999 coming out of a hardware store.

hare
308 Happy the hare at morning,

harlow
290 is silent - as in Harlow'.

harm
1019 said ever did me any harm.
1902 be kept from doing harm.
2488 do me no harm because
2999 may do you extreme harm.
3106 should do the sick no harm.
4151 What harm have I ever done

harmonies
1760 who uses harmonies instead of

harmony
2376 disposed to harmony. But

harpic
496 As I read the Harpic tin.

harpists
160 Harpists spend half their life

harvard
1976 is to send a son to Harvard.
2797 Yale College and my Harvard.
2964 the glass flowers at Harvard'.

harvest
2096 and she laughs with a harvest.
3269 the bite of a harvest apple.

harvesting
1490 resources we're not harvesting.

hashish
3552 I puffed hashish, but I

haste
4454 always in haste, I am

hat
58 a woman with his hat on.
3014 to get ahead, get a hat.
4431 come out of an empty hat.
4524 the right hat to wear on

hatch
3888 - you'll hatch out

hatched
40 before they are hatched.

hatches
2240 under hatches .. Rain!

hate
986 We hate some persons
1306 I hate quotations.
1483 and hate what's
1562 I hate all Boets and
2811 I hate all sports as
2824 Women hate revolutions and
2842 There's no hate lost
2961 town and hate each other
4119 I hate and detest
4319 Hate is such a luxurious

hated
1516 I never hated a man enough

hateful
2079 to the eye, hateful to the

hates
2988 He who hates vice hates
3563 authority, Hates a
3616 Any man who hates dogs and

hating
509 he'll end up hating you.
3051 a fool, But hating, my boy,
3680 Hating anything in the way

hatred
785 Now hatred is by far the
2358 more like hatred than like

hats
536 their hats Come
4443 bad hats in my
4490 Hats divide generally into

haughty
3627 this that haughty, gallant,

haunt
3309 glide, And haunt the places

have
400 If you have it, you
4562 got to have We plot to

have to
4191 you have to go round.

hazard
92 hazard of being a

hazards
2743 The hazards of computing are

hazy
3171 is so hazy, he really

head
828 on your head- Do you
838 to get one's head cut off.
1284 you shorter by the head.
1285 but for your good head.
1435 into his head, no one
1683 one small head could
1711 have his head examined.
2288 put his head down close

head-in-air
1914 there, Little Johnny Head-In-Air!

headache
1602 a dismal headache, and

headlight
1125 is the headlight of an

headmaster
922 Headmasters have powers at their

heads
2453 live; Their heads are green,

heals
1431 God heals, and the doctor

health
10 Health is the thing that
1164 you have both it's health.
1443 fatal to health than an
1799 yet met a healthy person
2938 in the health even of
3395 men when in the worst health.
3744 more than health and a poor

healthy
663 healthy man, the
3932 it is a kind of healthy grave.
4205 'Tis healthy to be sick

heap
3869 I was struck all of a heap.

hear
745 who do not wish to hear it.
1325 that we may hear from
1831 could they hear all that
1983 if people ever hear of him.
3610 a first hearing, and I

heard
1426 what you heard, not what
1649 generally heard, and if it
2026 right to be heard does not

3327 Have you heard it's in the
3492 The more he heard, the less
4485 never heard of either

hearing
2748 of the best hearing aids a man

hears
1829 If a man hears much that a

heart
581 take their heart in one
690 She had A heart - how shall
895 eye to the heart that does
1961 in your heart, you have
1973 not your heart away; Give
2301 giving your heart to a dog
2360 always fooled by the heart.
3218 ease the heart Like a
3831 Irishman's heart is nothing
4100 Of every heart: It pains
4148 I writ; My heart did do it,
4343 you her heart, you can

hearts
1597 Hearts just as pure and fair
3038 their hearts and minds
3900 of their hearts for sins
4434 women's hearts So far

heat
3929 Heat, ma'am! It was so
4348 stand the heat, get out

heathen
2279 The 'eathen in 'is blindness
2280 The 'eathen in 'is blindness

heaven
398 Heaven for climate, hell for
1458 concept of heaven is, they
1675 hell, you will be in heaven.
1762 Heaven is the place where
3384 If heaven made him, earth
3906 But; Heaven will
3963 their place in heaven also.
3968 you, Heaven would be
4118 If Heaven had looked upon
4302 cigars in heaven, I shall
4556 better in heaven, my friend

heavier
2516 age, weighs heavier in the

heavy
3802 doth make a heavy husband.

hedge
2147 a clipped hedge is to a

hedgehogs
2263 throwing hedgehogs under me,

hedges
4120 tongues, and hedges ears.

heels
4 Time wounds all heels.

heffalump
2886 decided to catch a Heffalump.

height
1469 makes up in height for what
heights
4352 great heights only by
heir-apparent
3787 in thine own heir-apparent garters!
hell
39 Hell to ships, hell to
162 Hell is truth seen too
398 climate, hell for
529 Hell, madame, is to love
1130 I go to hell?' 'No,'
1396 and the hell of horses.
1675 to love hell, you will
1762 his carrot: hell is the
2572 Oh hell, say that I am
2727 go through hell to get it.
2818 to go to hell without
3290 gates of Hell - but no
3838 it would be hell on earth.
3850 working definition of hell.
3963 said that hell is paved
3968 bear, And Hell would not
4060 to go to hell in such a
4076 the news and raise hell.
4086 connected with it to hell.
4253 public] hell. I just
4440 Hell is not other people,
hellhound
4576 you like, a hellhound is always
help
51 with the help of too
128 present help in time of
306 on earth to help others;
2952 Worrying helps you some.
helpless
1311 baby - so helpless and
hen
751 A hen is only an egg's
3471 where the hen crows and
henry viii
1058 Henry VIII had so many wives
herd-instinct
3091 is the herd-instinct in the
here
218 Here's tae us; wha's like
455 We're here because we're
1616 Here's a state of things!
3012 I'm only here for the
4193 Here lies a man who never
heredity
709 Heredity is nothing but stored
1924 Heredity is an omnibus in
heresy
3856 believes be heresy? It is a
hero
1307 Every hero becomes a bore
1308 A hero is no braver than

1386 Show me a hero and I will
1450 A hero is a man who stands
1670 no man is a hero to his
2411 before The hero arrives,
3580 of being a hero, about the
3581 Being a hero is about the
heroes
2108 Heroes are created by
2834 Thoughts of heroes were as
2902 the movie heroes are in the
heroic
1906 In a truly heroic life there
2081 to make heroic decisions
hesitation
4147 yeast, salt and hesitation.
heterodoxy
4404 is my doxy; heterodoxy is another
hew
3320 to hew blocks
hi diddle
4415 Hi diddle dee dee (an actor's
hidden
1580 eyes, Hidden, ever and
hide
498 trying to hide anything,
hierarchy
3265 In a hierarchy every employee
high
1378 a permanently high plateau.
high mass
2689 on her return from High Mass.
high-tech
1907 thing with high-tech is that
highbrow
1873 A highbrow is the kind of
2772 A highbrow is a person
4390 What is a highbrow? He is a
higher
3360 Stuart or Nassau go higher?
3885 shall shoot higher than who
himself
378 about himself and called
521 is demolished but by himself.
2594 party - an' thet is himself.
hindsight
4547 Hindsight is always
hindu
3865 or turns Hindoo, His best
hip
864 feel in my hip pocket.
hire
627 and some hire public
2739 are men who hire out their
2975 do. I hire him to
hirelings
3354 twenty-two hirelings kick a

hissing
972 with the least hissing.

historian
1883 historian will
3094 The historian looks backward.
4010 for a historian is to have

historians
748 the past, historians can; it is

historical
4347 a famous historical figure who

history
34 History is the sum total of
258 you wonder about history.
565 History, n: an account mostly
659 first rough draft of history.
758 The history of art is the
855 History doesn't pass the
1141 Read no history: nothing but
1226 lessons of history is that
1404 History is more or less bunk.
1428 summary of history to say
1537 History never looks like
1779 History repeats itself.
2237 suicide note in history.
2421 men of history are
3768 History is not what you
3824 What will history say?
4058 a thread to hang history from.
4152 History gets thicker as it
4517 we owe to history is to

hit
58 wouldn't hit a woman
531 think and hit at the
3600 of making a hit every time
4627 if he is hit by a

hitler
1891 cancel out Hitler through
2588 war. Even Hitler and
3260 Mister Hitler? If you

hobby
163 A hobby is hard work you

hoe
2096 her with a hoe, and she

hog
2862 the whole hog, you know.

hogs
4036 Eat Frogs. Hogs Eat

holding
3582 A holding company is the

hole
368 of a better 'ole, go to it.
670 to the hole when the
3141 A hole is nothing at all,
3452 cat there's a hole nearby.

holey
3560 hands in holey pockets;

holiday
3657 to take a holiday would
3850 A perpetual holiday is a good

holland
1956 Holland .. lies so low

hollywood
1915 In Hollywood they don't feel
2902 years in Hollywood and I
3536 In Hollywood, if you don't have

holy
41 I'm so holy that when I

home
38 A House is not a Home.
194 you get home from
335 staying at home for real
545 no place to stay home from.
638 Boston, The home of the
1026 children to come back home.
1044 that has been kept at home!
1172 to found a home discovers
1459 wouldn't have in your home.
1463 Home is the place where,
1771 good of a home if you are
1905 into the home - where it
1999 his own home is always
2006 it ought t' stay at home.
2253 you get it home, but it
2976 Home is not where you live
3139 a computer in their home.
3306 there's nobody at home.
3500 to his wife away from home.
3529 get you home by nine

homely
491 face was homely as a
2114 homely - even, on
3222 makes you homely, make you

homer
520 you must not call it Homer.

homesick
4324 you can be homesick for while

homicidal
4072 The great homicidal classics?

homogenized
1461 against a homogenized society

honest
226 good to be honest and true,
856 he is only honest who is not
1506 none but honest men, must
1656 you're an honest man, or
1784 Honest women are
2062 An honest God is the noblest
2495 Men are so honest, so
2759 if a man is honest - ask him.
3781 I am as honest as any man
3812 naturally honest, I am so
4071 quotable than to be honest.
4275 the man looked honest enough.
4401 anglers, or very honest men.

286

honester
3526 The honester the man, the

honesty
493 Honesty is as rare as a man
1115 easy - honesty most of
2054 that honesty is always
2721 honesty is a good thing but
3068 than out of the honesty.
4477 Honesty is the best policy;

honey
2880 bear likes honey? Buzz!
4384 pouring honey into a

honeysuckle
3502 roadside honeysuckle. That's

honour
1191 trouble; Honour but an
1299 of his honour, the
1740 loss of honour was a
2196 Honour! tut, a breath,
2534 for the honour of the
2628 tribe and honour the
2752 woman's honour .. which
3194 Honour is like a match, you
3309 where their honour died. See
3789 Honour pricks me on. Yea,
4162 the hurt that Honour feels.

honourable
1356 strictly honourable, as the

honoured
942 an honoured old age,

hoofbeats
3950 you hear hoofbeats, think of

hookah
2275 from the hookah-mouth.

hoover
1765 onto the board of Hoover.

hope
358 Hope is a good breakfast,
1437 lives upon hope will die
1547 is the only hope that keeps
2065 said that hope is the
2141 triumph of hope over
2352 Hope, deceitful as it is,
2620 is past hope, the heart

hopeless
2156 is more hopeless than a

hoppy
1292 Bowery, Hoppy, Croppy,
2212 ajog, hoppy on akkant

horde
781 polished horde, Formed of

horizontal
312 none But the horizontal one.
967 Life is a horizontal fall.
3821 of a horizontal desire.

hornpipes
725 There's hornpipes and

horny
3512 I get horny for my

horribilis
1286 out to be an 'annus horribilis'.

horrid
2573 she was bad she was horrid.

horror
835 'The horror of that moment,'

horse
274 heard no horse sing a
453 A Protestant with a horse.
991 abuses his horse or his
1491 he'll not come back a horse.
1687 is a good horse in the
1729 be a man, a horse, a dog or
1820 in one's horse as he is
2154 a stately horse and make
2278 for the horse is drawn
3446 rise and steal a horse.
3638 about the horse And one of
3807 indeed, a horse of that
4160 dearer than his horse.
4497 I owe it to horse and hound.

horse-sense
2769 Horse-sense is something a horse

horseback
733 a beggar on horseback, and he

horseguards
3524 be in the Horseguards and still

horsepond
3236 almost always a muddy horsepond.

horses
1081 Horses and jockeys mature
2171 given to horses, but in
3950 think of horses before
4176 sir, in hosses, dawgs,

horseshit
3004 plants .. and horseshit.

hospital
3106 in a hospital is that it

host
444 all that a host and
4425 Perhaps host and guest is

hosts
442 classes: hosts and

hot spot
2892 and a swinging hot spot.

hot-bed
2146 raised in a hot-bed; and they

hot-water
2845 English have hot-water bottles.

hotel
2892 With a pink hotel, A

hound
881 a slepyng hound to wake.
4105 that I loves the 'ound more.
4497 I owe it to horse and hound.

hour
1986 in an hour than
1987 only an hour's drive
3399 is but an hour a day
3644 At such an hour the

hours
344 Foster, the hours I've put
1227 twenty-four hours and too
1255 for two hours, you think
2710 two golden hours, each set

house
38 A House is not a Home.
1599 in that House MPs
1601 The House of Peers,
2991 But a house is much more to
3458 buy the house; buy the
3471 Woe to the house where the
4114 to sell his house, and
4456 man in the house is worth

house of lords
4067 The House of Lords, an illusion to

housekeeper
1513 excellent housekeeper. Everytime
4549 to make a housekeeper think

housekeeping
4286 so-called housekeeping where they

housewife
545 being a housewife is you
3299 and love - except the housewife.
3399 a good housewife and a bad

housewives
4608 who are housewives, and other

housework
1329 Housework is what woman does

how-de-doo
1615 Here's a how-de-doo!

howl
2637 done and let them howl.

huff
2753 leave in a huff. If

hugo
968 Victor Hugo was a madman

hum
1665 and hideous hum Indicat

human
936 is simply a human organism
998 are only human .. But it
1026 Human beings are the only
1074 Only a few human beings
1419 It is human nature to think
1823 of the human race
2039 Why should human females
2382 The human species,
2621 then, so are human beings.
2917 the less human for being
3158 thing that human beings
3516 I loved the Human Race; I
4189 .. least human of all

humanities
3114 but the Humanities live for

humanity
601 unremitting humanity soon had

humble
55 I am, it's hard to be humble.
2792 Don't be so humble. You're

humbug
1120 said Scrooge. Humbug!'
3202 Yes we have. Humbug.

humility
604 Humility is a good quality,
1303 the naughtiness of humility.
1504 perceiving humility
2524 accuracy - whimpering humility.
2708 its own humility, which is
4600 humility. I chose

humorist
1105 the word humorist - I feel
1885 A humorist is a man who feels

humorous
1879 too humorous to

humour
47 but no sense of humour.
367 or lacking a sense of humour.
678 Humour is just another
799 sense of humour from
1471 Humour is the most engaging
1523 Humour is richly rewarding.
1540 Humour is an affirmation of
2431 of humour I know is:
2441 sense of humour is to give
2977 Humour is the contemplation
4217 Humour is emotional chaos

hump
4173 a positive hump, may marry

hunger
1967 Hunger is not debatable.
3403 ought to begin with hunger.

hungry
3416 you ask the hungry man how
3485 I am not hungry; but thank
4042 A hungry man is not a free

huns
2897 better than Huns or Wops,

hunted
2517 by their hunted

hunter
308 read The Hunter's waking

hunting
76 go a hunting, For fear
731 my life to hunting and
3480 ain't the 'unting as 'urts

hunting-field
2997 a decent death on the hunting-field.

hunts
4161 a dog, he hunts in dreams.

hurry
2508 'No hurry, no hurry,' said
4056 He sows hurry and reaps
4454 I am never in a hurry.

hurt
1392 wouldn't hurt the place.
2541 I know will not hurt me.
3195 ain't likely to hurt you.
4096 They never hurt a hair of
4162 helps the hurt that
4279 to hurt you to the

hurting
3074 stop hurting because

husband
96 surrender value of a husband.
106 having one husband too many.
164 A husband always prefers his
507 Being a husband is a
879 over hir housbond as hir
1287 the words 'My husband and I'.
1362 animal, a husband and wife.
1925 Husband and wife come to look
2074 A good husband should always
2755 The husband who wants a happy
3629 A husband is what is left of
3634 trust a husband too far,
3802 doth make a heavy husband.
4149 who has an ideal husband.

husbands
381 majority of husbands remind me
1268 reasons for husbands to stay at
2654 way to get husbands to do
3325 cast, When husbands or when
3974 Husbands don't really count

hustles
1233 to him who hustles while he

hybrid
4337 is a hybrid of a

hygiene
3911 part of the hygiene of older

hymns
2371 amorous hymns, and

hypochondria
2 cure for hypochondria is to

hypochondriac
4061 being a hypochondriac these days

hypocrisy
2354 Hypocrisy is a tribute which
2775 Hypocrisy is the most difficult
3098 oneself is a form of hypocrisy.
4507 time. That would be hypocrisy.

hypocrite
2163 No man is a hypocrite in his
3382 Hypocrite - mouth one way,

hypocrites
1837 are the only honest hypocrites.
1840 We are not hypocrites in our
4029 the cant of hypocrites may be the

hypotenuse
1639 the square on the hypotenuse.

hypothesis
2043 a beautiful hypothesis by an ugly
2584 a pet hypothesis every day

hysteria
2425 manipulated hysteria as the
3037 the moment of deepest hysteria.

i
1543 I am I plus my

ice
291 lies to ice a wedding
1468 Some say in ice. From what
3347 The ice of her Ladyship's

icebergs
1777 between passing icebergs.

iced
280 and three parts iced over.

icicle
844 age like an icicle down my

iconoclasm
1931 Rough work, iconoclasm, but the

idea
37 contain a single idea.
229 puts a new idea across he
299 man with an idea has at
672 the impact of a new idea.
2016 of an idea whose time
2722 does get an idea he usually
3543 suffering than an idea.
4534 with an idea, and grew
4602 An idea is salvation by

ideal
3560 the realms of the ideal.
4149 An ideal wife is any woman

ideas
517 of genuine ideas, Bright
759 Our ideas. They are for
976 possess ideas; the
1184 to crown Ideas flow up
1234 am long on ideas, but short
1291 Big ideas are so hard to
1387 of foolish ideas have died
3945 What two ideas are more
4018 without his ideas get
4312 marriage of ideas which,
4488 Ideas won't keep: something

identity
2665 sense of identity is our

idiosyncrasy
2086 Pound - idiosyncrasy on a

idiot
566 Idiot, n: a member of a
883 Any idiot can face a crisis
1610 The idiot who praises, with
2849 like an idiot, babbling,

idle
1502 He is idle that might be

imperfect
2077 He was imperfect, unfinished,
imperfection
2869 flawless imperfection of a New
imperialism
2484 Imperialism is the monopoly stage
impertinence
3732 symbol of impertinence and
importance
1209 tell me of importance, for God's
2559 nothing of importance can happen
important
743 three most important things a
2085 there is is very important .'
3445 wildcat is very self important.
3657 is terribly important, and that
4358 The important thing is not what
imposes
1195 the child imposes on the
impossibility
1310 man is an impossibility until he
impossible
80 what is impossible for talent
236 Nothing is impossible for the
2240 It is impossible to live in a
2246 flying machines are impossible.
3019 - the impossible takes a
3243 is always impossible to live
3254 I see it is impossible for the
imposture
2776 them to carry on the imposture.
impotence
3705 as he is of impotence.
4424 Impotence and sodomy are
impressed
690 Too easily impressed: she liked
impression
1124 left an impression more
imprisoned
1010 Imprisoned in every fat man a
improper
3914 An improper mind is a
impropriety
2780 Impropriety is the soul of wit.
improve
431 greatly improve his
improvement
608 Improvement makes straight roads;
1947 social improvement, or read
3752 children for signs of improvement.
impudence
3653 of Cockney impudence before
inaccuracy
742 lying, but I hate inaccuracy.
3686 A little inaccuracy sometimes
incapable
2929 but I am incapable of taking

incapacity
3505 in proportion to his incapacity.
incest
414 excepting incest and
inch
244 by the inch and
713 have an inch of dog
1196 Every inch that is not
4468 Every other inch a
inches
2186 to their inches.
incisors
363 into incisors and
include
1713 Gentlemen, include me out.
income
332 A large income is the best
3071 my net income with my
3922 a good income is of no
income tax
3528 as an income tax refund.
incomes
3678 their incomes nowadays,
incommunicable
4047 is for the most part incommunicable.
incompetence
3265 rise to his level of incompetence.
3268 their level of incompetence.
incompetent
390 Only an incompetent mind is
incomplete
1515 A man is incomplete until he has
incongruities
2431 of the incongruities of life,
inconsistency
3908 Inconsistency is the only thing in
inconvenience
3541 through the inconveniences of life.
inconvenient
591 but the most inconvenient one, too.
3937 it is confoundedly inconvenient.
incurable
1039 Life is an incurable disease.
indebted
3871 is indebted to his
indecent
2420 will be Indecent .. 10
3419 An indecent mind is a
indeed
2003 in need is a friend indeed.
indefatigable
3969 That indefatigable and unsavoury
independence
1347 we call it independence. When men
3770 step toward independence is a

independent
2593 Ain't to be inderpendunt, why, wut

indian
132 American Indians made a
1095 what the Indians called

indifference
825 Indifference may not wreck a man's
4052 you with an indifference closely

indigestion
266 complains of moral indigestion.
4056 sows hurry and reaps indigestion.

indignation
1305 A good indignation brings out all
3028 mists of righteous indignation.
4452 Moral indignation is jealousy

indiscretion
2671 a cliché and an indiscretion.

indispensable
1524 are indispensable when you
2002 that they seem indispensable.

individual
1051 educate an individual - educate
2325 of the individual was: a
3091 herd-instinct in the individual.

individually
56 of men who individually can do

indoors
1 - clean, indoors and no
2687 given us indoors and

inefficiency
1075 God of inefficiency, but when

inelegance
328 a continual state of inelegance.

inevitable
2600 with the inevitable. The only

inexperienced
181 of the inexperienced giving

infancy
2543 of man are infancy,

inferior
3599 you feel inferior without

inferiority
889 enjoy the inferiority of their
2124 of an inferiority, from his

infidel
568 Infidel, n: in New York, one

infinite
2292 a man of infinite-resource-a
2977 point of view of the infinite.

infirmities
1357 the natural infirmities of those

inflation
168 Inflation is defined as the
1455 Inflation is one form of
3588 Invest in inflation. It's the

influence
2169 things he cannot influence.

information
3999 much common information all day

infuriating
250 A word to the wise is infuriating.

ingenuity
2789 about the ingenuity or the

ingredients
2982 are three ingredients in the
3988 most useful ingredients of family

inhale
3552 hashish, but I didn't inhale.
4046 that is, if you don't inhale.

inherit
2728 they shall inherit the earth.

inheritance
871 For an inheritance to be really

iniquity
3721 to have them, what iniquity!

injuries
2957 is adding insult to injuries.

injury
887 An injury is much sooner

injustice
626 taken to maintain injustice.
2812 Injustice is relatively easy to

ink
199 buys his ink by the
3003 worthless by applying ink.
3796 he hath not drunk ink.

innkeeper
3432 The innkeeper loves the

innocent
597 The truly innocent are those
808 The innocent is the person who
1593 As innocent as a new-laid egg.
3166 until they are proved innocent.

innocuous
1728 lambent but innocuous.

insane
1813 obviously he must be insane.

insanity
570 a temporary insanity often
2507 genius and insanity. I have
2513 Insanity is hereditary - you

inscription
564 n: an inscription on a tomb

insect
2154 is but an insect, and the

insects
2529 certain insects come by

inseparable
3945 are more inseparable than Beer

inside
207 the lady inside And a
1070 lived inside myself,
1336 lot of people inside me.
1715 that great inside thing that

insignificance
1849 to see the insignificance of human
insincerity
3159 language is insincerity. When
inspiration
3522 at the mercy of inspiration.
inspire
987 you cannot inspire a woman
instinct
760 all healthy instinct for it.
765 he was, his instinct told him
institution
1317 are in the institution wish to
2097 ancient institution, the old
3302 is a great institution, and no
4463 is a great institution, but I am
institutions
3552 of institutions. Even in
4408 greatest institooshuns of which
instruction
1489 is that no instruction book came
instrument
428 legs an instrument capable of
insufferable
446 that has made me insufferable.
insular
1148 An insular country, subject
insult
887 forgotten than an insult.
2957 is adding insult to
insulted
1073 me to get insulted in places
2751 been so insulted in my
insulting
3115
intellect
895 not go through the intellect.
1252 to make the intellect our god;
2360 The intellect is always fooled
2385 feather to tickle the intellect.
intellectual
316 The word Intellectual' suggests
810 An intellectual is someone whose
1256 An intellectual is a man who takes
2622 - the intellectual cripple's
2680 An intellectual is someone whose
intellectuals
4601 I hate intellectuals. They are
intelligence
2622 substitute for intelligence.
2772 educated beyond his intelligence.
4499 Intelligence appears to be the
intelligent
375 The intelligent are to the
978 she is intelligent demands
1078 Many highly intelligent people are
3296 Marry an intelligent person.

intention
602 slightest intention of
3143 - attention without intention.
intentions
3963 with good intentions. They
intercourse
2409 Sexual intercourse began In
interest
937 loses interest in
1024 take it out, you lose interest.
2596 But oh, I du in interest.
interested
2 and get interested in someone
912 the more interested he is in
1128 man is more interested in a woman
interesting
588 the most interesting things he
1372 They are interesting to look
3045 much more interesting than any
3061 to make other people interesting.
4090 not nice, but it's interesting.
4390 more interesting than
interests
3707 sharing the interests of others.
interference
730 without interference. They
interior
1871 by interior blessings.
international
574 n: in international affairs, a
internet
4552 to the Internet, we know
interrupt
2227 for itself, don't interrupt.
interrupted
2465 you get interrupted when you
3556 truly enjoyed must be interrupted.
interstices
2150 with interstices between
interval
3708 save to enjoy the interval.
intimate
541 us, the intimate roof of
intimidating
4180 should be intimidating. There's
intolerable
4345 possession of it is intolerable.
intoxicated
2128 when he is intoxicated, has not
intrusion
3966 education, I call it intrusion.
invaded
2478 Remorse, Invaded with a
invalid
3412 Invalids live longest.
3421 Every invalid is a physician.

invent
4010 to have no ability to invent.
4129 What some invent, the rest

invented
1047 necessity invented stools,
2706 have invented in order
3281 artist. He invented the

invest
3588 Invest in inflation. It's
3605 Never invest your money in

invested
922 have never yet been invested.

invisible
696 who has no invisible means of

invisibly
4219 dripping invisibly all over

involuntarily
2848 it is done involuntarily by

involuntary
2249 It was involuntary. They sank my

ireland
552 who left Ireland at
2214 Ireland is the old sow that
2960 Ireland is a fatal disease;

irish
456 that the Irish are
2962 dissatisfied. I'm Irish.
3134 An Irish queer: a fellow

irishman
3831 An Irishman's heart is nothing

irishmen
452 like true Irishmen - locked

iron
2677 iron.

irrelevancies
445 free of irrelevancies and loose

irritable
3880 some people are very irritable.

irritate
2771 as to irritate the person

irritating
3243 and even irritating to live
3880 carry on irritating some

island
549 This island is made mainly
1117 snug little Island, A right
3119 Englishman is an island.
4322 little island huffing

it
3387 to know it, don't do

italian
656 rival. The Italian woman
2822 as baseball in Italian.

italians
2106 Italians come to ruin most

italy
718 here after seeing Italy.
2124 not been in Italy, is always
3941 from Italy a greater

itch
2587 once the itch of
3396 As old as the itch.

itches
231 To scratch when it itches.

ivy
26 poison ivy is another

jabberwock
831 'Beware the Jabberwock, my son!

jackass
3527 Any jackass can kick down a

jade
1687 an arrant jade on a

jail
2175 being in a jail, with the

jam
833 rule is, jam tomorrow

jane
4438 Me Tarzan, you Jane.

jargon
517 we have jargon; instead

jaw-jaw
929 To jaw-jaw is always better

jaws
827 With gently smiling jaws!

jazz
1760 A jazz musician is a

je-ne-sais-quoi
1634 piminy, Je-ne-sais-quoi young

jealousy
2185 Jealousy is all the fun you
4452 is jealousy with a

jeepers
2833 Jeepers Creepers - where'd

jelly
3453 you, even jelly breaks

jellybeans
3531 by his way of eating jellybeans.

jest
272 and a jest which will

jesting
2493 empty and meaningless jesting.

jesuit
2272 a thing, a tool, a Jesuit.

jesus
1962 is that Jesus is coming
4096 When Jesus came to

jew
1149 Yes, I am a Jew, and when
1253 declare that I am a Jew.
2862 really a Jew . Just

jewel
4200 eye is the jewel of the

jewellery
2485 you, just rattle your jewellery.

jewish
679 Look at Jewish history.
3617 A Jewish man with parents

jews
1337 Of God To choose The Jews.
1680 The Jews have always been
2793 We Jews have a secret

jilted
802 courted and jilted Than never

jingling
4162 But the jingling of the guinea

job
1 the sort of job all
1790 he creates a job vacancy.
1815 a hell of a job. I have
2219 fifth and lost the job.
2907 It's an odd job, making
3790 as poor as Job, my lord,

jockeys
1081 Horses and jockeys mature

jog
2395 a man might jog on with.
4023 As we jog on, either

jogging
3741 Jogging is very beneficial.

john brown
3046 this slab John Brown is stowed.

johnny
1914 at little Johnny there,

johnson
3247 Dr Johnson's sayings would

joined
3830 God hath joined together

joint
4082 was out of joint, and he

joke
1014 face of a joke upon the
1612 Life is a joke that's just
3096 A joke is an epigram on
3940 to get a joke well into

jokes
1462 my little jokes on Thee
3425 He that jokes confesses.

jotting
2446 you. The jotting is

journalism
279 Journalism is literature in a
1795 essence of journalism is to know

journalist
4580 the British journalist. But,
4615 by rote; A journalist makes up

journey
581 the journey of life,
1604 on that journey you find

joys
4496 lasting joys the man

judas
4516 is always Judas who writes

judge
99 gives a judge an
197 the living judge - Too
2814 A judge is a law student
2994 We judge ourselves by our
3348 I am no judge of such
3610 One cannot judge
4158 mistake to judge people by
4543 a time they judge them;

judgement
20 give his judgement rashly,
154 Good judgement comes from
693 nor enough judgement to be
806 the last judgement. It
1826 independent judgement is being
2359 one complains of his judgement.
3186 Judgement of beauty can err,

judges
2013 is what the judges say it is.
2996 [Irritable judges] suffer

judging
840 In judging others, folks will

juliet
3889 the Nurse, not Juliet.

jumblies
2453 were the Jumblies live;

jumping
4101 the cat is jumping. The

june
3464 June's too soon, July's

jupiter
4210 its hands and pray to Jupiter.

jury
1472 A jury consists of twelve
1498 be on the jury at a

just
172 Just when you thought it
649 on the just And also

justice
173 were any justice in the
504 price of justice is eternal
1170 Justice is too good for some
1775 Lord Chief Justice of England
1936 man, not a court of justice.
2770 In England, justice is open to
2812 I justice is relatively easy
3175 line about justice - not only
3801 ducats! Justice! the law!

justify
1972 can To justify God's ways

kaiser
1288 put the kibosh on the Kaiser.

keep
221 Keep a thing seven years
484 she'll have to keep it.
973 from seeing you keep yours.
1169 eye. To keep him - two.
1791 than to let him keep her.
1832 We should keep the Panama
4457 always say, keep a diary
4488 Ideas won't keep: something

key
502 for the key. I wonder

keyhole
4330 size of the keyhole, today's

keys
1743 half that's got my keys.'

khatmandu
1835 north of Khatmandu, There's a

kibosh
1288 put the kibosh on the

kick
916 with a kick and not a
3108 hands, I want to kick them.
3223 thinks he may kick at him.
4421 They may kick you out,

kicked
25 He had been kicked in the
244 shall be kicketh by the

kicks
2856 is what kicks you in the

kid
4606 you're a kid, you see

kiddie
3051 Any kiddie in school can

kiddies
537 You kiddies have

kidding
3260 you are kidding, Mister

kids
2416 have any kids yourself.
2986 with our kids - they've

kill
927 you have to kill a man it
959 shalt not kill; but
1269 will kill a man so
1320 a king you must kill him.
2444 get out and kill something.
3084 at all but kill animals
3195 may kill you, but
3575 war they kill you in a
3614 Kill a man, and you are an
3970 trying to kill, but which
4371 well to kill an admiral
4622 likely to kill you is

killed
2347 one has killed the beast.

killing
3897 In reality, killing time Is
3970 but which ends in killing him.

kills
528 it kills all its

kin
3044 one's own kin and kith

kind
1069 their own kind. The
1353 naturally kind, you

kindly
3691 the KCMG (Kindly Call Me

kindness
2006 Kindness goes a long way lots

king
687 The King to Oxford sent a
823 is a born king of
1097 to be king for a
2878 The King asked The Queen,
3253 esteem of a king, that he
3254 for the King to have
3365 What is a King? - a man
3566 and mighty king Whose
3639 go For your King and your
3757 A king is a thing men have
4237 The King, observing with

king george
2695 King George, passing slowly in a

kings
832 - and kings - And why
1186 and ruin kings.
1343 only five Kings left - the
2677 Bind-their kings-in-chains-
4264 All kings is mostly

kinquering
3980 Kinquering Congs their titles

kipling
4013 cease from kipling And the

kiss
418 Kiss till the cow comes
1072 "I'd luv to kiss ya, but I
1730 the first kiss after men
1887 would I kiss my Julia's
2891 A kiss can be a comma, a
2923 say a kiss on the
2935 my deary! kiss me, and be
3230 take his kiss!' '"Tis

kissed
248 they are kissed; some call
868 one wants to be kissed.
877 mouth he kiste hir naked
2303 Being kissed by a man who
4126 said when she kissed her cow.
4233 young, I kissed my first

kisses
1964 who throw kisses are
2295 Christian kisses on an
2618 cards for kisses, Cupid

631 Laughter is the shortest
780 Mirth and Laughter Sermons
1289 recipe like Laughter. Laugh it
3239 Laughter is pleasant, but the
4327 Laughter .. the most
4331 Laughter would be bereaved if

laundry-list
3608 Give me a laundry-list and I'll

law
175 The law locks up both man
626 Law and order is one of
1595 The Law is the true
1811 The aim of law is the
1876 The Common Law of England
1936 a court of law, young
2546 Law .. begins when
2785 from th' law of
3001 in the law. Nothing
3809 the windy side of the law.

lawbreaking
3646 opposed to lawbreaking, he is not

laws
578 that the laws of the
622 can be made so by laws.
2557 broke the laws of God and
3116 Laws were made to be

lawsuit
1479 successful lawsuit is the one
4377 I lost a lawsuit, and once

lawyer
752 A lawyer's dream of heaven -
1472 who has the better lawyer.
1949 knife, as a lawyer's mouth
2975 as I want a lawyer to tell me
4566 to be a lawyer, but now I

lawyers
1118 would be no good lawyers.
1554 I know you lawyers can, with
2739 Lawyers are men who hire out
3303 To some lawyers, all facts

lay
764 one can lay it on so
1007 She lays it on with a
2220 that a man lay down his
4213 that he lay down his

lazier
2353 We are lazier in our minds

laziness
3544 for laziness: there is

lazy
310 tends to be lazy, craves
367 for anyone lazy.
1964 kisses are hopelessly lazy.
2204 Men get lazy, and
3431 to send a lazy man for
3641 ugly women, only lazy ones.
4351 The lazy are always
4583 The lazy man gets round

lead
1216 You can lead a man up to
2684 foremost To lead such dire

leader
1093 A true leader always keeps
1327 is no ethical leader for me.
1892 European leaders actually
2471 them - I am their leader.

leafage
4568 important than his leafage.

lean
4215 face as lean over too

leaping
1820 one's horse as he is leaping.

leaps
346 in mighty leaps, It leaps

lear
2455 to know Mr Lear!' Who has

learn
14 who know how to learn.
644 we don't learn from it.
1324 First learn the meaning of
2201 To teach is to learn twice.
3304 We live and learn, but not
3625 those who learn; poetry
3769 don't want to learn - much.
4000 You have to learn to do
4572 on hand to learn them a bit
4606 more you learn to see

learned
101 have not learned from
219 what you learned this
797 If I've learned anything in
956 I know I learned after I
1311 he has learned the
2704 in my life learned anything
2725 who have learned to do
4308 old man had learned in seven
4445 time we've learned, it's too

learning
754 public and learning the
1699 and learning, Good
2982 good life; learning, earning
3240 a little learning was
3933 with learning, but stood
4237 loyal body wanted learning.

learnt
4402 it can never be fully learnt.

leathern
2744 moist Their leathern boats

leave
2579 old adage, Leave them while
3596 done, and leave out the

leave-taking
747 but I don't like the leave-taking.

led
2288 nose .. Led go! You

4201 have not stood up to live.
4288 I can live for two months
4445 We should live and learn;

lived
1546 should have lived
1918 Well, I've lived my life as
2061 I have lived to thank God
4193 who never lived, Yet still

lives
1065 half of our lives is ruined
1957 But human creatures' lives!
2341 of their lives to making

living
97 It's living together
197 of the living can the
278 The living need charity more
322 The art of living is more
1002 like living together
2005 to stop living on account
3440 make a wonderful living.
4366 Living? The servants will

livingstone
3987 Dr Livingstone, I presume?

llama
474 The Llama is a woolly sort

lloyd george
234 Lloyd George knew my father, My

loafing
4159 cricket as organized loafing.

loan
345 have him on loan from

loaves
3416 two, he replies four loaves.

local
1923 But nothing local, as one

location
3193 on location is in

lodgings
3949 in frowzy lodgings, where

logically
298 facts, it logically ought to

london
1177 London, that great cesspool
2417 thought of London spread out

lonely
2104 I may be lonely, and the
2979 No man is lonely while

lonesome
3420 be quarrelling than lonesome.

long
222 is his long staying.
667 they last too long.
2137 Mr Long's character is
3053 but it's gone on too long.
3282 It takes a long time to
3377 would live long, but none

longer
1308 is brave five minutes longer.
1447 live longer; it just
2310 takes a little longer.

longest
3412 Invalids live longest.

longevity
1399 Longevity conquers scandal
1940 Longevity is having a chronic

look
2091 When I look in the glass I
2398 people will look at
2597 you can look or listen.
3542 shall still look for Him.
4111 If I look like this, I
4236 Look in my face. My name

looked
2871 The more he looked inside the

looking
87 as much as looking at things
650 dark room - looking for a
1370 I'm looking for loopholes.
2254 you start looking very
2816 that someone may be looking.
4011 all night looking for them

looks
690 on, and her looks went
982 A woman as old as she looks.
4257 needs good looks. From 35

loopholes
1370 I'm looking for loopholes.

loose
2030 I can pry loose is not

lord
32 The good Lord set definite
1283 My Lord, I had forgot the
2641 o' my soul, Lord God; As I

lords
1702 I see the lords of human
2951 Great lords have their
3112 House of Lords as from

lordships
100 for their lordships on a hot

lose
217 his side shall lose him.
973 Many people lose their
1041 that you'll lose your mind
2460 day you may lose them all';
2463 But to lose our teeth
2502 does not lose his reason
3639 want to lose you but we
3718 a portrait I lose a friend.
3843 One is to lose your
4509 To lose one parent, Mr

loser
3567 gracious loser, and I'll

loved
460 of Balliol loved and led
717 He may have loved before; I
1552 sighed, he loved, was
1783 handle loved, May be
2656 has ever loved anyone the
2852 And if I loved you
3516 I wish I loved the Human

loveliness
1621 miracle of loveliness. People

lovely
2029 has got, A lovely woman in a
2920 Ah, it's a lovely thing, to

lovemaking
1912 keeping. Lovemaking is

lover
1011 searching for a new lover.
1632 Peripatetic Lover, he lived
1669 you can still be a lover.
3204 Scratch a lover, and find a
3629 left of a lover, after the
4216 not a dog lover. To me, a
4246 with her lover's mind if
4557 to her lover -

lovers
860 two were lovers or no,

loves
482 as good as what he loves.
2640 that a man loves And when

loving
2966 can help loving the land
4543 begin by loving their

low
1956 .. lies so low they're
1988 is a very low grade of

lower
4508 if the lower orders

loyalty
4237 body wanted loyalty; To

lubricates
3751 A dinner lubricates business.

lucifer
2836 Prince Lucifer uprose.

luck
494 hard luck - well, we
527 The luck of having talent
646 average luck to survive
1159 Luck is being ready for
1334 old enemy down on his luck.
1660 With luck on your side you
2435 believer in luck. I find
2986 had bad luck with our
3526 the man, the worse luck.
3601 the good luck of the
3991 believes in luck and sends

luckiest
311 are the luckiest of mortals

lucky
1373 - a man's lucky if he gets
3380 Throw a lucky man into the
3459 were born lucky, even your

lumber
1175 away in the lumber room of
3314 of learned lumber in his

luminous
2452 The Dong with a Luminous Nose!'

lumps
4016 There are lumps in it.

lunatics
3637 The lunatics have taken charge

lunch
187 for life, not for lunch.
227 such thing as a free lunch.
1364 the cork out of my lunch.

luncheon
477 to spend At luncheon with a

lurch
2476 me in the lurch, Lor' how

lust
846 women with lust. I've
2188 do thou lust after that

luxuries
951 One of the luxuries of a
3005 Give us the luxuries of life,
4598 to save the luxuries until I

luxurious
1301 are most luxurious. They

luxury
1047 And luxury the
3150 Every luxury was lavished on

lying
592 the truth without lying.
742 do not mind lying, but I
765 amount of lying go the
1409 the use of lying when
2202 of hard lying in the
3217 this: One of you is lying.
4447 is legalized lying.

lymphomaniac
791 Does that mean I'm a lymphomaniac?

macavity
1274 Macavity, Macavity, there's no

macbeth
444 in general Macbeth and Lady

machine
611 ingenious machine for
2245 the machine is fast,

machines
4444 that these machines will ever

macho
1514 Macho does not prove mucho.

mad
424 are born mad. Some
1136 Don't get mad, get even.

1563 Mad, is he? Then I hope
2300 or less mad on one
2648 football mad And the
3948 nation is mad - and the
4300 we are all mad, the

made
858 is as God made him and
4078 think nobody never made me.

madeira
1393 Have some madeira, M'dear.

madman
968 Hugo was a madman who
1802 up than a downright madman.

madmen
1133 is only the noise of madmen.
3318 worst of madmen is a saint

madness
1318 woman, has a dash of madness.

magazines
1510 the women's magazines. It may

magic
866 kiss is magic, the
3654 given by magic the power
4139 men mistook magic for

magical
404 as a purely magical object.

magnetic
1632 While this magnetic,

magnetized
2711 it is not magnetized. Lay it

maid
1058 he saw a maid of honour.
1355 an old maid is like

maids
1613 little maids who, all

major-general
1638 model of a modern Major-General.

majority
3278 on God's side is a majority.
3563 Reaching majority, Seizing
4265 big enough majority in any

make
399 a Scotsman on the make.
431 do not make the man;
1216 you can't make him think.
3273 The man who makes no

make out
3958 for, I could not well make out.

make-believe
1842 Man is a make-believe animal - he

makes
294 mind until he makes it up.

male
402 to be so male that when
2423 the male of the
4498 the true male never yet

malevolence
2577 is detached malevolence.

malice
589 with malice than with
3725 Malice is of a low stature,

malign
2362 had rather malign oneself

malt
1972 Malt does more than Milton

mama
1511 but I believe it is Mama.

mammon
3916 God and Mammon soon

man
184 If every man would mend a
200 Man is more mushroom than
273 The young man who wants
443 make a man by
598 When a man comes to me
599 When a man gets talking
600 A man is a person who
646 Every man, even the most
653 Only man, among living
654 I'm a man more dined
884 A man and a woman marry
1302 Every man is wanted, and
1351 A man of fifty looks as
1541 A man .. is so in the
1685 The man recovered of the
1814 To find the Inner man.
1843 Man is the only animal
1911 there a man with hide
1982 A man should be taller,
2164 Every man has, some time
2245 Man is a slow, sloppy and
2291 ever tasted Man?' 'No,'
2293 get to a man in the
2416 Man hands on misery to
2537 Every man over forty is
2705 Man is a dog's ideal of
2747 A man is only as old as
2790 I met a man who wasn't
2919 Man, I can assure you, is
3123 of plain is your only man.
3131 No man is as
3218 Where's the man could ease
3244 every great man there is a
3720 Every man in the world is
3775 A man isn't a man until
3799 let him pass for a man.
3902 Man, an animal that makes
3975 Man is a social animal.
4119 called man; although
4150 of any man
4182 A man you don't like who
4220 Man is flying too fast
4278 Man is the Only Animal
4456 "A man in the house is
4470 The only man who can

me
2035 - But the One was me.

meal
3248 A good meal makes a man
3403 A good meal ought to begin
3447 face is half the meal.

meals
2505 just meals on heels.

mean
3345 most people mean, even if
4020 ever I do a mean action, it
4250 even if you don't mean it.

meaning
1648 with hidden meaning - like
1860 The true meaning of life is
1933 to have a meaning that one
4392 sure of her meaning before she

means
4410 within our means, even if
4539 have to die beyond my means.

measles
2095 is like the measles; we all
2102 like the measles - all the

measure
4147 in little measure and evil

measured
1273 I have measured out my life

meat
4401 The dish of meat is too

media
4068 The media. It sounds like

medical
270 where the medical profession
2239 In disease Medical Men guess:
4577 in advance of medical thought.

medicinal
346 Medicinal discovery, It moves

medicine
1381 practice of medicine is a
3177 to take medicine is perhaps
3178 masses not to take medicine.
4139 magic for medicine; now, when
4248 In medicine, sins of

medicos
3519 And of medicos marvelling

medieval
949 Medieval marriages were

mediocre
1855 are born mediocre, some men
2855 and a mediocre one

mediocrity
2063 republic of mediocrity, genius is

mediterranean
3776 from the Mediterranean - from

medley
3205 of song, A medley of

meek
2728 Pity the meek for they

meet
2933 And we meet with champagne
3280 Every man meets his

meetings
1524 Meetings are indispensable

megalomania
304 States is megalomania, that of

mellow
2928 Indeed is too mellow for me.

melody
3328 You're a melody From a

member
1258 a standing member: an
2754 will accept me as a member.

memoirs
3261 write one's memoirs is to
3596 did do - well, that's memoirs.

memorandum
835 don't make a memorandum of it.'

memories
397 God gave us memories that we
3883 ought to have good memories.
4058 The memories of men are too

memory
185 he has a very good memory.
593 imagination for their memory.
874 Memory is the thing you
2134 say, 'His memory is going'.
2305 in a man's memory if they
2359 of his memory, but no
2940 good enough memory, he should
3087 of a bad memory is that
3121 am speaking only from memory.
3504 should have a good memory.
3546 remarkable memory; I forget
3744 health and a poor memory.
3871 to his memory for his
3872 say, quite from your memory.

men
39 hell to men, hell to
82 We men have got love well
114 his men were
186 marriage, men would
239 What men usually ask of
249 W men have their faults
255 knew what men meant When
331 Men are all so good for
682 Men build bridges and
913 I love men, not because
990 Men will wrangle for
1231 us that men and
1264 Men's men: be they gentle
1312 Men are what their
1392 old bald men wouldn't
1957 O! men with sisters dear,
2341 majority of men devote the
2495 like a man? Men are so

2556 Some men are good for
2795 I want is men who will
2819 Men have a much better
2927 consists of men, women,
3039 though he had 200,000 men.
3250 Men are generally more
3488 our best men are dead!
3539 the wisest men make fools
3676 I like men to behave like
3774 I see of men, the more
3864 When men reach their
4007 the men we wanted
4234 to know of men, the more
4460 not the men in my life
4476 to expect men to do all
4608 sexes: men, women who

mend
184 man would mend a man,
480 tried to mend the
2954 worst, they generally mend.

mentality
2511 with the mentality of a fox

mentioned
4242 family that is never mentioned.

mentioning
3534 without mentioning a single

mercury
2549 to pick up mercury with a

mercy
1361 and leaving mercy to heaven.
2641 Hae mercy o' my

merit
1313 The merit claimed for the

mermaid
2241 than the Mermaid Tavern?

merriment
2156 than a scheme of merriment.

merry
226 good to be merry and wise,
3760 never was a merry world

merry-go-round
2672 no go the merry-go-round, it's no
4191 on the merry-go-round, you have

mess
1817 fine mess you've
2832 Don't mess with

message
171 pay for a message sent to
340 electric message came: `He

messages
1712 messages should be

messing
1747 as simply messing about in

met
373 I met a lot of people in
2496 We met at nine. We met at

metaphysic
769 as high As metaphysic wit can

metre
2557 of God and man and metre.
3502 though its metre was to

mexico
1116 Poor Mexico, so far from God

mice
4098 Like little mice, stole in

mickey mouse
3328 sonnet, You're Mickey Mouse!

microbe
461 The Microbe is so very small

microbes
190

microscope
461 To see him through a microscope.

microscopic
3315 not man a microscopic eye? For

middle
551 stay in the middle of the

middle age
11 centre of middle age. It occurs
191 Middle age is when you have a
1028 Middle age is when your broad
3048 Middle age: when you're sitting
3057 begins And middle age ends, The
3529 Middle age is when you're faced
3640 I am old. Middle age was the

middle ages
637 than in the Middle Ages, when one
3924 live in the Middle Ages And be

middle class
467 The Middle Class was quite
3165 the sinking middle class .. may

middle classes
1594 ye lower middle classes! Bow, bow,

middle east
1916 The Middle East is a region where

middle-aged
2053 Middle-aged people are often
2134 a young or middle-aged man, when
3752 watches her middle-aged children
4211 length, the middle-aged man

middle-class
4424 control is flagrantly middle-class.

middlesex
538 Elysium - rural Middlesex again.

midge
536 And lightly skims the midge.

midnight
313 room at midnight See us
3806 a-bed after midnight is to be

might
4428 Britons alone use Might'.

mighty
4489 down the mighty from their

migrations
1705 and all our migrations from the

mile
713 of dog than miles of
1074 the square mile; they are
3379 walked a mile in his

military
954 to entrust to military men.
1397 toys but of no military value.
3840 When the military man

milk
1589 seem, Skim milk
1778 with the milk of human
3015 Drinka Pinta Milka Day.
3041 is moo, the other, milk.

millennium
2024

million
2011 to make a million .. the
2522 you make a million? You start

millionaire
3233 marrying a millionaire, to fall
3834 I am a Millionaire. That is my

millionaires
1376 All millionaires love a baked
4294 opposed to millionaires, but it

milton
1972 more than Milton can To
2143 Milton, Madam, was a genius

mind
43 My mind is not a bed to be
78 see are the mind's best bet
271 has a good mind and sorry
384 My mind is very, very
439 matter of the made-up mind.
711 make up her mind to be
794 enters the mind through
810 whose mind watches
900 an open mind is
1028 your broad mind and narrow
1034 that my mind has not
1041 lose your mind when you
1067 what the mind is
1217 further impaired his mind.
2680 whose mind watches
3047 think my mind is
3149 body, his mind would be
3154 keep your mind
3289 classical mind at work,
3292 When the mind is thinking,
3359 your padlock - on her mind.
3368 activity of mind. Genius
3419 An indecent mind is a
3496 - Never mind. What is
3715 Free your mind and your
3994 is to the mind what
3997 writes her mind but in her
4246 her lover's mind if she
4352 The mind reaches great
4470 change his mind is the man
4581 sick, it's all in the mind.

minded
4022 to it, had minded what they

minds
606 many open minds should be
1110 Minds are like parachutes.

minefield
2713 fat, is a minefield - you have

mineral
1638 animal, and mineral, I am the

minimum
3152 paper work down to a minimum.

mink
251 needs a mink coat but a
380 of wearing mink is to look

minority
77 people to make a minority.
3563 How a minority, Reaching
3626 A minority group has 'arrived'

minstrel
1607 A wandering minstrel I - A

minute
394 a sucker born every minute.
1255 it's only a minute. But when
2753 leave in a minute and a

minutes
2710 diamond minutes. No

miracle
2944 monster or miracle in the
4260 prays for a miracle. Every

miracles
4439 Miracles sometimes occur, but

miraculous
4506 have a miraculous power of

mirage
1225 a receding mirage in an

mirror
1063 just had a mirror put over
1734 break her mirror early.
2525 A book is a mirror: if an ass
3712 The mirror is the conscience
3736 toilet without a mirror.

mirthfulness
436 Mirthfulness is in the mind and

misanthropy
1841 obvious resource of misanthropy.

mischief
3078 knowest the mischief done!

misdemeanour
4560 Dullness is a misdemeanour.

miserable
753 two people miserable instead of
2153 the world miserable has always
4155 it is very miserable, and

misery
1180 for the misery of being
2416 hands on misery to man. It
2589 amount of misery which it

misfortune
562 has had the misfortune to
693 is a great misfortune neither to
1232 What a misfortune it is to be
4509 as a misfortune; to lose

misfortunes
2601 The misfortunes hardest to bear
2783 Few misfortunes can befall a boy
3323 another's misfortunes perfectly

misleading
277 contains a misleading

misled
1195 have been misled; So they

mispronounce
2983 language: all men mispronounce it.

misquotation
3241 Misquotation is, in fact, the

miss
1041 you won't miss it very

missed
178 would have missed her; Had
1609 would be missed - who

missionaries
3576 horse racing and missionaries.

missionary
1130 the local missionary priest,
4500 would eat a missionary, Cassock,

mist
3393 A Scotch mist may wet an

mistake
622 The great mistake is that of
1266 forms of mistake, prophecy
1644 Man is Nature's sole mistake!
1851 to make a mistake, your
2181 recognize a mistake when you

mistaken
577 to be mistaken at the top

mistakes
203 with making mistakes. Just
1111 forget his mistakes - no use
1784 for the mistakes they
3273 makes no mistakes does not
4523 one gives to their mistakes.
4599 bury his mistakes, but an

mistress
350 but the worst mistress.
1790 marries his mistress, he
1816 and America as my mistress.
3310 And mistress of herself,
4609 A mistress should be like a

mistresses
419 better price than old mistresses.

mists
536 And low the mists of evening

mix
3144 I mix them with my

moanday
2211 All moanday, tearsday,

mobile
3334 being that he is mobile.

moccasins
3379 walked a mile in his moccasins.

model
1237 possible models for men

moderate
2395 a year a moderate income -

moderation
192 Even moderation ought not to be
2177 a thing as moderation, even in
2697 long as it isn't in moderation.

modern
807 suffice for modern man: he
935 Modern art is what happens
1813 the first modern man - so

modest
1983 A modest man is usually
3533 Modest? My word no .. He
4269 I was born modest; not all

modesty
289 His modesty amounts to
698 Enough for modesty - no more.
2941 aside her modesty with her
3230 true.' 'O modesty!' ''Twas
3894 cultivate modesty .. But I

moment
4395 I am in a moment of pretty

moments
3611 has lovely moments but awful

monarch
1432 greatest monarch on the

monarchial
2391 is to enjoy monarchial

monarchy
3174 Monarchy is the gold filling

money
17 put your money in your
27 how to get money except by
69 Money is better than
148 far as your money will go.
240 really big money, you
285 Money is something you got
326 may bring money, but
355 Money is like muck, not
374 Money, it turned out, was
389 thinks of money, you have
470 Rhyme. But money gives me
518 Making money is fun, but
648 marries for money, thee
739 demand your money or your
934 after the money is gone.
1113 make more money in private
1164 have any money, the
1208 It's other people's money.
1333 Money is the wise man's

1388 Her voice is full of money.
1422 sex for money and sex
1440 old dog, and ready money.
1458 - all the money to buy
1470 ask of money spent
1718 pay good money to go out
1751 There's no money in poetry,
1758 how to get money without
1870 between money and sex
1960 lend you money if you can
1998 to spend money where it
2075 there's money in muck."
2103 Running for money doesn't
2123 wrote, except for money.
2179 havin' money made it
2430 enough to get money from it.
2586 don't like money actually,
2661 of saving money: to be
2664 Money is the poor people's
2779 Money is like a sixth sense
2867 Money couldn't buy friends
3233 marries for money; they are
3293 bring money along with
3422 Money swore an oath that
3438 you or to lend you money.
3439 With money in your pocket,
3461 have to eat money, but
3466 me advice, give me money.
3493 pays your money and you
3541 Money is good for bribing
3582 give your money to while
3590 lots of money to even
3619 you to love money - it's
3643 up against money, for if
3672 got the money, so we've
3716 where the money went - it
3734 Money is human happiness in
3881 need the money, he
3989 Money is the most
4001 Money is always there but
4059 you've got too much money.
4063 Money isn't everything -
4163
4290 Make money and the whole
4354 Money has no smell.
4382 question of money, everybody
4585 a barrel of money, Maybe
4587 Money dignifies what is

mongrels
1377 of energetic mongrels.

monk
651 he vowed a monk to be; But

monkey
547 attack the monkey when the
1330 of the monkey at the zoo
1576 best is only a monkey shaved!
4085 a fiendish monkey at an
4501 his descent from a monkey?

monkeys
1746 Monkeys .. very sensibly
4552 a million monkeys banging on

monogamy
106 too many. Monogamy is the

monopoly
1894 best of all monopoly profits is
2484 is the monopoly stage of

monotony
3557 to a monotony of
4014 articulate monotony, And

monster
2944 a greater monster or miracle

monstrous
1362 That monstrous animal, a

montezuma
2678 imprisoned Montezuma, and who

monument
1277 Their only monument the
2086 - idiosyncrasy on a monument.

moo
3041 One end is moo, the

moon
673 promise the moon and mean
1677 when he landed on the moon.
2097 at the new moon, out of
4211 to the moon, or

moonlecht
2419 braw brecht moonlecht necht, Yer

moonshine
3673 atoms is talking moonshine.

moral
830 got a moral, if you
3839 he is moral when he is
4199 not be too moral. You may

morality
3091 Morality is the herd-instinct
3666 kinds of morality side by

morals
668 comes first, then morals.
1646 with the morals of a
2827 even in the field of morals.
3852 Have you no morals, man?

more
738 who knows more and more
2301 arrange for more? Brothers
3105 The more you let yourself
4612 believing more and more

morning
2418 up in the mornin', But it's
2547 me on a morning when he
3570 find next morning that it
4190 fact, are better by morning.

moron
220 the happy moron, He
3136 is not a moron; she's

mortal
1686 Her last disorder mortal.
3114 are mortal, but the
4248 are mortal, sins of

moses
2014 If Moses had been a

mosquito
3140 get into a fool or a mosquito.

mother
183 gave her mother forty
194 A mother is a person who if
509 hates his mother, because
2876 Care of his Mother, Though he
3456 love is a mother's; then
3472 An ounce of mother is worth a
3752 how old a mother is, she
4219 Her own mother lived the
4584 .. never called me mother.

mother-in-law
164 his wife's mother-in-law to his
1446 his mother-in-law are
1836 wife and a surprised mother-in-law.
2806 is a mother-in-law whose

mothers
1228 Tired mothers find that
1312 what their mothers made them.
3441 and therefore he made mothers.

motivation
692 The whole motivation for any

motives
2994 by our motives and others

moulting
3040 they're moulting They're

mountain
76 Up the airy mountain, Down the
3773 isn't the mountain ahead that

mountains
3713 toward high mountains - he

mourners
2993 of mourners he is

mouse
3452 When the mouse laughs at

moustache
2303 wax his moustache was - like

mouth
384 open, and so is my mouth.
1251 is keeping your mouth shut.
1530 is, one's mouth what one
2746 whispering in her mouth.
4044 problem with an open mouth.

mouths
3794 she made mouths in a

move
647 A high altar on the move.

moves
95 If it moves, salute it; if

movies
1663 Movies should have a
2630 of American movies abroad
3574 kill the movies, and that

mozart
632 Ah Mozart! He was happily
2474 that when Mozart was my

mp
1 Being an MP is the sort

mps
1600 lot Of dull MPs in close

much
4342 Much of a muchness.
4459 Too much of a good thing

muchness
1264 they're much of a muchness.
4342 Much of a muchness.

mucho
1514 Macho does not prove mucho.

muck
355 is like muck, not good
2075 there's money in muck."

mug
1276 Poetry is a mug's game.

mule
3451 None but a mule deserves

mules
3060 world of mules there are

multifarious
3897 of the multifarious ways By

multitude
2325 was: a multitude of one

mum
2415 up, your mum and dad.

mumble
630 (3) When in doubt, mumble.

mummy
2292 He had his Mummy's leave to

murder
1905 back murder into the
2050 Murder is a serious
2515 Murder, like talent, seems

muscular
195 Muscular Christianity.

museum
3700 may visit a museum but only a
3967 the British Museum Reading

mushroom
200 Man is more mushroom than
1015 too short to stuff a mushroom.

music
126 and guitar music is on the
274 All music is folk music, I
429 not like music, but they
1022 words about music, one of
2037 the inexpressible is music.
2168 Music .. the only sensual

2860 before the music begins
3313 but the music there.
3608 and I'll set it to music.
4327 civilized music in the

music-hall
1619 The music-hall singer attends a
2784 Music-hall songs provide the

musician
4301 Wagner, a musician who wrote

mussolini
2588 Hitler and Mussolini were,

mustard
1655 'Pass the mustard', and they

my-lorded
4174 him, and my-lorded him as

myself
342 If I am not myself, who will
393 I find I'm talking to myself.
1017 I like myself the best.
1070 inside myself, and she
2944 in the world than myself.
3894 busy thinking about myself.
4164 closest relation is myself.

mysteries
4309 mad, the mysteries disappear

mystery
662 grasped the mystery of the
2574 and a mystery to the
4528 The true mystery of the

mystic
1992 Mystic: a person who is

mythical
1876 about a mythical figure -

nail
3429 The nail that sticks out

nailed
2030 is not nailed down is

nails
3001 clean finger nails.

naked
550 Secretary naked into the
775 Half naked, loving,

nakedness
3287 stratagem to cover nakedness.

name
188 My name is George
629 that his name is worth
1121 with your own name.
2667 The name of a man is a
3962 a terrible name - A name
3977 your name perfectly,
4094 easier to name 10 artists
4106 'oss, my wife, and my name.
4236 face. My name is

names
3606 you forget names, then you

napoleon
2033 man is Napoleon; hence the
3767 Napoleon's armies always used

narrative
2088 is a prose narrative of some

narrow-souled
3322 It is with narrow-souled people as

nasal
2478 tread My nasal organ.

nastiest
1678 and say The nastiest thing in

nasty
1572 Something nasty in the
2114 turn very nasty at short
2919 you, is a nasty creature.

nation
178 Still better for the nation:
2307 and lazy nation, To puff
3365 burden of the nation's care.
3948 half of the nation is mad -

national
111 of grave national stress,

nationalism
48 Nationalism is a silly

nations
1231 men and nations behave

native
2118 in his native place.
3370 Yorker is a native of the

natives
3764 were only natives at the

natural
1692 he was natural, simple,
3180 The natural man has only two

nature
281 Nature, with equal mind,
437 is human nature so weak as
590 Nature never makes any
617 Nature thrives on patience;
824 joy in nature is the
1314 Nature is reckless of the
1325 Nature has given to men one
1598 comical How Nature always
1644 Man is Nature's sole
1930 Nature, when she invented,
2060 whole of nature is a
2196 thing in nature; a mere
2338 Mother Nature
2837 not Eternities!' Says Nature.
2985 the habit from nature.
3018 Death [is] nature's way of
3383 comb that Nature gives us
3408 a banker provided by nature.
3706 By nature's kindly
4471 much human nature in some
4480 Yes madam, Nature is
4481 Nature is usually wrong.
4555 stuff that nature replaces

natures
1315 Some natures are too good to

naught
2583 for nobody for naught.

navel
3426 Below the navel there is

navy
842 head of the Navy is that I
1586 Ruler of the Queen's Navee!
1588 Rulers of the Queen's Navee!
2679 in the navy of Charles

nbc
4398 information NBC piles on

neat
1350 much as a neat, clean,
1886 about baldness - it's neat.

necessary
4374 a very necessary thing.

necessities
3005 dispense with its necessities.
4598 The necessities were going by

necessity
1047 Thus first necessity invented
1085 the door of necessity, not at

neck
1004 he sticks his neck out.
3141 can break your neck in it.

need
1053 Women need a reason to
1960 that you don't need it.
2003 ain't in need is a
3639 Country both need you so.
4111 like this, I need the trip.

needed
2912 What's needed in this world
3741 It makes it feel needed.

needs
653 says prayers. Or needs to.

negative
2630 unfinished negative of which
2832 the negative Latch on

neglect
4192 to the neglect of his

negotiating
2549 Negotiating with de Valera .. is

negro
1073 the average negro could

neigh
90 me to neigh, grind my

neighbour
897 makes our next-door neighbour.

neighbourhood
3458 the house; buy the neighbourhood.

neighbours
1458 little more than the neighbours.
1474 Good fences make good neighbours.

neptune
2937 said to Neptune during a

nero
2802 by night. Nero fiddled,

nerve
3629 after the nerve has been

nerves
2586 but it quiets my nerves.

nervous
2239 disease, they call it nervous.

nest
1917 not throw it into the nest.

net
850 Net - the biggest word in

network
2150 Network. Anything

neuroses
6 is how to use your neuroses.

neurosis
4228 Neurosis is the way of
4315 A neurosis is a secret you

neurotic
129 and a neurotic. A
663 For the neurotic, the
1574 the neurotic, the
2830 Neurotic means he is not as

never
52 Never eat at a place called
802 jilted Than never be courted
1583 What, never? No, never!
2601 are those which never come.
3555 always, by God, never.
3592 used to be and never was.
4077 Never was born!' persisted
4421 but they never let you

new
226 you are on with the new.
2058 'This is new, therefore
3225 nothing new. The

new york
568 n: in New York, one who
1114 not in New York you are
2260 here in New York. There is
2981 New York, the nation's thyroid
2984 Like so; N'Yawk, N'Yawk.'

new yorker
2869 imperfection of a New Yorker.
3370 A natural New Yorker is a native

new-laid
1593 As innocent as a new-laid egg.

news
659 News is the first rough
1639 a lot of news, With many
1962 The good news is that
2486 I heard the news today, oh
3271 tension out of the news.
4076 It is a newspaper's duty

newscasters
1889 and it drives newscasters berserk.

newspaper
1339 One newspaper a day ought to be
2724 The art of newspaper
4076 It is a newspaper's duty to

newspapers
3279 of men and morning newspapers.
4069 It's the newspapers I can't
4441 impossible? Read the newspapers.

newton
2035 another Newton, a new

next
104 happens next is much

nice
852 of saying nice doggie'
2418 O! it's nice to get up in
2903 Be nice to people on your
3501 thoroughly nice people

nicer
83 really much nicer than men:
4563 But it's nicer, much nicer

nicest
1678 thing in the nicest way.
2978 the very nicest people.

nickname
1847 A nickname is the heaviest

night
4609 only for a night and away.

nights
2597 makes sech nights, all white

ninety
534 Ninety per cent of this game
1941 A man over ninety is a great

ninety-nine
1254 and years. Ninety-nine times, the

nip
3565 but I'll nip him in the

no
811 A man who says no.
1735 No' and 'Yes' are words
2209 Ulysses] No, it did
3984 to say No'; it will

noah
2035 one poor Noah Dare hope

noble
983 the spur of noble minds, the
2117 too, has noble wild

noblemen
1641 are all noblemen who have

nobles
3360 Nobles and heralds, by your

noblesse
4241 the French noblesse had been

noblest
2062 God is the noblest work of

nobody
171 sent to nobody in
1442 Who is that? Nobody.
4307 he knew nobody had said

noise
429 love the noise it makes.
1038 The noise, my dear! And the
1049 till they make a noise.
2316 A loud noise at one end and
3322 the more noise they make
4291 Noise proves nothing.

non-being
4228 of avoiding non-being by

non-fiction
344 use of her non-fiction tickets.

nonconformity
3162 history of Nonconformity behind

none
2835 None of your dam
3398 days is none of these
4618 a good one and none at all.

nonsense
180 A little nonsense now and then
317 It is nonsense to speak of
447 The nonsense which was
512 is simple nonsense: natural
740 home, are nonsense; but some
2776 what nonsense this was
3342 A little nonsense now and then
3555 your damned nonsense will I put
4034 The nonsense of the old women

nookie
1723 occasional satisfying nookie.

noon
1985 riser may sleep till noon.

normal
3169 God we're normal, Yes, this

norman
114 While the Norman Baron lay,
345 feel with Norman that I

north
2645 about the North, but live

norway
2117 Norway, too, has noble wild

nose
691 Any nose May ravage with
1501 has a great nose thinks
2288 his little nose .. 'Led
2346 further than his own nose.
3227 Cleopatra's nose been
3433 back and breaks his nose.
3612 A large nose is in fact
3732 lights upon his very nose.
4450 is not a nose at all,

noses
1845 very nice noses, or will

nostalgia
202 Nostalgia ain't what it used to
379 Nostalgia is a seductive liar.

not
354 young man not yet, an
475 Gun, and they have not.
970 I'm not ok - you're not
1142 is better not, she would
3449 to be than not to be.
4356 We are not amused.

note
2475 the very note, This is

notes
3731 The notes I handle no

nothin'
594 Pity costs nothin' and ain't
2285 'e wore Was nothin' much

nothing
56 can do nothing but as a
236 Nothing is impossible for the
238 What costs nothing is worth
331 so good for nothing, and
344 she was nothing. Nothing
808 person who explains nothing.
880 than a good womman? Nothyng.
886 about nothing - and then
927 it costs nothing to be
988 you have nothing to say,
1226 is that nothing is often a
1412 Nothing in human life, least
1601 war, Did nothing in
1718 bad television for nothing?
1737 at eighty, nothing at all.
1747 There is nothing -
1808 stand for nothing fall for
1844 There is nothing good to be
1952 Nothing ever tasted any
1989 - do nothing, say
2130 to say nothing, when he
2158 should have done nothing else.
2198 that doing nothing was a sin.
2269 Nothing to do but work,
2547 when he had nothing else to
2583 Nobody does nothing for nobody
2924 true I had nothing on. I had
2942 and nothing
3141 A hole is nothing at all, but
3352 can settle down to do nothing.
3467 Drink nothing without seeing
3469 it is to do nothing, and then
3491 Nothink for nothink 'ere, and
3837 He knows nothing; and he
3862 to know nothing than to
3992 labour of doing nothing.
4028 Toby, 'but nothing to this.'
4097 not love, Nothing can make
4110 as having nothing a-year,
4165 Nothing has yet been said

4338 void. Nothing in the
4526 Nothing that is worth knowing
4569 Nothing was ever done so

notices
1329 that nobody notices unless she

notion
1617 seem to suit her notion.

nouns
2963 is all nouns and verbs.

novel
2088 The novel is a prose
2662 A novel must be
3998 of the novel is that

novels
2676 child you lose two novels.
2781 half the novels that are

nowhere
2269 't is gone; Nowhere to fall
2270 Nowhere to go but out,
4486 up, with nowhere to go.

noxious
2267 Of all noxious animals, too,

nubbly
2291 Fish. 'Nice but nubbly.'

nude
2269 from going nude. Nothing

nuisance
1293 of one nuisance for

null
3125 city, is Null an' Void!

number
4267 the number of things

numbing
2667 a man is a numbing blow from

nun
3148 a nun would envy

nuptials
2244 day set apart for her nuptials.

nurse
465 a-hold of Nurse For fear
3107 of what a nurse should be
3889 offered the Nurse, not

nurseries
1358 are the nurseries of all

nurses
353 age, and old men's nurses.

nuts
3409 gives the nuts, but he
4181 - where the nuts come from.

oar
1560 of grab an oar and row

oath
3422 swore an oath that
3855 I utter an oath again may

oats
2171 Oats: A grain which in

3828 do for the old, to shock
3964 am putting old heads on
3996 can grow old with a
4090 Growing old - it's not
4273 than an old bird of

old age
405 To me, old age is always
3064 But when old age crept over
3309 frolics, and old age of cards.
4537 tragedy of old age is not

old man
1224 that an old man has for
1943 called an old man for the
2134 in an old man, people
2449 was an Old Man with a
3781 that is an old man and no

old men
208 Old men and far travellers
256 men think old men fools and

olden
3326 In olden days a glimpse of

older
33 is to go on getting older.
1035 As one gets older, one
2946 more, as I grow older.
3981 as you grow older that the
4347 growing older is that it
4606 The older you get, the more

omelette
473 admirable omelette and the
3404 as a pretty good omelette.

omnibus
1924 is an omnibus in which

omnipotence
1104 of God's omnipotence that he

omniscience
3946 forte, and omniscience his

once
2520 only live once - but if
2526 at least once a year; a
3194 you can only use it once.

one
3398 One of these days is none
3520 more than one man in bed
3674 of one gets

one up
3332 How to be one up - how to

one-and-twenty
1973 When I was one-and-twenty I heard a

one-eyed
1835 There's a one-eyed yellow idol

oneself
3098 to talk of oneself is a form

onion
3785 live in an onion that
3938 Let onion atoms lurk within

only
3698 It's the only thing.

oozing
2494 Oozing charm from every

open
384 very, very open, and so is
553 If you open that Pandora's
2027 yourself open to what is

opening
900 object of opening the mind,
3063 Opening night is the night

opens
3276 When a man opens the car

opera
267 language an opera is sung in
1016 The opera ain't over 'til
1534 Opera is when a guy gets
2822 Opera in English is, in the
2971 to the opera, like
3609 wonderful opera would be
4624 than of a grand opera.

operate
3881 really operate unless it

operatic
3373 so romantic, so operatic.'

opinion
315 a whole climate of opinion.
503 His opinion of himself,
1657 what a poor opinion I have of
1703 was ever of opinion, that the
2606 of public opinion is like
3267 I want your opinion I'll give
3576 of opinion is what
3737 your true opinion of

opinions
743 and his religious opinions.
1528 great many opinions in this
2603 never change their opinions.
2653 or so bad as their opinions.
2945 were two opinions alike in
3655 man's opinions are much
4565 made up of opinions and

opportunities
4173 with fair opportunities and

opportunity
2226 is only opportunity in work
3631 when he had the opportunity.
3694 Equality of opportunity is an
3845 with the maximum of opportunity.

opposite
3926 moving in opposite

opposition
916 an opposition is
1099 duty of an Opposition [is] very

optimist
789 The optimist proclaims that we
1994 to live with an optimist.
2008 An optimist is a fellow who
2091 - I remain an optimist.
2719 an optimist is a guy that has

oracular
3875 use of my oracular tongue,

oratory
3277 Oratory: the art of making

orchestra
426 for an orchestra: start
4143 to the orchestra, not

orchid
1210 isn't an orchid, he must

order
1663 necessarily in that order.'
1729 in that order. In
2711 things in order - God does
4420 with a wig to keep order.

ordering
1560 in just ordering people to

ordinary
1308 than an ordinary man, but
2404 or upon one of ordinary size.
2700 duke as an ordinary man is

organ
74 my second favourite organ.
547 when the organ grinder is

organism
757 of every organism to live

organized
3591 gets you organized for the

organizing
549 Only an organizing genius

organs
872 cry from suffering organs.

orgasm
3029 The orgasm has replaced the

orgies
2034 routine punctuated by orgies.

orgy
3028 An orgy looks particularly
3554 late. The orgy has moved

original
1764 profoundly original art looks
2166 good and original; but the

original sin
3294 did researches in original sin.

originality
2059 What is originality? Undetected

originals
3226 we do not admire the originals.

orphan
4449 'I'm a Norfan, both sides,'

orthodox
1977 preaching, that's not orthodox.
4083 not orthodox. She felt

orthodoxy
4404 Orthodoxy is my doxy;

ostrich
2681 wings of an ostrich. It

other
2209 did lots of other things
3545 bourgeois are other people.

others
306 to help others; what on
1919 is composed of others.
2357 in noticing them in others.
3826 not do unto others as you

ought
2053 that they ought to be..
2436 , 'so he ought to be'.

ounce
3472 An ounce of mother is worth

ours
1095 Indian said simply Ours'.

ourselves
421 old, but more like ourselves.
4231 in this together - by ourselves.

out
126 music is on the way out.
1512 They go out when
2270 to go but out, Nowhere
2473 you get out of it
3127 to keep it out of as many

out-of-doors
2687 indoors and out-of-doors, we should

outlast
2084 that will outlast it.

outlived
849 eighty has outlived probably

outposts
2247 who has outposts in your

outrageous
4008 Outrageous acts and everyday

outside
85 Outside every fat man there

over
532 game isn't over until it's
2853 damn thing over and over.
4461 to put it all over you."

overcare
1443 health than an overcare of it.

overcoat
2600 is to put on your overcoat.
3560 pockets; my overcoat also was

overcomes
1450 end victoriously overcomes him.

overdeveloped
1526 the more overdeveloped the women.

overdone
604 but it can be overdone.

overfed
4244 Overpaid, overfed, oversexed,

overflowed
3933 He not only overflowed with

overheateth
1801 but it overheateth the oven.

overlook
2107 everything: overlook a great

overpaid
1874 Is grossly overpaid; There
4244 Overpaid, overfed, oversexed,

oversexed
4244 overfed, oversexed, and over

overtaxed
524 against the overtaxed.

overthrow
4004 to overthrow my

overtime
166 three overtime hours to
840 will work overtime for no

owed
1060 what he owed to others.
2661 to be owed by someone

owl
2457 The Owl and the Pussy-Cat
2873 He respects Owl, because
2884 Owl hasn't exactly got
3492 was an old owl lived in

own
57 want to own anything
1372 wouldn't like to own one.
2530 only to those who own one.

oxen
2144 drives fat oxen should

oxford
446 .. It is Oxford that has
1444 in the Oxford sense: you
1745 men at Oxford Know all
1774 it to be a street in Oxford.
2208 long be popular in Oxford.
3484 House to Rome, Oxford.
3979 will leave Oxford by the
3991 and sends his son to Oxford.
4237 To Oxford sent a

oxtail
2220 to the university of Oxtail.

oxygen
223 enough oxygen for two

oyster
490 eating one oyster cracker or
1949 open an oyster without a
2854 world is an oyster, but you
3868 An oyster may be crossed in
4113 man that first ate an oyster.

oysters
3681 Oysters are more beautiful

pacify
3197 down and pacify it with

pack
282 while, So pack up your

paddington
814 As London is to Paddington.

paddle
2292 leave to paddle, or else
2734 Every man paddle his own

padlock
3359 clap your padlock - on her

page
700 They have no page two.
1948 (moving the page back and

paid
694 but he will be well paid.
3354 these men paid their

pain
138 'Although pain isn't
139 I feel no pain dear mother
3761 the intermission of pain.

painful
1881 the painful publicity

pains
4100 heart: It pains a man when

paint
95 pick it up, paint it white.
616 attempt to paint the colour
3547 I paint with my prick.
3653 a pot of paint in the

painted
441 so young as they are painted.

painter
3548 A painter who has the feel of

painters
935 when painters stop

painting
573 Painting, n: the art of
3226 How vain painting is, exciting
3717 is a painting with

palaces
2047 of mock palaces clearly

pale
1651 I was a pale young curate

pall mall
2990 sweet shady side of Pall Mall!

panama
1832 keep the Panama Canal.

pandora
553 open that Pandora's Box, you

panther
3294 in panther skin Mona

pants
584 wears the pants in a
2749 like the pants of my blue
2850 public with his pants down.
3059 limbs in pants; Yours are
4385 seat of the pants to the
4417 who can't put his pants on.

paper
3003 like paper, and make
3796 not eat paper, as it
3995 of this paper appears

paper work
3152 to keep the paper work down to a

papers
25 he read in the Sunday papers.
3573 is what I read in the papers.

par
4296 shall not be taken at par.

parable
2934 sweetly in parable told, We

parachute
885 with a parachute packed by

paradise
1396 is the paradise of women,
2396 Same old glimpse of Paradise.
2892 They paved paradise And put up
3709 is the paradise of

paradox
4534 and winged it with paradox.

parallelogram
2437 is a parallelogram - that is,

parcels
4436 it in small parcels, That she

pardon
1725 Pardon me boy is that the
1853 God will pardon me. It's

parent
4387 As a parent you just hang on
4509 To lose one parent, Mr

parenthood
4229 Parenthood remains the greatest

parents
1 class parents want for
101 which parents have not
1236 is the way parents obey their
3043 that's what parents were
3266 our parents'
4257 needs good parents. From 18
4543 their parents; after a
4582 and parents exist to

paris
269 when they die, go to Paris.
552 of living in Paris.
1774 a suburb of Paris, until I
3406 could put Paris into a
4295 In Paris they simply stared

parking lot
2892 put up a parking lot, With a

parliament
3836 It enables Parliament to do

parliamentary
1727 has got the Parliamentary Party by

parochial
2077 provincial - he was parochial.
2393 hopelessly parochial when not

parrot
1023 morning, a parrot that

parsley
3049 Parsley is gharsley.

parson
903 him the parson ran, the
1048 The parson knows enough who
1178 creed no parson ever knew,
1683 too, the parson owned his
1909 years, If Parson lost his
3760 and the Parson left

part
1708 I read part of it all the
2090 to whom the part is greater

partialities
4272 and our partialities and

particular
1465 father's. He's more particular.

parties
787 Like other parties of the

partner
1558 Is judged a partner in the

party
121 huge garden party, faintly
1137 Stick to your party.
2312 people at a party, they
2625 The party needs a good
2683 was for a party; Then all
3327 What a swell party this is.
3583 that each party is worse
3585 organized party, I'm a

pass
759 trying to pass them on
4527 is to pass it on. It

passage
3882 frequent passage from hand

passes
3211 seldom make passes At girls
3298 don't make passes at female

passing
2695 George, passing slowly in

passion
1414 Passion destroys passion; we
2244 of a passion for a man,
2493 What is passion? That
3217 he vows his passion is
3338 and it is a passion to which
4020 betwixt one passion and
4160 when his passion shall have
4170 hopeless passion is my
4624 of a 'grand passion' than of a

passionate
314 any romance, however passionate.

passions
3180 two primal passions, to get
4027 but his passions which have

past
445 The past is a work of art,
3173 forward to the past.

3695 you the past is a
3703 the past are
3924 the past And

pasteur
3190 Louis Pasteur's theory of

pastime
2647 to a national pastime here.

pate
3306 beat your pate, and fancy

paternity
3721 the bond of paternity, which is

pathetic
2887 Pathetic,' he said. 'That's

patience
617 thrives on patience; man on
870 neither respect nor patience.
888 Patience is a most necessary
2070 Patience has its limits. Take
3391 handful of patience is worth
4320 in other people's patience.
4561 the patience of a

patient
3790 my lord, but not so patient.

patiently
1509 to bear patiently with bad
4092 a week patiently waiting if

patients
2905 time with patients; and if

patrician
1592 crust, A regular patrician.

patriot
1190 Never was patriot yet, but

patriotism
48 Patriotism is a lively sense of
2119 Patriotism is the last refuge of
2428 Patriotism is when you risk your

patron
2172 Is not a patron one who

patter
1649 patter Isn't

paul
3827 to pay Paul can always

pauses
3731 But the pauses between

pay
600 who will pay two
732 Pay, pack, and follow at
1559 going to pay every
2304 two ye must pay for one by
2307 therefore pay you cash
3390 does not pay weekly,

paying
2183 when they're paying for it.
3593 government we're paying for.
3626 entire group paying for it.

payroll
3775 he has to meet a payroll.

pc
3334 isn't a PC. It is a

pea-green
2457 a beautiful pea-green boat. They

peace
574 Peace, n: in international
2080 like the peace of God;
2467 as inner peace. There is
2498 They made peace between us;

peace-maker
3779 is the only peace-maker; much

peaceable
3661 peacocks are peaceable birds.

peacock
1737 a man is a peacock, at thirty
3661 that any peacock envies
4530 She is a peacock in

peal
1909 The wildest peal for years,

peanut
490 one half of a salted peanut.

peasant
3886 a stalwart peasant in a

peasants
4241 with their peasants, their

peculiar
1830 Funny peculiar or funny

pedant
3700 but only a pedant can live

pedestrians
1109 classes of pedestrians in these

pedigree
1123 The pedigree of honey Does not

peel
3130 Peel's smile: like the

peepers
2833 get those peepers? Jeepers

peepshow
2672 and a ticket for the peepshow.

peerage
3118 I want a peerage, I shall
4544 study the Peerage, Gerald

peerless
2557 lies that peerless paper peer

peers
1642 we love our House of Peers.
2525 if an ass peers into it,
2699 Peers: a kind of eye-shade

pelican
2839 bird is the pelican! His beak

pen
1796 Some with a fountain pen.
2516 The pen, in our age,
2587 the scratching of a pen.
4349 been rescued by his pen.

penalised
3341 penalised for a

pence
773 not of pounds, but of pence.
2608 care of the pence, and the

penetrate
4339 To penetrate one's being, one

penetrating
1360 requires a penetrating eye to

penny
1606 are a penny, and ever
2695 worn penny in the

pension
2673 hang your hat on a pension.

people
173 the world, people would be
275 are some people that if
661 Few people would not be the
719 all the people who know
998 of course, people are only
1038 my dear! And the people!
1212 that when people have no
1277 godless people: Their
1658 The people work with
1884 a nice way to start people.
1984 What people say behind your
2031 When people don't want to
2131 there are people whom one
2398 proved that people will look
2464 People don't ask for facts
2536 People who like this sort of
2768 you can give to some people.
3031 to see some people before
3067 People are like birds - from
3880 some people because
4044 Some people approach every
4440 not other people, hell is

peradventure
1906 there is no peradventure. It is

perceiving
2083 faculty of perceiving in an

percentage
423 It's a reasonable percentage.

perfect
4512 of us are perfect. I myself

perfection
716 to think of perfection; but it's
1695 The very pink of perfection.
2773 husbands a perfection that
3517 closest to perfection a person
4016 is death. Perfection is

performance
3792 so many years outlive performance?

performer
692 for any performer is 'Look

perish
939 Perish the thought!
1468 it had to perish twice, I

perished
4349 Caesar had perished from the

permanent
1124 more delightful than permanent.

pernicious
1042 Pernicious weed! whose scent the

perpendicular
3200 leaning out of the perpendicular.
3821 is] a perpendicular expression

perpetual
3914 mind is a perpetual feast.

perseverance
432 between perseverance and
4024 the name of perseverance in a good

persians
1750 Persians do not

person
131 of the person you would
315 no more a person now but a
819 the sort of person you and I
1799 a healthy person who
2723 there is a person born who
4622 The person by far the most

personal
1890 and permanently personal.
1933 be something personal about it.

personality
1252 muscles, but no personality.
2926 develop a personality once and
4565 personality, more made

personnel
1722 great men could pass Personnel.

persons
1845 Persons who undertake to pry

perspire
2290 dig till you gently perspire.

persuade
2365 faults to persuade people
3649 ways to persuade others is

pessimism
1993 Pessimism is only the name that
2091 face means pessimism, but in
3615 My pessimism goes to the point

pessimist
789 and the pessimist fears this
1994 A pessimist is one who has been
4531 Pessimist - one who, when he

peter
2557 peer Lord Peter, Who broke

peter pan
4314 in Peter Pan , and you

petitioner
578 of a single petitioner

pets
1023 have three pets at home

petticoat
2941 it on again with her petticoat.
4098 beneath her petticoat, Like

philadelphia
1367 I went to Philadelphia, but it

philanthropist
575 Philanthropist, n: a rich (and

philistine
2224 of the Philistine is his

philistines
1631 Though the Philistines may

philosopher
941 but some philosopher has said
1239 to be a philosopher; but, I
3783 never yet philosopher That could

philosophers
2186 All men are Philosophers, to their
3503 of philosophers into sages

philosophies
740 All philosophies, if you ride them

philosophize
317 he eat than that he philosophize.

philosophy
1267 faced with philosophy and
1687 This same philosophy is a good
2255 to build a philosophy. It
2576 a simple philosophy. Fill
3710 a system of philosophy to be
3740 a new philosophy - I only
4019 Philosophy has a fine saying for

phone
4224 did you answer the phone?

phrases
1630 in novel phrases of your

physical
1671 about his physical or moral
3103 by a little physical antipathy.

physician
694 to live, a physician will be
3178 of the physician is to
3364 died last night of my physician.
3421 Every invalid is a physician.
4618 a good physician and a bad

physicians
51 the help of too many physicians.
464 Physicians of the Utmost Fame
3510 drunkards than old physicians.

physics
2821 resort to physics and
3671 is either physics or stamp

pianist
3731 than many pianists. But the
4515 shoot the pianist. He is

picasso
1873 sausage and thinks of Picasso.
2868 divides them like Picasso.
4485 can't stand Picasso, those who

piccadilly
1631 walk down Piccadilly with a

pick
95 move, pick it up; and
189 to' don't pick no cotton.
273 should pick out a good

picket-guard
1941 he is a picket-guard at the

picking
575 is picking his

picture
1939 painting a picture, not doing
3011 Every picture tells a story.

pictures
826 'without pictures or
1712 Pictures are for
4603 Pictures deface walls oftener

piddles
3023 I write as a sow piddles.

pie
53 want no pie in the sky
387 buttons on a custard pie.
3331 put into a pie by Mrs

pie-crust
4123 and pie-crust are made

pig
911 with a pig. You get
2458 'Dear Pig, are you
4262 selling of pig in a poke.

pig-woman
2187 of the pig-woman's booth

pigeons
173 to fly over pigeons for a
4003 Pigeons on the grass alas.

piglet
2871 the more Piglet wasn't

pigs
832 And whether pigs have

pile-driver
928 Use a pile-driver. Hit the

pill
4188 take the pill. Roman

pillow
1798 the feather pillow, bears the

pillows
3444 faster, we need the pillows.

pills
2469 you bitter pills in sugar
2831 some 'do-give-a-damn' pills.

piminy
1634 miminy, piminy,

pimpernel
3147 That demmed, elusive Pimpernel?

pin
3569 have heard a pin drop.

pineapple
3874 is the very pineapple of

pink
1695 The very pink of

pinko-grey
1406 races are really pinko-grey.

pins
2293 as a row of pins - For the

pint
3123 A pint of plain is your

pioneer
3167 the clarity of a pioneer axe.

pious
1185 In pious times, ere

pipe
388 in your pipe, my Lord

piracy
576 Piracy, n: commerce without

pirate
1636 thing To be a Pirate King.
2521 was his pirate ship but

piss
1539 a pitcher of warm piss.

pissed
1962 that he's really pissed off.

pissing
2113 the tent pissing out than

pistol
2385 pun] is a pistol let off at

pit
2079 of the pit that is

pitcher
1539 worth a pitcher of warm

pitt
814 Pitt is to Addington As

pity
594 Pity costs nothin' and
2728 Pity the meek for they

place
466 know their place, and not
497 us in our place is
1053 sex - men just need a place.
3317 Get place and wealth, if
3748 God! this is an awful place.
3901 A place for everything, and

placebos
2635 be cured by his own placebos.

plagiarism
2059 Undetected plagiarism.
2904 it's plagiarism; if you

plagues
812 But of all plagues, good

plain
1706 me pretty plain, that they
1869 the really plain people
2935 Be plain in dress, and
2989 is that plain' cooking

plainer
2462 Tree The plainer than ever

plaintiff
944 argument, abuse the plaintiff.

plans
2349 we are making other plans.

plant
1304 a weed? A plant whose

planted
1074 commonly planted too close.

plateau
1378 a permanently high plateau.

platitude
2724 to stroke a platitude until it
4079 is a solemn platitude gone to a

plato
1631 à la Plato for a
4093 with Plato, and more

play
276 What we play is life.
281 her sons at play, Sees man
459 a pretty play fellow for
1251 is x; y is play; and z is
1275 A play should give you
1965 If you play it, it's
2394 you have played it
2504 this may be play to you,
2939 When I play with my cat,
3063 before the play is ready

playboy
4134 the only Playboy of the

played
2618 my Campaspe played At cards

player
4011 hurt a ball player. It's

playing
160 other half playing out of
2375 only play at playing at them.
3000 work terribly hard at playing.

pleasant
1690 all that was pleasant in man.
2455 'How pleasant to know Mr
2953 something pleasant happens to
4102 be very pleasant if it were

please
2733 If you please, ma'am, it was
4131 is - try to please everybody.

pleased
19 He more had pleased us, had he
1494 is good when he is pleased.

pleases
3967 think it pleases a man when

pleasure
266 fool bolts pleasure, then
357 a lie doth ever add pleasure.
364 The great pleasure in life is
428 of giving pleasure to
470 gives me pleasure all the
562 pursued pleasure that he
737 To make pleasure pleasant,
792 only as far as the pleasure."
1052 only safe pleasure for a

policy
554 [foreign] policy is to be
2054 the best policy. It is
3689 English policy is to float
3849 My only policy is to profess
4477 is the best policy; but he

polished
1586 And I polished up the

polite
927 costs nothing to be polite.

politeness
788 glance of great politeness.
2314 When suave politeness, tempering
3874 the very pineapple of politeness!

political
362 death of a political economist.
1223 he ducks political meetin's,
2826 that of a political aspirant
3766 for fear of Political Economy.
3837 clearly to a political career.

politician
586 is the Politishun's golden
623 art of a politician is to
796 An honest politician is one who
951 of a politician's life is
1055 a politician is an arse upon
1091 Since a politician never
1556 That politician tops his part,
2550 A politician was a person with
2708 taste, especially a politician.
2722 that when a politician does get
3099 A politician divides mankind
3344 For a politician to complain
3345 A politician crystallises what
3604 successful politician is he who
3795 a scurvy politician, seem To
4254 A politician is a man who
4405 I'm not a politician and my

politicians
2261 Politicians are the same all
3342 would we politicians be if we
4094 any century than 10 politicians.
4558 Politicians make good company for

politics
334 From politics, it was an easy
367 Politics is not a good
614 Politics is like football - it
1092 Politics are too serious a
1136 Laws of Politics: 1. Get
1761 They politics like ours
1899 taken the politics out of
2636 women would have on politics.
2758 Politics doesn't make strange
2987 Politics is a field where
3221 enter local politics solely as
3530 Politics is supposed to be the
3583 about this Politics thing, you
3587 truth into politics you would
3590 Politics has got so expensive

3870 than it has with politics.
4203 Politics is the gizzard of
4341 Politics is the art of
4614 Russian Or on Spanish politics?

pollution
1490 Pollution is nothing but
2338 Air pollution is turning Mother
3969 engine of pollution, the dog.

polo
3132 Sex - the poor man's polo.

polygamy
1185 Before polygamy was made a
1996 Polygamy: an endeavour to get

ponder
630 in charge, ponder. (2) When

pondering
3071 find myself pondering on how to

ponies
1909 blind, pit ponies, And

pooh
2874 Pooh began to feel a

poor
61 - the best poor man's
327 for being poor - which is
349 but it keeps them poor.
1756 Too poor for a bribe, and
1773 I am a poor man, but I
2057 saints were poor, it does
2225 and the poor get
2683 helped the poor, And the
3440 them, the poor would make
3461 luckily the poor provide
3722 The poor don't know that
3790 I am as poor as Job, my
4171 rich woman as a poor woman.

pop
2707 goes - Pop goes the

pope
605 should the Pope be any
4089 a President, not a Pope.

popular
2208 long be popular in Oxford.
2863 bad she was very very popular.

popularity
3249 Avoid popularity; it has many

population
404 by a whole population which
1703 and only talked of population.
1919 the entire population of the
3518 about the population explosion,

porcupine
1783 The porcupine, whom one must
2263 a couple of porcupines under

port
519 It would be port if it
2127 for boys; port, for men;
4446 All port tastes the same

portioned
2683 were fairly portioned; The

portrait
2315 same, of a portrait, in frame,
3717 A portrait is a painting with
3718 I paint a portrait I lose a

position
4294 to offer me the position.

positive
577 To be positive: to be mistaken
2832 the positive

posse
18 nothing; in posse I am

possessed
976 mankind are possessed by them.

possession
50 The possession of gold has
4084 perpetual possession of being
4345 but the possession of it is

possibility
2044 to deny the possibility of

possible
1577 probable, possible shadow of
4441 Possible? Is anything

post
525 come. Lie follows by post.

postal
2417 sun, Its postal districts

poster
292 is, at least, a great poster.

posterity
24 decided to write for posterity.
1155 go down to posterity talking

posthumously
3093 either; some are born posthumously.

postponed
2008 going to be will be postponed.

postponement
2857 most of us one long postponement.

postscript
3997 her mind but in her postscript.

pot
193 - where the pot calls the
2216 make them in the one pot.

potato
3183 is like a potato - the only

potency
1457 highest expression of potency.

potentiality
3705 as full of potentiality as he is

pound
3472 is worth a pound of clergy.

pounds
773 Pounds are the sons, not of
2606 is sixteen pounds to the
2608 and the pounds will take

poverty
69 better than poverty, if only
365 Poverty is an anomaly to rich
458 Come away; poverty's
3937 Poverty is no disgrace to a
4311 honest poverty a little,

power
16 A friend in power is a
88 Power is like a woman you
241 who has the power and skill
471 accursed power which
518 use the power it brings.
1061 If absolute power corrupts
2042 some great power would
3161 Liberal - a power worshipper
3237 Without the power to drink
3673 a source of power from the
3989 It confers power on whoever
4136 authority and minimal power.
4506 miraculous power of turning

powerful
1148 and with a powerful middle
1442 Who is powerful? He that

powers
922 have powers at their
1305 brings out all one's powers.

practical
851 Practical, simple, cheap and
2051 a most practical plan: You

practice
3624 a very good practice always to
3666 but do not practice, and the
3857 put it in practice not only

practise
3867 you would practise this

practised
2775 be practised at spare
3632 is still very much practised.

praise
435 kind of praise is that
1315 good to be spoiled by praise.
1405 Praise the Lord and pass the
1438 Praise to the undeserving is
1527 where men praise courage
2308 shall praise us, and
2331 without the praise of the
2363 To refuse praise reveals a
2738 They praise those works, but
3956 everybody praise the Duke,

praised
2401 God be praised the

praising
764 doing one's praising for
3924 are always praising the past

pram
1009 than the pram in the

pray
239 when they pray is that

393 When I pray to Him I
434 a man to pray cream and
578 Pray, v: to ask that the
3931 going to pray for you at

prayer
117 is the Tory party at prayer.
2197 Common Prayer, The organ
2306 he made his prayer (Even as
4271 relief denied even to prayer.
4296 In prayer we call ourselves

prayers
530 that has said its prayers.
653 says prayers. Or needs
1909 with angry prayers For tamed
2061 that all my prayers have not
3065 our prayers and

praying
3182 No praying, it spoils
4142 you are praying; if God

prays
4260 a man prays for, he

preach
3411 the fox preaches, look to
3666 which we preach but do not

preachers
2571 When I need preachers I buy 'em
3762 Preachers say, Do as I say, not

precedency
2142 point of precedency between a

precisian
2765 The devil turned precisian!

predatory
3747 person with predatory instincts

predecessor
731 Unlike my predecessors I have

predict
2066 can only predict things

predicted
2232 have predicted that by

pregnancy
2503 a kind of hysterical pregnancy.
2821 to avoid pregnancy by a

pregnant
2248 could get pregnant, abortion

prejudice
1643 everybody's prejudice I know a
4305 is fatal to prejudice, bigotry

prejudices
2818 the moral prejudices of the
3935 it; it prejudices a man so.

prepared
59 of being totally prepared.

preparedness
1666 guns? .. preparedness makes us

prerogative
2391 to enjoy monarchial prerogatives.

presence
892 It is the presence of mind
2072 need your presence more than
3497 better than presence of mind in

present
2914 Always present your front to

presented
91 One was presented with a small

presents
28 not for the presents, an
2072 more than your presents.
2377 Presents, I often say, endear

presidency
387 to make the presidency work these
1221 Th' prisidincy is th' highest

president
735 as the President's spouse.
952 be right than be President.
1020 ass as a president, and I
2022 by the president it keeps.
2802 any other President, whether
3109 not their President is a
4037 may become president, and I
4089 elected a President, not a
4251 being a president is like
4252 All the President is, is a
4561 office of president requires

press
3344 about the press is like a

pressure
2606 The pressure of public opinion

presume
3987 Dr Livingstone, I presume?

presumption
4221 be amused by its presumption.

pretend
1064 I do not pretend to know what

pretending
4507 life, pretending to be

pretty
1391 girl can be pretty - but a
3350 Which is sometimes so pretty.
3374 us leave pretty women to
4423 plain. The pretty can get

prevents
992 but prevents others
2769 has that prevents him

prey
1761 The greater prey upon the
4121 that on him prey; And these

price
137 A fair price for oil is
214 will not raise your price.
483 have a price tag on the
504 The price of justice is
1492 me in the price but not in
2180 use at a price you can't
3401 The price spoils the

3835 Wot prawce Selvytion nah?
4065 is a high price to pay for
4522 knows the price of

prick
3547 with my prick. (possibly

pricking
3973 knight was pricking on the

pricks
2110 has the pricks on the
3789 Honour pricks me on. Yea,

pride
992 paradox in pride: it makes
1504 Pride, perceiving humility
1505 Pride had rather go out of
1552 Parthenia's pride! He saw,
1608 my family pride is
1702 Pride in their port,
2139 fellow whom pride, or
3735 Pride is the direct

priest
4132 actor and a priest both

primal
3180 only two primal passions,

prime
510 48 - in the prime of my
3965 One's prime is elusive.

prime minister
467 be The next Prime Minister but three:
1727 The Prime Minister has got the
2794 girl or a turned-out Prime Minister.
3909 when the Prime Minister tries to
4180 the Prime Minister should be

prime ministers
376 wild flowers, and Prime Ministers.
922 with which Prime Ministers have never
3688 know that Prime Ministers are wedded

primitive
27 A people so primitive that they
2628 is the last primitive society in

principle
338 though not in principle.
2334 go on the principle that it
2497 a simple principle for the
2570 men to rise above principle.
2596 believe in princerple, But oh, I
4367 The first principle of war is:

principles
1137 Damn your principles! Stick to
2592 It ain't by princerples nor men My
4039 fight for principles than to

print
2967 'tis devils must print.
4196 own licence to print money.

printing
821 Gunpowder, Printing, and the
2132 for not printing any list

private
255 to dine; Private room,

318 Private faces in public
743 his private parts, his
1113 more money in private life.
1212 for private usefulness
1856 field to private industry.
2595 trusts To very privit uses.

privilege
471 stands on Privilege (And goes
1525 People of privilege will always
1579 But the privilege and pleasure

privileges
2828 is not rights, but privileges.

probability
1732 the laws of probability, North

probable
1577 doubt - No probable, possible

problem
700 has a real problem. They
1112 are confronted with a problem.
1176 a three-pipe problem, ..
2243 now it is a problem to be
3888 A problem left to itself
4044 every problem with an

problems
1719 in your problems, and they
2701 kinds of problems, except

procession
4284 in that procession but
4574 room, a solemn procession of one.

procrastination
2718 procrastination is the art of keeping

produceful
3052 consumeful or very produceful.

productions
3568 all the new productions must do as

profanity
4271 profanity furnishes

professed
1528 of them are professed by people

profession
3530 oldest profession. I have
3581 profession on earth.

professionals
2230 Amateurs hope. Professionals work.

professions
4206 one of the professions which are

professor
319 A professor is one who talks in
2220 regius professor of French

profit
2674 blow the profit. The glass

profitability
1182 Profitability is the sovereign

profitable
2721 it is not profitable to its

profits
624 It profits a man nothing to

profundity
3100 Profundity of thought belongs to

programme
232 So Much a Programme, More a
4554 not making programmes for the

progress
81 retreat; that is progress.
757 All progress is based upon a
1004 He makes progress only when
1293 we call progress' is the
3053 Progress might have been all

prohibition
3594 is like prohibition, it's a

project
1804 The project as understood by

prolonging
1262 interest in prolonging the lives

promise
484 about the promise of spring
673 can promise the moon
1207 boy the promise of a man,
2261 over. They promise to build a
2262 we should promise people
3566 king Whose promise none

promises
406 the man who promises least;
4123 Promises and pie-crust are

pronounce
4285 Vinci and pronounce it Vinchy;

proof
2165 'Tis a proof that he
3442 'For example' is not proof.

property
898 respect property. They
949 a matter of property, and, as

prophecy
1266 of mistake, prophecy is the

prophesy
2599 Don't never prophesy - unless

proportion
3219 in inverse proportion to the sum
4212 is rich in proportion to the
4273 well the proportion of things.

propose
1099 and propose nothing.

prose
1934 write in prose you say
4012 curse Of a prose which

prospect
1600 The prospect of a lot Of dull

prosper
1821 doth never prosper, what's

prosperity
1650 say, Of more prosperity than A.

prostrate
3237 is he, who prostrate lies,

protect
2699 glass, to protect us from
4364 - I can protect myself

protected
3151 squirrels, must be protected.

protecting
573 the art of protecting flat

protestant
453 PAT: A Protestant with a
1151 A Protestant, if he wants aid or
4188 Protestant women may take the

protoplasmal
1608 back to a protoplasmal primordial

proud
1756 and too proud to
2170 is always proud of himself
3656 are always proud of the

prove
2808 trying to prove that the
3549 Prove to me that you're no

provence
4556 Than you found it in Provence?

proverb
2242 A proverb is no proverb to
3670 A proverb is one man's wit

proverbs
3064 wrote the Proverbs And King

providence
1150 thanks to Providence that his

provincial
2077 worse than provincial - he was

prudence
336 forced into prudence in her
4277 and the prudence never to

pry
1845 to pry into, or

psalms
3064 King David wrote the Psalms.

pseudonym
1416 is the pseudonym of God

pseudopodium
3879 A lonely pseudopodium I wandered

psychiatrist
1711 goes to a psychiatrist should

psychiatry
212 Psychiatry is the care of the id
3266 Psychiatry enables us to correct

psychoanalysis
902 Psychoanalysis is confession without

psychotherapy
145 word for psychotherapy is 'talk'.

psychotic
2830 I am, and psychotic means he's

pub
964 and the pub opening

raised
4077 I was raised by a

rake
798 on the prongs of a rake.

ramble
1796 world I ramble, I see

rape
3367 rape is said to

raphael
4485 can't stand Raphael and those

raphaels
1693 of their Raphaels,

rapscallions
4264 All kings is mostly rapscallions.

rapturous
2479 The rapturous, wild, and

rarer
2348 nothing rarer than the

rarest
4207 thought was the rarest.

rascality
3982 relieved by rascality.

rat
3565 I smell a rat; I see him

ratiocination
767 And pay with ratiocination.

rational
324 he can be rational and
1171 work in a rational and

ratomorphic
2326 the rat, a ratomorphic view of

rats
3121 500 million rats in the

rattle
2485 you, just rattle your

raven
2602 with his raven like

razor
2930 a polished razor keen,
3320 to hew blocks with a razor.

reach
3045 everybody's reach, And it is

reaction
523 productive reaction against

read
463 but his books were read.'
807 and read the
2411 Don't read too much now:
2738 works, but read these.
3241 A widely read man never
3314 ignorantly read, With
3489 I never read books - I
3568 attempts to read all the
3654 power to read each
4441 Read the
4625 for people who can't read.

readers
1851 your readers might like

reading
1249 Reading after a certain
1417 know any reading more easy,
3152 Reading isn't an occupation
3866 writing's vile hard reading.
3893 people now reading and
3915 thing, but I prefer reading.
3994 Reading is to the mind what
4025 the soul of reading; take them

ready
993 and ready for more.
3063 the play is ready to open.
4463 I am not ready for an

real
233 reason and the real reason.

realistic
2631 to make a realistic decision',

reality
213 Reality is an illusion caused
663 over reality. For the

reaps
4056 hurry and reaps

rears
343 S-E-X ever rears its ugly

reason
233 are two reasons for doing
686 Fell, The reason why I
760 love - all reason is against
794 through reason can be
1053 need a reason to have
1542 listen to reason .. Reason
2493 vanish at reason's
2502 lose his reason over
2972 was neither rhyme nor reason.
3811 a woman's reason: I think
4027 is not his reason, but his
4095 die than it is to reason why.
4411 What is the reason of this
4553 Reason is an emotion for the

reasonable
1876 figure of 'The Reasonable Man'.

reasoning
1809 Man is a reasoning, rather than
3291 who was capable of reasoning.

reasons
2514 and has its reasons which are

rebel
811 What is a rebel? A man who

rebellion
4008 acts and everyday rebellions.

receipt
2000 like they expected a receipt.

receiver
2327 left the receiver off the

recent
4152 it approaches recent times.

1145 of the same religion.' ' And
1333 is the wise man's religion.
1412 of all in religion, is ever
1700 I take my religion from the
2011 is to start your own religion.
2056 Religion is a way of walking,
2825 fellow's religion, but only
3127 to bring religion into it.
3426 is neither religion nor truth.
3681 than any religion ..
3834 That is my religion.
3944 England but vice and religion!
4027 against religion, always
4139 when religion was strong
4382 is of the same religion.

religions
4372 forty-two religions and only

relished
180 and then is relished by the
1222 an' thin is relished by th'

remain
424 born mad. Some remain so.

remains
2309 cut up what remains Just roll

remarkable
2051 This very remarkable man

remarks
1163 said our remarks before us.

remedies
4135 are some remedies worse than

remedy
411 As a remedy against all ills
3514 a sharp remedy, but a

remember
185 a man can remember what he
974 point to remember is that
1027 best way to remember your
1126 thing to remember: writers
1168 Remember me when I am dead And
1730 Women still remember the first
2496 Ah yes! I remember it well.
2509 quite remember whether he
3703 who cannot remember the past
3768 It is what you can remember.
4094 good to remember that
4267 that I can remember, as the
4310 I could remember anything,

remembered
2161 will be remembered, and

remembering
1111 two people remembering the same

remorse
30
1045 Remorse, the fatal egg by

renewing
3546 constantly renewing itself for

rent
142 buy it, rent it.

repair
818 you can't repair it

repairing
3606 that cats or needs repairing.

repairs
606 should be closed for repairs.

repartee
904 is the unbearable repartee.

repay
459 Tiger well repay the

repeat
1018 be called on to repeat it.
1779 History repeats itself.
3703 are condemned to repeat it.

repel
296 and cheek repel me. I am

repent
3754 to give them time to repent.

repentance
1200 Repentance is but want of power
3381 is the best part of repentance.
4613 who feels Repentance on a

repented
783 and much repented, And

repertoire
2969 one's repertoire, the

replaced
386 has been replaced, as he has

reply
1858 tempted to reply, 'Who

reports
4300 The reports of my death are

reprehend
3875 Sure, if I reprehend anything

republic
2895 in a republic is like a

reputation
2955 my reputation will take
3728 I am better than my reputation.

reputations
1263 large home of ruined reputations.

required
1423 I am not required to do

requirement
1951 The first requirement for a
3106 very first requirement in a

requited
3188 are alike requited, God is

rescued
4349 sword been rescued by his

research
666 Basic research is when I'm
1451 years of research into the
1866 What is research, but a blind
2206 Research' is a mere excuse
2584 for a research scientist
2904 steal from many, it's research.

resemblance
3226 by its resemblance to things
3530 very close resemblance to the

resemble
559 that resemble, but do

resent
999 don't resent having

resignation
2754 accept my resignation. I don't

resist
4458 unless I can't resist it.
4520 I can resist everything
4529 to it. Resist it, and

resolution
550 carry this resolution you will

resolutions
771 Of great and mighty resolutions.

resolve
1447 If you resolve to give up
4621 purpose to resolve; In all

resolved
2631 that he has resolved to do

resort
157 is the last resort of the

resorts
2500 Pleasure resorts are like

respect
456 lack of respect for
870 neither respect nor
898 Thieves respect property.
2825 We must respect the other
3224 and starves your self respect.
3274 his respect for those
3658 as a rule respect public
3772 Let us respect grey hairs,
4289 at least respect his

respectability
386 West, with respectability and
3356 outside respectability and keep

respectable
1789 the most respectable woman has
2959 can go is considered respectable.
3678 who aren't respectable live

respected
1783 May be respected, but is

respecting
2873 can't help respecting anybody

responsibility
2316 no sense of responsibility at the
4067 subscribe - responsibility without

responsible
2537 forty is responsible for his

rest
3245 It is no rest to be idle.
3469 and then rest afterward.
4419 needs more rest if one
4550 life. The rest is merely

restaurant
297 a good table at a restaurant.
1679 tablecloth restaurant is still
2465 at a good restaurant, but not

resting
3644 in bed resting up from

result
4536 you get the result.

results
1235 Results! Why, man, I have

retainer
466 The Old Retainer night and

reticulated
2150 Anything reticulated or

retire
510 my life. Retire? Retire
995 length of time to retire.
1152 for him to retire from the
3864 sixties and retire, they go

retired
1077 role of a retired person is

retirement
3133 Retirement: statutory senility.

retiring
2152 think of retiring from the

retract
2637 Never retract, never explain,

retreat
81 ninety-nine retreat; that is
4609 country retreat near the

retreating
3059 you seen yourself retreating?

retrograde
2192 be not retrograde; But

returned
703 way And returned on the

returns
1420 nobody ever returns them; the

revelations
4542 garden. It ends with Revelations.

revenge
1791 no better revenge than to
4376 he took his revenge by

reversed
1729 the order would be reversed.

review
3538 I have your review in front

reviewing
3935 book before reviewing it; it

reviews
2523 When the reviews are bad I

revivals
758 art is the history of revivals.

revolt
1343 world is in revolt. Soon

revolting
3040 They're pretty revolting.

revolution
146 passion for revolution but an
1484 who rejects the Revolution.
2262 than only revolution, they
3591 One revolution is like one

revolutionists
2824 and revolutionists. They

revolutions
706 Revolutions are not made with
3675 like revolutions, should
3847 Revolutions have never lightened

reward
1345 are their own rewards.
1944 The reward of a general is
2710 No reward is

rewrite
4517 to history is to rewrite it.

rhetorician
768 For all a rhetorician's rules
1146 sophistical rhetorician,

rheumatism
1331 believe in rheumatism and true

rhubarb
2320 blancmange and rhubarb tart.

rhyme
1934 write in rhyme you say
2972 now it is rhyme; before,
3319 can, All rhyme, and

rhyming
878 Thy drasty rymyng is nat

rhythm
2104 between two rhythms, the

rib
3668 his rib. But male

ribs
642 all his ribs in his
1655 they roar their ribs out!

rich
46 happy to be rich, I'm
365 anomaly to rich people: it
575 n: a rich (and
854 you aren't rich, you
1385 the very rich. They are
1460 are like a rich father who
2225 surer, The rich get rich
2958 I am rich beyond the
3242 that of the rich for
3440 If the rich could hire
3461 The rich would have to eat
3652 ourselves a rich nation,
3918 we could be rich and not
4171 to marry a rich woman as a
4212 A man is rich in
4311 to become rich, so that I

riches
231 better than riches To scratch

350 Riches are a good handmaid,
2616 gives riches to those
4118 looked upon riches to be a

rid
3955 indeed am I rid of it all
4012 Which shall rid us from

ridden
2534 and ridden out of

riddle
2332 can make a riddle out of an

riddles
2480 'I'm bad at riddles; But I

ride
207 from the ride With the
2788 you cannot ride two horses
4013 the Haggards ride no more.
4387 just hang on for the ride.

ridiculous
47 of the ridiculous, but no
992 some men ridiculous, but
1742 the Sublime To the Ridiculous.'
3305 Alive, ridiculous, and dead
3386 be certain is to be ridiculous.

riding
4483 life In riding to and

rifle
2309 on your rifle and blow

right
62 Only if it's done right.
176 going to turn out all right.
235 who is right - only who
383 wrong than weakly right.
584 has a good right to them.
764 exactly in the right places.
890 all he does is right.
901 is all right; it is the
952 rather be right than be
1043 and then be right by chance.
1246 prove me right; a single
1254 hundredth time I am right.
2026 The right to be heard does
2042 do what is right, on
2129 man has a right to utter
2298 - of - them - is - right!
4141 make a right, but they

righteous
3028 mists of righteous

righting
2556 good for righting wrongs,

rights
512 Natural rights is simple
978 equal rights with men.
1848 things to rights have no
2828 is not rights, but

rimbauds
3209 he was always chasing Rimbauds.

ring
365 do not ring the bell.

1054 pierced the outer ring.
2458 Your ring?' Said
2841 not get the ring without

rise
950 thrive Must rise at five;
3237 floor Can rise alone and

risen
503 having once risen, remained

riser
1985 be an early riser may sleep

risk
695 runs the risk of
2004 without the risk.
2428 is when you risk your life
2638 equals risk plus
2690 a proxy for risk and a

risks
4037 one of the risks he takes.

ritz
2770 all - like the Ritz Hotel.

river
2261 even when there is no river.

rivers
2934 and like rivers grow cold.

road
895 There is a road from the
3046 the ads, And not the road.

roads
608 straight roads; but the

roam
1044 sent to roam Excels a
1701 Where'er I roam, whatever

roar
1495 your will roar when your
1655 and they roar their ribs

roareth
1665 this that roareth thus? Can

rob
1356 that is, to rob a lady of
1796 men, Some rob you with a
2190 nightly rob the dairy.

robbed
3076 once we've robbed a couple

robbery
657 the benefit of the robbery.

robbing
669 What is robbing a bank

robs
3827 which robs Peter to

rock
852 till you can find a rock.
4625 Rock journalism is people

rocket
3198 rose like a rocket, he fell

rogue
1196 that is not fool is rogue.

rogues
3356 keep them rogues and

role
1077 The role of a retired

roman
903 Before the Roman came to
3764 The Roman Conquest was,

romance
314 than any romance, however
336 she learned romance as she
847 historical romance is the
3947 Romance without finance is no
4545 years of romance make a

romances
4099 Are like romances read, or

romans
1854 The Romans would never have
2683 sold: The Romans were like
2685 To whom the Romans pray, A

romantic
1628 ruin that's romantic; Do you
2448 of all romantic poets
3551 much more romantic I'd be But

rookery
3372 that cawing rookery of

room
1772 I left the room with
2402 men can find room for.
3603 There is no room in this

roosevelt
1714 If Roosevelt were alive he'd

roost
3960 always come home to roost.

rooster
3459 even your rooster will lay
3471 and the rooster keeps

root
2078 is the root of all

rootage
4568 A man's rootage is more

roots
845 of these is roots, the
1872 is destroying his roots.

rose
691 with impunity a rose.
2730 dropping a rose petal down
3366 that, says Rose, I'll die:
4002 Rose is a rose is a rose

roses
2757 two dozen roses to Room
3952 coming up roses.

rosewater
706 are not made with rosewater.

rotted
3047 late, Or simply rotted early?

rotten
3888 up or goes rotten. But
4617 good feel rotten.

roughly
829 Speak roughly to your little

round
1475 only way round is
4220 that is round. Soon he

roundheads
3765 and the Roundheads (Right but

routine
866 third is routine. After

rovers
541 us are Rovers and

row
1560 an oar and row with them.

royalties
284 fond of fresh air and royalties.

royalty
2699 the full glare of Royalty.

rub
3643 try to rub up against

rubbish
1171 deal of rubbish, and yet
3154 a lot of rubbish into it.

rubs
159 The hard rubs of the world

rude
1529 rude as the
4538 never unintentionally rude.

rudeness
1913 Rudeness is the weak man's

rug
1433 snug As a bug In as rug.

rugged
1741 O'er the rugged mountain's
2125 is a rugged being.

ruin
425 a bit of a ruin that
2106 come to ruin most
2552 a bit of a ruin that
4545 look like a ruin; but

ruined
50 of gold has ruined fewer men
508 has been ruined by
1065 lives is ruined by our
4377 I never was ruined but twice

rule
143 can make a rule, and every
833 The rule is, jam tomorrow
932 make it a rule never to
1242 The first rule of
2813 made it a rule never to
2840 to obey the more they rule.
3128 It's my rule never to lose
3307 gen'ral rule That every
4108 infallible rule we know

ruler
2040 not a ruler but the

rulers
565 about by rulers, mostly
2761 are rulers who always

rules
217 the rules, his side
3060 of mules there are no rules.

run
296 of woman I would run from.
551 road. They get run down.
979 it over and try to run it.
2255 It doesn't have to run.
2515 to run in
2540 trying to run away, it
2681 him to run, though
3260 on the run? We are
4202 I should run for my

runcible
2456 He weareth a runcible hat.

running
836 all the running you can do
3301 man who teaches running.

runs
140 fights and runs away, May

rural
2029 woman in a rural spot!

rushed
3579 we have rushed through

russell
2922 me as you did my Lord Russell.

russia
3079 Russia has two generals in
4324 Russia is the only country

russian
170 Intelligent Russian once
1282 nice: her Russian eye Is
1591 have been a Roosian, A French,

rust
22 away the rust of the
4487 wear out than to rust out.

rustics
1683 the gazing rustics ranged

rutherford
4317 Margaret Rutherford is that

sack
3788 If sack and sugar be a

sacrament
1068 minor sacrament .. I am

sacrifices
3632 times, sacrifices were made

sadder
779 of woe, Sadder than

saddest
2826 The saddest life is that of a
3349 scenes Saddest this sight

safe
172 it was safe to go back
1106 is like a safe to which
2973 see me safe up, and my

safeguards
1428 that the safeguards of liberty

safest
1411 it is the safest thing we

safety-pin
111 for the big safety-pin at the top

sagacity
3642 who gains sagacity in youth,

sage
3222 you homely, make you sage.
3711 most foolish woman, a sage.

sages
3503 into sages and cranks

said
20 might be said on both
1019 I never said ever did
1183 things are said over
1426 you heard, not what I said.
1590 himself has said it, And
3225 is not be said that I
3771 what I have said, I envy
4122 as well said, as if I
4165 yet been said that's not
4307 - when he said a good

saint
3158 that a saint must
3318 madmen is a saint run mad.
3745 in order to be a saint.

saints
2057 most of the saints were poor,
3166 Saints should always be

sake
3757 their own sakes, for

salad
1689 Garrick's a salad; for in
2109 shit from chicken salad.

salary
1570 he had a salary to
4226 yearly salary, double

salisbury
1605 crossing Salisbury Plain on a

salmon-fishers
2744 But now the salmon-fishers moist

salt
4147 yeast, salt and
4469 having salt rubbed

salt water
4091 is like salt water, good to

salute
95 it moves, salute it; if it

salvation
3835 Wot prawce Selvytion nah?
4602 An idea is salvation by

same
340 he is much the same'.
836 keep in the same place. If
1035 exactly the same with
1500 are seldom the same man.
2396 Same old slippers, Same
3450 are not the same thing.
4446 tastes the same after

sanctuary
376 which need sanctuary more than

sand
3773 grain of sand in your

sandals
3428 wears out a thousand sandals.

sandwiches
655 freedom and sandwiches they will

sane
3836 that no sane person

sanguine
461 But many sanguine people

sanity
1289 It it's sanity you're after
1318 Sanity is very rare; every
3854 be achieved by brute sanity.

sank
2249 They sank my boat.

sans
1383 to lie, Sans wine, sans

santa claus
1351 as old as Santa Claus to a girl

sardines
502 a tin of sardines - we are

saskatchewan
2440 wheat' and Saskatchewan was born.

sat
1055 has sat except a
1798 person who has sat on him!

satan
4289 may not pay Satan reverence,

satire
1438 undeserving is severe satire.
2184 it's satire, but when
2235 Satire is what closes
2930 Satire should, like a
4112 Satire is a sort of glass,

satirist
1903 What satirist ever toppled the
2626 A satirist is a man who

satisfaction
2004 subtle satisfaction without

satisfied
4246 would be satisfied with her

satisfying
993 be a wholly satisfying link

saturday
1162 Empire on a Saturday night
2235 is what closes Saturday night.
3048 at home on Saturday night and

satyr
3284 either a stoic or a satyr.

sauces
4372 and only two sauces.

sauntering
798 you can go sauntering along for

sausage
1873 looks at a sausage and thinks

savage
936 A savage is simply a human
1446 untutored savage
2731 As savage as a bear with a

savagely
4369 they are fighting so savagely.

savages
1149 were brutal savages in an

save
1242 is to save all the
4156 It takes time to save time.
4364 God save me from my

saved
423 thieves was saved. (Pause)

saving
2113 you're saving your face

savings
2741 is past savings

saw
3192 I came, I saw, I
4443 I never saw so many
4567 No man ever saw a

say
283 you have something to say.
930 Say what you have to say
988 nothing to say, say
1018 you don't say anything,
1260 nothing to say, abstains
1402 to decide is what to say.
1418 people say a foolish
2575 you can't say something
3762 Preachers say, Do as I

saying
4019 has a fine saying for
4571 the art of saying nothing in

says
2626 and then says them about
3912 not what he says, but what
4015 man who says frankly

scalded
1507 The scalded cat fears even

scale
1379 The best scale for an

scallywag
366 Women love scallywags, but some

scandal
1359 Love and scandal are the best
1399 conquers scandal every
3271 public scandal is good

scare
1981 A good scare is worth more

scared
1480 afraid of like scared people.

scarlet
463 sins were scarlet, but his
1953 loves a scarlet coat
2193 though clothed in scarlet.

scars
1990 or diplomas, but for scars.

sceptic
2044 much of a sceptic to deny

scepticism
3723 only her scepticism kept her

schizophrenia
304 of Canada is paranoid schizophrenia.
4142 to you, you have schizophrenia.

schlemiel
3433 The poor schlemiel is a man who

schmuck
1097 than a schmuck for a

school
3000 At school I never minded the
3684 he's been to a good school.

schoolboy
2678 Every schoolboy knows who

schoolgirl
1611 Pert as a schoolgirl well can

schoolmasters
657 to some schoolmasters if they
1699 Let schoolmasters puzzle their
4582 Schoolmasters and parents exist to

schools
849 three new schools of
3592 The schools ain't what they
4128 in the schools, That

science
1267 and investigated by science.
2043 tragedy of Science: the
2335 fact that science, which can
2430 as the science of
3348 Of science and logic he
3625 Science is for those who
3671 All science is either physics
3946 Science is his forte, and
4139 strong and science weak, men
4335 Whenever science makes a
4536 is a science. If you

scientific
689 averred, A scientific faith's
1395 not very scientific, but it
1638 I know the scientific names of
4611 No scientific theory achieves

scientists
4189 behavioural scientists .. least

scintillations
1728 Let the scintillations of your wit

scissors
1907 always end up using scissors.

score
4222 kept the score Man wants

scorn
1596 virtuous scorn The

scotch
3393 A Scotch mist may wet an
3940 well into a Scotch

scotchman
2117 which a Scotchman ever sees,
2167 made of a Scotchman if he be

scotchmen
2378 to like Scotchmen, and am

scotland
2171 but in Scotland supports

scotsman
399 than a Scotsman on the

scoundrel
2119 the last refuge of a scoundrel.
3846 man over forty is a scoundrel.
4118 given them to such a scoundrel.

scow
1135 - an old scow which

scratch
428 all you can do is scratch it.
2576 full. And scratch where it
3204 Scratch a lover, and find a

scratching
2587 it but the scratching of a pen.

screwing
2560 I gave up screwing around a

scribblative
3959 arts babblative and scribblative.

scribble
1867 Always scribble, scribble,
3319 scrawl, and scribble, to a man.

scripture
2371 texts of scripture, I got my

scrivener
2380 and cropt scrivener - one that

scrooge
1120 'Bah,' said Scrooge.

scrub
2625 a good scrub with a

scythe
4451 Time with a scythe of my own.

sea
98 And all the sea were ink,
842 I am very much at sea.
1588 never go to sea, And you
2099 Love the sea? I dote

2101 and England is - the sea.
2215 snotgreen sea. The
3344 complaining about the sea.

seamen
2679 there were seamen in the

searched
3582 to while you're being searched.

seas
1518 troubled seas of

seaside
2609 to the seaside, is said

seasons
2837 'I play for Seasons; not

seat
1228 to the seat of the
4385 the seat of the

seatbelts
1071 your seatbelts. It's

seats
633 bought two or three seats.

second
1390 are no second acts in
3610 to hear it a second time.

second-rate
430 so many second-rate ones of
1968 up with poets being second-rate.

secret
1444 A secret in the Oxford
3092 me! The secret of reaping
3142 The secret of business is to
4315 is a secret you don't

secretary
4041 We hear the Secretary of State

secrets
1049 Secrets with girls, like
2823 so many secrets, we cease

secure
332 may secure all the

seduced
2794 from a seduced

see
103 man can see much
728 gie us To see oursels as
951 is that you see yourself
1005 can't go to see somebody.
2107 See everything: overlook
3031 gie us to see some
3795 politician, seem To see
4467 and see me?"
4606 learn to see what

seeing
1508 Seeing's believing, but
2138 Worth seeing, yes; but not
3424 Seeing's believing - but

seek
1555 alone I seek to please.
3147 We seek him here, we seek
3508 am going to seek a great

seen
1202 see and be seen, in heaps
2124 not having seen what it is
3175 but must be seen to be
4144 has seen and
4491 when you've seen one

sees
1032 woman never sees what we do
2308 Thing as he sees It for the
2947 A wise man sees as much as

seldom
2400 we knew how seldom they did.

self-abuse
1103 is the worst form of self-abuse.

self-denial
2508 that air of self-denial that

self-enjoyment
4558 do - their self-enjoyment is

self-esteem
681 to our self-esteem as to find

self-made
3991 A self-made man is one who

self-pity
493 rare as a man without self-pity.

selfish
338 have been a selfish being all
4055 slack and selfish, and

sell
243 enough to sell the stuff.
2347 Never sell the bear's skin

seminary
1613 Come from a ladies' seminary.

senate
1135 The U.S. Senate - an old
2628 The Senate is the last

send
2605 God'll send the bill to
4086 I could send everyone

senescence
3057 Senescence begins And middle age

senility
3133 Retirement: statutory senility.

seniors
2590 in and the seniors take none

sensation
1614 the sensation of a

sensational
4513 something sensational to read in

sense
47 have a fine sense of the
839 care of the sense and the
1100 Common sense is the best
2366 common sense except to

2648 o' the wee bit sense he had.
2779 a sixth sense without
2799 loses his sense of
2811 sports hates common sense.
3001 but common sense, and
3999 lose their common sense.

sensible
1145 Sensible men are
1319 No sensible person ever made

sensual
2168 the only sensual pleasure

sentence
807 A single sentence will suffice
2740 is not a word but a sentence.

sentimental
1631 Then a sentimental passion of a

separate
1997 it is to separate the wheat
2778 on they can separate, but if

separately
1439 we shall all hang separately.

separateness
1461 of their separateness; I'm

separation
747 bear the separation, but I
3879 Anon came separation, by

sequel
336 the natural sequel of an

serenity
181 is little serenity comparable
1427 apparent serenity of the

serge
2749 of my blue serge suit."

serious
339 is a very serious business.
954 War is too serious a matter
1092 are too serious a matter
1415 to look serious; because
1787 to be serious, but you
1833 for serious minds, a
2050 Murder is a serious business.
3814 much more serious than that.
4326 a funny way of being serious.

seriousist
1105 with the word seriousist.

seriously
2026 the right to be taken seriously.

sermon
662 the Sermon on the
3248 whole world than any sermon.
3509 hearing a sermon or praying

sermons
780 Laughter Sermons and

servant
1743 said, 'Your servant's cut in
3892 a civil servant. He was

servants
4366 The servants will do

serve
2956 We also serve who only
3916 set out to serve both God

service
3274 of no possible service to him.
4015 is doing a public service.

services
629 worth more than his services.

serving-men
2289 six honest serving-men (They

setting
1848 are fond of setting things to

seven
221 a thing seven years and
1129 be there at seven and get
1425 they are seven and anyone
1597 lowly air Of Seven Dials.

seventeen
4186 Seventeen and never been sweet

seventy
263 you are seventy, nearly
1946 To be seventy years young is

severe
2266 little too severe - like

sewer
1845 of a common sewer, either
2473 is like a sewer. What you
2901 through a sewer in a
4388 through a sewer in a

sewing
682 the job of sewing on a

sex
62 Is sex dirty? Only if
64 it. It's sex with
65 that sex is a
70 the answer, sex raises
75 Once sex rears its ugly
343 Delia, if S-E-X ever rears
374 like sex, you
392 you darling after sex.
710 know about sex and how
993 Sex ought to be a wholly
1025 Sex is the great amateur
1053 to have sex - men just
1063 place of sex in my
1164 money, it's sex. When you
1422 between sex for money
1517 about sex, because I
1782 apart and started sex.
1870 money and sex appeal,
1974 Sex is like petrol. It's
2426 said about sex, it cannot
2558 having sex and not
2560 that sex is a
2690 risk and a dummy for sex.
2845 people have sex life; the

2859 Sex is one of the nine
2965 another form of safe sex.
3069 in the sex
3132 Sex - the poor man's
3559 friendship, sex and death.
3724 is another name for sex.
4389 is like sex. When

sexes
997 within the sexes than
1911 says two sexes aren't
3927 are three sexes - men,
4608 have three sexes: men,

sexless
4553 is an emotion for the sexless.

sexton
1954 told the sexton, and The

sexual
1452 unnatural sexual behaviour
1731 Of all sexual aberrations,
2512 Sexual revolution has

sexually
156 Life is a sexually transmitted

shake
1626 With a shake of his

shakespeare
1849 should read Shakespeare. If we
2023 Playing Shakespeare is very
2035 to be Shakespeare, another
2147 is to Shakespeare .. as a
2194 honour to Shakespeare that in
4552 works of Shakespeare. Now,

shaking
2928 without shaking, Indeed is

shallow
127 Deep down he is shallow.
4528 It is only shallow people who

shame
1013 but for the shame of it.
2620 the heart is past shame.

shanks
271 a good mind and sorry shanks.

share
3976 child will share willingly
4334 a right to share your

shared
699 everybody shared enough,

shares
1606 The shares are a penny, and

sharing
3707 consists in sharing the

shave
1081 are old enough to shave.
4483 A man who shaves and takes

shears
3926 a pair of shears, so joined

sheba
3879 Queen of Sheba, or I King

sheep
920 A sheep in sheep's
1166 man, while sheep in
2055 for the sheep to pass
2889 else their sheep, Was all
3238 mountain sheep are
4014 half-witted sheep Which

shelf life
4243 The shelf life of the modern

shell
196 that gloomy shell He does

shelled
215 We shelled the Turks from 9

shepherds
4378 need both shepherds and

shield
247 often a shield than a

shifted
3847 have only shifted it to

shilling
2458 for one shilling Your
3354 paid their shillings to watch

shillings
1773 give ten shillings to find

ship
2175 Being in a ship is being

ships
39 Hell to ships, hell to men,

shiraz
611 red wine of Shiraz into

shirt
1605 In your shirt and your

shiver
506 should shiver on the

shock
1614 sharp shock, From a
3828 the old, to shock them and
4204 receive a shock unless you

shocking
3326 something shocking Now,

shocks
3667 that shocks the

shoe
3773 grain of sand in your shoe.

shoes
832 things: Of shoes - and
1700 I take my shoes from the
3755 for his old shoes; they were
3810 than over shoes in love.
4183 in, mind it wipes its shoes.

shoestring
4590 and runs it into a shoestring.

shoot
454 they could shoot me in my
907 man were to shoot his
1320 If you shoot at a king you
1818 war is! You shoot a fellow

1901 where I am about to shoot.'
3340 you could shoot snipe off
3885 Who shoots at the mid-day
4494 Shoot, if you must, this
4515 do not shoot the

shooting
3160 sport is war without shooting.
3475 thinking is shooting without

shopocracy
3117 hear you abuse the shopocracy.

shopping
369 Shopping is the perfect model
3716 I don't even like shopping.

short
2137 is very short . It is
3095 times too short for us to
3270 up some children is short.
4155 is very short, so it is

shortage
549 produce a shortage of coal

shortcoming
222 His shortcoming is his long

shorten
737 pleasure pleasant, shorten.

shorter
114 crying, Shorter hours and
1284 make you shorter by the

shortest
1102 and one of the shortest lived.

shot
907 him a good shot, but not
3528 to being shot at and

shoulder-blade
1621 have a left shoulder-blade that is a

shoulders
3964 your young shoulders .. all my

show
2658 if we are going to show.
4417 Show me a man with both

show business
4389 Show business is like sex. When

shower
675 an abundant shower of curates
2642 to have a summer shower'.
3169 this is our finest shower!

showery
1292 Blowy, Showery, Flowery,

showing
73 Showing up is eighty percent

shrapnel
4490 defensive hats, and shrapnel.

shrieks
3325 Not louder shrieks to pitying

shrimp
2259 until a shrimp learns to

shuffled
2559 pack is shuffled and cut -

shunting
731 my life to shunting and

shut
2755 his mouth shut and his
3308 Shut, shut the door, good

shut up
2408 tenderly. Shut up he

shutter
4169 her on a shutter, like a

sick
1204 are always sick. Most of
1316 falls sick but the
2133 to be at when he is sick.
2260 It would make a stone sick.
2391 To be sick is to enjoy
3366 you not extremely sick?
4193 Who, if not sick, was never
4205 to be sick sometimes.
4353 When we are sick our
4581 think we're sick, it's all

side
260 is on his side. The rich
736 on the side of big
741 heard one side of the
2682 Are on our side to-day.
3278 on God's side is a
4265 town on our side? and ain't
4585 a song, Side by side.

sidearms
1677 carried no sidearms when he

sieve
2453 they went to sea in a Sieve.
2454 aloud 'Our Sieve ain't big,

sigh
4346 we sigh for an

sight
2441 be that his sight is not

sights
399 impressive sights in the

sign
72 some clear sign! Like
1121 Never sign a walentine
3467 seeing it; sign nothing

signals
1777 exchange of signals between
4143 suggestive signals to the

signatures
4551 put their own signatures on them.

silence
351 Silence is the virtue of
763 Silence is not always tact,
904 Silence is the unbearable
1213 about silence: The
1271 that silence is always
1806 more manageable than silence.
2037 After silence, that which
3817 of silence and could
3934 flashes of silence, that make

silent
290 The 'T' is silent - as in
787 was first silent, then
955 pleasures in life are silent.
2318 Absolutely silent and
3414 Better silent than stupid.

silk
1888 Whenas in silks my Julia

sillier
853 is nothing sillier than a

silly
135 says it's a silly, childish
2433 too much, and he gets silly.
3564 are as silly as our

silver
546 the thirty pieces of silver.
3130 like the silver plate on a

similies
3786 the most unsavoury similies.

simple
1655 thus with simple folk - an

simplest
1819 are the simplest, and so

simplify
1168 am dead And simplify me when

sin
496 and full of sin, Cold the
1068 a sin of some
1185 polygamy was made a sin.
1200 but want of power to sin.
2198 was a sin. I had to
2304 For the sin ye do by two
2554 ay, as sin, And
3628 greatest sin, except to
3683 beauty is only sin deep.

since
4314 in Peter Pan ever since.

sincere
4250 Always be sincere, even if

sincerity
661 worse for complete sincerity.
3615 the sincerity of the
4518 A little sincerity is a

sing
3439 and you sing well too.

singer
1661 an aging singer who had to

singers
2969 For most singers the first
3609 be if there were no singers.

singing
1977 like the singing better
4585 along Singin' a song,

single
360 wife, But single thraldom,
1703 continued single and only

singles
540 strenuous singles we played

sings
1534 of bleeding, he sings.

sink
3165 We of the sinking middle

sinks
1135 very fast, but never sinks.

sinned
1000 The people sinned against

sinners
3644 an hour the sinners are still

sinning
3381 The sinning is the best part
3644 from their sinning of the

sins
2046 sins, in the
3900 hearts for sins they have
4248 medicine, sins of

sire
2851 him for a sire, and her

sissy
3295 A rose-red sissy half as

sisters
1585 so do his sisters, and his
2293 O'Grady Are sisters under
3551 hadn't had sisters How much

sit
496 Here I sit, alone and
1255 When you sit with a nice
1860 you do not expect to sit.
2023 get to sit down,
2290 is not to sit still, Or
2575 someone, sit right here
3117 I cannot sit still,
4270 cat that sits down on a

sits
3495 Sometimes I sits and

sitting
2283 and sitting in the

situation
2179 been in no situation where

sixpence
3491 precious little for sixpence.

sixties
2510 they divided up the Sixties.
3864 reach their sixties and

sixty
1569 you going sixty miles an

size
1257 the size of the dog

skeleton
427 Like two skeletons copulating
2692 becomes a skeleton in the

skies
3818 whose God is in the skies.

skill
241 power and skill To stem

skilled
413 to become a skilled

skllls
4132 similar skills - dressing

skin
35 A thick skin is a gift
569 give up his skin for the
3393 an Englishman to the skin.

skip
1389 easier to skip it and go

skirmish
1750 The trivial skirmish fought

skittles
795 beer and skittles; They are

skunk
2539 kills a skunk is the

sky
1321 The sky is the daily

slab
3046 this slab John Brown

slag-heap
1179 slag-heap covered in

slamming
469 Little Girls is slamming Doors.

slander
4279 the one to slander you and

slang
3696 Slang is a language that

slashing
4172 For a slashing article, sir,

slave
676 Better be a slave at once!

slaves
572 and two slaves, making,

slay
2682 But slay, and slay,

sleep
66 girl to sleep with me,
242 his first sleep should be
319 in someone else's sleep.
1840 not hypocrites in our sleep.
2468 to do when you can't sleep.
3444 Sleep faster, we need the
3509 I never sleep in comfort
3556 Sleep, riches and health to
3656 men who sleep badly, are
3798 sleep, Dreaming
4419 been to sleep for over a

sleeping
881 good a slepyng hound to
3072 art tha sleepin' there
3101 Sleeping is no mean art. For
4429 fuss about sleeping together.

sleeps
3415 An arch never sleeps.

sleeves
2629 with its sleeves rolled.
3696 up its sleeves, spits on

slept
2802 Coolidge] slept more than
3230 thought he thought I slept.'

slice
4576 Slice him where you like, a

slip
1824 me while I slip into

slogans
517 principles, slogans; and,

slop
3933 but stood in the slop.

sloppy
4249 Sloppy, raggedy-assed old

slough
539 and fall on Slough! It isn't

slow
2535 I'm a slow walker, but I
3018 telling you to slow down.

slowest
2106 family chose the slowest one.

sluggard
4418 of the sluggard; I heard

small
3443 big. You are not so small.

smaller
168 larger and candy bars smaller.
1827 out a great many smaller ones.
3212 an inch smaller and it

smallest
3538 in the smallest room in my

smallpox
3394 to the face than smallpox.

smart
2420 its time Smart Dowdy ..
2627 coach who's smart enough to

smart-asses
3298 make passes at female smart-asses.

smarter
300 themselves smarter. But he
1401 with people smarter than I am.

smash
1805 never smash in a face.

smell
2268 says the smell of fish
3565 Speaker, I smell a rat; I
4354 Money has no smell.

smelt
2322 The room smelt of not

smile
207 rode with a smile on a tiger
224 A smile is a curve that can
282 bag, And smile, smile,
864 gave me a smile I could

2040 last fading smile of a
2407 other a smile with a
3753 frown or smile, Sat and

smiling
3108 when I'm smiling and
3447 A smiling face is half the

smily
2598 All kin' o' smily round the

smith
1932 him by naming him Smith.

smoke
388 my Lord Otto, and smoke it.
1825 you guine do wid de smoke?
2276 but a good cigar is a Smoke.
4302 If I cannot smoke cigars in

smoked
2187 the brain smoked like the
2322 of not having been smoked in.
4233 woman, and smoked my first

smoking
641 Smoking is a dying habit.

snake
1369 I see a snake - which I

snares
3249 it has many snares, and no

sneak
2324 works, sneak attack is

sneaky
3083 a little snouty, sneaky mind.

sneer
3199 Who can refute a sneer?

sneering
1608 help it. I was born sneering.

sneeze
2424 like having a good sneeze.

snigger
1375 a eunuch and a snigger.

snob
2623 The true snob never rests;

snobbery
4331 be bereaved if snobbery died.

snobbish
2565 'Don't be snobbish, we seek

snobs
42 Snobs talk as if they had

snotgreen
2215 The snotgreen sea. The

snow
2302 buried in snow to the
3036 African who dreams up snow.

snow-white
4464 used to be snow-white .. but I

snowy
1292 Snowy, Flowy, Blowy,

snuff
1693 and only took snuff.

soporific
3330 too much lettuce is soporific'.

sordello
3337 can be but the one Sordello'.

sore
969 who is sore about
2731 as a bear with a sore head.

sorrow
2301 There is sorrow enough in
3210 Sorrow is tranquillity
3785 should water this sorrow.

sorrows
3922 are few sorrows, however

sorry
525 Very sorry can't come. Lie
2152 will be sorry that you

sort
931 This is the sort of English

soul
624 to give his soul for the
1654 mum, Whose soul was sad,
1799 much about his own soul.
3855 may my soul be blasted
3966 the pupil's soul. To Miss
4225 it has no soul to be

souls
2299 About their blessed souls.
3917 sell their souls, and live

sound
126 like their sound, and
1806 they think sound is more
3948 the other not very sound.

sounds
839 and the sounds will take
3120 is better than it sounds.
4301 is better than it sounds.

soup
3430 better with soup than

south
2645 live as far south as

sovereign
4391 Ours is a sovereign nation Bows

sovereignty
879 to have sovereynetee As wel

sow
2214 is the old sow that eats
3023 I write as a sow piddles.

sows
4056 He sows hurry and reaps

space
673 of the space age -
1814 Outer Space, To find
1987 Space isn't remote at all.

spade
2192 nominate a spade a spade.

spaghetti
2979 eating spaghetti - it

spaniards
356 and the Spaniards seem wiser

spanish
2762 are fond of Spanish wine, and

spanking
1228 find that spanking takes less

spat
4386 The times spat at me. I

speak
1322 Speak what you think today
1324 you say, and then speak.
2340 some who speak one moment
2362 than not speak of oneself
2736 gets up to speak and says
3261 is to speak ill of
3777 when I think, I must speak.
3962 no one can speak, and no
4049 true, And speak when he is

speaker
1124 of the speaker have left
1871 A dull speaker, like a plain

speakers
1294 the great speakers were bad

speaking
1501 everybody is speaking of it.
3475 Speaking without thinking is

speaks
244 inch and speaketh by the
4357 He speaks to me as if I was

specialist
1382 The specialist is a man who

speciality
2577 My speciality is detached

spectacle
4548 and there's a spectacle.

spectators
1969 lists and the spectators laugh.

speculator
4077 raised by a speculator, with lots

speech
1271 Speech may be barren; but it
1287 begin my speech with the
1402 to make a speech, the first
1681 true use of speech is not so
1746 from speech, lest they
1852 make your speech not too
2345 make your speech
3045 any other form of speech.
3179 and grunt. Speech was given
3287 looking at speech is to say
3832 the power of speech.
3875 my parts of speech! was ever
3990 Speech happens not to be his

speeches
2025 thought my speeches were too

speechless
1963 literally speechless. Where

spell
3572 here for a spell, get all
4285 They spell it Vinci and

speller
4409 the wuss speller I know of.

spelling
2873 right; but spelling isn't
2883 My spelling is Wobbly. It's
2891 basic spelling that every

spend
2084 life is to spend it for
2256 am going to spend the rest

spender
1470 Where the spender thinks it

spendthrift
3726 Love is a spendthrift, leaves its

spent
1429 can scarce ever be spent.
2132 that I have spent all the
4160 shall have spent its novel

spermatozoa
2035 million Spermatozoa, All of

spherical
2456 perfectly spherical, He

spice
3853 It adds spice to my

spiders
174 me; No more spiders in my bath

spinach
26 ivy is another man's spinach.

spirit
1812 The spirit of liberty is the

spiritualists
4068 like a convention of spiritualists.

spit
4386 at me. I spit back at
4391 They spit on

spiteful
2424 when I feel spiteful; it's like

spits
3696 sleeves, spits on its

splashing
2024 I'll be splashing around in the

spoiled
4283 Golf is a good walk spoiled.

spoke
3492 the less he spoke; The less
4258 English as she is Spoke.

spoonfuls
4085 so much as spoonfuls of boiling

spoons
1273 my life with coffee spoons.
1299 faster we counted our spoons.
3840 up its spoons and packs

sport
1749 love as in sport, the
2787 of war and sport.
3160 sport is war

sports
2811 I hate all sports as rabidly

sportsman
2337 of God, we call him a sportsman.
2444 A sportsman is a man who, every

spots
3701 people are friends in spots.
4269 not all over, but in spots.

spouse
735 President's spouse. I wish

spread
355 not good except it be spread.
4227 Boredom is rage spread thin.

spring
484 promise of spring is that
4484 day of spring was once

spur
983 is the spur of noble

spurn
1596 Spurn not the nobly born

spurts
4352 great heights only by spurts.

squandering
1189 In squandering wealth was his

squares
2417 packed like squares of wheat.

squeak
1559 - until the pips squeak.

squeezed
1559 going to be squeezed as a lemon

squeezing
1696 you in the squeezing of a

squelching
3621 and fifty seconds of squelching.

squire
1119 Bless the squire and his

squirm
3206 a stab nor squirm To tread

squirrels
3151 like red squirrels, must be

stabbed
1534 a guy gets stabbed in the

stag
2511 The Stag at Bay with the

stage
1199 for love, but on the stage.
1692 On the stage he was

stagecoach
1079 faults in a stagecoach may

stages
2543 The four stages of man are

stagnation
715 then keeps life from stagnation.

stain
1496 leave a stain behind

stair
2790 up the stair I met a

stake
3924 at the stake as witches

stamp
3671 physics or stamp

stamps
3084 animals and stick in stamps.

stand
4427 I will not stand for being

standards
499 of date. Standards are always
4062 of lowering your standards!

standing
1984 is your standing in the

star
899 more distant than any star.
1073 Being a star has made it

stardom
347 Stardom isn't a profession;

stars
2457 up to the Stars above And
3327 it's in the stars, Next July
4346 look at the stars without
4435 merely the stars'
4521 us are looking at the stars.

start
426 orchestra: start together
933 the family start? It
2522 You start with

starter
300 was even a starter. There

startled
1943 is always startled when he

starvation
3658 to avoid starvation and to

state
1616 Here's a state of things!
2683 for the state; The the
3372 The State, that cawing

stately
2777 and round a stately park and

stately homes
4586 as the stately homes of

statesman
5 of a statesman is that he
1089 European statesman who will
1188 fiddler, statesman, and
1691 nice for a statesman, too proud
2550 did agree, he was a statesman.
2604 A ginooine statesman should be
4048 firm is a statesman, and a

statesman
4254 A statesman is a
4413 show us a statesman who can
4615 A statesman is an easy man, He

statesmen
1148 class, requires grave statesmen.

station
538 concrete station With a
1119 know our proper stations.

stationary
1775 its horn and each stationary.

statisticians
4222 Though statisticians in our time

statistics
2405 He uses statistics as a drunken

statue
124 to die Seldom rates a statue.

statues
228 bunk, Epp's statues are junk,

stature
3725 is of a low stature, but it

status quo
3986 be!' restored the status quo.

stay
3214 I shall stay the way I am
3350 in heaven Stay there And

staying
4011 It's staying up all

steal
657 they would steal two hours
961 shalt not steal; an empty
1278 imitate; mature poets steal.
1791 When a man steals your
2904 If you steal from one
2968 days Is to steal a few
3418 is when I steal other
3446 rise and steal a horse.

stealth
2081 good by stealth and being

steamer
1603 about in a steamer from

steel
2888 is clad in complete steel.

steer
75 it's time to steer clear.

stein
228 called Stein, There's

step
334 was an easy step to

sterilized
1833 recognized is a bias sterilized.

stick
417 of it will always stick.
2157 to a stick and a
3155 of a stick inside a
3198 he fell like the stick.

stigma
1776 Any stigma, as the old

still
3070 is to stand still for six

stilts
512 - nonsense upon stilts.

stimulant
1369 a supply of stimulant handy in

sting
54 butterfly, sting like a
225 is thy sting-a-ling-a-l
3246 it is a sting, It is a

stir
1645 You must stir it and stump

stock
3577 some good stock and hold
3961 see how his stock went on.

stock exchange
2691 onto the Stock Exchange missing

stocking
3326 glimpse of stocking Was looked

stocks
1378 Stocks have reached what

stoic
3284 either a stoic or a

stole
1832 all we stole it fair

stolen
2093 to be sweet must be stolen.

stomach
1160 - I have no stomach for such
2344 A hungry stomach has no ears.
3197 If your stomach disputes you,
3767 on their stomachs shouting:
3770 is a good-humoured stomach.

stone
1847 heaviest stone that the
2931 gout, give them the stone!

stools
1047 invented stools,

stoops
1707 woman stoops to folly

stop
2031 nothing will stop them.
2703 Stop, Sir, stop - go away:
3073 Stop the world, I want to
3260 who will stop your

stopped
2750 or my watch has stopped."
4597 But it stopped short - never

stories
1918 wicked stories about me.
2067 to believe of my own stories.

storm
2937 a great storm, 'O God,

story
508 many a good story has been

3011 Every picture tells a story.
3669 Every story has three sides
4033 is all this story about?' 'A

stove-lid
4270 on a hot stove-lid. She will

straight
224 that can set things straight.

strain
3020 the train take the strain.

strange
2758 make strange
3255 Strange to see how a good

strangeness
410 their degree of strangeness to us.

stranger
3044 of the stranger If one's

strangers
3778 we may be better strangers.
4006 myself and strangers. The

stratagem
3287 a constant stratagem to cover

straw
3758 Take a straw and throw it

stray
1548 fondly stray. Over the

street
800 it in the street and
4456 is worth two in the street."

streets
489 Streets Flooded. Please

strength
439 Strength is a matter of the
1913 man's imitation of strength.
2658 Our strength is often composed

stretched
1928 Man's mind stretched to a new
4263 which he stretched, but

strife
360 thraldom, or a double strife?
915 for the sake of strife.

strike
620 I write, I strike out three.

string
2439 model has a string to each

strip club
2965 The Strip Club is another form

struck
2087 to be struck by
3869 I was struck all of a heap.

struggle
1355 after you cease to struggle.
4623 the eternal struggle between

struggled
4489 having struggled so hard to

students
937 loses interest in students.

1680 always been students, and their
2251 sex for the students, athletics
3503 Students of the heavens are

studious
1555 Studious of elegance and ease,

study
2619 you are in some brown study.

stuff
1015 short to stuff a

stumble
1533 you stumble into when

stupid
3414 Better silent than stupid.
3550 half as stupid as my
4138 The stupid neither forgive

stupidity
32 on his stupidity - and
2330 Stupidity is an elemental force

stygian
2079 horrible Stygian smoke of

style
3281 has no real style. He just

styles
4375 All styles are good except

subject
926 and won't change the subject.

subjects
1382 who fears the other subjects.
3578 only on different subjects.
4558 favourite subjects -

sublime
599 and often reaches the sublime.
1742 from the Sublime To the

submission
1265 for submission
3658 voluntary submission to an

submits
3089 times; he submits to

subscribers
2132 any list of subscribers; one, that

substitute
517 the age of substitutes: instead

subtle
928 try to be subtle or clever.
1510 may not be subtle, but

succeed
1839 that it shall never succeed.
3026 To succeed pre-eminently in
4303 rest of us could not succeed.
4376 able to succeed in the

succeeds
1900 Nothing succeeds like one's
4362 a friend succeeds, a little

success
7 Success has made failures of
230 to be a success, but time
348 owes his success to his

526 thing about success is that
644 fails like success because we
1251 If A is a success in life,
1298 which can do without success.
1715 From success you get a lot of
2018 bows to success, even
2429 Success is not the result of
2613 Success is that old A B C -
2826 and his success is
3544 is also the success of others.
3598 failure on the way to success.
3693 marriage a success and only
3743 secret of success is to go
3921 isn't a success? Have I
3931 very lively hope of success.
3971 to success in life is
4131 formula for success, but I can
4536 Success is a science. If you

successes
3640 to have successes with women

successful
683 every successful man
865 the title of a successful book.
1571 who is successful before he
1673 every successful man you'll
2729 The successful people are the
2998 Being successful in England is a
4195 to do to be successful, most

successor
1900 like one's own successor.

sucker
394 There's a sucker born every
1368 give a sucker an even

sudden
1143 Departure should be sudden.

suddenly
2223 No one ever suddenly became

suez
2296 east of Suez, where the

suffer
2996 judges] suffer from a bad

suffering
3543 causes less suffering than an

sugar
2469 pills in sugar coating.

suggest
2654 is to suggest that

suicide
253 if it's just a suicide note.
1627 from the suicide's grave
2237 The longest suicide note in

suit
908 have chosen a suit by it.

suited
3613 are well suited when both

sum
1939 picture, not doing a sum.
3219 to the sum involved.

summer
100 on a hot summer afternoon.
452 day of high summer like true
3464 July's too late - for summer.
4394 to ensure summer in England

sun
3885 the mid-day sun, though he
4183 you let the sun in, mind

sunday
22 Sunday clears away the rust
215 it being Sunday, had

sundial
481 I am a sundial, and I make a

sundown
3589 between Sundown and Sun-up

sung
3336 Bah! I have sung women in

sunset
2696 may make a fine sunset.
3373 a horror of sunsets, they're

sunshine
4025 are the sunshine; they are

superfluities
1557 or no, we must have superfluities.

superfluous
4374 The superfluous, a very necessary

superior
188 I am a most superior person.
2224 for the superior tastes of
2964 to say, Superior people

superiority
1540 of man's superiority to all

superstition
2258 American superstition is belief

superstitious
2528 are more superstitious than they

supper
358 but it is a bad supper.
1238 I consider supper as a

supplied
1100 he is well supplied with it.

supply
595 is, the supply has always
1748 The supply of good
2406 The supply of government

support
916 to support the
2028 a loss to support a flagging
2795 who will support me when I

suppose
3918 To suppose, as we all

supposed
89 All you're supposed to do is
4252 they are supposed to do

sure
462 What nobody is sure about!
2607 you may be sure of, be

surgeon
2566 better than a plastic surgeon.

surgery
1381 practice of surgery a

surgical
3940 requires a surgical operation

surprise
1093 element of surprise up his

surprised
1091 he is quite surprised to be
3203 I wouldn't be at all surprised.
3244 man there is a surprised woman.

surrender
96 the cash surrender value of a
1525 rather than surrender any

survive
646 luck to survive this
1766 up if we are to survive.

survives
3899 is what survives when what

survivors
1575 are no winners, only survivors.

susceptible
4512 peculiarly susceptible to

suspecting
3615 point of suspecting the

suspense
4514 This suspense is terrible. I

suspicion
448 by the suspicion that they
2202 characters are above suspicion.

suspicions
2900 fool usually has his suspicions.

sustains
2614 What sustains the human spirit

swagger
3356 they would swagger more now,

swagman
3229 a jolly swagman camped by

swallow
4091 swim in but hard to swallow.

swallowed
1486 are being swallowed up by the
4251 to keep riding or be swallowed.

swallowing
1365 act of swallowing, I will

swat
948 just a bit harder to swat.

swayed
1637 she be swayed by quite

swear
4298 when very angry, swear.

sweet
4186 never been sweet in the

sweeteners
1359 are the best sweeteners of tea.

tangled
2218 the dark tangled curls of

tank
3013 Put a tiger in your tank.

taradiddles
2480 are sent For telling taradiddles.'

target
1054 a moving target; he never

tarred
2534 man who was tarred and

tarzan
4438 Me Tarzan, you Jane.

tasmanians
2774 that the Tasmanians, who never

taste
1174 has acquired a taste for it.
1261 of taste in jokes
1384 Taste is the feminine of
2205 worse taste, than in a
2323 not the taste of water I
2715 with no taste, etiquette
2820 the taste of the
3333 than the taste, and vice
3363 They never taste who always
3500 is better taste somehow
3876 You had no taste when you

tasted
2291 you ever tasted Man?'
3979 you have tasted two whole

tastes
3826 you. Their tastes may not be
4432 it never tastes quite the

tatters
2910 Rags and tatters, if you

tattoo
685 attempt to tattoo soap

taught
2289 (They taught me all I
2966 that has taught us Six
3857 I was taught when I was
4526 worth knowing can be taught.

tavern
1172 opened a tavern for his
2120 as by a good tavern or inn.

tax
1903 one small tax changed in
3586 The income tax has made

taxation
972 The art of taxation consists
1455 one form of taxation that can

taxes
134 State Building after taxes.
1434 except death and taxes.
2894 Death and taxes and

taxi
2753 leave in a taxi you can

taxicabs
719 driving taxicabs and

taxing
2589 less of a taxing machine

taxpayer
4624 The average taxpayer is no more

tea
479 word for Tea? Upon my
2216 I makes tea I makes
2712 warming the teapot. He's
2777 having tea just too
3487 I want tea; but if
3535 sooner the tea's out of

teach
768 rules Teach nothing
2201 To teach is to learn twice.
3769 wants to teach there are

teacher
265 is a good teacher, but she
528 is a great teacher, but
2422 the worst teacher; it gives
4136 A teacher should have maximal

teaches
3844 does. He who cannot, teaches.

teaching
219 secret of teaching is to

teapot
2712 warming the teapot. He's a

tears
3785 Indeed the tears live in an

teary
2598 lips, An' teary round the

teases
829 Because he knows it teases.

teat
2709 a full teat for

technique
3522 infallible technique and then

technological
994 single technological resource
2612 Technological man can't believe in

technology
1456 Technology - the knack of so

tediousness
49 his own tediousness has yet to

teenager
1454 The teenager' seems to have

teeth
363 like teeth, are
3477 bite, don't show your teeth.
4332 children cut their teeth.
4339 must go armed to the teeth.

teetotaller
3162 a secret teetotaller and often
3819 only a beer teetotaller, not a

telegrams
3375 of those telegrams of which

telephone

37 The telephone book is full of
237 This telephone' has too many
994 The telephone is the most
3009
3048 and the telephone rings and

television

413 through the television set.
700 Television has a real problem.
1036 heavens, television is
1459 Television is an invention that
1718 and see bad television for
1905 Television has brought back
2398 Television has proved that
2564 Television is a gold goose that
3746 Television? The word is half
4604 Television is chewing gum for

tell

275 know, you can't tell 'em.
1444 you may tell it to only
1795 find out who will tell you.
2737 and I can't tell you why;
3483 doing, and tell her she
4397 I always tell a young man
4541 a woman who tells one her

telling

4059 way of telling you you've
4479 with you - I am telling you.

tells

4154 him how he is, tells you.

temper

973 lose their tempers merely
1467 losing your temper or your
3128 to lose me temper till it
4023 - only keep your temper.

temperance

1327 Temperance is the control of all
2115 for me as temperance would be

temperature

3193 to the mean temperature of the

temptation

1258 a dangerous temptation to foreign
1739 better of temptation is just to
2307 is always a temptation to a rich
2497 to resist an adequate temptation.
3845 maximum of temptation with the
4157 Temptation rarely comes in
4458 avoid temptation unless I
4520 everything except temptation.
4529 rid of a temptation is to

temptations

191 of two temptations and choose
1591 of all temptations To belong
3529 with two temptations and you
4503 There are no temptations there.

tempted

2231 I'm tempted to reply,

tennis

1482 playing tennis with the
2675 every tennis player

tennis-balls

4435 the stars' tennis-balls, struck

tennyson

2217 Lawn Tennyson, gentleman poet.

tension

3271 - takes the tension out of the

tent

2113 inside the tent pissing

terminated

307 to be terminated when one

terra firma

2236 I like terra firma - the more

terrible

3962 came, A terrible man with a
4184 life a terrible thing,
4514 suspense is terrible. I hope

terror

4240 adds a new terror to life

test

1509 What is the test of good
1826 The true test of
3056 I test my bath before I
3858 The test of a man or

tested

4240 I have tested your

thames

536 I see the Thames again? The
4393 God! the Thames is between

thanked

1371 I never even thanked her.

thankful

3593 Be thankful we're not getting
3607 is really thankful, and has
4303 Let us be thankful for the

thanks

1150 grateful thanks to

that

2760 thrown away for that.

theatre

45 goes to the theatre unless he
1545 go to the theatre instead.
3736 go to the theatre is like
4316 an evening in the theatre.

thee

2317 as without Thee We are not

theme

3998 The central theme of the

themselves

1680 greatest study is themselves.

theories

2299 Art, And theories' and

theory

1141 that is life without theory.

1253 If my theory of relativity
2825 respect his theory that his
4062 in the theory that

therapist
815 goes to a therapist, is a
1971 a very effective therapist.

therapy
4399 point of therapy is to get

there
68 want to be there when it
110 I? I'm already there.'
2790 who wasn't there. He wasn't
4005 you get there, there
4606 a kid, you see what's there.

thereafter
2252 is that thereafter you have

thermometer
1927 of inverted thermometer, the bulb

thickens
4365 the plot thickens very much

thieves
423 One of the thieves was saved.
898 Thieves respect property.

thin
1010 fat man a thin one is
1012 way to get thin is to
1662 Thin people are beautiful

thing
179 is no such thing as a
2272 is become a thing, a tool, a
2536 sort of thing will find
3246 What thing is love for
3258 is such a thing as too
3404 is no such thing as a

things
1235 thousand things that won't
1589 Things are seldom what they
2874 Think of Things, you find

think
531 You can't think and hit at
1112 We only think when we are
1187 of such Who think too little
1216 you can't make him think.
1254 I think and think for
1275 to think about.
1419 nature to think wisely and
2001 what they think wouldn't
2038 What we think and feel and
2051 you don't think you can't,
2340 moment before they think.
2343 not the one you would think.
2445 begin to think, it is
2501 Think wrongly, if you
2578 with them besides think.
2729 ones who think up things
3058 I think that I shall never
3665 sooner than think; in fact,
3672 so we've got to think!
3811 reason: I think him so,

3823 expect a soldier to think.
3942 who could think for two
3985 I'm not so think as you
4080 I don't think much of
4293 how much we think of
4358 what they think of me, it
4392 know what I think till I see

thinker
1078 are poor thinkers. Many
2245 brilliant thinker; the

thinking
1249 into lazy habits of thinking.
1587 thought of thinking for myself
1937 who are thinking about
2328 ways save us from thinking.
3292 the mind is thinking, it is
3346 And I'm a fool for thinking.
3604 is thinking most often
3636 lie awake thinking about

thinks
260 Every man thinks God is on
2228 that which he thinks he has.
3495 I sits and thinks, and then

thinner
2463 and keep on growing thinner.
2483 to grow thinner, diminish

third-rate
430 all these third-rate foreign

thirst
2296 an' a man can raise a thirst.
3507 drink for the thirst to come.

thirty
280 I am past thirty, and three
956 I learned after I was thirty.
1217 when he was thirty will get a

thorn
1659 Licking honey From a thorn.

thought
229 ten men who thought of it
374 sex, you thought of nothing
939 Perish the thought!
1193 he went, for want of thought.
1735 amount of thought before you
1852 If no thought your mind does
2001 be so bad if they thought.
2400 what people thought of us if
3100 of thought belongs to
3179 was given to conceal thought.
3230 kept: He thought me asleep;
3346 is worth a thought, And I'm a
3516 I wish I thought What
3655 be if he thought for
4144 what nobody has thought.

thoughts
2151 man mistake words for thoughts.
3197 pacify it with cool thoughts.
3564 people's thoughts are as
3654 other's thoughts, I suppose

thousand
4177 if I had five thousand a year.

thousands
3312 But thousands die, without or

thread
3797 out the thread of his
4058 too frail a thread to hang

threat
1207 girl the threat of a

three
109 half a boy; three boys are
837 I tell you three times is
1481 In three words I can sum up
1611 Three little maids from
1613 Three little maids who, all
2876 he was only three. James

three-pipe
1176 is quite a three-pipe problem,

three-sided
2949 they would make him three-sided.

thrice
3861 Thrice is he armed that hath

thrive
950 that would thrive Must rise

throat
474 undulating throat Like an
1476 of taking life by the throat.
3176 in the throat and one in
4615 you by the throat; So stay

throats
1688 each other's throats, for pay.

throne
1432 proudest throne is obliged

through
36 you can get through, but
1475 The only way round is through.
1708 of it all the way through.
2095 we all have to go through it.
4218 you've been through with

throw
422 I would throw it out of
1929 and hug, or throw themselves

thrown
2760 All this thrown away for

thrust
1855 mediocrity thrust upon them.
3808 greatness thrust upon them.

thumb
862 the thumb is born

thunderstorm
2087 out in thunderstorms, to be

thursday
2852 love you Thursday - So much

thus
4411 Why is this thus? What is

thwackum
1361 Thwackum was for doing

thyroid
2981 the nation's thyroid gland.

tiber
2685 Oh, Tiber! father Tiber To

ticket
554 to take a ticket at
2672 and a ticket for the

tide
777 There is a tide in the

tie
2778 It's a tie that only

tiger
207 smile on a tiger They
459 The Tiger, on the other
3013 Put a tiger in your tank.
4251 riding a tiger. A man

tigers
924 and fro on tigers from which
3417 fro upon tigers from which
3445 are no tigers, a wildcat

tigress
579 She was a tigress surrounded

tile
3172 red brick, but white tile.

tiller
2937 holding my tiller straight.'

tilt
541 With the tilt of her

timbuctoo
4500 plains of Timbuctoo, I would

time
4 Time wounds all heels.
169 Time wastes our bodies and
230 It takes time to be a
401 women and so little time.
528 Time is a great teacher,
867 There is time for work.
1161 Time goes, you say? Ah no!
1227 too much time on the
1234 short on time. I expect
1736 Time and I against any
2327 hook, and time is running
2420 before its time Shameless
2496 I was on time. No, you
2570 The time has come for all
2827 Time is a great legalizer,
2882 Time for a little
2908 it's for such a long time!
3093 My time has not yet come
3173 spend their time mostly
3217 By the time you say you're
3219 Time spent on any item of
3222 Let time that makes you
3295 sissy half as old as time.
3463 done at any time will be
3579 do with the time we have
3897 killing time Is only
3970 Time: That which man is

4082 The time was out of joint,
4156 It takes time to save
4192 What time he can spare
4208 Time is but the stream I
4383 This is no time for making
4451 of Father Time with a

time-table
2781 read a time-table or a

times
4386 The times spat at me. I

ting-a-ling
225 is thy ting-a-ling-a-ling O

tinkering
1242 intelligent tinkering is to save

tired
333 can ever be tired of Bath!
612 you got tired of
756 process of getting tired.

tiresome
4375 good except the tiresome kind.

tiring
2023 is very tiring. You
2896 Wooing, so tiring.

title
865 A good title is the title

titled
3242 that of the titled for

titles
3980 Congs their titles take.

tits
3890 have their tits somewhere

titwillow
1626 Willow, titwillow,
1627 'Oh willow, titwillow,

toad
1745 As intelligent Mr. Toad.
2413 I let the toad work
2414 arm, old toad; Help me
4381 Ask a toad what is beauty?

toast
3138 all the toasts of the
3235 a piece of toast

toasted
120 England is just toasted milk.

tobacco
2188 that tawney weed tobacco.
2384 thy sake, Tobacco, I Would
2389 leave off tobacco! Surely
2906 without tobacco is not
4233 any more time on tobacco.

tobacconist
2187 of the tobacconist are

today
30 immense, Today I feel
1322 you think today in words
3490 Never do today what you can

toes
2460 who has no toes Had once

together
4231 all in this together - by

toilet
3736 one's toilet without a

told
779 phrase, 'I told you so.'

tolerant
4535 wonderfully tolerant. It

tolerates
748 that He tolerates their

tomb
3913 the gilded tomb of a

tombstone
2297 fight is a tombstone white,

tomorrow
1322 balls, and tomorrow speak what
3470 Tomorrow is often the busiest
3490 you can put off till tomorrow.

tongue
130 hold his tongue in ten
876 wel they tonge, and thenk
1325 to men one tongue, but two
1424 a fool who holds his tongue.
3231 customs, politics and tongue.
3476 The tongue ever turns to the
4620 her eternal tongue, For ever

took
819 you and I took me for.

tools
768 but to name his tools.
4261 fools) Their working tools.

tooth
3453 jelly breaks your tooth.
3476 turns to the aching tooth.

toothache
3074 Toothache doesn't stop hurting
3783 endure the toothache patiently.

toothpaste
1800 Once the toothpaste is out of

top
2559 who comes top of the
3328 You're the top! You're
3553 just about top of the
4601 from the top down. I

top-boots
3714 pleasure me in his top-boots.

tories
116 Mamma, are Tories born
687 horse, For Tories own no
2114 Tories, in short, are

torments
938 how many torments lie in the

torontonian
457 A Torontonian is a man who leaves

tribe
566 powerful tribe whose

tribes
781 two mighty tribes, The Bores

trick
380 The trick of wearing mink
469 A Trick that everyone

tried
905 not been tried and found
921 have been tried from time
3820 if anyone ever tried it.
4465 one I've never tried before.

trimming
2969 the second half trimming it.

trinkets
2287 to your trinkets; then ye

trip
2901 A trip through a sewer in
4060 look forward to the trip.
4111 like this, I need the trip.

triumph
4361 A triumph of the embalmer's

trojan
553 know what Trojan 'orses

trombone
1948 The trombone age (moving the

trouble
128 help in time of trouble.
401 The trouble with life is that
1069 kind. The trouble lies in
1082 In trouble to be troubled Is
1528 have never been in trouble.
1961 worst kind of heart trouble.
1980 is in trouble, don't
2226 Trouble is only opportunity
2717 in time of trouble when it is
3595 gives us trouble, it's what
3651 stirring up trouble somewhere.
4449 of one who had seen trouble.

troubled
2962 I'm troubled. I'm

troublemakers
2657 and its dead troublemakers.

troubles
52 woman whose troubles are
282 up your troubles in your

trousers
506 Trousers should shiver on the
2049 one's best trousers to go out

trout
4198 you find a trout in the

trowel
1007 She lays it on with a trowel.

truck
2254 hit by a truck - if you

truck drivers
3272 language truck drivers are using,

trudged
1193 He trudged along unknowing

true
688 He said true things, but
772 was proved true before,
837 you three times is true.
2368 perfectly true is
2594 He's been true to one
2852 Thursday - So much is true.
3710 to be substantially true.
4502 ear, 'You are not true'.
4552 we know this is not true.

trumpet
1693 shifted his trumpet, and only

trumps
2373 dirt were trumps, what

trust
601 You can trust all
761 put one's trust in God is
2113 ass. Never trust a man
4541 never trust a woman

truth
162 Hell is truth seen too
210 handle the truth
277 economical with the truth.
377 trusted to speak the truth.
595 scarce as truth is, the
971 but truth, and too
1054 Truth for him was a moving
1244 the truth, leave
1409 lying when truth, well
1449 discovers the entire truth.
1533 Truth is something you
1931 way to get at the truth.
2129 he thinks truth, and every
2177 even in telling the truth.
2207 have sought truth, and
2434 A half truth, like half a
2527 but not on truth saying.
2946 I speak the truth, not so
3081 else you tell the truth to.
3424 feeling is God's own truth.
3426 neither religion nor truth.
3436 Truth is the safest lie.
3521 Truth may be stranger than
3587 injected truth into
3688 to the truth, but like
3690 is only one truth,
4045 telling the truth about
4253 tell the truth, and they
4263 mainly he told the truth.
4276 Truth is the most valuable

truthful
4350 are born truthful, and die

truths
707 tell him disagreeable truths.
803 call first truths those we

1819 greatest truths are the
2045 held truths may be
3816 All great truths begin as

truthtelling
211 the honest truthtelling there is

trying
414 a point of trying every
4256 while I was trying to be

tube
1800 out of the tube, it is

tuesday
2873 can spell TUESDAY, even if
3111 it good - we want it Tuesday.

tumble
3515 bags And tumble victuals

tumbled
1742 time She tumbled off a bus,

tumbling
750 ladder without tumbling off.

tumult
2320 The tumult and the shouting

tune
547 about the tune, there is
2376 I am incapable of a tune.

tunes
1895 have all the good tunes.

tuning
160 their life tuning and the

tunnel
1125 end of the tunnel is the

turd
878 is nat worth a toord!'

turkey
3080 Turkey is a dying man. We

turned
24 After being turned down by

turning
2439 face for turning its head
4179 The lady's not for turning.

turnip
2165 the man who turnips cries,

turnpike
1238 supper as a turnpike through

turtle
1004 Behold the turtle. He makes

tutors
1503 Old foxes want no tutors.

twenty
1429 thinks twenty shillings

twenty-twenty
4547 Hindsight is always twenty-twenty.

twice
834 as life and twice as
836 at least twice as fast as

2363 to be praised twice over.
2984 name her twice, Like so;
4495 must do twice as well as

twin
2482 was born a twin And not a

twins
1741 threw the twins she
2694 is to have been born twins.

twist
1554 with ease, Twist words and
3329 for I have NO MORE TWIST.

two
65 between two people.
239 is that two and two
995 Two weeks is about the
2714 has to suffice for two.

typewriters
4552 a million typewriters will

typing
816 not writing, that's typing.

tyranny
3658 to an unnecessary tyranny.
3847 burden of tyranny: they have
4370 benevolent tyranny tempered

tyrant
561 n: a tyrant's
3069 of a cruel tyrant. Enjoy!'

uglinesses
1309 with its uglinesses the

ugly
75 rears its ugly 'ead it's
702 with an ugly woman than
1652 Elderly ugly daughter.
1764 art looks ugly at first.
3641 are no ugly women,

ulcers
161 He'd give the devil ulcers.

umbrage
3481 have taken umbrage. The deuce

umbrella
649 steals the just's umbrella.

un-wholesome
2379 they are un-wholesome companions

unaggressive
2649 well groomed and unaggressive.

unattended
1512 They go out when unattended.

unattractive
1625 la, A most unattractive old thing,
1871 surface so unattractive must be

unaware
892 makes me unaware of

unbecoming
1006 more unbecoming a man of

unbent
2374 She unbent her mind

unbribed
4580 man will do unbribed, there's

uncertain
113 Life is uncertain - eat dessert
3386 To be uncertain is to be

uncertainty
1374 capacity to endure uncertainty.

unclad
2668 uncertain, unclad and

uncle
3805 grace, nor uncle me no

uncomfortable
1537 and it always feels uncomfortable.
3839 moral when he is only uncomfortable.

uncommunicating
2381 The uncommunicating muteness of

unconcern
2172 looks with unconcern on a man

unconquerable
2389 which this unconquerable purpose

unconvincing
1623 bald and unconvincing narrative.

uncorseted
1282 emphasis; Uncorseted, her

under-dogs
4422 among the under-dogs - except

underachieve
2329 United States, you underachieve.

underdeveloped
1526 The more underdeveloped the country,

undergraduates
447 Undergraduates owe their happiness

underground
3183 belonging to him is underground.

underneath
31 In uplifting, get underneath.

undersized
1604 He's a bit undersized, and you

understand
228 And no one can understand Ein.
267 is a language I don't understand.
1031 my life to understand that it is
2427 meant to understand - They're
2569 adores what he cannot understand.
2976 but where they understand you.
3231 ne'er quite understand The
4004 I understand you undertake to
4295 idiots understand their own

understanding
792 "My understanding of Women goes
2080 of God; they pass all understanding.
2116 likely to propagate understanding.
2135 to find you an understanding.
2499 only the understanding that one's
4296 of tacit understanding that the

understands
1992 but who understands the

undertaking
4004 to overthrow my undertaking.

undertaxed
524 long as the undertaxed can defend

undeserving
1438 to the undeserving is severe

undivided
3879 Alone and undivided, we lived

undone
1202 undo, and some to be undone.
3329 .. I am undone and worn

undress
544 you have to undress in front
1122 women - and I undress for men.
4623 unadmitted desire to undress.

undying
3217 Infinite, undying - Lady,

uneatable
4540 full pursuit of the uneatable.

uneducated
923 for an uneducated man to
4409 was so unedicated. He's the

unemployment
1021 out of work, unemployment results.

unendurable
298 seldom as unendurable as, to

unequal
1290 division of unequal earnings.
4434 Unequal nature, to place

unfaithful
3500 should be unfaithful to his

unfettered
2693 to have an unfettered

unfinished
177 is always unfinished business.

unfit
2808 party is unfit to rule -

unforgiving
3878 An unforgiving eye, and a damned

ungainly
3110 is more ungainly than a

unhabitual
2083 perceiving in an unhabitual way.

unhappiness
2726 between periods of unhappiness.
4306 There is no unhappiness like the

unhappy
371 I've had an unhappy life,
2341 their remaining years unhappy.
3656 Men who are unhappy, like men
4573 All the unhappy marriages

unhooked
4399 is to get unhooked, not to

uniform
1953 coat Should be more uniform.
2285 The uniform 'e wore Was

unimportant
2859 The other eight are unimportant.
3077 be very busy with the unimportant.

unintelligible
787 then unintelligible, then

unintentionally
149 anyone's feelings unintentionally.

union
1102 The proper union of gin and
3701 always the union of a part
4312 their union, were not

unitarian
2782 A Unitarian very earnestly

united
1089 will be united by the

united states
1116 and so close to the United States.
1486 of the United States, but then
1520 die in the United States of too
2329 die in the United States, you
3121 rats in the United States; of
4567 of the United States, but I

unites
2868 Nothing unites the English

unity
643 no cultural unity, no

universal
1262 is coming. Universal peace is

universe
1106 The universe is like a safe to
1243 plays dice with the universe.
1919 of the universe, with one
3004 about the universe. There's

universities
359 Universities incline wits to

university
937 A university is what a college
1216 up to the university, but you
3172 Jimmy's university.
3240 to the university, where it
3983 the High; We are the University.

unjust
649 also on the unjust fella: But

unknowable
2823 in the unknowable. But

unknown
3286 and the unknown, what else

unlabelled
2046 to go about unlabelled. The

unlike
4578 is! So unlike anything

unlucky
2723 who is so unlucky that he

unmarried
3842 to keep unmarried as long as

unmuzzled
2046 the police do an unmuzzled dog.

unnatural
336 of an unnatural beginning.
1452 The only unnatural sexual

unnecessary
1822 the unfit, to do the unnecessary.
4607 agree, one of them is unnecessary.

unobtrusiveness
3679 respectful unobtrusiveness of one

unorthodox
498 anything unorthodox goes on

unpleasant
3534 anything unpleasant , at all.

unpopular
446 I was not unpopular [at school]
4038 it is safe to be unpopular.

unpunished
680 good deed ever goes unpunished.

unsaid
2855 or four things a day unsaid.
4571 practically nothing unsaid.

unsatisfied
4533 leaves one unsatisfied. What

unsavoury
3786 the most unsavoury similies.

unselfishness
3707 Real unselfishness consists in

unspeakable
4540 a fox - the unspeakable in full

unspoiled
1037 utterly unspoiled by

unstuck
111 of coming unstuck, thank

unsuccessful
683 a lot of unsuccessful years.

untie
2200 cut what you can untie.

untravelled
1701 My heart untravelled fondly

untrue
316 A man who's untrue to his

unwilling
1822 of the unwilling, picked

unworthy
370 a small and unworthy goal for

up
1466 know why it was put up.
2707 Up and down the City
2903 on your way up because

up to date
3828 them and keep them up to date.

upbringing
3148 I'd the upbringing a nun would

uplift
391 give gentle uplift and

uplifting
31 In uplifting, get underneath.

3349 Who died to make verse free.
3357 others in verse: but I
4012 And an unmelodious verse ..
verses
2080 Dr Donne's verses are like
4085 The verses, when they were
vertical
312 we can The vertical man Though
vertigo
2660 of death: We die of vertigo.
vestry
3930 you in the vestry after
veterans
3309 world its veterans rewards! A
vetoes
1184 flow up And vetoes down.
vibrates
4620 skill she vibrates her
vibration
1888 That brave vibration each way
vicar
2315 Evangelical vicar, in want
vice
623 to render vice
746 function of vice to keep
1085 Vice came in always at the
1222 Vice goes a long way
1358 of all vice and
1827 One big vice in a man is
2004 Gossip is vice enjoyed
2168 pleasure without vice.
2354 which vice pays to
2775 vice that any
2988 who hates vice hates men.
3944 England but vice and
4396 by not having been vice.
vice-presidency
1539 The vice-presidency isn't worth a
vices
640 but most vices may be
917 none of the vices I admire.
2222 their vices may be of
2369 When our vices leave us, we
3257 fit can enjoy their vices.
4548 man has no vices, he's in
vichyssoise
2238 me of vichyssoise - it's
vicious
3684 a boy to be vicious till he's
victim
1552 Behold the victim of
1609 that a victim must be
victims
1755 The little victims play! No
victoria
3371 Queen Victoria - a mixture of

victorian
2926 In Victorian times the purpose
victory
3956 'But 'twas a famous victory.'
victuals
795 to please About their victuals.
view
2877 a wonderful view Of
vigilance
2775 unceasing vigilance and a rare
vigorous
1301 are least vigorous, or when
2670 people more vigorous than we
vigour
296 My vigour, vitality and
vile
2401 reckoned Vile, but viler
vilely
3791 it not show vilely in me to
vilify
417 Vilify! Vilify! Some of it
villa
2990 must have a villa in summer
village
1682 The village all declared how
villainy
4247 There is no villainy to which
4275 of villainy which we
violin
381 trying to play the violin.
754 playing a violin solo in
3259 a distant violin - it's the
virginity
3366 no; for my virginity, When I
4238 little more virginity, if you
virgins
4484 the young virgins into the
virtue
351 is the virtue of fools.
623 to the cause of virtue.
746 to keep virtue within
809 to believe in pure virtue.
2354 which vice pays to virtue.
2714 A woman's virtue ought
2912 accommodating sort of virtue.
2932 maxim be my virtue's guide:
2999 The virtue of much
3090 makes a necessity of virtue.
3841 What is virtue but the Trade
4396 Virtue knows to a farthing
virtues
917 all of the virtues I dislike
1345 like virtues, are their
1871 all the virtues, for we
2222 have no virtues, their
2356 greater virtues to bear

1414 passion; we want what puts
1959 you do want in case
2159 from want to want,
2727 what they want and are
2872 'I don't want him,' said
2915 unbridled, now Just want.
3111 We don't want it good - we
3733 feels the want of what it
4167 When you want to, they
4345 The want of a thing is

wanted
1302 man is wanted, and no

wants
600 item he wants. A woman
1295 to have few wants, and to
1681 express our wants as to
3628 when a man wants her is a
4222 score Man wants a great

war
235 War does not determine
929 better than to war-war.
954 War is too serious a
1191 War, he sung, is toil and
1218 game is war - crool,
1415 Men love war because it
1487 War appeals to young men
1818 and curious war is! You
1856 get out of war altogether
2275 Horses and Power and War.
2588 against war. Even
2593 We've a war, an' a debt,
2787 of war and sport.
2868 like war. Nothing
3022 Make love, not war.
3160 sport is war without
3575 in every war they kill
3697 give a war and nobody
4153 Crimea: The War That Would
4367 of war is: For

war office
3825 except the British War Office.

warfare
1575 nuclear warfare. There

warm
3427 fire let us warm ourselves.

warming
2712 than warming the

warming-pans
2834 were as good as warming-pans.

warmth
3129 except its occasional warmth.

warns
2816 voice which warns us that

wars
3714 from the wars today and

wary
3355 feeling wary when I

wash
894 that wash most are

washed
1072 but I just washed my hair."

washing
4185 only washing. And

washington
1527 Washington is a place where men
2047 Washington is an endless series
4391 cough in Washington They spit
4564 office in Washington either

washup
2213 dumbly, only to washup.

waste
131 to be is to waste the person
169 Time wastes our bodies and
603 treats me like toxic waste.

waste basket
3891 The waste basket is a writer's

waste-paper
495 file your waste-paper basket for
4433 is the waste-paper basket of

watch
481 done much better by a watch.
1036 appear on, you don't watch.
1965 If you watch a game, it's
2750 dead, or my watch has
4384 fine Swiss watch:

watching
533 observe a lot just by watching.

water
41 wine, it turns into water.
172 to go back in the water.
1970 by drinkers of water.
2216 I makes water I makes
3455 times - in water, in butter
3478 she falls into the water.
4146 into the water for the

watergate
1738 little bit of Watergate in him.

waterloo
3280 man meets his Waterloo at last.

way
1541 so in the way in the
1838 to find my way across the
1922 - but woman has her way.
2112 her own way, and the
2654 The best way to get

weak
555 The weak have one weapon:
983 end and aim of weak ones.

weak-minded
1798 A very weak-minded fellow I am

weaken
697 life if you don't weaken.

weakness
1626 'Is it weakness of intellect,
2658 of the weakness that we're

weaknesses
2786 the encounter of two weaknesses.

wealth
1080 The solid wealth of
1115 Wealth makes everything easy
1519 greater the wealth, the
3317 place and wealth, if

wealthy
633 extremely wealthy town; I
2509 wealthy, and yet

weapon
555 have one weapon: the
2793 a secret weapon in our
3909 to select a weapon it is the

wear
1673 who has nothing to wear.
2980 to learn to wear it over
4487 better to wear out than

wearing
380 trick of wearing mink is to

weasel
1364 Some weasel took the cork
2707 goes - Pop goes the weasel!
3288 The weasel under the

weather
328 hot weather we have!
2155 first talk is of the weather.
2674 you won't hold up the weather.

weathered
491 Lincoln's) weathered face was

wed
947 trouble I wed again, and

wedding
21 bought her wedding clothes.
1893 Wedding is destiny, and

wedding-cake
305 like a wedding-cake left out

wedding-ring
938 the small circle of a wedding-ring!

weed
1304 What is a weed? A plant

weeds
3397 like a garden full of weeds.

week
22 the rust of the whole week.
1986 than others can in a week.

weekly
3390 not pay weekly, but he

weep
848 one end and weep for her
1740 Weep not for little Léonie

well
435 speaks well of a man,
1204 are always well and those
1565 I am not well; pray get
1601 And did it very well.

2879 perfectly well and she
3275 done rather well under very
3488 feeling very well myself.

well conducted
4109 like a well conducted person,

well-bred
745 thoroughly well-bred and soon

well-connected
1596 virtuous scorn The well-connected.

well-looking
1694 one of my well-looking days,

well-remembered
1205 forgiven is usually well-remembered.

well-spent
820 as rare as a well-spent one.

well-written
820 A well-written Life is almost as

wellness
4395 in a moment of pretty wellness.

wench
2716 besides, the wench is dead.

west
1759 Go West, young man, and

west end
3905 running farce in the West End.

western
4491 seen one Western you've

western union
1712 be delivered by Western Union.

wet
3340 He's so wet you could

whack
928 time - a tremendous whack!

whacks
183 forty whacks; When she

whaleship
2797 A whaleship was my Yale College

what
769 He knew what's what, and
2289 names are What and Why
2489 Ah! What is man?

wheat
152 amorous Over Shredded Wheat.
1997 the wheat from the
2440 there be wheat' and

wheels
1398 do not let the wheels show.

whereabouts
3481 they have! Whereabouts is that?

wherefore
2489 is man? Wherefore does he

wherever
84 bed for it; Wherever you may

wherewithal
3362 But had not always wherewithal.

windy
3809 keep o' the windy side of

wine
41 I touch wine, it turns
302 to put new wine into old
412 a bottle of wine, a wife is
701 about wine, I did
780 Let us have Wine and Women,
1030 drink wine by
1549 glass, for wine inspires
3186 with the wine and the
3339 - the wine was a
3455 in butter and in wine.
4506 of turning wine into

wing
1625 under my wing, Tra la, A

wings
845 is roots, the other, wings.
2213 whitespread wings like he'd

wink
2809 sinner and wink your eye

winning
59 Winning can be defined as the
2568 Winning isn't everything. It
3698 Sure, winning isn't

winter
23 out in the Middle of Winter.
786 The English winter - ending
3335 Winter is icummen in, Lhude

wipes
4183 in, mind it wipes its shoes.

wireless
171 The wireless music box has no

wires
340 Across the wires the

wisdom
32 on man's wisdom, but set
880
1046 so much; Wisdom is humble
1206 All human wisdom is summed
1380 up facts; wisdom lies in
1421 the indifference of wisdom.
1522 of economic wisdom is to know
1991 every day; wisdom consists
1993 weak nerves give to wisdom.
2784 provide them with wisdom.
3228 is the beginning of wisdom.
3670 wit and all men's wisdom.
4270 only the wisdom that is in

wise
354 one of the wise men that
563 to the wise and
822 man half as wise as he
1173 It takes a wise man to
1194 The wise, for cure, on
1424 more like a wise man than a
1442 Who is wise? He that
1973 I heard a wise man say,
2370 is not as wise as he

2947 A wise man sees as much as
3179 Look wise, say nothing,
3430 you are wise, and you
3492 all like that wise bird!
4048 said that a wise man who
4619 Be wise with speed; A fool

wisecrack
2506 Epigram: a wisecrack that has

wisecracking
3216 between wisecracking and wit.

wisely
1231 behave wisely once they

wiser
318 places Are wiser and nicer
356 French are wiser than they
1672 I stand no wiser than
2776 they are wiser than they,
3304 but not the wiser grow.
3321 that he is wiser to-day

wisest
180 relished by the wisest men.
3539 Even the wisest men make

wish
2118 a lurking wish to appear
3516 I wish I loved the Human

wit
182 Little wit in the head
247 Wit is far more often a
272 examination is false wit.
769 As metaphysic wit can fly.
873 a great man pass for wit.
1850 Wit is the salt of
2413 I use my wit as a
2780 is the soul of wit.
2784 the dull with wit, just
3216 and wit. Wit has
3306 and fancy wit will come:
3670 one man's wit and all
4148 did do it, And not my wit.
4262 either, let wit bear a
4312 Wit is the sudden

withdrawn
916 should be withdrawn at the

withering
2489 Whither is he withering?

within
1878 when once it is within thee.

without
1959 is going without something
3207 been better without: Love,
3951 many things I can do without!

witticism
695 away a witticism if he

witty
349 dull men witty, but it
1787 can't pretend to be witty.
2368 true is perfectly witty.

wives
353 Wives are young men's
1058 had so many wives because
1788 only my wives. But you,
1957 mothers and wives! It is not
2921 three wives at a time,
3064 many, many wives; But when
3418 people's wives and

wobbles
2883 but it Wobbles, and the

woe
779 notes of woe, Sadder
3471 Woe to the house where
4355 Woe is me, I think I am

wolf
651 The wolf was sick, he
2055 while the wolf remains of

wolves
1166 are wolves for

woman
88 is like a woman you want
118 cleverest woman finds a
330 of ten, a woman had better
584 when a woman wears the
722 and a good woman - or a bad
880 wisedoom? Womman. And what
882 A woman knows how to keep
912 husband any woman can have.
963 If a woman likes another
977 is for the woman; but the
978 The woman who thinks she is
1032 A woman never sees what we
1040 But what is woman? - only
1153 Every woman should marry -
1207 girl the threat of a woman.
1229 done with a woman. You can
1232 be born a woman! .. Why
1265 A woman dictates before
1281 When lovely woman stoops to
1344 No woman can be a beauty
1371 It was a woman who drove me
1451 is 'What does a woman want?'
1673 find a woman who has
1998 than a woman if you
2244 stages in a woman's life,
2276 And a woman is only a woman
2447 Woman, a pleasing but a
2495 Why can't a woman be more
2517 the sort of woman who lives
2541 A woman is the only thing I
2649 to a woman being a
2817 happily a woman may be
2891 that every woman ought to
2941 A woman who goes to bed
3088 Woman was God's second
3102 goest to woman, take thy
3103 A woman may very well form
3104 Has a woman who knew that
3187 A woman is always buying
3231 A woman is a foreign land,

3478 A beautiful woman who is
3628 her is a woman's greatest
3777 know I am a woman? when I
3794 yet fair woman but she
3842 It is a woman's business to
3997 A woman seldom writes her
4009 A woman without a man is
4149 wife is any woman who has an
4173 A woman with fair
4222 below And Woman even more.
4223 Woman's place is in the
4343 When once a woman has given
4408 The female woman is one of
4427 called a woman in my own
4541 trust a woman who tells

womankind
3840 and packs off its womankind.

womb
2189 The very womb and bed of

women
82 without it. Women don't seem
83 Women are really much nicer
248 Some women blush when they
264 now is, are women persons?
327 Single women have a
331 and hardly any women at all.
401 beautiful women and so
441 Most women are not so young
739 your life; women require
780 Wine and Women, Mirth and
792 of Women goes only
799 humour from women? So that
879 quod he, Wommen desiren to
913 because they are not women.
1127 Most women set out to try
1138 possible to women. They ask
1267 Plain women he regarded as
1268 function of women, if it is
1326 to 'cuckold' for women.
1730 Women still remember the
1765 to get women out from
1766 Women must learn to lighten
1804 is making women more like
1810 turn into American women.
1865 knew how women pass the
2076 Women never dine alone.
2153 been thrown upon the women.
2275 things are, Women and Horses
2342 Women run to extremes; they
2425 as the Women's
2582 about Women's
2636 effect women would have
2650 Women do not find it
2829 Women have simple tastes.
2840 Women are perfectly well
2927 of men, women, and
3185 or refuse, women are glad
3336 I have sung women in three
3374 pretty women to men
3539 about women, and even

works
4075 could add: 'and it works'.
4519 put my talent into my works.

world
61 man's country in the world.
98 If all the world were
159 rubs of the world are what
184 all the world would be
610 at the end of the world.
618 The whole world is about
914 test; The world wil give
971 The world is too dangerous
1152 to retire from the world.
1259 advantage i' this world.
1373 a funny old world - a man's
1434 In this world nothing can
1814 The World would be a safer
2372 can see the world hath more
2554 The world's as ugly, ay, as
2644 The world belongs to the
2727 Ours is a world where
2745 the whole world cannot
2818 live in the world without
2831 What the world needs is
2854 The world is an oyster, but
2912 in this world is an
2927 This world consists of men,
3073 Stop the world, I want to
3124 The whole worl's in a state
3189 All the world is queer save
3651 of the world are asleep
3750 half of the warld thinks the
4398 on in the world from one
4502 cow of the world, and as we
4596 good, The world would be

worldly
2451 were all his worldly goods.

worm
1626 tough worm in your
2157 with a worm at one end
3206 upon a worm. 'Aha, my
3601 bad luck of the early worm.

worms
918 We are all worms, but I do
4296 ourselves worms of the

worn
136 if it had worn out two
3329 I am worn to a ravelling

worried
185 what he worried about last

worries
1799 person who worries very much
2169 but a fool worries about
3430 Worries go down better with

worry
1979 Farmers worry only during
2400 We wouldn't worry so much
2720 oh i should worry and fret

worrying
282 the use of worrying? It never
2952 Worrying helps you some. It
4346 without worrying whether

worse
116 born wicked, and grow worse.
465 of finding something worse.
858 a good deal worse.
1445 bad that I don't feel worse.
2010 day - then worse again in
2179 money made it any worse.
3583 party is worse than the
4127 her person for the worse.
4532 the world worse than being

worship
2628 We still worship the elders

worshipped
3149 if he thee worshipped with his

worst
438 The worst thing in this
660 be good to know the worst.
1056 hope nobody gets the worst.
2551 they prepared for the worst.
2954 come to the worst, they
3085 The worst thing, I fear,
3395 when in the worst health.
3402 The worst is not always

worth
238 nothing is worth nothing.
594 and ain't worth nothin'.
906 a thing is worth doing, it
2138 Worth seeing, yes; but not
4526 that is worth knowing

worthless
3003 and make it worthless by

worthy
1650 Yet B is worthy, I dare
2906 is not worthy to live.

wotthehell
2720 but wotthehell wotthehell oh i

wound
1066 Next to the wound, what
2042 clock and wound up every
2930 razor keen, Wound with a
4469 into their wounds, even if

wounded
2309 When you're wounded and left

wren
513 Christopher Wren Said, 'I
2012 with the wings of a wren.

wrestle
911 never to wrestle with a

wrestling
322 that of wrestling than of

wretches
1665 How shall wretches live like

wrinkle
1197 the first wrinkle and the

writ
4148 And this I writ; My heart

write
82 enough; They write about it.
253 Write something, even If
1682 he could write and cypher
1934 When you write in prose you
2136 know how to write trifles
2424 I like to write when I feel
2531 I can write better than
3023 I write as a sow piddles.
3319 who cannot write, and those
3489 read books - I write them.
3866 You write with ease, to
4006 I write for myself and
4201 sit down to write when you
4625 who can't write

writer
1859 for a good writer is a
2332 A writer is someone who can
2465 fame is a writer's fame;
3505 of a writer is
3891 basket is a writer's best
4243 hardback writer is

writers
363 Writers, like teeth, are
1126 remember: writers are always
1279 are failed writers - but so
1341 kinds of writers - the
1963 are my writers when I

writing
283 said that writing comes more
701 it came to writing about
816 That's not writing, that's
1413 Writing is easy: all you do
2153 faculty of writing has
2194 that in his writing,
2446 Writing is no trouble: you
2472 love, but get it in writing.
2556 And some for writing verses.
4026 Writing, when properly

written
1717 the paper it is written on.
4268 man himself cannot be written.

wrong
383 be strongly wrong than
688 called them by wrong names.
901 American who is all wrong.
1000 kinds of wrong. The
1101 are always in the wrong.
1246 can prove me wrong.
1521 majority is always wrong.
1641 who have gone wrong!
1848 to setting them wrong.
1898 really wrong with him -
1910 but being wrong ain't one
2088 has something wrong with it.
2722 usually gets it all wrong.
2795 me when I am in the wrong.
2883 get in the wrong places.

3321 been in the wrong, which is
3332 has gone wrong, however
3717 something wrong with the
4168 comes easy, comes wrong.
4223 place is in the wrong.
4466 women go wrong, men go
4481 Nature is usually wrong.
4620 most divinely in the wrong.

wrongdoing
1945 A sense of wrongdoing is an

wrongly
2501 Think wrongly, if you please,

wrongs
4141 Two wrongs don't make a

wrote
3502 tackle, I'm glad I wrote it.
4301 who wrote music

y-shaped
3153 the grave in a Y-shaped coffin.

yale
2797 was my Yale College
3203 the Yale Prom were

yawns
4239 the grave yawns for him.

year
10 the best time of the year.

yearning
2982 learning, earning and yearning.

years
1220 at all ivry fifty years.
1227 the last six thousand years.
1429 and twenty years can scarce
4043 is not the years in your

yeast
4147 in large: yeast, salt and

yellow
1835 a one-eyed yellow idol to

yes
1735 'No' and Yes' are words

yesterday
2718 of keeping up with yesterday.

yet
320 continence, but not yet.

yid
3618 PUT THE ID BACK IN YID!

yield
1739 is just to yield to it.
4529 is to yield to it.

yorkshireman
3446 over a Yorkshireman's grave,

you
225 For you but not
1793 You know I know you know
3009 It's for you-hoo!
3468 gossips to you will
3643 for if you rub up

young
11 you are too young to take up
33 to make me young again.
765 Young as he was, his
1882 Only the young die good.
2167 if he be caught young.
2584 It keeps him young.
3085 no longer young, is that
3282 a long time to become young.
3640 When I was young, I used to
3828 that the young can do for
3911 of the young is a
4233 I was very young, I kissed
4273 to be a young June bug,
4537 old, but that one is young.

young man
1759 Go West, young man, and grow up
4050 give me the young man who has

young men
256 Young men think old men fools
3910 than young men can

young people
2915 civility; Young people
3035 it gets young people to bed at

younger
4310 When I was younger, I could

yourself
1573 Be yourself. Who else is
2655 go to bed with is yourself.
2767 if you have to do it yourself.
4622 likely to kill you is yourself.

youth
257 This is a youth-oriented
1084 age is youth without
1224 have in our youth is
1224 have in our youth is
1332 If youth knew; if age was
3100 belongs to youth, clarity
3622 sign of an ill-spent youth.
3642 sagacity in youth, but
3798 hast nor youth nor age;
4211 The youth gets together

zeal
2314 bigot zeal, Corrected
2732 All zeal .. all zeal, Mr

zipper
3606 pull your zipper up, then